750 Italian Verbs
and Their Uses

Also in the *750 Verbs Series*

750 French Verbs and Their Uses
750 German Verbs and Their Uses
750 Russian Verbs and Their Uses
750 Spanish Verbs and Their Uses

750 Italian Verbs and Their Uses

Brunella Notarmarco Dutton

Series Editors
Jan R. Zamir, Ph.D.,
and
Sonia Nelson Zamir, M.A.

JOHN WILEY & SONS, INC.
New York • Chichester • Weinheim • Brisbane • Singapore • Toronto

Published by John Wiley & Sons, Inc.
Published simultaneously in Canada.

This publication is designed to provide accurate and authoritative information in regard to the subject matter covered. It is sold with the understanding that the Publisher is not engaged in rendering professional services. If professional advice or other expert assistance is required, the services of a competent professional person should be sought.

Library of Congress Cataloging-in-Publication Data

Dutton, Brunella Notarmarco.
    750 Italian verbs and their uses / Brunella Notarmarco Dutton :
  edited by Jan Zamir and Sonia Nelson Zamir.
      p. cm. — (750 verbs and their uses)
    ISBN 0-471-01627-6 (pbk. : alk. paper)
    1. Italian language—Verbs. 2. Italian language—Usage.
  I. Zamir, Jan R. II. Zamir, Sonia. III. Title.
  IV. Series.
  PC1271.D88   1996
  458.2'421—dc20   95-44005

Printed in the United States of America

10 9 8 7 6 5 4 3 2 1

Contents

Preface

The main purpose of this book is to give the reader a clear picture of the uses of 750 common Italian verbs, with their prepositions shown in the proper contexts. A number of illustrative sentences for each entry implicitly reflect the various usages of the verb and its prepositions in context.

For the most part, each verb is introduced first without a preposition in order to show the basic and most common usage of the verb. If the verb is associated with a certain preposition, we provide the preposition within the meaning of the entry—and under the same entry, we give examples that illustrate the verb with the preposition. If there is a strong link between the existing verb and the preposition, we present the verb with its preposition as a subentry and provide examples of its use as a phrasal verb. Herein lies one of the major contributions of this book.

In presenting the verbs with their prepositions, we thus distinguish between two types of verbal expressions. First are the verbs that are predominantly fixed to their prepositions, and these will often represent a meaning distinct from that of the main verb. (For example, in English we have such phrasal verbs as "hold up," "hold out," "hold back," "hold down," "hold in," "hold off," and "hold with.") Second, we have many common verbs that are not linguistically linked with the prepositions in a fixed way but are found with certain prepositions in frequent contexts. (For example, we find in English the expressions "to speak up" or "to speak out" as being bound and constituting a phrasal verb. However, we find it useful for the reader to be aware also of the association of "to speak" with commonly used prepositions, as in "to speak on the phone" or "to speak over the loudspeaker," "to speak under his breath," "to speak in a whisper," etc.) For pedagogical reasons we found it useful to include both types.

We have made several critical decisions in the format of this book that make it especially valuable. First, we have varied the number of examples for English speakers. Hence, the more unusual expressions are treated more extensively. Second, the examples attempt to give as wide a semantic range as possible for each verb, and they include a number of nouns and idiomatic expressions. Third, where appropriate, we attempt to present the examples in a structurally diversified manner so as to show various tenses. Finally, we have frequently attempted to elucidate the subject-verb-object relationship. Most noticeably, whenever the forms of the direct and indirect object pronouns coalesce (*Giovanni mi vede/mi parla*), we provide in our example a third-person form (*Giovanni lo vede/gli parla*) in at least one of our Italian sentences. As the distinction between the direct and the indirect object pronoun is often clearer in the third person in Italian, we believe this will help to illustrate this rather difficult aspect of the Italian language for English speakers. We would also like to add here that our examples in this book are based on current, everyday usage of the language. Thus, we have tried to avoid pedantic and unusual prescriptive structure.

This book of Italian verbs and their respective prepositions can be used at all levels of competency—both as an independent source and as a supplementary aid for developing writing skills, providing grammatical practice, and so on.

Terms and Abbreviations Used in This Book

English	Abbreviation	Italian
adjective	*adj*	aggettivo
adverb	*adv*	avverbio
for example	*e.g.*	per esempio
et cetera	*etc.*	eccetera
figurative	*fig*	figurativo
formal	*formal*	formale
gerund	*ger*	gerundio
idiomatic	*idiomatic*	espressione idiomatica
that is	*i.e.*	cioè
infinitive	*inf*	infinito
informal	*informal*	familiare
literally	*literally*	letteralmente
literary	*lit*	letterario
noun	*noun*	nome
oneself	*oneself*	-si
or	*or*	o
past participle	*ptp*	participio passato
proverb	*proverb*	proverbio
somebody	*sb*	qc (qualcuno)
slang	*slang*	gergo
something	*sth*	qco (qualcosa)
subject	*subject*	soggetto
subjunctive	*subj*	congiuntivo

abbandonare   to leave, abandon, forsake, desert; to give up; to neglect; to fail; to drop

- Molti uomini avevano già abbandonato il loro paese.
  Many men had already left their country.

- Il prigioniero fu abbandonato su un'isola deserta.
  The prisoner was abandoned on a desert island.

- Non si abbandona un amico nel bisogno!
  One does not forsake a friend in need!

- Suo cugino ha abbandonato moglie e figli (/il suo posto).
  Her cousin deserted his wife and children (/his post).

- Non posso credere che Maria abbia abbandonato l'insegnamento.
  I can't believe that Mary has given up teaching.

- Il loro giardino era abbandonato.
  Their garden was neglected.

- Le forze lo abbandonavano.
  His strength was failing him.

- Il vecchio abbandonò il capo sul petto e morì.
  The old man dropped his head on his chest and died.

  abbandonarsi   to let oneself fall, give oneself up; to give way to; to sink

  - Il loro figlio si abbandonò al vizio.
    Their son gave himself up to vice.

  - Giulia si abbandonò alla disperazione (/al dolore).
    Julia gave way to despair (/to grief).

  - La ragazza si abbandonò sulla poltrona. (*fig*)
    The girl sank into the armchair.

abbassare   to lower; to turn down; to pull down; to dim

- Quel quadro va abbassato.
  That picture must be lowered.

- Abbassate il sipario!
  Lower the curtain!

- La ragazza abbassò gli occhi (/la voce).
  The girl lowered her eyes (/voice).

- Prima di tutto si dovrebbero abbassare i prezzi (/i costi/i salari).
  First of all, prices (/costs/salaries) should be lowered.

- Puoi abbassare la radio (/la televisione/la luce/il gas), per favore?
  Can you turn down the radio (/television/light/gas), please?

- Tutte le saracinesche (/le leve) erano già state abbassate.
  All the rolling shutters (/levers) had already been pulled down.

- Con la nebbia è consigliabile abbassare i fari.
  When there is fog, it is advisable to dim the headlights.

  abbassarsi to bend down; to drop; to go down; to abase oneself

  - Il ragazzo si abbassò per raccogliere la penna (/il libro/il giocattolo).
    The boy bent down to pick up the pen (/book/toy).

  - Il barometro si è abbassato.
    The barometer has dropped.

  - Il livello dell'acqua si era finalmente abbassato.
    The water level had finally gone down.

  - Non credevo che un uomo si potesse abbassare così.
    I did not think a man could abase (or lower) himself that way.

abbattere to pull down, demolish, knock down; to shoot down; to slaughter; to dishearten

- Tutti quei vecchi palazzi sono stati abbattuti.
  All those old buildings have been demolished.

- Tre aerei nemici furono abbattuti quella notte.
  Three enemy planes were shot down that night.

- Il bestiame dovette essere abbattuto.
  The cattle had to be slaughtered.

- La notizia della loro morte l'ha abbattuta molto.
  The news of their death greatly disheartened her.

  abbattersi to fall down, to get depressed/disheartened; to break

  - Improvvisamente si abbatté al suolo, morto.
    Suddenly he fell to the ground, dead.

  - Eugenio non è un tipo che si abbatta facilmente.
    Eugene is not the kind who gets easily depressed.

  - Una terribile tempesta si è abbattuta sulla città.
    A violent storm broke over the city.

abboccare to bite; to be taken in

- I pesci non abboccavano quando mio padre lá.
  The fish were not biting when my father was there.

- Qualunque proposta gli facciano, Giorgio abbocca.
  Whatever proposal they make, George is taken in.

  abboccarsi to have a meeting, confer

  - Si abboccheranno domattina.
    They will have a meeting tomorrow morning.

abbonare qc a qco   to make sb a subscriber to sth

■ L'ho abbonata al *Corriere della Sera.*
I made her a subscriber to the Corriere della Sera.

abbonarsi a qco   to subscribe to sth/get a subscription to sth

■ Mi sono abbonato a una rivista (/alla radio/ai concerti della Scala).
I got a subscription to a magazine (/the radio/the La Scala concerts).

abbottonare   to button (up); to be reserved

■ Abbottona il cappotto (/la camicia/la giacca) del bambino.
Button the child's coat (/shirt/jacket).

■ Dove si abbottona questo golf?
Where is this sweater buttoned?

■ Suo marito sembra una persona molto abbottonata.
Her husband looks like a very reserved person.

abbottonarsi   to button (one's clothes up)

■ Abbottonati il cappotto (/la camicia/la giacca).
Button up your coat (/shirt/jacket).

■ Se Lei non si abbottona, prende freddo.
If you do not button up, you'll catch cold.

abbracciare   to embrace, hug; to espouse to take up to comprise or include; to grasp; to see; to surround

■ Il piccolo abbracciava l'orsacchiotto (/la mamma).
The little one was hugging his teddy bear (/mother).

■ Decisero di abbracciare la sua causa.
They decided to espouse his cause.

■ Anna vuole abbracciare una carriera negli affari.
Ann plans to take up a career in business.

■ Si parla di un impero che abbraccia dodici nazioni.
One talks of an empire comprised of twelve nations.

■ La mente non può abbracciare tutto.
The mind cannot grasp everything.

■ Da qui l'occhio abbraccia tutta la valle.
*From here one can see (*literally: *embrace) the whole valley.*

■ Una palizzata abbraccia tutto il campo.
A fence surrounds the whole field.

abbracciarsi   to hug one another

■ I due fratelli si abbracciarono prima di partire.
The two brothers hugged each other before leaving.

abbreviare   to shorten, make short, curtail

■   Non potremmo abbreviare il discorso (/la predica/la parola)?
Couldn't we shorten the speech (/sermon/word)?

■   Per abbreviarla, finirono per comprare quella casa.
To make a long story short, they ended up buying that house.

■   Questa è la forma abbreviata di quella parola?
Is this the abbreviated form of that word?

abdicare a qco   to abdicate sth

■   Il re abdicò al trono in favore del figlio.
The king abdicated the throne in favor of his son.

abitare   to live in, inhabit, dwell in; to occupy

■   Dove abiti? —Abito a Milano (/Roma/Firenze/qui/là).
Where do you live? —I live in Milan (/Rome/Florence/here/there).

■   Abitano in Italia (/in Messico/negli Stati Uniti) da molti anni.
They have been living in Italy (/Mexico/the United States) for many years.

■   Le piace abitare in campagna (/città/centro/un sobborgo), signor Rosi?
Do you like living in the country (/in the city/downtown/in a suburb), Mr. Rosi?

■   Da quanto tempo abitano in quella casa (/quell'appartamento)?
How long have they been living in that house (/apartment)?

■   A Tommaso piacciono gli animali che abitano la savana.
Thomas likes the animals that inhabit the savanna.

■   Credono che quella casa sia abitata dagli spiriti.
They believe that house is inhabited by ghosts.

■   La loro casa non è abitata da molto tempo.
Their house has not been occupied for a long time.

abituare qc a + *inf*   to accustom sb to + *ger*

■   La devi abituare a farsi il letto (/mettere in ordine la sua stanza/fare colazione).
You should accustom her to making her bed (/tidying up her room/eating breakfast).

abituarsi a qco/*inf*   to get accustomed to sth/*ger*

■   Tu ti devi abituare a questo nuovo tipo di vita.
You have to get accustomed to this new kind of life.

■   Quando si abitueranno ad alzarsi presto (/a lavorare fino a tardi/a vivere qui)?
When will they get accustomed to getting up early (/working late/living here)?

abolire to abolish sth; to abrogate; to give up; to suppress

- La pena di morte è stata abolita in molti stati.
  The death penalty has been abolished in many states.

- Questa legge va abolita.
  This law must be abrogated.

- Il dottore mi ha detto di abolire il caffè (/le sigarette/la birra).
  My doctor told me to give up coffee (/cigarettes/beer).

- Quell'ordine religioso è stato abolito molti anni fa.
  That religious order was suppressed many years ago.

abortire to have a miscarriage, abort; to have an abortion; to fail

- Si dice che abbia abortito due mesi fa.
  They say she had a miscarriage two months ago.

- Tu pensi che il marito l'abbia fatta abortire?
  Do you think that her husband made her have an abortion?

- Il loro tentativo è abortito.
  Their attempt has failed.

abusare di qco to abuse sth; to overindulge in + *ger;* to take advantage of sth

- Il loro padre ha sempre abusato della sua autorità (/della sua salute/delle sue forze).
  Their father has always abused his authority (/health/strength).

- Non voglio abusare della sua gentilezza (/pazienza/bontà).
  I don't want to take advantage of your kindness (/patience/goodness).

accadere (auxiliary *essere*) to happen

- È accaduto un fatto inspiegabile.
  An inexplicable thing happened.

- Che vi è accaduto?
  What happened to you?

- Accadeva spesso che non si vedessero per settimane.
  It often happened that they would not see each other for weeks.

  accadere di + *inf* to happen to + *inf*

  - Gli accadde di incontrarli.
    He happened to meet (run into) them.

accalorare to rouse, heat

- La discussione li accalorò.
  The discussion roused them.

  accalorarsi to get excited/heated

  - Il padre di Gianni si accalorò nel raccontare la vicenda.
    Johnny's father got excited as he was recounting the event.

accampare to assert (rights); to bring forward (make excuses, claims)

■ Il fratello del signor Arnaldi accampava diritti sulla proprietà.
Mr. Arnaldi's brother asserted his rights to the property.

■ Quel tuo amico accampa sempre pretesti (/pretese).
That friend of yours is always making excuses (/claims).

> **accamparsi** to camp, live temporarily as in a camp
>
> ■ Ci accampammo vicino al lago (/nel bosco/in montagna).
> *We camped near the lake (/in the woods/on the mountain).*

accarezzare to caress, fondle, stroke; to cherish; to thrash

■ La ragazza accarezzò il viso del bambino.
The girl caressed the baby's face.

■ Non accarezzare il cane contropelo.
Don't stroke the dog the wrong way.

■ Antonio accarezzava l'idea (/la speranza) di tornare in Italia un giorno.
Anthony cherished the idea (/hope) of going back to Italy one day.

■ Gli hanno accarezzato le spalle (/il groppone).
They thrashed his shoulders (/back) soundly.

> **accarezzarsi** to stroke
>
> ■ L'avvocato si accarezzò il mento (/la barba) con la mano.
> *The attorney stroked his chin (/beard) with his hand.*

accavallare to overlap; to cross

■ Non accavallare i cavi.
Don't overlap the cables.

■ Non accavallare le gambe.
Don't cross your legs.

> **accavallarsi** to build up, pile up
>
> ■ I ricordi si accavallavano.
> *The memories were building up (or piling up).*

accecare to blind

■ La luce degli abbaglianti accecò la lepre.
The headlights blinded the hare.

■ Suo marito era accecato dalla luce intensa (/dalla passione).
Her husband was blinded by the intense light (/passion).

accelerare to accelerate, increase the speed, go faster; to hasten, quicken

■ Quando accelero, si sente uno strano rumore.
When I increase the speed, one hears a strange noise.

■ Perché non acceleri?
Why don't you go faster?

■ Non potresti accelerare il passo?
Couldn't you quicken your pace?

accelerare qco   to speed up sth

■ Dovreste accelerare il movimento (/ritmo).
You should speed up the movement (/rhythm).

■ Questo medicinale accelererà il processo di guarigione.
This medication will hasten the healing process.

accendere   to light; to turn on; to strike

■ La ragazza accese la sigaretta e cominciò a parlare.
The girl lit a cigarette and started to speak.

■ Accendi la luce (/la radio/la televisione), per favore!
Turn on the light (/radio/television), please!

■ Accendi un fiammifero, per piacere.
Strike a match, please.

accendersi   to light up; to come on; to get excited

■ Il fuoco si è acceso subito.
The fire lit up right away.

■ La luce non si accende.
The light does not come on.

■ Tu ti accendi per un nonnulla.
You get excited over nothing.

accennare   to mention

■ Come accennato più sopra, la riunione si terrà giovedì prossimo.
As mentioned above, the meeting will be held next Thursday.

accennare a qc/qco   to speak briefly of/about sb/sth; to point out, refer to, hint about sb/sth

■ Il conferenziere accennò al problema dei senzatetto.
The lecturer spoke briefly of the problem of the homeless.

■ A chi (/cosa) accennavi?
Whom (/What) were you referring to?

accennare a + *inf*   to show signs of + *ger*

■ L'inflazione non accenna a diminuire.
Inflation does not show signs of decreasing.

accennare di sì (col capo)   to nod (the head)

■   Il professore non disse "sì" ma accennò di sì col capo.
The professor did not say "Yes" but nodded his head.

accennare a qc di + *inf*   to signal sb to + *inf*

■   Il direttore (della scuola) mi accennò di avvicinarmi (/parlare/tacere).
The principal signaled me to come closer (/to speak/not to speak).

accentuare   to stress, emphasize; to point out; to accentuate

■   Questi fattori hanno accentuato la crisi.
These factors have emphasized (or underlined) the crisis.

■   Vorremmo accentuare certi aspetti del problema.
We would like to point out certain aspects of the problem.

accentuarsi   to become more marked (noticeable)

■   Il malinteso fra i due si è accentuato.
The misunderstanding between the two has become more marked.

■   La crisi si sta accentuando.
The crisis is getting worse (or more serious).

■   Con l'età si accentuò in lui la pigrizia (/l'instabilità dell'umore).
His laziness (/moodiness) became more noticeable with age.

accerchiare   to encircle

■   Il nemico fu accerchiato dalle nostre truppe.
The enemy was encircled by our troops.

accertare   to check; to ascertain; to assess

■   Dovresti accertare questi dati (/la veridicità del suo racconto).
You should check these data (/the truth of his story).

■   Sì deve accertare l'entità dei danni.
Damages must be assessed.

accertarsi di qco/che + *subj*   to ascertain; to make sure

■   Dobbiamo accertarci della realtà dei fatti.
We must ascertain the facts.

■   Accertatevi che vengano.
Make sure that they come.

accettare qc/qco   to accept sth; to admit sb; to agree to sth; to follow sth

■   Sono sicuro che sua madre accetterà l'invito (/il regalo/l'offerta).
I am sure his mother will accept the invitation (/the gift/the offer).

- Il loro padre accettò la carica (/la sfida/le condizioni).
  Their father accepted the appointment (/the challenge/the conditions).

- L'hanno accettato nella società (/nel circolo).
  They admitted him into the partnership (/into the club).

- Non abbiamo accettato la proposta (/la transazione).
  We did not agree to the proposal (/the transaction).

- Perché non accettate il loro suggerimento (/i consigli del medico)?
  Why don't you follow their suggestion (/the doctor's advice)?

  accettare di + *inf*   to agree to + *inf*

  - Pensavo che il signor Grimaldi avrebbe accettato di presiedere la riunione (/ridurre le spese/assumere più persone).
    I thought Mr. Grimaldi would agree to chair the meeting (/reduce expenses/hire more people).

acclamare   to acclaim, to hail

- Il gruppo acclamò il nuovo presidente.
  The group acclaimed the new president.

- Lo acclamarono imperatore.
  They hailed him as emperor.

accogliere   to receive, welcome; to record; to consent; to grant; to uphold

- L'hanno accolta a braccia aperte (/freddamente).
  They received her with open arms (/coldly).

- Marco è stato ben accolto dai miei amici.
  Mark was welcomed by my friends.

- Questa parola non è stata ancora accolta nel dizionario.
  This word has not been recorded in the dictionary yet.

- Spero che accolgano la vostra proposta.
  I hope they will consent to your proposal.

- La nostra richiesta non è stata accolta.
  Our request was not granted.

- Il vostro ricorso sarà certamente accolto.
  Your appeal will certainly be upheld.

accomodare   to fix, repair, mend; to suit

- Hai fatto accomodare le mie scarpe?
  Did you have my shoes repaired?

- Questo non gli accomoda.
  This does not suit him.

- La nostra amica fa solo quello che le accomoda.
  Our friend does as she pleases.

accomodarsi   to come in; to make oneself comfortable; to sit down, take a seat; to come to an agreement on sth; to work out

- Si accomodi.
  Come on in (or Make yourself comfortable or Have a seat).

- Non state in piedi, per favore, accomodatevi.
  Don't stand up. Please sit down.

- Sul prezzo ci accomoderemo.
  We'll come to an agreement on the price.

- Vedrai che tutto si accomoderà.
  You'll see that everything will work out.

- Si accomodi da questa parte, prego.
  This way, please (or Come this way, please).

accompagnare   to accompany; to escort; to close gently; to follow

- Devo accompagnarla a scuola (/al pronto soccorso/alla stazione/al commissariato/in biblioteca/dal dentista/dovunque vada).
  I have to accompany her to school (/the emergency room/the station/the police station/the library/the dentist's office/wherever she goes).

- Quella cantante era accompagnata al piano da un pianista di Milano.
  That singer was accompanied on the piano by a pianist from Milan.

- In quel garage chiedi che qualcuno ti accompagni alla macchina.
  In that garage ask for someone to escort you to your car.

- Accompagna la porta, non sbatterla.
  Close the door gently; don't slam it.

- Il padre li accompagnò con gli occhi.
  Their father followed them with his eyes.

accompagnarsi   to match

- Questi colori si accompagnano bene.
  These colors match well.

accontentare qc   to please sb; to grant

- Lo accontentano in tutti i suoi desideri.
  They grant all his wishes.

accontentarsi di qco/*inf*   to be content with sth/*ger*

- Si accontentano di quello che hanno.
  They are content with what they have.

- Si accontenterebbero di lavorare poche ore al giorno (/dormire sul divano/mangiare un panino).
  They would be content with working a few hours a day (/sleeping on the couch/eating a sandwich).

accorgersi di + *inf*   (auxiliary *essere*) to notice; to perceive; to realize

■ Non ti sei accorta di essere seguita (/sorvegliata)?
  Didn't you notice you were being followed (/watched)?

■ L'ho fatto senza accorgermene.
  I did it without realizing it.

■ Ti sei accorto che stavi girando a destra?
  Did you realize you were turning right?

■ Non si era accorto che nevicava.
  He was not aware it was snowing.

accusare (qc di qco)   to charge (sb with sth); to blame; to feel , *acknowledge*

■ L'imputato è accusato di furto (/rapina/omicidio).
  The defendant is charged with theft (/robbery/murder).

■ Puoi accusare soltanto la tua cattiva sorte.
  You can blame only your bad luck.

■ Il paziente accusa da due giorni un forte dolore al ginocchio destro.
  The patient has been feeling a strong pain in his right knee for two days.

■ Accusano ricevuta della sua lettera.
  They acknowledge receipt of his letter.

   accusare qc di + *inf*   to accuse sb of + *ger*

   ■ Lo hanno accusato di aver falsificato la firma di suo padre (/aver accettato delle tangenti).
     They accused him of forging his father's signature (/of accepting kickbacks).

   accusarsi   to accuse oneself/each other/one another

   ■ Per salvarla si accusò di un delitto che non aveva commesso.
     In order to save her, he accused himself of a crime he had not committed.

   ■ I due criminali continuarono ad accusarsi.
     The two criminals kept on accusing each other.

acquistare (qco da qc)   to purchase (sth from sb); to acquire; to win; to improve

■ L'ho acquistato da una ditta americana.
  I purchased it from an American company.

■ Come hanno acquistato onori e ricchezze?
  How did they acquire honors and wealth?

■ Il romanzo gli acquistò molta fama.
  The novel won him great renown.

■ Il vino acquista invecchiando.
  Wine improves with age.

adattare   to adapt; to turn; to adjust

■   Questo romanzo sarà adattato per il teatro.
This novel will be adapted for the stage.

■   Hanno adattato una scuola a ospedale.
They turned a school into a hospital.

■   La nonna le adattò il vestito da sposa della mamma.
Her grandmother adjusted her mother's wedding gown for her.

adattarsi   to adapt oneself; to adjust; to be suitable for, suit

■   Vi manca la capacità di adattarvi alle circostanze (/a un ambiente diverso).
You lack the ability to adapt to circumstances (/to different surroundings).

■   La madre di Barbara non sa adattarsi a vivere da sola.
Barbara's mother cannot adjust to living alone.

■   Dobbiamo adattarci.
We must make the best of things.

■   Quella parte non gli si adatta.
That part is not suitable for him.

■   La nuova casa si adatta ai suoi gusti.
The new house suits her tastes.

addolcire   to sweeten; to alleviate, mitigate; to mellow; to soften

■   È così amaro che neanche lo zucchero lo può addolcire.
It is so bitter that even sugar can't sweeten it.

■   Le parole della loro amica addolcirono il loro dolore.
Their friend's words alleviated their sorrow.

■   Il dolore (/L'età) ha addolcito il suo carattere.
Suffering (/Age) has mellowed his character.

■   Se l'acqua è dura, va addolcita.
If water is hard, it must be softened.

addolcirsi   to mellow; to soften

■   I suoi lineamenti si sono addolciti.
Her features have softened.

addolorare   to grieve; to distress

■   La notizia ci addolorò molto.
The news grieved us a lot (or We were greatly grieved at the news).

■   Mi addolora sapere che voi non tornerete.
It grieves me to hear that you will not come back.

- Le tue parole l'hanno addolorata.
  Your words have distressed her.

addolorarsi per qco   to be distressed by sth

- Si è addolorata per la tua risposta (/l'accaduto).
  She was distressed by your answer (/what happened).

addormentare   to make sleepy, put to sleep, lull; to sleep; to be boring; to anesthetize

- Il vino fa addormentare il nonno.
  Wine makes Grandpa sleepy.

- Questa ninna-nanna lo fa addormentare.
  This lullaby puts him to sleep.

- È' un libro che addormenta.
  It is a boring book.

- Lo hanno addormentato prima dell'operazione.
  They anesthetized him before the operation.

addormentarsi   to fall asleep; to go to sleep

- Giovanni si è addormentato subito.
  John fell asleep right away.

- Mi si è addormentata la mano.
  My hand has gone to sleep.

- Non addormentarti sui libri.
  Don't sleep on your books.

addossare (qco a qc/qco)   to place, lean, lay (sth against/on sb/sth)

- Potresti addossare la scala alla parete.
  You could lean the ladder against the wall.

- Il signor Gori addossa sempre la responsabilità di tutto agli altri.
  Mr. Gori always lays the responsibility of everything on others.

- A chi addossano la colpa?
  Whom are they blaming?

addossarsi   to lean against sth; to crowd together

- Il vecchio si addossò alla porta.
  The old man leaned against the door.

- Tutti gli scioperanti si addossarono gli uni agli altri nella sala.
  All the strikers crowded together in the hall.

- Lei non deve addossarsene tutta la responsabilità, signor Guerini.
  You should not take all the responsibility of it upon yourself, Mr. Guerini.

aderire   to stick, adhere, to fit; to support; to comply with; to join (a political party)

■   La tappezzeria non aderisce bene al muro.
    The wallpaper does not stick to the wall.

■   L'abito le aderiva come una seconda pelle.
    Her dress fit her like a second skin.

■   Avevano subito aderito a quell'idea.
    They had immediately supported that idea.

■   Pietro aderiva a tutti i tuoi desideri (/tutte le tue richieste).
    Peter would comply with all of your wishes (/requests).

■   A diciotto anni quello scrittore aderì al partito comunista.
    At eighteen years of age that writer joined the Communist Party.

adorare   to adore, worship, love

■   Adora sua moglie.
    He adores his wife.

■   Liliana adora le patatine fritte (/quell'attore tedesco).
    Lillian loves (or adores) French fries (/that German actor).

■   I Romani adoravano molti dei.
    The Romans worshiped many gods.

adottare   to adopt, choose; to take

■   Hanno adottato una bambina.
    They have adopted a little girl.

■   Dovrebbero adottare criteri più moderni (/un atteggiamento positivo).
    They should adopt more modern criteria (/a positive attitude).

■   Adotteremo una nuova tattica.
    We'll adopt (or choose) a new strategy.

■   Saremo costretti ad adottare severe misure.
    We'll be forced to take serious measures.

affannare   to trouble, worry

■   Questi pensieri la affannano.
    These thoughts trouble (or worry) her.

affannarsi per qc/qco/ *or* + *inf*   to worry (oneself) over sb/sth; to toil, work to + *inf*

■   Non affannarti per noi (/per un nonnulla).
    Don't worry about us (/over nothing).

■   Si affannano per accumulare denaro.
    They work (or toil) to accumulate wealth.

afferrare   to grasp; to seize; to get hold of

■ Mi domando se afferri il concetto.
I wonder whether you grasp the concept.

   afferrare qc per qco   to catch sb by sth

   ■ Lo afferrarono per il collo (/un braccio/una gamba).
   They caught him by the neck (/arm/leg).

   afferrarsi a qc/qco   to catch sth; to cling to sb; to clutch or hold tight to sth

   ■ La bambina cercò di afferrarsi a lui.
   The little girl tried to cling to him.

   ■ Cercavono di afferrarsi al remo (/al ramo).
   They were trying to clutch at the oar (/branch).

   ■ Afferratevi al corrimano.
   Hold tightly to the handrail.

affettare   to slice; to feign; to affect

■ Hai già affettato il pane (/il prosciutto)?
Have you already sliced the bread (/prosciutto)?

■ C'era una nebbia da affettare. (*fig*)
There was an extremely dense fog.

■ La loro figlia affettava un'aria disinvolta.
Their daughter feigned indifference (or put on a casual air).

■ Tutti affettavano una grande ammirazione per lui.
They all affected a great admiration for him.

affezionarsi a qc/qco   (auxiliary *essere*) to grow fond of sb/sth; to get to like sth

■ Olga si è affezionata molto al tuo bambino (/al nuovo maestro/al gattino).
Olga has grown very fond of your child (/the new teacher/the kitten).

■ Pietro si è affezionato al suo lavoro.
Peter got to like his work.

affidare (qco a qc)   to entrust (sb with sth); to assign; to confide; to commit; to grant custody

■ Gli aveva affidato tutti i suoi averi (/una lettera/i suoi gioielli).
She had entrusted him with all her belongings (/a letter/her jewels).

■ Pensavo che gli avessero affidato un incarico importante.
I thought they had assigned him an important task.

■ Non affidare un segreto a qualcuno che non conosci bene.
Do not confide a secret to someone you do not know well.

- Affidiamo l'anima a Dio.
  Let's commit our souls to God.

- Il giudice ha affidato i bambini alla madre (/ai nonni).
  The judge granted custody of the children to their mother (/grandparents).

  affidarsi a qc/qco   to trust in sb; to rely on sth

  - Affidati a Dio (/alla fortuna/al caso).
    Trust in God (/good fortune/fate).

  - Mi affido alla tua discrezione (/al tuo buon senso/alla tua generosità).
    I rely on your discretion (/good sense/generosity).

affittare   to rent; to let; to lease

- La signora Anselmi ha affittato una camera a uno studente.
  Mrs. Anselmi rented out (or let) a room to a student.

- Camere d'affittare.
  Rooms for rent.

- Dovremo affittare una macchina per andare là (/un appartamento in centro).
  We'll have to rent a car to go there (/an apartment downtown).

- Pensano di affittare un podere in Toscana.
  They plan to lease some (agricultural) land in Tuscany.

affogare   (auxiliary *essere;* if the verb is followed by a direct object, auxiliary *avere*)
to drown

- Il bambino affogò nel fiume.
  The child drowned in the river.

- Il ragazzo ha affogato il gattino nel lago.
  The boy drowned the kitten in the lake.

- A te piacciono le uova affogate?
  Do you like poached eggs?

- Suo marito affoga i dispiaceri nel vino. (*fig*)
  Her husband drowns his sorrows in wine. (fig)

- Tu affoghi in quella giacca. (*fig*)
  That jacket is much too big for you.

- Credo che Giorgio sia affogato nei debiti. (*fig*)
  I think George is up to his ears in debt.

affondare   to sink

- Pensano di aver affondato due navi nemiche.
  They think they sank two enemy ships.

- La barca a vela affondò.
  The sailboat sank.

affondare in qco   to sink into sth

- I nostri piedi affondavano nella neve (/nel fango).
  Our feet were sinking into the snow (/mud).

affondare qco in qco to thrust sth into sth; to drive sth into sth

- L'assassino gli affondò il pugnale nel petto.
  The murderer thrust the dagger into his chest.

- Hanno affondato un grosso palo nel terreno.
  They drove a big stake into the ground.

- Non affondare il dito nella piaga! (*fig*)
  Don't pour salt on the wound! (fig)

affrettare   to hasten, hurry

- Puoi affrettare il passo?
  Can you quicken your pace?

affrettarsi   to hurry (up), hasten

- Affrettati, se vuoi arrivare in tempo.
  Hurry up if you want to arrive on time.

affrettarsi a + *inf*   to hurry (up), to hasten to + *inf*

- Affrettatevi a tornare (/scendere/salire).
  Hurry back (/down/up).

- Ci affrettammo ad andarcene (/a dirglielo/a rispondere alla lettera).
  We hastened to leave (/tell him/answer the letter).

affrontare qc/qco   to face, confront sb/sth; to tackle sth

- Quel nostro amico non ha paura di affrontare il pericolo.
  That friend of ours is not afraid to face (or afraid of facing) danger.

- I soldati affrontarono il nemico.
  The soldiers confronted the enemy.

- Bisogna che affrontiate il problema.
  You need to tackle the problem.

aggiornare   to adjourn; to bring, keep up-to-date

- La seduta è aggiornata al 15.
  The meeting is adjourned until the 15th.

- Questo dizionario è stato aggiornato.
  This dictionary has been updated.

- Non mi sembra che tu sia aggiornato su questi argomenti.
  I do not think you are up-to-date on these topics.

aggiornarsi   to get oneself up-to-date

- Perché non ti aggiorni?
  Why don't you get yourself up-to-date?

aggiungere   to add

- Non ho altro da aggiungere.
  I have nothing to add.

- Dovresti aggiungere un po' di sale (/l'interesse al capitale).
  You should add some salt (/the interest to the capital).

aggiungersi   to join

- A Firenze un nuovo viaggiatore si aggiunse al gruppo.
  A new traveler joined the group in Florence.

- A questo si aggiunse la malattia del loro figlio.
  On top of this came their son's illness.

aggiustare   to repair, fix, mend; to settle

- Devo fare aggiustare il mio orologio (/le scarpe).
  I must have my watch (/my shoes) repaired.

- La mamma ha aggiustato tutte le calze.
  Mother has mended all the socks.

- Hanno aggiustato la controversia (/le cose/i conti). (*fig*)
  They settled the dispute (/matters/the accounts).

- Lo hanno aggiustato per le feste. (*idiomatic*)
  They gave him a good thrashing.

aggiustarsi   to come to an agreement, an understanding

- Sull'affitto ci aggiusteremo.
  We'll come to an understanding about the rent.

aggravare   to increase; to make worse (more serious); to overload

- Hanno aggravato la pena.
  They increased the sentence.

- Non aggravare la responsabilità di quel ragazzo!
  Don't increase that boy's responsibility!

- Questi scioperi aggravano la situazione.
  These strikes make the situation more serious.

- Tu non fai che aggravare le cose.
  You are only making things worse.

aggravarsi   to get more serious; to get worse

■   Le condizioni del paziente si sono aggravate.
The patient's condition has gotten worse.

■   La situazione politica in quel paese si è aggravata.
The political situation in that country has grown more serious.

agire   to act, operate, work; to behave; to take legal steps

■   Hanno agito di comune accordo.
They acted by mutual consent.

■   Questa medicina agisce sul sistema cardio-vascolare.
This medication acts on the cardiovascular system.

■   Quel medicinale non sembra agire.
That drug does not seem to work.

■   Questo congegno agisce rapidamente.
This device works fast.

■   Non si agisce così.
That's not the way to behave.

■   Tuo genero ha agito da gentiluomo (/da delinquente/bene/male).
Your son-in-law behaved like a gentleman (/like a criminal/well/badly).

■   Dovremo agire contro di loro.
We'll have to take legal steps against them.

agitare   to wave, shake; to agitate; to stir (up); to discuss

■   L'uomo agitava il cappello (/il fazzoletto/la mano) in segno di saluto.
The man was waving his hat (/handkerchief/hand) as a sign of greeting.

■   Agitare prima dell'uso.
Shake before using.

■   Lo scopo dell'uomo politico era di agitare le masse.
The politician's goal was to stir up the masses.

■   Il vento agitava le foglie.
The wind was stirring the leaves.

■   Agitarono a lungo la questione dei licenziamenti.
They discussed the matter of layoffs for a long time.

agitarsi   to toss; to agitate; to get upset

■   Il paziente (/Il bambino) si agitava nel sonno.
The patient (/child) was tossing in his sleep.

■   Quando arrivò la polizia, la folla cominciò ad agitarsi.
When the police arrived, the crowd became agitated.

■   Le acque del fiume (/lago) cominciarono ad agitarsi.
The river (/lake) waters began to get rough.

agitarsi per qco   to agitate for; to get upset over sth

- Gli operai si agitano per un aumento di salario.
  The workers are agitating for a salary increase.

- Tu ti agiti per così poco.
  You get upset over so little.

aiutare (qc/qco)   to help (sb); to aid (sb/sth); to stimulate (sth)

- Aiutami!
  Help me!
- Si devono aiutare i bisognosi.
  The needy must be helped.
- In casi di questo genere la memoria del paziente va aiutata.
  In cases like this, the patient's memory must be stimulated.

aiutare qc a + *inf*   to help sb with/into/out/down + *inf*

- La mamma lo aiuta sempre a fare il compito.
  Mom always helps him with his homework.

- Perché non la aiuti a salire in (/a scendere dalla) macchina?
  Why don't you help her into (/out of) the car?

- Aiutami a fare il letto (/pulire la casa/preparare la cena).
  Help me make the bed (/clean the house/get supper ready).

aiutarsi   to help onself/each other/one another

- Aiutati, che Dio ti aiuta. (*proverb*)
  God helps those who help themselves. (proverb)

- I due fratelli si erano sempre aiutati.
  The two brothers had always helped each other.

allargare   to broaden, widen; to enlarge; to increase; to spread; to open (up); to stretch; to let out

- Stavano allargando la stradina.
  They were widening the little road.
- Devono allargare le loro vedute.
  They have to broaden their views.
- Allargò le braccia scoraggiato.
  Discouraged, he opened his arms.

■ Queste scarpe sono troppo strette, devo farle allargare.
These shoes are too tight; I must have them stretched.

■ Hai fatto allargare la tua gonna?
Did you have your skirt let out?

allargarsi   to expand; to broaden; to spread out, widen out

■ L'attività si è allargata recentemente.
Activity has expanded recently.

■ Dopo questa ansa il fiume si allarga.
After this bend the river broadens.

■ Ho provato a usare uno smacchiatore, ma la macchia si è allargata.
I tried using a stain remover, but the stain has spread out.

alleggerire qc/qco (di qco)   to lighten; to relieve sb/sth (of sth)

■ Hanno alleggerito la barca.
They lightened the boat.

■ Devo alleggerire il mio bagaglio.
I must make my luggage lighter.

■ Fu alleggerito di molte responsabilità (/di quell'obbligo).
He was relieved of many responsibilities (/that obligation).

alleggerirsi (di qco)   to relieve oneself of sth; to put on lighter clothes

■ Si è alleggerito di quella responsabilità.
He relieved himself of that responsibility.

■ Confessando il ragazzo si alleggerì dei rimorsi. (*fig*)
By confessing, the boy unburdened his guilt.

■ Non fa ancora abbastanza caldo per alleggerirsi.
It is not yet warm enough to put on lighter clothes.

allenare   to train, coach

■ Un mio amico allena quella squadra di calcio (/quei cavalli da corsa) da molto tempo.
A friend of mine has been coaching that soccer team (/those racehorses) for a long time.

■ È un atleta ben allenato.
He is a well-trained athlete.

allenarsi   to train

■ Si stanno allenando per l'incontro di domenica (/le Olimpiadi).
They are training for the Sunday match (/the Olympics).

allentare (to loosen, slacken; to relax)

■ Dovresti allentare la fasciatura (la stretta).
You should loosen the bandage (your hold).

■ Angelo spera che suo padre allenti i cordoni della borsa. (*fig*)
Angelo hopes his father will loosen his purse strings. (fig)

■ Allentiamo il passo (/la cintura di sicurezza).
Let's slacken the pace (loosen the seatbelt).

■ È consigliabile non allentare la disciplina.
It is advisable not to relax discipline.

allentarsi   to get less rigid; to loosen

■ Mi sembra che la sorveglianza si sia allentata.
It seems to me that supervision has become less rigid.

■ Perché non ti allenti la cravatta?
Why don't you loosen your tie?

alleviare   to alleviate, make sth lighter/easier

■ La morfina alleviò le sofferenze del malato.
Morphine alleviated the sick man's suffering.

■ Questo alleviò la nostra fatica.
This made our hard job easier.

allontanare   to move, send away; to banish; to alienate; to dismiss

■ Allontana quella sedia dal caminetto: potrebbe bruciarsi.
Move that chair away from the fireplace; it could get burned.

■ La hanno allontanata.
They sent her away.

■ Questo contribuì ad allontanare ogni sospetto.
This helped banish any suspicion.

■ Il suo comportamento allontana tutti.
His behavior alienates everyone.

■ Un altro impiegato è stato allontanato per la stessa ragione.
Another employee was dismissed for the same reason.

allontanarsi   to go, draw away; to leave; to wander

■ Si sono allontanati senza salutare.
They went away without saying goodbye.

■ Era d'aspettarsi che la moglie s'allontanasse da lui.
It was to be expected that his wife would leave him.

■ Io penso che tu ti stia allontanando dall'argomento.
I think you're wandering from the subject.

alludere a qc/qco   to allude to sb/sth

- Penso di sapere a chi (/che cosa) volete alludere.
  I think I know to whom (/what) you want to allude.

- Durante la riunione si alluse al problema economico.
  The economic problem was alluded to during the meeting.

allungare   to lengthen; to prolong; to stretch; to give; to pass; to dilute; to reach out

- Io credo che dovresti allungare la gonna (/il suono di quella vocale).
  I think you should lengthen your skirt (/the sound of that vowel).

- Vorrei che potessimo allungare le vacanze.
  I wish we could prolong our vacation.

- Il ragazzo allungò il collo, ma non riuscì a vederla.
  The boy stretched his neck, but he couldn't see her.

- Allungami il giornale (/quel libro), per favore.
  Pass me the newspaper (/that book), please.

- Il ladro allungò le mani sui gioielli.
  The thief got a hold of (or laid hands on) the jewels.

- Mio fratello beve sempre il vino allungato con l'acqua.
  My brother always drinks wine diluted with water.

- Non potreste allungare il passo? Siamo già in ritardo.
  Couldn't you speed up? We are already late.

  allungarsi   to get longer; to stretch out; to grow taller

  - Hai notato che le giornate cominciano ad allungarsi?
    Have you noticed that the days are getting longer?

  - Sono stanco: vorrei allungarmi un po' sul letto.
    I am tired; I'd like to stretch out on the bed for a while.

  - Come si è allungato suo figlio!
    How tall your son has grown!

alzare (qco)   to raise, lift (sth); to build

- Non c'è bisogno di alzare la voce!
  There's no need for you to raise your voice!

- Lo studente alzò la mano per rispondere.
  The student raised his hand to answer.

- Non hanno alzato un dito per aiutarla. (*fig*)
  They did not lift a finger to help her. (fig)

- Alza quella sedia, per favore.
  Lift that chair, please.

- Per favore, alza il finestrino, ho freddo.
  Please roll up the window. I'm cold.

■ Hanno alzato un muro fra di loro.
They built a wall between themselves.

■ Chi alzerà la bandiera?
Who'll raise the flag?

■ Il ragazzo alzò le spalle.
The boy shrugged his shoulders.

alzarsi   to get up, rise, raise; to get tall

■ Mia nipote si alzava sempre tardi (/presto/alle sette).
My niece would always get up late (/early/at seven).

■ Il sipario (/Il sole) si alza alle otto (/alle cinque).
The curtain (/The sun) rises at eight (five).

■ Lo studente si alzò per prendere il libro.
The student rose to get the book.

■ Mia figlia si è alzata molto.
My daughter has gotten very tall.

amare   to love

■ Francesca lo amava alla follia.
Frances loved him to distraction.

■ Roberta ama la musica classica (/gli impressionisti/gli animali/la cucina francese/la poesia/il nuoto/la giustizia/le comodità).
Roberta loves classical music (/the impressionists/animals/French cooking/poetry/ swimming/justice/comfort).

amarsi   to love each other/one another; to love oneself

■ Si amano nonostante la differenza d'età.
They love each other despite the difference in ages.

ammalarsi   (auxiliary *essere*) to fall ill, take ill

■ Il nonno di Giuseppe si ammalò seriamente un anno fa e morì.
Joseph's grandfather was taken seriously ill a year ago and died.

■ La bambina si è ammalata di bronchite.
The little girl got bronchitis.

ammazzare   to kill, murder, slaughter

■ Quell'uomo ha ammazzato cinque persone.
That man killed (or murdered) five people.

■ Il caldo ci ammazza oggi.
The heat is killing us today.

■ Mio nonno ammazza il tempo leggendo.
My grandfather kills time by reading.

ammazzarsi   to kill oneself, get killed

- Si è ammazzato.
  He killed himself.

- Suo figlio si è ammazzato in un incidente di macchina (/scalando il Cervino).
  His son got killed in a car accident (/climbing the Matterhorn).

- Perché ti ammazzi di lavoro?
  Why do you work yourself to death?

ammettere   to admit; to allow (in); to accept; to assume

- Solo pochi candidati sono stati ammessi agli esami.
  Only a few candidates have been admitted to the exams.

- Lo ammetto.
  I admit it.

- Non si ammettono reclami.
  No complaints are allowed.

- Non credo che siano ammessi gli animali nel negozio.
  I don't think animals are allowed in the store.

- La sua richiesta non è stata ammessa.
  Her application has not been accepted.

- Ammettiamo che sia accaduto.
  Let's assume that it happened.

- È una verità ammessa da tutti.
  It is a truth recognized by everyone.

ammettere di + *inf*   to admit (that . . .); to admit to + *ger*

- Ammetti di aver sbagliato?
  Do you admit you made a mistake?

- L'accusato ha ammesso di aver rubato i gioielli.
  The accused admitted to having stolen the jewels.

ammirare   to admire

- Ho sempre ammirato quei quadri (/il tuo comportamento/il loro ingegno).
  I have always admired those paintings (/your behavior/their intelligence).

- Ammiro la tua sfrontatezza.
  I admire (or am amazed at) your audacity.

andare   (auxiliary: *essere*) to go, fly, drive; to fit; to match (clothing); to like; to feel like; must; to sell (well); to be fashionable; to be needed; to walk; to run

- Dove siete andati ieri sera?
  Where did you go last night?

- Vanno sempre a piedi a scuola.
  They always walk to school.

- Questo vestito non mi va più.
  This dress does not fit me anymore.

- Questa borsa non va con questo vestito.
  This handbag does not go with this dress.

- Questo non mi va per niente.
  I don't like this at all.

- Non mi va di andare a teatro stasera.
  I do not feel like going to the theater tonight.

- Il vino bianco va servito freddo.
  White wine must be served chilled.

- Questo prodotto va molto quest'anno.
  This product is selling well this year.

- Ci andranno almeno otto metri di stoffa.
  At least eight meters of fabric will be needed.

andare a qco   to go + *ger;* to run on sth

- Mio fratello è andato a caccia (/pesca/cavallo) domenica scorsa.
  My brother went hunting (/fishing/horseback riding) last Sunday.

- La loro macchina va a metano.
  Their car runs on methanol.

andare a +   to go + *town/city*

- Sua sorella va a Roma (/Chicago) il mese prossimo, signora Sacchi?
  Is your sister going to Rome (/Chicago) next month, Mrs. Sacchi?

andare a +   to go to + *somewhere (specific place)*

- Non vado a casa (/a letto/a scuola/alla lezione/a teatro) stasera.
  I am not going home (/to bed/to school/to class/to the theater) tonight.

- Sei andato al cinema (/allo stadio/all'aeroporto/alla posta centrale) ieri?
  Did you go to the movies (/stadium/airport/central post office) yesterday?

andare a + *inf*   to go + *ger/inf*

- Perché non andiamo a ballare?
  Why don't we go dancing?

- I bambini sono andati a dormire presto ieri sera.
  The children went to sleep early last night.

■ La settimana prossima devo andare a trovare i miei genitori.
Next week I have to visit my parents.

andare in + *country singular*   to go + *country singular*

■ Vorrei andare in Italia (/Olanda/Grecia) la prossima estate.
I'd like to go to Italy (/Holland/Greece) next summer.

andare in + **article** + *country plural*   to go + *country plural*

■ Andranno negli Stati Uniti appena potranno.
They'll go to the United States as soon as they can.

andare in + *means of transportation*   to go by + *means of transportation*

■ Tu andrai in bicicletta (/moto[cicletta]/scooter/macchina/auto[mobile]/treno/aereo/barca)?
Will you go by bike (/motorcycle/moped/car/automobile/train/airplane/boat)?

andare in + *somewhere/room of house*   to go into/to + *somewhere/room of house*

■ Quando andate in campagna (/montagna/piscina/palestra/banca/chiesa/albergo/ufficio)?
When are you going to the countryside (/mountains/swimming pool/gym/bank/church/hotel/office)?

■ Vado in cucina (/camera da letto/bagno/soggiorno/sala da pranzo).
I'm going into the kitchen (/bedroom/bathroom/living room/dining room).

andare da (*article***)**   to go to sb's house/apartment/restaurant/sb's office (that of a professional, e.g., doctor, dentist, attorney, architect, etc.)/a store

■ Lei pensa che siano andati dal loro zio (/da Maria/dal dottore/dalla signora Anselmi/da Giannino/dal panettiere/dal parrucchiere)?
Do you think they went to their uncle's place (/Maria's/the doctor's/Mrs. Anselmi's/Giannino's restaurant/ the baker's/the beauty salon)?

andar via   to go away, leave; to come off (stains)

■ Papà è appena andato via.
Dad has just left.

■ Mi dispiace, ma questa macchia non va via.
I am sorry, but this stain does not come off.

andarsene   to leave; to get out

■ Finalmente se ne sono andati!
Finally they left!

■   Vattene!
Get out! (Go away!)

animare   to animate; to enliven, liven up; to encourage

■   L'arrivo di Luca (/La sua presenza) animò la festa (/la conversazione).
Luke's arrival (/His presence) enlivened the party (/the conversation).

■   Cosa possiamo fare per animare la festa?
What can we do to liven up the party?

animarsi   to come to life; to become livelier; to light up

■   Di notte quella parte della città si animava.
At night that part of the city would come to life.

■   La conversazione si anima.
The conversation becomes livelier.

■   Il viso del bambino si animò lentamente.
The child's face lit up slowly.

annoiare qc (con)   to bore sb (with)

■   I suoi discorsi mi annoiano a morte.
His speeches bore me to death.

■   Non annoiarmi con le tue chiacchiere (/le tue prediche).
Don't bore me with your idle talk (/your sermons).

annoiarsi   to get bored

■   Ai concerti il padre di Anna si annoiava e si addormentava.
At the concerts Ann's father would get bored and fall asleep.

■   Si sono annoiati a quelle riunioni (/quegli spettacoli).
They got bored at those meetings (/those shows).

annoiarsi a + *inf*   to get bored + *ger*

■   Sua nonna si annoia a non far nulla (/leggere/guardare la tv).
Her grandmother gets bored doing nothing (/reading/watching TV).

annullare   to annul, cancel; to undo

■   Pensano che il loro matrimonio possa essere annullato.
They think their marriage can be annulled.

■   Il contratto (/L'ordine) è già stato annullato.
The contract (/order) has been canceled already.

■   L'impiegato deve annullare i francobolli con un timbro.
The employee has to cancel the stamps with a postmark.

■   Sfortunatamente questo annullerà i benefici della cura.
Unfortunately, this will undo the benefits of the treatment.

anticipare / to move up; to arrive; to pay in advance; to come early; to disclose /

- Devono anticipare la partenza (/la data del matrimonio).
  They have to move up their departure (/the date of their wedding).

- Gli hanno anticipato un mese di stipendio.
  They paid him a month's salary in advance.

- L'autobus (/Il signor Rossi) ha anticipato di un'ora.
  The bus (/Mr. Rossi) arrived an hour early.

- Il freddo (/Il caldo/La primavera/L'inverno) ha anticipato.
  The cold (/The warm weather/Spring/Winter) has come earlier.

- Il segretario del ministro ha anticipato alla stampa i risultati dell'inchiesta.
  The minister's secretary has disclosed the results of the inquiry to the press.

apparire a qc   (auxiliary *essere*) to appear to sb

- Le apparve in sogno il figlio morto.
  Her dead son appeared to her in her dreams.

  apparire (a/in)   to appear (on/in); to loom /

  - Il sole è apparso all'orizzonte (/a est).
    The sun appeared on the horizon (/in the east).

  - Da questa deposizione appare la sua colpevolezza.
    From this testimony it appears that he is guilty.

  - La costa apparve nell'oscurità.
    The coast loomed in the darkness.

  apparire + *adj*   to look + *adj*

  - Il tuo amico vuole apparire elegante (/aggiornato/raffinato).
    Your friend wants to look elegant (/up-to-date/refined).

appartenere a qc/qco   to belong to sb/sth, be a member of sth

- Questa terra appartiene a loro da secoli.
  This land has belonged to them for centuries.

- Mio marito non appartiene più al circolo filatelico.
  My husband is no longer a member of the philatelic club.

applaudire   to applaud, clap; to approve

- Il pubblico applaudì i musicisti per un quarto d'ora.
  The public applauded the musicians for fifteen minutes.

- Tutti hanno applaudito la proposta del sindaco.
  Everyone approved of the mayor's proposal.

applicare (qco a/su)   to stick sth on, apply sth (on/to)/to enforce

- Devi applicare due francobolli sulla lettera (/un'etichetta sulla bottiglia).
  You have to stick two stamps on the letter (/a label on the bottle).

- Il dottore mi ha detto di applicare dell'unguento sulla ferita.
  My doctor told me to apply some ointment on the wound.

- Stanno applicando i risultati della loro ricerca.
  They are applying the results of their research.

- Bisogna che tu applichi la mente a quello che fai.
  You need to apply your mind to what you're doing.

- La legge va applicata.
  The law must be enforced.

   applicarsi   to apply oneself

   - È un ragazzo molto intelligente, ma non si applica.
     He is a very intelligent boy, but he doesn't study (or apply himself).

appoggiare   to lay; to lean; to rest; to second; to support

- Appoggia il piatto sul tavolo.
  Lay the plate on the table.

- Perché non appoggiamo la scala alla parete?
  Why don't we lean the ladder against the wall?

- La statua appoggia su una base di marmo.
  The statue rests on a marble base.

- Noi tutti appoggiammo la mozione.
  We all seconded the motion.

- Appoggeremo la vostra petizione (/il vostro candidato/la vostra proposta).
  We will support your petition (/candidate/proposal).

   appoggiarsi   to lean

   - La vecchia si appoggiò al braccio del nipote.
     The old woman leaned on her grandson's arm.

   - Nei momenti difficili ci si appoggia alla famiglia.
     In difficult times one leans on one's family.

approfittare   to take advantage of sth; to avail oneself of sth

- Approfittarono dell'occasione per fare un viaggio.
  They took advantage of the opportunity to take a trip.

- Voglio approfittare della loro offerta.
  I want to avail myself of their offer.

approfittarsi di qco   to take advantage of sth

■   Antonio si approfitta dell'ingenuità della moglie.
Anthony takes advantage of his wife's naïveté.

aprire   to open (up); to lead; to start; to turn on

■   Apri la mano, per favore.
Open your hand, please.

■   Credo che il cancello sia stato aperto dai bambini.
I think the gate was opened by the children.

■   Oggi vado in banca ad aprire un nuovo conto.
Today I am going to the bank to open a new account.

■   Credi che quel negozio sia ancora aperto? —No, è chiuso.
Do you think that store is still open? —No, it is closed.

■   Il vescovo apriva la processione.
The bishop was leading the procession.

■   Il conferenziere aprì il discorso dicendo "Cari amici!"
The lecturer started his speech by saying, "Dear friends!"

■   Hanno aperto una sottoscrizione per i senzatetto.
They have started a subscription fund for the homeless.

■   Perché hai aperto la radio (/la televisione/la luce)?
Why did you turn on the radio (/the television/the light)?

■   Apri bene gli occhi (/le orecchie)!
Keep your eyes (/ears) open!

aprirsi   to open; to bloom; to begin

■   Il dialogo si aprì subito.
The dialogue opened at once.

■   Le finestre della camera da letto si aprono sul mare.
The bedroom windows open on the sea.

■   Si sono aperti i primi fiori.
The first flowers have bloomed.

■   La stagione della caccia si è aperta il sedici agosto.
The hunting season began on the sixteenth of August.

arrendersi   to surrender; to yield

■   Le truppe nemiche si arresero a discrezione.
The enemy troops surrendered unconditionally.

■   Mi sono dovuto arrendere alle preghiere degli amici.
I had to yield to my friends' entreaties.

■   Dobbiamo arrenderci all'evidenza.
We must face the facts.

arrestare   /to stop/ to arrest, capture; to halt

- Signor Baldini, arresti il motore.
  Mr. Baldini, stop the engine.

- Non si può arrestare il progresso.
  Progress can't be stopped.

- Il polizotto lo ha arrestato per furto con scasso.
  The policeman arrested him for burglary.

- Dope tre anni non hanno ancora arrestato l'evasore fiscale.
  After three years the tax evader is still at large.

- Speriamo che possano arrestare il nemico.
  Let's hope they can halt the enemy.

arrestarsi   to stop, come to a halt; to pause

- L'orologio si arrestò a mezzanotte.
  The clock stopped at midnight.

- Il treno si è arrestato improvvisamente.
  The train came suddenly to a halt.

1. arrivare   (auxiliary *essere*) to arrive

- Quando arrivano i tuoi amici? —Arrivano domani (/giovedì/la settimana prossima/fra un mese).
  When do your friends arrive? —They arrive tomorrow (/Thursday/next week/in a month).

arrivare a + *somewhere*   to arrive at + *somewhere*

- Loro sono arrivati a scuola (/a casa/a lezione/a teatro/alla stazione/all'aero-porto/allo stadio) tardi.
  They arrived at school (/home/class/the station/the airport/the stadium) late.

arrivare a   to go as far as

- Arriviamo alla chiesa (/alla piazza) e poi torniamo.
  We are going as far as the church (/square), and then we are coming back.

arrivare a + *town/city*   to arrive at + *town/city*

- Arriverò a Milano (/Roma/Firenze) giovedì prossimo.
  I'll arrive in Milan (/Rome/Florence) next Thursday.

arrivare in + *country singular*   to arrive in + *country singular*

- Arrivarono in Messico (/in Italia) nel 1910.
  They arrived in Mexico (/Italy) in 1910.

arrivare in + *article* + *country plural*   to arrive in + (*country plural*)

■ È appena arrivata negli Stati Uniti.
   She has just arrived in the United States.

arrivare in + *means of transportation*   to arrive by + *means of transportation*

■ Mia sorella è arrivata in macchina (/treno/aereo).
   My sister arrived by car (/train/plane).

arrivare a + *time*   to arrive at + *time*

■ A che ora arriveresti? —Potrei arrivare a mezzogiorno (/all'una/alle sette).
   What time would you arrive? —I could arrive at noon (/one/seven).

arrivare a qco/arrivarci   to reach sth; to come up

■ Dobbiamo assolutamente arrivare a un accordo (/una decisione).
   We absolutely must reach an agreement (/a decision).

■ L'acqua le arrivava già al petto.
   The water already reached her chest.

■ Quel cassetto è troppo alto: non ci arrivo.
   That drawer is too high; I can't reach it.

2. arrivare   to arrive; to happen

■ Il tuo libro mi è arrivato ieri.
   Your book arrived yesterday.

■ Non si può mai sapere cosa può arrivare.
   One can never know what might happen.

arrivare a + *inf*   to manage, be able to + *inf*

■ Arriveremo a finirlo (tradurlo/impararlo) per le tre?
   Will we manage to finish (/translate/learn) it by three o'clock?

asciugare   to dry

■ Non le piace asciugare i piatti.
   She doesn't like to dry the dishes.

■ La mamma le asciugò le lacrime.
   Her mother dried her tears.

asciugarsi   to dry oneself (off)

■ I bambini non si sono asciugati.
   The children did not dry themselves off.

- Devo asciugarmi i piedi (/i capelli).
  I have to dry my feet (/hair).

ascoltare (qc/qco)   to listen to sb/sth; to attend sth; to obey sb; to grant sth; to pay attention

- I ragazzi stanno ascoltando un disco (/un loro amico/un discorso).
  The kids are listening to a record (/a friend of theirs/a speech).

- Perché non mi ascolti?
  Why don't you listen to me?

- Quegli studenti non ascoltavano le lezioni regolarmente.
  Those students would not attend classes on a regular basis.

- Quei bambini non ascoltano mai i genitori.
  Those children never obey their parents.

- Speriamo che Dio ascolti le nostre preghiere.
  Let's hope God will grant our prayers.

- Ascolta!
  Pay attention!

aspettare qc/qco   to wait for sb/sth

- Chi aspetti? —Aspetto mia moglie.
  Whom are you waiting for? —I'm waiting for my wife.

- Che cosa aspetta? —Aspetto la posta (/l'autobus).
  What are you waiting for? —I'm waiting for the mail (/the bus).

- Il professore lo (/la/li) aspetta da dieci minuti.
  The professor has been waiting for him (/her/them) for ten minutes.

- Aspettiamo il momento propizio (/un'occasione favorevole) per agire.
  We are waiting for the right moment (/a favorable occasion) to act.

aspettare di + *inf*   to wait + *inf*

- Aspettavamo di sapere qualcosa di suo padre (/essere mandati all'estero/ottenere la promozione).
  We were waiting to hear something about his father (/to be sent overseas/to get a promotion).

aspettare che qc/qco + *subj*   to wait for sb/sth + *inf*

- Aspetti che venga tua zia (/il bel tempo/la posta)?
  Are you waiting for your aunt (/good weather/the mail) to come?

- Aspettavano che avvenisse qualcosa di nuovo.
  They were waiting for something new to happen.

aspettarsi qco (da qc)   to expect sth (of sb)

- Non mi aspetto niente di buono da loro.
  I don't expect anything good of them.

- I genitori si aspettavano molto (/troppo) da lui.
  His parents expected a lot (/too much) of him.

- Questo loro se l'aspettavano.
  They were expecting this.

aspettarsi di + *inf*   to expect + *inf*

- Non ci aspettavamo di vederlo là.
  We didn't expect to see him there.

- Si aspetta di essere pagato (/chiamato) domani.
  He expects to be paid (/called) tomorrow.

aspettarsi che qc/qco + *subj*   to expect sb/sth + *inf*

- Si aspettava che lui tornasse (/la guerra finisse presto).
  She expected him to come back (/the war to end soon).

aspirare   to inhale; to draw away; to aspirate

- Quando fumo non aspiro.
  When I smoke, I don't inhale.

- Si dovette aspirare l'acqua con una pompa.
  The water had to be drawn away with a pump.

- In inglese l'acca è quasi sempre aspirata.
  In English, h *is almost always aspirated.*

aspirare a qco   to aspire to sth

- Quel pittore aspirava al successo (/alla fama/all'immortalità).
  That painter aspired to success (/fame/immortality).

aspirare a + *inf*   to aim at + *ger*

- Aspirava a diventare sindaco (/scrittore/chirurgo/astronauta/attore).
  He aimed at (or His goal was) becoming mayor (/a writer/a surgeon/ an astronaut/an actor).

assegnare   to assign; to award; to fix

- Ci hanno assegnato un compito gravoso (/un lavoro pesante).
  They assigned us an irksome task (/a heavy job).

- L'hanno assegnata a un altro reparto (/alla sede di Milano).
  They assigned her to another department (/the Milan office).

- Gli hanno assegnato il premio Bancarella.
  They awarded him the Bancarella prize.

- Il tempo assegnato per questo lavoro è scaduto.
  The time limit fixed for this job has expired.

assicurare   to guarantee, assure

■ Ti posso assicurare un buon stipendio (/una carriera).
I can guarantee you a good salary (/a career).

assicurare qc che   to assure sb that

■ Ti assicuro che verrò alla prossima riunione (/non è vero).
I assure you that I'll come to the next meeting (/it isn't true).

■ Ci assicurò che le avrebbe parlato.
He assured us that he would talk to her.

assicurare qco a qc   to secure sb sth

■ Voleva assicurare alla sua famiglia una vacanza serena (/ai figli un avvenire).
He wanted to secure a peaceful holiday for his family (/a future for his children).

assicurare qc/qco a qco   to secure sb/sth to sth; to insure sth

■ Dovresti assicurare la fune all'albero (/il bambino al seggiolino dell'auto).
You should secure the rope to the tree (/the child in the car seat).

■ Perché non assicuri la porta con una catena?
Why don't you fasten the door with a chain?

■ Hai assicurato la lettera (/il pacco)?
Did you insure the letter (/the package)?

assicurare qco contro qco   to insure sth against sth

■ Hanno assicurato la casa contro gli incendi (/i suoi gioielli contro il furto).
They have insured their house against fire (/her jewels against theft).

assicurarsi qco   to secure sth for oneself

■ Voglio assicurarmi una copia del suo ultimo articolo.
I want to secure myself a copy of his last article.

assicurarsi che + *subj*   to make sure (that)

■ Assicurati che non ci sia nessuno (/abbiano comprato il giornale).
Make sure no one is there (/they bought the newspaper).

assicurarsi a qco   to fasten oneself to sth

■ Ti sei assicurato al cavo?
Did you fasten yourself to the cable?

assicurarsi contro qco   to insure against sth

■ Vi siete assicurati contro il furto (/gli incendi)?
Did you insure yourselves against theft (/fire)?

■   Mi sono assicurato sulla vita.
    I took out a life insurance policy.

assicurarsi di qco/di + *inf*   to make, be sure of sth/make sure (that)

■   Si sono assicurati della sua innocenza?
    Did they make sure of his innocence?

■   Assicurati di poter venire (/avere i soldi) prima di far promesse.
    Make sure you can come (/you have the money) before making promises.

assistere   to attend; to assist, give assistance to; to look after

■   Nicola ha assistito a tutte le lezioni (/alla Messa).
    Nicolas attended all the classes (/Mass).

■   Assistilo come puoi.
    Give him all the assistance you can.

■   Madre Teresa assisteva i lebbrosi.
    Mother Teresa looked after the lepers.

associare   to associate; to join, pool; to make a member of

■   Non li avevo associati con quell'avvenimento.
    I hadn't associated them with that event.

■   Associamo i diversi concetti (/la sostanza e l'immagine).
    Let's join the different concepts (/substance and image).

■   Hanno associato i loro capitali.
    They pooled their capital.

■   Ho associato mio nipote al nostro circolo.
    I made my nephew a member of our club.

associarsi   to join; to share

■   Si sono associati al circolo (/al nuovo partito).
    They joined the club (/the new political party).

■   Ci associamo al dolore (/alla gioia) di Diana.
    We share Diane's sorrow (/joy).

assolvere (da/per)   to absolve (of/from); to acquit; to accomplish

■   Il sacerdote lo assolse da tutti i suoi peccati.
    The priest absolved him of all his sins.

■   Fu assolto dal suo giuramento.
    He was absolved from his oath.

■   Sperano che sia assolto per insufficienza di prove.
    They hope he will be acquitted for lack of evidence.

- Dovete assolvere quel compito.
  You must accomplish that task.

assorbire   to soak up, absorb; to engross, to take up; to assimilate

- La carta da cucina assorbirà l'acqua.
  The paper towel will soak up (or absorb) the water.

- Quel lavoro ha assorbito tutte le mie forze.
  That job took up all my strength.

- Quel programma televisivo assorbiva l'attenzione dei ragazzi.
  The kids were engrossed in that TV program (literally: That TV program engrossed the kids' attention).

assumere   to assume; to put on; to take on; to hire; to raise

- Credo che quella scrittrice abbia assunto uno pseudonimo.
  I think that female writer assumed a pseudonym.

- Il padre di Giovanni assunse il comando della spedizione (/la responsabilità dell'impresa).
  John's father assumed the command of the expedition (/the responsibility of the enterprise).

- Si assume che siano morti.
  It is assumed that they died.

- Il signor Carlini assume sempre quell'aria annoiata (/quell'aria distaccata).
  Mr. Carlini always puts on that bored expression (/air of detachment).

- Quel fatto ha assunto grande importanza.
  That event has taken on great importance.

- Hanno assunto nuovi operai.
  They took on (or hired) new laborers.

- Dobbiamo assumere informazioni su di lei.
  We have to make inquiries about her.

- Il cardinale poi fu assunto al pontificato.
  The bishop then was raised to the papacy.

   assumersi   to take (upon oneself); to accept

   - Ci dobbiamo assumere tutti i rischi.
     We must take all the risks.

   - Si è assunto l'incarico.
     He accepted the assignment.

astenersi da qco   (auxiliary *essere*) to abstain from sth/+ *ger*

- Il dottore gli ha detto che deve astenersi dal fumo.
  The doctor told him that he must abstain from smoking.

- Molti si sono astenuti dal voto.
  Many abstained from casting their vote.

  astenersi dal(l') + *inf*   to abstain, refrain from + *ger*

  - Devo astenermi dall'esprimere la mia opinione (/dal farlo).
    I have to abstain from expressing my opinion (/doing it).

  - Decidemmo d'astenerci dal fare domande.
    We decided to refrain from asking questions.

attaccare   to attack; to attach; to be tied; to paste up; to harness; to hang; to start; to catch, be catching, be contagious; to take root

- È stato attaccato da due passanti.
  He was attacked by two passersby.

- Enrico attaccò le opinioni di tutti.
  Henry attacked everybody's opinions.

- Le ho attaccate insieme.
  I attached them together.

- Sei ancora attaccato alle sottane della mamma. (*fig*)
  You are still tied to your mother's apron strings. (fig)

- Hanno attaccato molti manifesti.
  They put up many posters.

- Attaccarono solo due cavalli al carro.
  They harnessed only two horses to the cart.

- Abbiamo attaccato uno specchio sopra il divano.
  We hung a mirror over the sofa.

- Gli operai attaccano alle sette.
  The workmen start work at seven.

- Questa malattia attacca.
  This disease is catching (contagious).

- Tu mi hai attaccato questo vizio (/il morbillo).
  I caught this bad habit (/the measles) from you.

- La pianta sta attaccando.
  The plant is taking root.

- Questa moda sta attaccando fra i giovani.
  This fashion is becoming popular with the young.

  attaccarsi   to cling; to stick; to grow fond of

  - Attaccati alla ringhiera.
    Cling to the rail.

  - L'arrosto si è attaccato al fondo del tegame.
    The roast stuck to the bottom of the pan.

- Ci siamo molto attaccati ai loro bambini.
  We have grown very fond of their children.

attirare   to attract; to appeal; to entice

- A tua sorella piace attirare l'attenzione di tutti.
  Your sister likes to attract everybody's attention.

- Siamo sicuri che questa mostra attirerà migliaia di visitatori.
  We are sure this exhibit will attract thousands of visitors.

- Questo genere di film (/Quel progetto) non mi attira.
  This kind of movie (/That plan) does not attract (or appeal to) me.

- L'hanno attirata con false promesse.
  They enticed her with false promises.

  attirarsi   to draw upon oneself; to win

  - Quell'uomo si è attirato l'odio di tutti.
    That man incurred (or drew upon himself) everybody's hatred.

  - Quei ragazzi si sono lasciati attirare dalla speranza di forti guadagni.
    Those boys let themselves be drawn in by the hope of large gains.

  - Tua madre sa come attirarsi la simpatia (/l'affetto) di tutti.
    Your mother knows how to win everybody's love (/affection).

attraversare   to cross; to go, ride, cycle, drive through; to run, swim across

- Non attraversare col rosso!
  Don't cross against a red light!

- Quell'idea non le attraversò la mente. (*fig*)
  That idea did not cross her mind. (fig)

- Quel mio studente sta attraversando un periodo molto difficile.
  That student of mine is going through a very difficult time.

- Attraversammo la città a piedi (/a cavallo/in bicicletta/in macchina).
  We walked (rode/cycled/drove) through the town.

- I bambini attraversarono il prato correndo.
  The children ran across the meadow.

- Decisero di attraversare il fiume a nuoto.
  They decided to swim across the river.

attuare   to carry out; to bring about

- Hanno attuato il loro piano.
  They carried out their plan.

- Dobbiamo attuare quella riforma.
  We must bring about that reform.

augurare qco a qc   to wish sb sth

- La sua amica gli augurò il buongiorno (/buon compleanno/buon Natale/buona Pasqua/buon viaggio).
  His girlfriend wished him good day (/a happy birthday/a merry Christmas/a happy Easter/a good trip).

- Ti auguriamo gioia (/fortuna/successo/ogni felicità).
  We wish you joy (/good luck/success/every happiness).

- Non augurare il male a nessuno.
  Don't wish anyone ill.

  augurare a qc di + *inf*   to wish (that) sb

  - Ti auguro di riuscire (/avere quello che vuoi/sposarla).
    I wish you would succeed (/get what you want/marry her).

aumentare   to increase; to go up; to rise; to raise

- La produttività va aumentata.
  Productivity must be increased.

- Il freddo sta aumentando.
  It's getting colder (The cold is increasing).

- Il livello del fiume è aumentato.
  The level of the river has risen.

- Le è aumentata la febbre.
  Her temperature has risen.

- Hanno aumentato gli stipendi (/i prezzi).
  They have raised salaries (/prices).

  aumentare (di)   to go up; to gain

  - L'olio (/Questo quadro) è aumentato di prezzo (/valore).
    The price of oil (/The value of this painting) has gone up.

  - Maria è aumentata di peso (/due chili).
    Mary has put on weight (/two kilos).

avanzare   (auxiliary *essere,* but if the verb is followed by a direct object, the auxiliary is *avere*) to advance; to put forward; to save; to be left

- All'alba le nostre truppe avanzeranno.
  At dawn our troops will advance.

- Avanzano nella foresta.
  They are advancing into the forest.

- Tuo figlio ti avanza di un bel pezzo.
  Your son is a lot taller than you are.

- Avanzarono una nuova proposta (/una teoria rivoluzionaria).
  They put forward a new proposal (/a revolutionary theory).

- Dovresti avanzare qualcosa per il futuro.
  You should save something for the future.

- Noi tutti avanziamo negli anni.
  We all are getting on in years.

- Non avanzò niente.
  Nothing was left.

avanzarsi   to advance; to come

- L'esercito ribelle si avanzava.
  The rebel army was advancing.

- L'inverno si avanza.
  Winter is coming.

1. avere   to have

avere (auxiliary verb)

- Carlo ha detto che non voleva mangiare perché aveva già mangiato.
  Charles said he did not want to eat because he had already eaten.

- Ha detto che l'avrebbe fatto.
  He said he would do it.

- Dopo aver studiato, sono andato a letto.
  After studying, I went to bed.

- Ti telefonerò appena gli avrò parlato.
  I'll call you as soon as I have talked to him.

- Lo avrei fatto, se avessi avuto tempo.
  I would have done it if I had had time.

avere qc/qco   to have sb/sth; to feel sth; to own sth

- Suo figlio ha molti amici.
  His son has many friends.

- Io non ho odio per nessuno.
  I do not feel hatred for anybody.

- Giuseppe ha il raffreddore (/la tosse/l'influenza/i reumatismi).
  Joseph has a cold (/a cough/the flu/rheumatism).

- Che cosa hai? (*idiomatic*)
  What's the matter with you?

- I loro parenti non hanno di che vivere.
  Their relatives have nothing to live on.

- Questo non ha niente a che vedere con quello che dicevi.
  This has nothing to do with what you were saying.

- Hanno diversi appartamenti in centro.
  They own several apartments downtown.

- Quanti ne abbiamo oggi? —Ne abbiamo dodici.
  What's the date today? —It is the 12th.

avere da + *inf*   to have to + *inf*

- Ho da scrivere oggi.
  I have to write today.

avere qco da + *inf*   to have sth + *inf*

- Abbiamo veramente molto da fare oggi.
  We really have a lot to do today.

- Mi dispiace, non ho niente da offrirti (/darti).
  I'm sorry, I don't have anything to offer you (/to give you).

avere + *(adj +) noun*   to have/feel (idiomatic) (+ *adv* +) *adj/noun*

- Avevi fame (/sete)? —Sì, avevo molta fame (/sete).
  Were you hungry (/thirsty)? —Yes, I was very hungry (/thirsty).

- Avete freddo (caldo/sonno)? —Sì, abbiamo molto freddo (caldo/sonno).
  Are you cold (warm/sleepy)? —Yes, we are very cold (warm/sleepy).

- La nipote della signora Pierucci ha paura dei cani (/vergogna).
  Mrs. Pierucci's granddaughter is afraid of dogs (/ashamed).

- Tu credi di aver sempre ragione, ma questa volta hai proprio torto.
  You think you are always right, but this time you are really wrong.

- Quel ragazzo ha molto coraggio (/molta fortuna).
  That boy is very brave (/very lucky).

- Quanti anni hai? —Ho dieci anni.
  How old are you? —I am ten years old.

- Lei ha sempre fretta, signora Rossi!
  You are always in a hurry, Mrs. Rossi!

- Avresti voglia di fare una passeggiata?
  Would you feel like taking a walk?

- Di quanti soldi hai bisogno? —Ho bisogno di novecentomila lire.
  How much money do you need? —I need nine hundred thousand lire.

2. avere   to wear

- Mi ricordo che la bambina aveva un vestito rosso.
  I remember that the little girl was wearing a red dress.

avvenire   (auxiliary *essere*) to happen, occur

- Qualunque cosa avvenga, conta su di me.
  Whatever happens, count on me.

avvertire   to let sb know; to notify; to realize; to notice; to feel

- Per favore, mi avverta quando se ne va, signora Galliani.
  Please let me know when you are leaving, Mrs. Galliani.

- Avete già avvertito la polizia?
  Have you already notified the police?

- Non so se avvertano l'importanza di questo fatto.
  I don't know if they realize the importance of this fact.

- Per fortuna la nonna avvertì l'odore di gas e riuscì a evitare una disgrazia.
  Luckily, Grandma noticed the smell of gas and was able to avoid an accident.

- Improvvisamente il ragazzo avvertì un dolore lancinante alla gamba.
  Suddenly the boy felt a stabbing pain in his leg.

avvicinare qco a qc/qco   to approach sth to sb/sth, draw sth near sb/sth

- Avvicina la panca al tavolo (/il libro alla luce).
  Draw the bench near the table (/the book near the light).

- Avvicinò il ministro per congratularsi con lui.
  He approached the minister to congratulate him.

  avvicinarsi   to approach, draw near

  - Si avvicina un temporale (/il treno/il freddo/l'inverno).
    A storm (/The train/The cold/Winter) is approaching.

  - L'ora di smettere si avvicina.
    The time to stop is drawing near.

  avvicinarsi a qc/qco   to approach sb/sth; to be close; to be like

  - La nave si avvicina al porto.
    The ship is approaching the port.

  - Un mendicante gli si avvicinò.
    A beggar approached him.

  - La traduzione (/La copia) si avvicina molto all'originale.
    The translation (/copy) is very close to the original.

  - Come carattere Leonardo si avvicina alla madre.
    Leonard is very much like his mother temperamentally.

avvisare   to inform, let sb know; to warn

- Perché non mi hanno avvisato del suo arrivo?
  Why didn't they inform me about his arrival?

- Avvisami quando vieni.
  Let me know when you are coming.

- Avrebbero dovuto avvisarla del pericolo.
  They should have warned her of the danger.

- Uomo avvisato, mezzo salvato. (*proverb*)
  Forewarned is forearmed. (proverb)

  avvisare qc di + *inf*   to advise sb + *inf*

  - Noi li avvisammo di non farlo.
    We advised them not to do it.

avvolgere   to wrap (up); to shroud; to roll up; to envelop

- Ho avvolto il regalo in un foglio di carta.
  I wrapped the gift in a sheet of paper.

- Hanno avvolto il bambino in uno scialle.
  They wrapped the baby in a shawl.

- La vita di quell'attore era avvolta nel mistero.
  That actor's life was wrapped in mystery.

- La campagna era avvolta nella nebbia.
  The countryside was shrouded in the mist.

- Dobbiamo avvolgere il tappeto per poterlo spostare.
  We must roll up the carpet in order to be able to move it.

- Una densa oscurità li avvolse.
  A thick darkness closed in on them.

- L'uomo era avvolto dalle flamme.
  The man was enveloped in flames.

  avvolgersi   to wrap oneself

  - La ragazza si avvolse nel mantello.
    The girl wrapped herself in the cloak.

B

baciare   to kiss

- Il nonno le baciò la mano.
  Grandfather kissed her hand.

- La ragazza lo baciò sulle guance (/sulla bocca/sulla fronte).
  The girl kissed him on the cheek (/mouth/forehead).

   baciarsi   to kiss each other

   - Si baciarono appassionatamente.
     They kissed passionately.

badare   to look out (for)

- Bada!
  Look out!

   badare a qc/qco   to look after sb/sth; to mind; to listen, pay attention to

   - La suocera di Grazia bada alla casa (/ai bambini/agli affari).
     Grace's mother-in-law looks after the house (/the children/the business).

   - Il pastore badava al gregge.
     The shepherd watched the flock.

   - Badate a quello che dico (/ai vostri affari).
     Mind what I say (/your business).

   - Non dovreste badare alle chiacchiere.
     You should not listen to gossip.

   - Davide non ci bada.
     David does not pay attention to it.

   - Loro non badano a spese.
     They spare no expense.

   - L'hanno fatto senza badare a spese.
     They did it regardless of expense.

   badare a + *inf*   to keep on + *ger;* to care about + *ger*

   - Badate a studiare.
     Keep on studying.

   - Tu badi solo a divertirti.
     All you care about is having fun.

   badare di + *inf*   to be careful (make sure) + *inf*

   - Bada di non farti male (/non perderti).
     Be careful not to get hurt (/not to get lost).

■ Bada di studiare.
Make sure to study.

bagnare   to wet; to soak; to dip; to water; to flow (through); to wash; to sprinkle; to celebrate

■ Il pavimento è bagnato.
The floor is wet.

■ Tua nipote era bagnata fino alle ossa.
Your niece was soaked to the skin.

■ Il bambino bagnò le mani nella fontana.
The little boy dipped his hands in the fountain.

■ Ricordati di bagnare le piante tutti i giorni.
Remember to water the plants every day.

■ L'Arno bagna Firenze. Torino è bagnata dal Po.
The Arno River flows through Florence. The Po River flows through Turin.

■ Napoli è bagnata dal Mare Tirreno.
Naples is washed by the Tyrrhenian Sea.

■ Caterina bagna sempre le camicie di cotone prima di stirarle.
Catherine always sprinkles cotton shirts before ironing them.

■ Dobbiamo bagnare la tua laurea.
We have to celebrate your graduation.

  bagnarsi   to get wet, soaked

  ■ Non avevo l'ombrello e mi sono bagnata.
  I did not have my umbrella, and I got wet.

  ■ Il bambino si è bagnato di nuovo.
  The baby got wet again.

  ■ Gli occhi della bambina si bagnarono di lacrime.
  Tears came to the little girl's eyes.

balbettare   to stammer; to babble

■ Balbettarono una scusa e se ne andarono.
They stammered out (mumbled) an excuse and left.

■ Il figlio di mia nipote balbetta già le prime parole.
My niece's son is already babbling his first words.

ballare   to dance; to roll; to be loose (tooth); to hang loosely; to shake; to fidget

■ Vuoi ballare con me?
Will you dance with me?

■ I bambini ballavano in tondo (/dalla gioia).
The children were dancing in a circle (/with joy).

■ Sai ballare il tango (/il valzer)?
Can you tango (/waltz)?

■ La barca ha ballato durante la burrasca.
The boat rolled during the storm.

■ Gli balla un dente.
He has a tooth loose.

■ Questa giacca ti balla addosso.
This jacket hangs loosely on you.

■ Il tavolo balla.
The table is shaking.

■ Il bambino ballava sulla seggiola.
The child was fidgeting in his chair.

■ Quando non c'è la gatta, i sorci ballano. (*proverb*)
When the cat's away, the mice will play. (proverb)

balzare (su qc/qco)   (auxiliary *essere*) to spring upon sb/sth; to jump on sth; to leap

■ Il leone (/Il gatto) balzò sulla preda (/indietro).
The lion (/The cat) sprang upon the prey (/back).

■ I due studenti sono balzati sull'autobus (/sul treno).
The two students jumped on the bus (/train).

■ Il cuore le balzava dalla paura (/dalla gioia).
Her heart was leaping from fear (/for joy).

balzare da qco   to jump from sth; to come out from sth

■ Il bambino balzò giù dal letto (/fuori dal nascondiglio).
The child jumped out of bed (/his hiding place).

balzare in qco   to jump into sth

■ Il ragazzo balzò in sella (/in avanti/in piedi).
The boy jumped into the saddle (/forward/on his feet).

balzare a qco   to jump down; to mount; to strike

■ Marco balzò a terra (/a cavallo).
Mark jumped down (/mounted his horse).

■ Balza subito agli occhi che sono innamorati.
It strikes one immediately that they are in love.

barattare qco (con qc/qco)   to exchange, swap sth (with sb/for sth)

■ Barattarono caffè con zucchero.
They exchanged coffee for sugar.

■ I due australiani barattavano qualche parola con la gente del posto.
The two Australians exchanged a few words with the locals.

■ I ragazzi barattarono i loro giocattoli.
The boys swapped their toys.

barcollare   to reel, stagger; to be shaky

■ L'ubriaco barcollò e cadde.
The drunkard reeled and fell down.

■ Gli detti un colpo che lo fece barcollare.
I gave him a blow that made him stagger.

■ Avanzavano (/camminavano) barcollando.
They were staggering forward (/along).

■ Il governo barcollava.
The government was shaky.

basare qco su qco   to base, found sth on sth

■ Questa accusa non è basata su dati certi.
This accusation is not based (or founded) on certain facts.

basarsi su qco   to go by, judge by sth

■ Non ci dobbiamo basare su quello che dice (/sulle apparenze).
We ought not go by what he says (/by appearances).

■ Io mi baso su prove documentate.
I go by documentary evidence.

bastare   (auxiliary *essere*) to be enough, sufficient; to suffice; to last

■ Ti basteranno diecimila lire?
Will ten thousand lire be enough for you?

■ Ci basta la tua promessa.
Your promise is enough for us.

■ Basta!
Enough!

■ Quello che ho guadagnato ci deve bastare tutto il mese.
What I earned must last us the whole month.

bastare per + *inf*   to be enough + *inf*

■ Basta un esempio per convincerla.
One example is enough to persuade her.

■ Non basteranno due ore per finire quel lavoro.
Two hours will not be enough to finish that job.

bastare + *inf*   to suffice + *inf*

■ Basti dire che tutti la conoscevano.
Suffice it to say that everyone knew her.

basta che + *subj*   to need (only) + *inf*

- Basta che voi lo chiamiate (/gli scriviate/glielo diciate).
  You need only call him (/write to him/tell him).

- Bastava che tu me l'avessi detto subito!
  If only you had told me right away!

battere   to beat, defeat; to scour; to tap; to knock; to clap; to blink; to throb; to type; to strike; to kick; to fly (a flag)

- La loro squadra ha battuto la nostra.
  Their team beat ours.

- Niente può battere questo prodotto.
  Nothing can beat this product.

- La notizia gli fece battere il cuore.
  The news made his heart beat stronger.

- Improvvisamente si resero conto che il cuore del figlio non batteva più.
  Suddenly they realized that their son's heart was no longer beating.

- Il nemico è stato finalmente battuto.
  The enemy has finally been defeated.

- La polizia batteva la zona alla ricerca dell'assassino.
  The police were scouring the area in search of the murderer.

- Daniela provò a battere sul vetro della finestra.
  Danielle tried tapping on the windowpane.

- Paola gli batté sulla spalla.
  Paula tapped him on his shoulder.

- Credo che qualcuno stia battendo alla porta.
  I think somebody is knocking at the door.

- Il motore della macchina batte in testa.
  The engine of my car is knocking.

- Il pubblico continuò a battere le mani.
  The public kept applauding (i.e., kept on clapping their hands).

- Io non sapevo dove battere il capo.
  I didn't know which way to turn.

- Quel bambino continua a battere gli occhi.
  That child keeps on blinking.

- Le tempie mi battevano.
  My temples were throbbing.

- La sua segretaria deve battere a macchina molte lettere.
  His secretary has many letters to type.

- Battono le cinque.
  It is just striking five.

- L'uccellino batteva le ali.
  The little bird was flapping its wings.
- Il calciatore batté il pallone (/un calcio).
  The soccer player kicked the ball (/took a penalty).
- Il bambino batteva i piedi.
  The child was stamping his feet.
- Credo che battano una pista sbagliata.
  I think they are off track.
- La nave batteva bandiera nera.
  The ship was flying a black flag.

battere di/da/per qco   to beat with, chatter with sth

- Il cuore le batteva di gioia (/per l'emozione).
  Her heart was beating with joy (/with feeling).
- Le battevano i denti dal freddo (/dalla paura/dallo spavento).
  Her teeth were chattering with cold (/fear/fright).

battere contro qco   to bump against sth

- Ho battuto il ginocchio contro la scrivania.
  I bumped my knee against my desk.

battere qc in/a qco   to beat sb in/at sth

- Nessuno lo batte in matematica (/francese/velocità).
  Nobody beats him in math (/French/speed).
- Credi di poterla battere a ping-pong (/tennis/scacchi/carte)?
  Do you think you could beat her at Ping-Pong (/tennis/chess/cards)?

battere su qco   to beat down on sth; to insist on sth

- La pioggia (Il sole) batteva sul tetto (/sulla mia finestra).
  The rain (/The sun) was beating down on the roof (/my window).
- Quell'insegnante ha battuto molto su quell'argomento.
  That teacher insisted a lot on that topic.

battersi   to fight, duel

- Si batterono da eroi.
  They fought like heroes.

battersela   to run away, beat it

- I due se la batteranno, son sicuro!
  The two will run away, I am sure!

battezzare   to baptize, christen; to call, nickname

- Battezzarono la nave con una bottiglia di champagne.
  They christened the ship with a champagne bottle.

- Lo avevano battezzato "l'americano".
  They had nicknamed him "The American."

- Lo battezzeranno Antonio, come il nonno.
  They'll call him Anthony, like his grandfather.

bendare   to bandage, wrap, dress; to blindfold

- Ricordo che la sua mano era bendata.
  I remember that his hand was bandaged.

- Devi bendare quella ferita.
  You must dress that wound.

- Gli hanno bendato gli occhi, prima di fucilarlo.
  They blindfolded him before shooting him.

benedire   to bless; to be lost

- Che Dio ti benedica!
  (May) God bless you!

- Il Papa benedisse i fedeli raccolti in piazza San Pietro.
  The pope blessed the faithful gathered in Saint Peter's Square.

- Tutto è andato a farsi benedire. (*fig*)
  Everything was lost.

bere   to drink; to swallow; to soak up

- Suo marito beve troppo (/poco/vino/come una spugna).
  Her husband drinks too much (/little/wine/like a fish).

- Dopo l'incidente si è dato al bere.
  After the accident he took up drinking.

- Beviamo alla tua salute!
  Let's drink to your health!

- La signora Gentili bevve il caffè a piccoli sorsi.
  Mrs. Gentili sipped her coffee.

- Questa non la bevo! (*idiomatic*)
  I am not going to swallow that one! (idiomatic)

  bersi   to drink away/in

  - Si è bevuto tutti i soldi che aveva. (*idiomatic*)
    He drank away all the money he had. (idiomatic)

  - Se la beveva con gli occhi. (*idiomatic*)
    He was drinking her in with his eyes. (idiomatic)

biasimare   to blame (sb for sth), disapprove of sth

- Voi dovete biasimare solo voi stessi.
  You have only yourselves to blame.

- Biasimarono la sua condotta.
  They disapproved of his behavior.

> **biasimarsi per qco/*inf***   to blame oneself for sth/*ger*
>
> - Non biasimarti per quello che è successo!
>   *Don't blame yourself for what happened!*
>
> - Vittorio si biasimò per non averla aiutata (/non essere stato gentile).
>   *Victor blamed himself for not helping her (/not having been kind).*

bilanciare   to balance (out/one another); to weigh

- Il carico deve essere bilanciato bene.
  The load must be well balanced.

- Vorrei che le entrate bilanciassero sempre le uscite.
  I would like the income always to balance the expenditure.

bisbigliare   to whisper; to gossip

- L'ho vista bisbigliargli qualcosa all'orecchio.
  I saw her whispering something in his ear.

- Si bisbiglia sul loro conto.
  There has been some gossip about them.

bisognare (qco)   (auxiliary *essere*) to need sth; to be necessary

- Gli bisognerebbe il nostro aiuto.
  He would need our help.

> **bisogna che** + *subj*   it is necessary (that)
>
> - Bisogna che io glielo dica.
>   *I need to tell him.*
>
> - Bisognava che voi studiaste di più.
>   *It was necessary for you to study more.*

> **bisogna** + *inf*   to have to, must
>
> - Bisogna mangiare per vivere.
>   *One has to eat to live.*
>
> - C'è lo sciopero dei mezzi di trasporto. Bisogna andare in macchina.
>   *All means of transportation are on strike. We must go by car.*

bisticciare (con qc per qco)   to quarrel (with sb over sth)

- Tu bisticci con tutti.
  You quarrel (or squabble) with everybody.

bloccare   to block; to stop, halt; to slam

- L'incidente ha bloccato il traffico per due ore.
  The accident blocked traffic for two hours.

- La palla è stata bloccata dal portiere dell'altra squadra.
  The ball was blocked by the goalkeeper of the opposite team.

- Il loro padre bloccò la macchina (/l'assegno).
  Their father stopped the car (/the check).

- Si devono bloccare i licenziamenti.
  Layoffs must be halted.

- Si dovrebbero bloccare gli aumenti.
  Increases should be frozen.

- Il guidatore bloccò i freni.
  The driver slammed on the brakes.

  bloccarsi   to stick, jam; to stall

  - La porta si è bloccata.
    The door got stuck.

  - Il motore si è bloccato.
    The engine stalled.

bocciare qc/qco   to fail sb; to reject sth

- L'hanno bocciato in latino (/matematica/inglese/storia dell'arte).
  They failed him in Latin (/math/English/history of art).

- Il progetto di legge (/la mozione) fu bocciato (/bocciata).
  The bill (/The motion) was rejected.

bollire   to boil, come to a boil; to feel hot

- L'acqua bolle a 100 gradi.
  Water boils (or comes to a boil) at 100 degrees centigrade.

- Il brodo bolle già?
  Is the broth already boiling?

- Oggi si bolle dal caldo.
  Today is boiling hot.

bombardare   to shell, bombard, bomb

- Le navi bombardarono il porto.
  The ships shelled the port.

- Lo hanno bombardato di domande. (*fig*)
  They bombarded him with questions. (fig)

- Due aeroplani nemici hanno bombardato la nostra città.
  Two enemy planes bombed our town.

brillare   to shine; to twinkle; to sparkle; to glitter; to blast; to hull   .

- Il viso della bambina brillava di gioia (/felicità).
  The little girl's face was shining with joy (/happiness).

- Le sette stelle dell'Orsa Maggiore brillavano in cielo.
  The seven stars of the Big Dipper were twinkling in the sky.

- Gli occhi del mio gatto brillavano nel buio.
  My cat's eyes were gleaming (or shining) in the dark.

- L'oro brilla.
  Gold glitters.

- Devono far brillare due mine.
  They must blast two mines.

- Il riso (/L'orzo) va brillato.
  Rice (/Barley) must be hulled.

brindare   to toast

- Dobbiamo brindare al trionfo.
  We must toast the victory.

- Brindiamo alla salute del signor Pasquini!
  Let's drink to Mr. Pasquini's health!

bruciare   to be on fire; to burn (down); to be very hot; to scorch; to smart; to sting; to cauterize

- La casa brucia.
  The house is on fire.

- La casa è bruciata.
  The house burned down.

- Non ho più legna da bruciare.
  I don't have any wood left to burn.

- Lorenzo bruciava di passione (/febbre/desiderio).
  Laurence was burning with passion (/fever/desire).

- Il pane sta bruciando.
  The bread is burning.

- Questo caffè (/La fronte della bambina) brucia.
  This coffee (/The little girl's forehead) is very hot.

- Hai bruciato la mia camicia?
  Did you scorch my shirt?

- Gli bruciano gli occhi.
  His eyes are smarting.

- Il dottore ha bruciato la verruca.
  The doctor cauterized the wart.

■ Il fumo ci bruciava gli occhi.
The smoke stung our eyes.

bruciarsi   to burn oneself; to burn out; to scald oneself

■ Mi sono bruciato il pollice.
I burned my thumb.

■ Credo che questa lampadina si sia bruciata.
I think this lightbulb has burned out.

■ Mi sono bruciata le mani con l'olio bollente.
I scalded my hands with hot oil.

bucare   to make a hole in; to have a flat tire; to punch

■ I ladri hanno bucato la parete.
The thieves made a hole in the wall.

■ Questa tovaglia è tutta bucata.
This tablecloth is full of holes.

■ La settimana scorsa ho bucato due volte.
Last week I had two flat tires.

■ Non hanno ancora bucato i biglietti.
They haven't punched the tickets yet.

bucarsi   to prick oneself; to inject drugs; to have a flat (tire)

■ Tua nuora si è bucata con l'ago.
Your daughter-in-law pricked herself with a needle.

■ Quel ragazzo si buca da anni.
That boy has been injecting himself with drugs for years.

■ Ho paura che si sia bucata una gomma.
I am afraid I got (or have) a flat.

burlarsi di qc/qco (per qco)   to make fun of sb, laugh at sth

■ Tutti si burlano di lui.
Everybody makes fun of him.

■ Si è sempre burlato della legge.
He has always laughed at the law.

bussare   to knock

■ Bussano, va' ad aprire la porta.
Somebody is knocking. Go open the door.

bussare a qco   to knock at sth

■ Perché non bussi alla porta del tuo vicino?
Why don't you knock at your neighbor's door?

buttare   to throw (away); to waste; to shoot

- Il suo bambino ha buttato la palla fuori dalla finestra, signora Salvi.
  Your child threw the ball out of the window, Mrs. Salvi.

- Il bambino le buttò le braccia al collo.
  The child threw his arms around her neck.

- Buttarono là la proposta di comprare un altro appartamento.
  They threw out the proposal to buy another apartment.

- Non mangiarlo: buttalo via.
  Don't eat it; throw it away.

- Non buttare il tempo (/il fiato). (*idiomatic*)
  Don't waste your time (/breath).

- Hai visto che le piante cominciano a buttare?
  Did you notice that the plants are starting to shoot?

buttare qco a qco   to turn sth upside down; to upset; to throw

- Buttò all'aria tutto l'ufficio per trovare quel documento.
  He turned the office upside down to find that document.

- Hanno buttato all'aria quel progetto.
  They threw out that plan.

buttare qc/qco in qco   to throw sb/sth in (into) sth; to hurl sth at sb

- Lo buttarono in carcere per dieci anni (/in mezzo alla strada).
  They threw him into prison for ten years (/into the gutter).

- Il loro amico buttò in aria il cappello (/la lettera nel fuoco).
  Their friend threw his hat up in the air (/the letter into the fire).

- Il figlio gli buttò in faccia la riposta. (*idiomatic*)
  His son hurled his answer at him. (idiomatic)

buttare giù qco   to throw sth down; to knock sth down; to swallow; to jot sth down; to make weak; to dishearten

- Non ho la chiave, buttamela giù, per piacere.
  I do not have the key. Throw it down to me, please.

- Hanno buttato giù molti vecchi edifici.
  They knocked down many old buildings.

- Non posso buttare giù niente.
  I cannot swallow anything.

- Ho buttato giù due righe sull'avvenimento.
  I jotted down two lines about the event.

- Questa influenza l'ha buttato giù molto.
  This flu has made him very weak.

■   La notizia li ha buttati giù.
    The news disheartened them.

buttarsi   to throw oneself; to pounce; to rush

■   I bambini si buttarono nell'acqua (/sul letto).
    The children threw themselves into the water (/onto the bed).

■   L'uomo si buttò ai piedi dell'amante.
    The man threw himself at his lover's feet.

■   La ragazza si buttò addosso il cappotto e uscì.
    The girl threw her coat on and went out.

■   Mia nipote si è buttata col paracadute dall'aereo.
    My niece parachuted from the plane.

■   Il gatto si buttò sul topo.
    The cat pounced on the mouse.

■   Il ladro si buttò giù per le scale.
    The thief rushed down the stairs.

buttarsi a + *inf* to throw oneself into

■   Si buttarono a lavorare (/studiare /fare piani).
    They threw themselves into their work (/studies/plans).

buttarsi in qco   to get deeply involved in sth

■   Mi buttai nel lavoro (/nella politica).
    I got deeply involved in my work (/politics).

C

cacciare to hunt, shoot; to throw out; to kick; to drive (away); to stuff; to stick; to push (back)

- Hanno cacciato tutto il giorno.
  They have been hunting all day.

- Gli piaceva cacciare la selvaggina (/i fagiani).
  He liked to shoot game (/pheasants).

- Lo cacciarono di casa (/dal ristorante).
  They threw him out of the house (/restaurant).

- Lo cacciarono da scuola.
  They expelled him from school.

- Lo cacciammo fuori a calci.
  We kicked him out.

- Cercammo di cacciargliela dalla mente.
  We tried to drive her out of his head.

- Cacciai due chiodi nel muro.
  I drove two nails into the wall.

- Claudia cacciò tutto nella sua borsa (/in un cassetto).
  Claudia stuffed everything into her bag (/into a drawer).

- Il bambino cacciò le mani in tasca.
  The little boy stuck his hands in his pockets.

- Gli cacciarono in corpo tre pallottole.
  They put three bullets into him.

- I poliziotti cercavano di cacciare indietro la folla.
  The police were trying to push back the crowd.

- La ragazza cacciò un grido.
  The girl let out a cry.

- Credono, in questo modo, di cacciare il malocchio.
  They believe, by so doing, that they will ward off the evil eye.

cacciarsi to thrust oneself, get into

- Voi vi cacciate sempre nei pasticci.
  You always get into a mess.

- Quando ti cacci qualcosa in mente!
  When you get something into your head!

1. cadere   (auxiliary *essere*) to fall (down)

■   Cadeva sempre molta neve in inverno.
A lot of snow would fall in the winter.

■   Quest'anno il mio compleanno cade di giovedì.
This year my birthday falls on a Thursday.

■   Molti edifici caddero durante quel bombardamento.
Many buildings fell during that bombardment.

■   Qualunque cosa lui faccia, cade sempre in piedi. (*idiom*)
No matter what he does, he always falls on his feet. (idiom)

cadere a qco   to fall to sth

■   Il colpo lo fece cadere a terra.
The blow made him fall to the ground.

■   Non caderle ai piedi appena la vedi!
Don't fall at her feet as soon as you see her!

■   Cadere dalla padella alla brace. (*idiom*)
To fall from the frying pan into the fire. (idiom)

cadere + *adj/ptp*   to fall + *adj/ptp*

■   Il ragazzo cadde ammalato (/addormentato/morto).
The boy fell ill (/fell asleep/dropped dead).

cadere da qco (su qco)   to fall from, tumble down sth (on sth)

■   Il gatto cadde dal tetto della casa sul tetto della macchina.
The cat fell from the roof of the house onto the roof of the car.

■   La nostra amica cadde da cavallo e si ruppe tre costole.
Our friend fell from her horse and broke three ribs.

■   Ieri sua madre è caduta dalle scale.
Yesterday his mother tumbled down the stairs.

cadere in qco   to fall in/into sth

■   Lo abbiamo visto cadere nell'acqua (/nel pozzo/nel crepaccio/nella piscina).
We saw him fall into the water (/water well/crevasse/swimming pool).

■   Sono caduti in disgrazia (/in una trappola).
They fell into disfavor (/in a trap).

2. cadere   to fail; to flop; to crash; to lose (hair or teeth); to drop, die, etc.

■   Molti studenti caddero in matematica.
Many students failed in math.

■   La commedia cadde.
The play flopped.

■ Due aerei nemici caddero in quel combattimento.
Two enemy planes crashed in that fight.

■ Gli sono caduti i capelli (/due denti).
He lost his hair (/two teeth).

■ Lasciamo cadere questo argomento.
Let's drop this topic.

■ Le è caduta la penna.
She dropped her pen.

cadere su qco   to turn to sth

■ La conversazione cadde sul problema della disoccupazione.
The conversation turned to the problem of unemployment.

calare   (auxiliary *essere* if the verb is not followed by a direct object) to lower (away); to cast off; to drop, let down; to fall; to strike

■ Avevano già calato tutte le scialuppe di salvataggio.
They had already lowered all the lifeboats.

■ La ragazza calò un cestino dalla finestra (/un secchio nel pozzo).
The girl lowered a basket from the window (/a pail into the well).

■ Calare una maglia alla fine di ogni ferro.
Cast off one stitch at the end of each row.

■ Si precipitarono a calare il sipario.
They hurriedly dropped the curtain.

■ Il vento (/Il livello dell'acqua) è calato.
The wind (/The water level) has dropped.

■ Il sole è già calato.
The sun has already set.

calare di (*measure*)   to decrease in sth; to go down; to lose

■ Sono calati di volume (/peso).
They decreased in volume (/weight).

■ I prezzi all'ingrosso (/al minuto) sono calati del cinque per cento.
Wholesale (/Retail) prices have gone down by five percent.

■ Sono calato di dieci chili.
I lost ten kilos.

calarsi   to let oneself down

■ Si calarono dal tetto.
They let themselves down from the roof.

calcare   to stamp on; to tread;Ú to stress; to exaggerate

- Calcano l'uva d'autunno.
  They stamp on grapes in autumn.

- Il loro figlio voleva calcare le orme del nonno.
  Their son wanted to follow in his grandfather's footsteps.

- Non dovresti calcare l'accento su quella sillaba (/sulla gravità della situazione).
  You should not stress that syllable (/the seriousness of the situation).

- Mi sembra che tu abbia calcato troppo la mano.
  I think you exaggerated.

  calcarsi qco su qco   to pull down sth on sth

  - Non calcarti il cappello sugli occhi!
    Don't pull your hat down over your eyes!

calmare   to calm (down); to soothe; to ease

- Le parole rassicuranti della mamma calmarono il bambino.
  His mother's reassuring words calmed the child.

- La medicina le calmò il dolore (/il mal di testa/lo spasmo).
  The medication soothed her pain (/headache/spasm).

- Non sono riuscito a calmare la sua rabbia (/il suo dolore).
  I couldn't ease his anger (/sorrow).

  calmarsi   to abate; to calm down

  - L'uragano (/Il vento) si calmò.
    The hurricane (/The wind) abated (or calmed down).

  - Calmatevi!
    Calm down!

calzare   to put on, wear (shoes); to provide shoes for; to fit (well)

- Che numero calza tua figlia?
  Which shoe size does your daughter wear?

- Quelle scarpe non calzano bene.
  Those shoes do not fit well.

- Ti calza a pennello! (*idiomatic*)
  It fits you like a glove! (idiomatic)

- Quell'esempio non calza.
  That example is not appropriate.

cambiare   (auxiliary *essere;* if the verb is followed by a direct object, auxiliary *avere*)
to change

- Niente cambiato dall'anno scorso.
  Nothing has changed since last year.

■ Le sue idee sono cambiate col tempo.
His ideas have changed over time.

■ Niente (/Tutto) è cambiato fra di noi.
Nothing (/Everything) has changed between us.

■ Il clima sta cambiando.
The climate is changing.

■ Per Milano si cambia.
You have to change for Milan.

cambiare qc/qco   (auxiliary *avere*) to change sb/sth

■ La guerra (/La scuola/Quella triste esperienza) l'ha cambiato.
The war (/School/That sad experience) changed him.

■ Credo che abbiano cambiato numero di telefono (/indirizzo).
I think they changed their telephone number (/address).

■ Quella ragazza ha cambiato parrucchiere (/dottore/dentista/sarta).
That girl changed her hairdresser (/doctor/dentist/dressmaker).

■ Perché non cambi marcia (/posto/modo di vivere/modo di pensare)?
Why don't you change gear (/your seat/your way of living/your way of thinking)?

■ Ho cambiato idea. Non vado al cinema.
I have changed my mind. I am not going to the movies.

■ Hai fatto cambiare l'olio (/le candele /le gomme)?
Did you have the oil (/spark plugs/tires) changed?

■ Per favore, può cambiarmi cento dollari in lire?
Can you change a hundred dollars into lire for me, please?

■ Puoi cambiarmi diecimila lire?
Can you give me change for ten thousand lire?

■ Hanno cambiato casa il mese scorso.
They moved (i.e., *changed their house*) *last month.*

camminare   to walk, tramp; to tread on; to stride along

■ Il bambino ha appena iniziato a camminare.
The baby just started walking.

■ Il ragazzo camminava di buon passo (/a testa alta/zoppicando).
The boy was walking at a good pace (/with his head held high/with a limp).

■ Camminavo in punta di piedi per non svegliare mio marito.
I was walking on tiptoe so as not to wake up my husband.

■ Meglio camminare sul sicuro.
It's better to walk on the safe side.

■ Il bambino camminava carponi.
The child was walking on all fours.

campeggiare   to camp; to stand out; to be prominent

■   Di solito campeggiavano sulla riva del lago di Garda.
Usually they camped by the shore of Lake Garda.

cancellare   to erase; to cross out, delete

■   Ho cancellato l'errore (/la lavagna).
I erased the mistake (/the blackboard).

■   Devi cancellare dalla mente questo triste ricordo (/questa offesa).
You must erase this sad memory (/this offense) from your mind.

■   L'insegnante ha cancellato le parole sbagliate (/dei nomi dalla lista).
The teacher crossed out the wrong words (/some names from the list).

> **cancellarsi**   to be erased
>
> ■   Temo che questo ricordo non le si cancellerà dalla mente.
> *I fear this memory will not be erased from her mind.*

cantare   to sing; to squeal; to talk; to chirp; to crow

■   Tuo cugino ci ha cantato una canzone (/un'aria/un motivo popolare).
Your cousin sang a song (/an aria/a pop song) for us.

■   Giorgio canta da tenore. Andreina canta da soprano.
George sings tenor. Andrea sings soprano.

■   Gli uccelli cantavano.
Birds were singing.

■   Dopo tre ore di interrogatorio, il complice ha cantato.
After being questioned for three hours, the accomplice squealed.

■   Gliele ho cantate. (*idiomatic*)
I gave him a piece of my mind. (idiomatic)

■   I grilli (/Le cicale) cantavano.
Crickets (/Cicadas) were chirping.

■   Alle cinque il gallo cantò.
At five the cock crowed.

capire   to understand, grasp

■   Non capisco cosa voglia da me.
I don't understand what he wants of me.

■   Non ho capito una parola (/un'acca).
I didn't understand a word.

■   Io non la capisco.
I don't understand her.

- Guglielmo capisce sempre una cosa per l'altra.
  William always misunderstands.

- Quel bambino capisce al volo.
  That child grasps things at once.

capire (capirla) che + *subj*   to realize that

- Finalmente hanno capito che dovevano andarsene.
  They finally realized that they had to leave.

- La vuoi capire che la situazione è molto difficile?
  Do you realize that the situation is very difficult?

capire di + *inf*   to realize

- Hanno capito di essere in pericolo (/avere torto/aver speso troppo).
  They realized they were in danger (/they were wrong/they had spent too much).

capirci   to understand (of it)

- Io ci capisco poco.
  I understand little (of it).

capirsi   to understand each other/one another

- Non ci capiamo più.
  We don't understand each other (/one another) anymore.

capitare   (auxiliary *essere*) to happen; to turn up

- Siamo capitati in piazza il giorno del mercato.
  We happened to be in the square on market day.

- Gliene sono capitate di tutti i colori.
  Everything possible happened to her/him.

- Se capitasse l'occasione, lo farei.
  Should the opportunity arise, I would do it.

- Metti il libro dove capita.
  Put the book anywhere you like.

- Io leggevo quanti libri mi capitavano.
  I would read as many books as came my way.

- Quel ragazzo mi capita sempre tra i piedi.
  That boy is always getting in my way.

capitare bene/male   to be lucky/unlucky

- Siamo capitati bene.
  We were lucky.

capitare di + *inf*   to happen + *inf*

- Se ti capita di vederlo (/parlargli), digli che venga a trovarmi.
  If you happen to see him (/speak to him), tell him to come and see me.

- Se mi capitasse di incontrarla (/parlarle/telefonarle), la potrei invitare.
  If I happened to meet her (/talk to her/call her), I could invite her.

capovolgere   to turn over, overturn; to change radically; to capsize

- Perché hai capovolto la tazza?
  Why did you turn the cup over?

- Questo ha capovolto la situazione.
  This has changed the situation radically.

- L'ondata capovolse la barca.
  The wave capsized the boat.

capovolgersi   to capsize

- La barca si capovolse durante la tempesta.
  The boat capsized during the storm.

caricare (qco)   to load (up) sth; to fill; to wind; to charge

- Pensi che abbiano caricato la nave oltre la sua portata?
  Do you think they loaded the ship beyond its capacity?

- I soldati caricarono il fucile (/il cannone).
  The soldiers loaded their rifles (/the cannon).

- Il vecchio caricò la pipa.
  The old man filled his pipe.

- La mattina il nonno caricava tutti gli orologi.
  In the morning Grandfather would wind all the clocks.

- Devo ricordarmi di far caricare la batteria della macchina.
  I must remember to have the car battery recharged.

caricare qc/qco di   to load (down) sb/sth with sth

- Caricarono il camion di sabbia (/sale).
  They loaded the truck with sand (/salt).

- Lo caricarono di debiti (/pacchetti).
  They loaded him down with debts (/packages).

caricare qc/qco su qco   to load sb/sth onto sth

- La signora Carini caricò i bagagli sul treno.
  Mrs. Carini loaded the luggage onto the train.

■   Caricarono i passeggeri sulla nave (/il bestiame su un camion).
They loaded the passengers on the ship (/the cattle onto a truck).

caricarsi di qco   to overburden oneself with sth

■   Non caricarti di lavoro (/debiti).
Don't overburden yourself with work (/debts).

cascare   (auxiliary *essere*) to fall (down); to tumble (down); to crash (down)

■   È cascato il quadro.
The picture fell.

■   I bicchieri cascarono sul pavimento.
The glasses crashed to the floor.

■   Il vaso (/Armando) cascò a pezzi (/morto).
The vase (/Armand) fell to pieces (/dropped dead).

■   I bambini cascano dalla fame (/dalla sete/dal sonno). (*fig*)
The children are very hungry (/thirsty/sleepy).

cascarci   to be had, taken in

■   Ci sei cascato!
You've been had (or You've been taken)!

catturare   to capture, seize, catch; to take prisoner; to arrest

■   Hanno catturato un animale selvatico.
They captured a wild animal.

■   La polizia ha catturato il ladro.
The police captured (or seized) the thief.

■   Furono catturati cinquecento soldati nemici.
Five hundred enemy soldiers were taken prisoner.

■   La pantera non è ancora stata catturata.
The panther is still loose.

■   Sono stati catturati dalla polizia.
They have been arrested by the police.

causare   to bring about; to cause; to give rise to

■   La guerra causò molti cambiamenti.
The war brought about many changes.

■   Quello può causare un incendio (/danni).
That may cause a fire (/damage).

■   Quello che hai detto potrebbe causare malintesi.
What you said could give rise to misunderstandings.

cavalcare   to ride (animals); to span

- Il principe cavalcava un cavallo bianco (/un mulo/un asino).
  The prince was riding a white horse (/a mule/a donkey).

cavare (qco da qco/a qc)   to draw out/from sth/sb; to extract; to gain from sth; to get sth out

- Gli hanno cavato molto sangue.
  They drew a lot of blood from him.

- Non si può cavar sangue da una rapa. (*idiom*)
  You can't draw blood from a stone. (idiom)

- Cavavano l'acqua da un pozzo.
  They used to draw water from a well.

- Il dentista gli ha cavato due denti.
  The dentist extracted two of his teeth.

- Che cosa ci hai cavato?
  What did you gain from it?

- Le hanno cavato il segreto di bocca.
  They got (or extracted) the secret out of her.

- Abbiamo cercato di cavargli di testa quell'idea balzana.
  We tried to get that strange idea out of his head.

  cavarsi   to take off; to satisfy; to quench; to get rid of sth

  - Cavati il cappotto (/il cappello/la giacca/le scarpe/le mani di tasca).
    Take off your coat (/hat/jacket/shoes/your hands from your pockets).

  - Spero che vi siate cavati la fame (/la curiosità/la voglia/la sete).
    I hope you satisfied your hunger (/curiosity/desire/quenched your thirst).

  cavarsela   to manage; to get out of it

  - Sai giocare a tennis? —Me la cavo.
    Can you play tennis? —I manage.

  - Se la sono cavata con un grande spavento.
    They got out of it with a big scare.

cedere   to yield; to give (in/way); to cave in; to cede; to transfer; to hand over

- Il padre cedette alle pressioni del figlio.
  His father yielded to his son's pressure.

- Il marito le ha ceduto tutto quello che aveva.
  Her husband gave her all that he had.

- Sono troppo ostinati, non cederanno mai.
  They are too obstinate; they'll never give in.

- Il terreno (/L'argine) cedette sotto la pressione dell'acqua.
  The ground (/embankment) gave way under the pressure of the water.

■ Il tetto ha ceduto sotto il peso della neve.
The roof caved in under the weight of the snow.

■ Tutto il territorio sarà ceduto all'Italia.
The whole territory will be ceded to Italy.

■ Pietro ha ceduto la cambiale (/i suoi diritti) all'altro socio (/al fratello).
Peter transferred the bill (/his rights) to the other partner (/his brother).

■ La direzione degli affari sarà ceduta a loro.
The management of the affairs will be handed over to them.

celebrare   to celebrate; to officiate; to observe; to hold *or* observe; to extol

■ I loro genitori hanno celebrato le nozze d'argento (/d'oro/di diamante).
Their parents celebrated their silver (/golden/diamond) wedding anniversary.

■ Quel sacerdote celebrerà le loro nozze.
That priest will officiate at their wedding.

■ Dovete celebrare le feste!
You must observe religious feast days!

■ Il processo si celebra in un'altra città.
The trial is being held in another city.

■ Tutti hanno celebrato i meriti di quello scienziato.
Everyone extolled the merits of that scientist.

cercare   to look for, seek, search; to look up/around; to fumble about for

■ Guido cercava moglie, Luisa cercava marito, e così si sono sposati.
Guy was looking for a wife, Louise was looking for a husband, and so they got married.

■ L'ho cercato per mare e per terra, ma non l'ho trovato. (*fig*)
I looked high and low (or everywhere) for it, but I didn't find it.

■ Dovresti cercare quelle parole nel dizionario.
You should look those words up in the dictionary.

■ Il marito la cercava con gli occhi.
Her husband was looking around for her.

■ Ho cercato le chiavi dappertutto ma non le ho trovate.
I searched everywhere for my keys, but I did not find them.

■ Cercavo a tentoni il buco della serratura.
I was fumbling for the keyhole.

cercare qc   to want to see sb

■ Lei chi cerca? —Cerco il direttore.
Whom do you want to see? —I want to see the manager.

cercare di + *inf*   to try + *inf*

- Cerca di sbrigarti (/dormire/venire).
  Try to hurry up (/sleep/come).

cessare   (auxiliary *avere* if the verb can be followed by a direct object; otherwise *essere*) to cease; to stop; to subside

- Cessate il fuoco!
  Cease fire!
- Il brutto tempo è cessato.
  The bad weather stopped.

cessare di + *inf*   (auxiliary *avere*) to stop + *ger;* to give up + *ger*

- Ha cessato di grandinare (/nevicare).
  It has stopped hailing (/snowing).

- Sua madre cessò di dipingere.
  His mother gave up painting.

chiacchierare   to chitchat; to gossip

- Quella ragazza sa solo chiacchierare.
  That girl knows only how to chitchat.
- Marta chiacchiera sempre sul conto di tutti.
  Martha always gossips about everybody.

chiamare   to call; to call for; to summon; to send for

- Può chiamarmi un taxi (/alle sei domani mattina)?
  Can you call me a cab (/at six tomorrow morning)?
- Hanno chiamato la primogenita Alessandra.
  They called their first born Alexandra.
- Le campane chiamano i fedeli.
  The bells summon the faithful.
- Dobbiamo chiamare il dottore (/il prete/la polizia/un'ambulanza).
  We must send for the doctor (/a priest/the police/an ambulance).
- Suo marito è stato chiamato alla presidenza della società.
  Her husband was elected president of the company.
- La soprano è stata chiamata alla ribalta quattro volte.
  The soprano took four curtain calls.
- L'hanno appena chiamata al telefono.
  They just phoned her.

chiamare a + *inf*   to call to + *inf*

- Lo chiameranno a dirigere l'orchestra (/presiedere il comitato).
  They'll call him to direct the orchestra (/to chair the committee).

chiamarsi   to call oneself; to be named

- Come si chiama? —Si chiama Anna.
  What's her name? —Her name is Anna.

- Non so come si chiama quest'aggeggio.
  I don't know what you call this gadget.

- Si deve chiamare sventurata se lo sposa davvero.
  She has to consider herself unfortunate if she really marries him.

chiarire   to clear up; to make clear

- Puoi chiarirmi un dubbio?
  Can you clear up a doubt for me?

- Il mistero non è ancora stato chiarito.
  The mystery has not been cleared up yet.

- Non posso chiarire tutto (/questa questione).
  I can't make everything (/this question) clear.

- L'accusato dovrà chiarire la sua posizione.
  The accused will have to make his position clear.

chiarirsi   to clear sth up

- Il mistero (/La situazione) non si è ancora chiarito (/chiarita).
  The mystery (/situation) has not been cleared up yet.

chiedere   to ask for (/about/after); to charge; to take; to beg

- Mi chiesero aiuto (/perdono/consiglio/il mio numero di telefono).
  They asked me for help (/forgiveness/advice/my telephone number).

- Mi chiedono sempre di lei (/di tuo padre/dei tuoi amici).
  They always ask me about her (/your father/your friends).

- Quanto chiede per una stanza?
  How much do you charge for a room?

- Non ti vergogni di chiedere?
  Aren't you ashamed to beg?

chiedere di + *inf*   to ask to + *inf*

- Non chiedergli di dirtelo (/farlo/partire/prestarti la macchina).
  Don't ask him to tell you (/to do it/to leave/to lend you his car).

chiedersi   to ask oneself, wonder

- Mi chiedo perché l'abbiano fatto.
  I ask myself why they did it.

■   Non ti chiedi se questo sia possibile?
Don't you wonder if this is possible?

chiudere   (auxiliary *avere* if the verb is followed by a direct object; otherwise *essere*)
to close (down), shut, turn off; to draw

■   I mercati (/Le scuole) chiudono alle sette (/il 15 giugno).
The markets (/Schools) close at seven (/on June 15).

■   L'argomento (/La seduta) è chiuso (/chiusa).
The matter (/The meeting) is closed.

■   Tu non chiudi mai la porta (/i cassetti/le finestre).
You never shut the door (/drawers/windows).

■   Gli hanno chiuso la bocca.
They shut him up.

■   Hai chiuso il gas (/la luce/il rubinetto/la radio/la televisione)?
Did you turn off the gas (/light/faucet/radio/television)?

■   Chiudono la porta col catenaccio (/lucchetto).
They bolt (/padlock) their door.

■   Quel ragazzo ha chiuso la porta con un calcio.
That boy kicked the door closed.

■   Chiudi le tende, per favore.
Draw the curtains, please.

■   Quest'anno abbiamo chiuso in attivo (/in perdita).
This year we showed a profit (/loss).

■   Il loro nome chiudeva la lista.
Their name came at the end of the list.

■   Chiudi la bocca.
Hold your tongue.

chiudere qc/qco in qco   to lock sb/sth in sth

■   Lo chiusero in prigione per dieci anni.
They locked him up in prison for ten years.

■   Faresti meglio a chiudere sempre i gioielli (/il denaro) in cassaforte.
You would be better off always locking your jewels (/money) in the safe.

■   Il padre li ha minacciati di chiuderli in collegio.
Their father threatened to send them away to boarding school.

chiudersi   to shut oneself, close; to heal; to cloud

■   Si è chiusa in casa (/nella sua stanza).
She shut herself in the house (/her room).

■   La porta si chiude da sé.
The door closes automatically.

- Sono preoccupato perché la ferita non si chiude.
  I am worried because the wound isn't healing.

- Il tempo si sta chiudendo.
  The weather is clouding over.

circondare   to surround; to enclose; to fence

- La città medievale è circondata da alte mura.
  The medieval town is surrounded by high walls.

- Hanno circondato quella parte del giardino con una siepe di ligustro (/un muro/ uno steccato).
  They surrounded that part of the garden with a privet hedge (/wall/fence).

  circondarsi   to surround oneself

  - Le piace circondarsi di poeti e scrittori.
    She likes to surround herself with poets and writers.

citare   to mention; to cite; to quote; to summon; to sue

- Hanno citato due casi di questo tipo.
  They mentioned two instances of this kind.

- Quel ragazzo è stato citato per la sua tenacia.
  That boy was cited for his perseverance.

- Quel professore cita sempre Dante.
  That professor always quotes Dante.

- Fu citato in tribunale come testimone.
  He was summoned to court as a witness.

- Sono sicuro che ti citeranno per danni.
  I am sure they will sue you for damages.

cogliere   to pick; to seize; to catch (out)

- Ai bambini piace cogliere le ciliege dall'albero.
  Children like to pick cherries from the tree.

- Colsero l'occasione per invitarla.
  They seized the opportunity to invite her.

- L'hanno colto in flagrante (/sul fatto/mentre rubava).
  They caught him red-handed (/in the act/stealing).

- La pallottola lo colse alla spalla.
  The bullet caught him in the shoulder.

- Riesci a cogliere il vero senso di quello che sta dicendo?
  Can you catch the true sense of what he's saying?

colare   (auxiliary *avere* if the verb is followed by a direct object; otherwise *essere*)
to strain; to pour; to ooze; to melt; to leak; to sink

- Devo colare la pasta (/il brodo).
  I must strain the pasta (/broth).

- L'olio va colato lentamente.
  The oil must be poured slowly.

- Sangue colava dalla bocca del soldato.
  Blood was oozing from the soldier's mouth.

- L'oro (/Il ferro) veniva colato.
  Gold (/Iron) was being melted.

- La mia borraccia (/Questa botte) cola.
  My flask (/This barrel) leaks.

- Il translantico è colato a picco (fondo).
  The transatlantic has sunk.

- Il sudore gli colava dalla fronte.
  Sweat was dripping from his forehead.

- Le lacrime colavano sulle guance della bambina.
  Tears were trickling down the little girl's cheeks.

collaborare   to collaborate; to contribute

- Molti avevano collaborato col nemico.
  Many had collaborated with the enemy.

- Nostro zio collabora a un quotidiano.
  Our uncle contributes to a daily newspaper.

- Indubbiamente tu hai collaborato alla riuscita del progetto.
  Undoubtedly you contributed to the success of the project.

collegare   to connect; to link (up)

- Non hanno ancora collegato i fili della luce.
  They haven't connected the electricity cables yet.

- La nuova autostrada (/Un servizio di autobus) collegherà diverse città
  (/i sobborghi col centro della città).
  *The new highway (/A bus service) will link up several towns (/the suburbs to the
  city's downtown area).*

  collegarsi   to connect, get through; to join forces

  - Non riusciamo a collegarci con Singapore.
    We can't get through to Singapore (by phone).

  - Le due nazioni si collegarono contro il comune nemico.
    The two nations joined forces against the common foe.

colpire   to hit; to strike; to affect; to shock

- L'hanno colpita con un bastone.
  They hit her with a stick.

- L'uragano ha colpito la zona costiera vicino a Genova.
  The violent storm hit the coastal area near Genoa.

- Io non colpisco mai il bersaglio.
  I never hit the target.

- La pietra (/Il proiettile) colpì il bambino alla testa.
  The rock (/The bullet) struck the little boy in the head.

- L'idea di un viaggio in quel paese gli aveva colpito la fantasia.
  The idea of a trip to that country had struck his imagination.

- L'assalitore lo colpì al cuore con un coltello.
  The assailant stabbed him in the heart with a knife.

- Il poliziotto lo colpì alla gamba con una revolverata.
  The policeman shot him in the leg with his revolver.

- L'influenza quest'anno colpisce soprattutto gli anziani.
  The flu this year mainly affects the elderly.

- Mi ha colpito la reazione del loro figlio (/il tuo comportamento).
  I was shocked by their son's reaction (/your behavior).

- Ci colpì la bellezza del paesaggio (/la cortesia della gente).
  We were impressed by the beauty of the landscape (/the people's courtesy).

coltivare   to cultivate, work; to plant; to grow; to train

- Sua moglie coltivava una passione per la musica.
  His wife cultivated a passion for music.

- Loro coltivano un podere.
  They work a farm.

- Coltivavano i campi a patate (/grano/soia).
  They used to plant the fields with potatoes (/wheat/soy).

- Coltivano grano (/lattuga/rose).
  They grow wheat (/lettuce/roses).

- Lei ha una bella voce; dovrebbe coltivarla, signorina!
  You have a beautiful voice; you should train it, Miss!

comandare   to command, order; to detail; to control; to operate; to rule

- Il padre di Antonio comanda una squadra di operai.
  Anthony's father commands a team of workers.

- Il capitano comandò ai suoi uomini di attaccare.
  The captain ordered his men to attack.

- Ci fu comandato di pattugliare la zona di confine.
  We were detailed to patrol the border.

- In casa mia comando io. (*idiomatic*)
  In my house I'm the boss. (idiomatic)
- Questo pulsante comanda le luci.
  This button controls the lights.
- L'apriporta si può comandare a distanza.
  The door opener can be operated by remote control.
- Il sergente comandò l'attenti (/il riposo).
  The sergeant called (them) to attention (/gave the order to stand at ease).
- La signora Dossi comanda tutti a bacchetta.
  Mrs. Dossi rules everyone with an iron rod.

combattere (contro/per)   to fight (against/for) sb/sth; to contend with

- Combatterono contro il nemico (/la fame/la miseria/le difficoltà).
  They fought (against) the enemy (hunger/poverty/difficulties).
- Loro hanno sempre combattuto il razzismo (/l'ignoranza).
  They have always fought racism (/ignorance).
- I dottori combattono l'epidemia di influenza.
  Doctors are fighting the flu epidemic.
- Dobbiamo combattere per la nostra patria (/un'idea/una società migliore).
  We must fight for our country (/an idea/a better society).
- Quella povera donna è stanca di combattere con i creditori.
  That poor woman is tired of contending with her creditors.

combinare   to arrange; to agree; to combine; to get something done; to match

- Hanno combinato una gita in comitiva.
  They arranged a group outing.
- Il matrimonio è stato combinato dai genitori.
  The marriage was arranged by their parents.
- Se combini idrogeno e ossigeno, cosa ottieni?
  If you combine hydrogen and oxygen, what do you get?
- Mi hai combinato un bel guaio!
  You have gotten me into a fine mess!
- Il mio bambino non combina che guai.
  My little boy does nothing but get into trouble.
- Tu non combinerai mai nulla.
  You'll never get anywhere.
- Oggi non ho combinato niente.
  I haven't gotten anything done today.

- Devi combinare bene i colori.
  You have to match the colors well.

  combinare di + *inf*   to arrange + *inf*

  - Abbiamo combinato di andare al cinema stasera.
    We arranged to go to the movies tonight.

  combinarsi   to combine; to go together; to fit in with

  - Questi due elementi non si combinano bene.
    These two elements do not combine well.

  - I nostri orari non si combinano.
    Our schedules don't fit in with each other.

cominciare   (auxiliary *avere* if the verb can be followed by a direct object; otherwise *essere*) to begin, start, commence

- Ho cominciato questo lavoro due giorni fa.
  I started this work two days ago.
- La lezione è cominciata alle nove.
  Class started at nine.
- A cominciare da oggi la lezione d'italiano finirà alle dieci.
  Starting from today, the Italian class will end at ten o'clock.

  cominciare a + *inf*   to begin + *ger/inf*

  - Cominciarono a lavorare (/mangiare/parlare/tradurre).
    They began working (/eating/speaking/translating).
  - Cominciò a nevicare (/fare caldo).
    It started to snow (/to get warm).

  cominciare col(l') + *inf*   to begin *or* start by + *ger*

  - Il direttore cominciò coll'elencare i problemi che dovevano risolvere.
    The manager started by listing the problems they were supposed to solve.

commentare   to comment upon; to criticize; to annotate; to write a commentary on

- Voglio commentare il discorso del presidente.
  I want to comment on the president's speech.
- Il tuo comportamento è stato commentato sfavorevolmente.
  Your behavior has been greatly criticized.
- Non so da chi sia stata commentata quell'edizione della *Divina Commedia*.
  I do not know who annotated that edition of The Divine Comedy.

■   Chi ha commentato quel passo della Bibbia?
Who wrote a commentary on that passage from the Bible?

commettere   to commit; to make

■   Hanno commesso un atroce delitto (/un furto/una rapina).
They committed a terrible crime (/a burglary/a robbery).

■   Io penso che tu stia commettendo un grosso sbaglio.
I think you are making a big mistake.

commuovere   to move (emotionally)

■   Le parole dei sopravvissuti commossero tutti.
The words of the survivors moved everybody.

■   La storia di quel ragazzo (/Quella musica) ci commosse profondamente.
The story of that boy (/That music) moved us deeply.

commuoversi   to be moved

■   Udendo quella notizia la mia amica si commosse.
Hearing that piece of news, my friend was moved.

■   La nonna di Roberto si commuove facilmente.
Robert's grandmother is easily moved.

compatire   to pity; to feel pity for; to be indulgent with

■   La compatisco perché ha avuto molti guai.
I pity her because she had a lot of problems.

■   Dobbiamo compatirlo.
We must feel pity for him.

■   Lo si deve compatire.
One has to be indulgent with him.

compensare   to compensate for; to make up for; to reward

■   L'assicurazione li compenserà dei danni.
The insurance will compensate them for the damages.

■   L'uomo compensava la sua bruttezza con un gran senso dell'umorismo.
The man compensated for his homeliness with a great sense of humor.

■   La ragazza lo compensò con un bacio.
The girl rewarded him with a kiss.

compiere   (used only in the present indicative/subjunctive, gerund, past participle; the
other tenses derive from *compire*)   to carry out; to do; to turn (*age*); to complete;
to cover

■   Hanno compiuto una missione importante (/un compito difficile).
They have carried out an important mission (/a difficult task).

- Devi compiere il tuo dovere.
  You have to do your duty.

- La figlia di Ernesto compirà sette anni il mese prossimo.
  Ernest's daughter will turn seven next month.

- Quando compi gli anni?
  When is your birthday?

- Mia cugina ha compiuto i suoi studi all'Università di Pavia.
  My cousin completed her studies at the University of Pavia.

- Hanno compiuto il percorso in due ore e venticinque minuti.
  They covered the distance in two hours and twenty-five minutes.

  compiersi   to (come to an) end; to be fulfilled; to come true

  - La seconda parte del viaggio si è compiuta senza incidenti.
    The second part of the journey came to its end without incident.

  - Il loro desiderio si è compiuto.
    Their wish has been fulfilled.

  - La predizione si è compiuta.
    The prediction came true.

comporre   to compose; to consist; to dial

- Federico Chopin compose questo notturno.
  Frédéric Chopin composed this nocturne.

- Una squadra di pallacanestro si compone di cinque giocatori.
  A basketball team consists of five players.

- Quell'appartamento si compone di tre vani.
  That apartment has (is made up of) three rooms.

- Per l'oroscopo di oggi, componete il seguente numero.
  Dial the following number for today's horoscope.

comportare   to entail; to involve

- Questa impresa comporta molti rischi.
  This enterprise entails many risks.

- Questo comportò molte spese.
  This involved many expenses.

  comportarsi   to behave

  - Comportatevi bene, bambini!
    Behave, children!

  - Si comportò da galantuomo (/male con gli amici).
    He behaved like a gentleman (/badly toward his friends).

comprare   to buy

- Mia figlia l'ha comprato all'asta (/all'ingrosso/al minuto/a buon mercato/ a credito/a rate/di seconda mano).
  My daughter bought it at an auction (/wholesale/retail/cheap/on credit/on the installment plan, secondhand).
- Ho comprato questa rivista in edicola (/in una libreria).
  I bought this magazine at the newsstand (/in a bookstore).

comprare qco da qc   to buy sth at (a store) *or* from sb

- Ho comprato il pane (/il latte/il pesce) dal fornaio (/lattaio/pescivendolo).
  I bought bread (/milk/fish) at the bakery (/dairy/fish market).
- Ho comprato questa macchina da lui.
  I bought this car from him.

comprare qc/qco   to bribe

- Hanno comprato il giudice (/i testimoni/i giurati).
  They bribed the judge (/the witnesses/the jury).

compromettere   to compromise; to endanger

- Non compromettere la tua libertà (/la tua reputazione/la tua salute/ il tuo avvenire/il tuo onore).
  Don't compromise your freedom (/reputation/health/future/honor).
- Il loro comportamento ha compromesso il risultato dell'impresa.
  Their behavior has endangered the outcome of the undertaking.

compromettersi   to compromise oneself

- Si è compromesso ammettendo di averle parlato.
  He compromised himself by admitting he had talked to her.

comunicare   to inform, tell; to broadcast; to instill; to transmit

- Chi le (/gli/vi) ha comunicato la notizia?
  Who told her (/him/you) the news?
- L'hanno appena comunicato alla tv (/radio).
  They have just broadcast it on TV (/the radio).
- Alice riesce a comunicare a tutti il suo entusiasmo (/la sua paura/la sua passione).
  Alice can instill her enthusiasm (/fear/passion) in everyone.
- Non si sa se questa malattia si possa comunicare facilmente.
  It isn't known if this disease can be easily transmitted.

comunicarsi   to take Holy Communion

- Ci si deve comunicare almeno a Pasqua.
  One must take Holy Communion at least at Easter.

concedere qco a qc   to grant sb sth; to bestow sth on sb; to admit

- L'agenzia le ha concesso l'aspettativa (/una dilazione di pagamento).
  The agency granted her a leave of absence (/an extension of payment).

- Pensiamo che gli concederanno la grazia (/un'udienza/una borsa di studio/ un sussidio/uno sconto del dieci per cento).
  We think they'll grant him a pardon (/audience/scholarship/subsidy/ten percent discount).

- Gli hanno concesso un favore.
  They bestowed a favor on him.

- Questo è discutibile, te lo concedo.
  This is debatable; I admit it.

- Mi concede questo ballo?
  May I have this dance?

concedere a qc di + *inf*   to allow sb + *inf*

- Concedetemi di parlare.
  Allow me to speak.

concedersi   to allow oneself

- Non posso concedermi una vacanza (/troppi svaghi).
  I can't allow myself a vacation (/too many diversions).

concentrare   to concentrate

- Vogliate concentrare l'attenzione su questo dettaglio (/problema).
  Please concentrate your attention on this detail (/problem).

concentrarsi   to concentrate; to be absorbed; to center

- Oggi non riesco a concentrarmi.
  I can't concentrate today.

- Il gruppo di scioperanti (/La maggior parte degli emigrati) si concentrava vicino alla piazza (/nelle grandi città).
  The group of strikers (/Most immigrants) concentrated near the square (/in large cities).

- Quando tu ti concentri nei tuoi pensieri non senti nemmeno il campanello!
  When you are absorbed in your thoughts, you don't even hear the bell!

- I sospetti si sono concentrati sul marito.
  Suspicion centered on the husband.

concludere   to conclude; to bring to an end; to infer; to close; to get done

- Il direttore concluse la serata con parole di elogio per tutti.
  The manager concluded the evening with words of praise for everyone.

- Le trattative non sono state ancora concluse.
  Negotiations haven't yet been brought to an end.

- Che cosa ne concludi?
  What do you infer from that?

- Abbiamo concluso un ottimo affare con loro.
  We closed on a very good business deal with them.

- Oggi non ho concluso niente.
  I didn't get anything done today.

concludere che   to come to a conclusion that

- Conclusero che era meglio dirlo a tutti (/non c'era più niente da fare).
  They came to the conclusion that it was better to tell everybody (/nothing more could be done).

concludere col/coll'/con lo + *inf*   to conclude by + *ger*

- Conclusero coll'ammettere di aver torto.
  They concluded by admitting they were wrong.

concludersi   to conclude, end up

- La riunione si concluse con una preghiera.
  The meeting concluded with a prayer.

- Pensano che il processo si concluderà con la condanna dell'imputato.
  They think that the trial will end in the conviction of the defendant.

condannare   to condemn; to convict; to give up hope; to ban; to demolish

- Tutti noi condanniamo il suo operato (/il suo comportamento).
  We all condemn his conduct (/his behavior).

- Dobbiamo condannare qualsiasi tipo di violenza.
  We must condemn any kind of violence.

- L'hanno condannata.
  They convicted her.

- I medici lo hanno condannato.
  The doctors gave up hope for him.

- Il Vaticano ha condannato le sue opere.
  The Vatican has banned his works.

- Questi edifici sono condannati.
  These buildings are to be demolished.

condannare qc a qco   to sentence, condemn sb to sth; to fine

- Lo hanno condannato a dieci anni di reclusione (/all'ergastolo/a morte).
  They sentenced him to ten years' imprisonment (/to life/to death).

- Fu condannato a una multa di centomila lire.
  He was fined one hundred thousand lire.

condannare qc per qco   to condemn sb for sth

- Fu condannato per omicidio (/furto/rapina a mano armata).
  He was condemned for murder (/theft/armed robbery).

condire   to season, flavor; to dress; to spice

- Hai condito quella pietanza?
  Did you flavor that dish?

- Condisci l'insalata con olio e aceto?
  Do you dress the salad with oil and vinegar?

- Tuo fratello condisce i suoi racconti con particolari molto interessanti.
  Your brother spices up his stories with very interesting details.

condurre   to lead; to take; to drive; to conduct

- Questa strada conduce a casa mia.
  This road leads to my house.

- La nostra squadra conduce per due a zero.
  Our team is leading by two to nothing.

- Mi condussero al commissariato (/a teatro).
  They took me to the police station (/theater).

- La condussero a casa in macchina.
  They drove her home.

- Il rame (/Questo metallo) conduce l'elettricità (/il calore).
  Copper (/This metal) conducts electricity (/heat).

confessare qc/qco a qc   to confess sb/sth (to sb)

- Hanno confessato il loro delitto (/la loro ignoranza/i loro peccati).
  They confessed their crimes (/ignorance/sins).

- Il prete confessò il condannato alla sedia elettrica.
  The priest heard the confession of the man sentenced to the electric chair.

confessare di + *inf*   confess to + *ger*

- L'uomo confessò di aver rubato i soldi.
  The man confessed to having stolen the money.

confessare che   to confess (that)

- Confesso che sono veramente stanco di tutto (/eccitato/spaventato).
  I confess (that) I am really tired of everything (/excited/frightened).

confessarsi   to confess; to plead guilty

- Il loro figlio si confessa tutte le settimane.
  Their son goes to confession every week.

- L'accusato si è confessato colpevole.
  The accused pleaded guilty.

confinare con qco   to border with sth

- L'Italia (La loro proprietà) confina con la Francia (/con la mia).
  Italy (/Their estate) borders with France (/mine).

confinare qc in   to intern, banish sb to; to shut sb up in; to be confined

- Quello scrittore fu confinato in un paesino del sud.
  That writer was banished to a small village in the south.

- La madre l'ha confinata nella sua stanza.
  Her mother shut her up in her room.

confinarsi   to retire, confine oneself; to shut oneself up

- I loro genitori si sono confinati in campagna.
  Their parents retired in the country.

- Quando devono studiare per un esame si confinano in casa.
  When they have to study for an exam, they shut themselves up in the house.

confondere   to confuse; to mix up; to mistake; to blur

- Lo confondi con tutte queste domande!
  You are confusing him with all these questions!

- La segretaria ha confuso le date (/le schede/i nomi).
  The secretary mixed up the dates (/cards/names).

- Questi occhiali mi confondono la vista.
  These glasses blur my vision.

confondersi   to get mixed up; to get confused; to mingle; to get disconcerted; to become confused; to blur

- Si è confuso e ha preso l'autobus sbagliato.
  He got mixed up and took the wrong bus.

- La ragazza si confuse sentendo quelle parole.
  The girl got confused hearing those words.

- Si confusero tra i turisti.
  They mingled with tourists.

- Maria si confonde sempre.
  Mary always gets disconcerted.

■ Tutto si confuse davanti ai miei occhi e svenni.
   Everything blurred before my eyes, and I fainted.

■ La costa si confondeva nella nebbia.
   The shoreline grew hazy in the fog.

confortare   to comfort

■ Tutti cercarono di confortarla.
   Everyone tried to comfort her.

    confortarsi   to comfort oneself; to console oneself

    ■ La ragazza si confortò pensando che le avrebbero trovato un altro lavoro.
   The girl consoled herself by thinking that they would find her another job.

congratularsi con qc   (auxiliary *essere*) to congratulate sb

■ Tutti si sono congratulati con te.
   Everybody congratulated you.

■ Mi congratulo con me stesso per averlo fatto.
   I congratulate myself for doing it.

conoscere   to know; to be familiar with; to meet for the first time; to be conversant
with; to recognize; to experience

■ Tuo padre conosce il suo mestiere (/la strada/la città/il mondo/i miei genitori/
   l'Italia/tutti).
   *Your father knows his job (/the road/the city/the world/my parents/Italy/every-
   body).*

■ Conosci qualcuno che sappia il cinese?
   Do you know somebody who knows Chinese?

■ Li ho conosciuti a casa dei Ferrari.
   I met them at the Ferraris'.

■ Lo conosco di vista (di fama/di nome/a fondo/personalmente).
   I know him by sight (/by reputation/by name/very well/personally).

■ Non conosco quell'autore (/quel musicista/quel tipo di macchina).
   I am not familiar with that author (/that musician/that kind of car).

■ Hanno conosciuto la miseria (/la felicità/il dolore).
   They experienced poverty (/happiness/sorrow).

    far conoscere qc a qc   to introduce sb to sb; to advertise

    ■ Fammi conoscere la tua ragazza.
   Introduce me to your girlfriend.

■ Dobbiamo far conoscere questo prodotto.
We must advertise this product.

farsi conoscere   to make a name for oneself

■ Si è fatto conoscere in breve tempo.
He made a name for himself in a short time.

conoscersi   to know oneself/each other/one another; to meet

■ Conosci te stesso.
Know thyself.

■ Ci conosciamo da molto.
We have known each other for a long time.

■ È un paesino dove si conoscono tutti.
It is a small village where everybody knows everybody else.

■ Credo che vi siate già conosciuti.
I think you've already met.

conquistare   to conquer; to take; to capture; to acquire; to win (over)

■ Abbiamo conquistato lo spazio (/tutto il paese/quella montagna).
We conquered space (/the whole country/that mountain).

■ Napoleone conquistò il potere quando era ancora molto giovane.
Napoleon came to power when he was still very young.

■ Conquistarono la fortezza nemica.
They captured the enemy fortress.

■ Conquistarono una grande ricchezza.
They acquired great wealth.

■ Adriano ha conquistato la stima di tutti (/il cuore della ragazza).
Adrian won everyone's esteem (/the girl's heart).

consegnare   to deliver; to hand in; to distribute; to confine to barracks

■ La merce deve essere consegnata entro il quindici di questo mese.
The goods must be delivered by the fifteenth of this month.

■ Hanno consegnato il prigioniero (/il ladro) alla polizia (alla giustizia).
They delivered the prisoner (/thief) to the police (/justice).

■ Non sono ancora riuscito a consegnare la mia traduzione.
I haven't been able to hand in my translation yet.

■ I telegrammi vanno consegnati a quello sportello.
Telegrams must be handed in at that counter.

■ Hanno appena consegnato le buste stipendio agli impiegati.
They have just distributed the pay envelopes to the employees.

■ Gli amici di mio figlio sono stati consegnati.
My son's friends have been confined to the barracks.

consentire   to allow, permit

■ Le mie possibilità non mi consentono questa spesa.
My means don't allow me this expense.

   consentire di + *inf*   to allow sb to + *inf*

   ■ Consentimi di dire (/spiegarti) quello che penso (/perché l'abbiamo fatto).
Allow me to tell you (/explain to you) what I think (/why we did it).

   consentire a qco/*inf*   to agree to sth/*inf*

   ■ Non hanno consentito alla nostra proposta (/al matrimonio della figlia/alla nostra richiesta di una dilazione del pagamento/a farlo).
They didn't agree to our proposal (/their daughter's marriage/our request for an extension of payment/to do it).

considerare   to consider; to think highly of; to weigh; to contemplate

■ Tutto considerato, credo che accetterò la tua offerta.
All things considered, I think I'll accept your offer.

■ Lo consideri fatto, signor Tallone.
Consider it done, Mr. Tallone.

■ I nostri superiori lo considerano molto.
Our superiors think highly of him.

■ Devi considerare il pro e il contro della loro proposta.
You have to weigh the pros and cons of their proposal.

■ Considero la possibilità di tornare in Italia.
I am contemplating going back to Italy.

   considerarsi   to consider oneself

   ■ Dovete considerarvi fortunati di non aver visto l'incidente.
You must consider yourselves lucky not to have seen the accident.

consigliare   to advise; to recommend

■ Le abbiamo consigliato la montagna (/il mare/il lago).
We advised her to go to the mountains (/seaside/lake).

■ Non te lo consiglio.
I advise you against it.

■ L'hanno consigliata bene (/male).
They gave her good (/bad) advice.

■ Che libro (/ristorante/piatto) ci consigli?
Which book (/restaurant/dish) do you recommend?

consigliare qc di + *inf*   to advise sb to + *inf*

- Ci consigliarono di rivolgerci a un avvocato (/non ripetere quello che avevamo sentito/noleggiare una macchina).
  They advised us to consult a lawyer (/not to repeat what we had heard/rent a car).

consigliarsi   to seek advice; to ask for advice; to have a consultation

- Mi sono consigliato con il mio avvocato.
  I have sought advice from my lawyer.

- Mi sono consigliato con loro.
  I asked for their advice.

- I soci si consigliarono.
  The partners had a consultation.

consistere di/in qco   (auxiliary *essere*) to consist of sth

- Quella enciclopedia (/La collezione) consiste di venti volumi (/mille pezzi).
  That encyclopedia (/The collection) consists of twenty volumes (/a thousand pieces).

consistere nel/nell'/nello + *inf*   to consist in + *ger;* to lie in + *ger*

- Il mio lavoro consiste nel controllare la merce.
  My job consists of checking the goods.

- La difficoltà consiste nel capire i dati.
  The difficulty lies in understanding the data.

consultare   to consult

- Perché non consulti il professore (/un dentista/l'elenco telefonico)?
  Why don't you consult the professor (/a dentist/the telephone book)?

- Devi consultare il tuo cuore (/la tua coscienza).
  You must examine your heart (/conscience).

consultarsi   to consult each other/with sb

- I generali della NATO si consultarono.
  The NATO generals consulted each other.

- Dobbiamo consultarci col nostro legale.
  We must consult with our attorney.

contare   to count (on/out); to be important; to take into account

- Il bambino della signora Govi sa glà contare fino a cento.
  Mrs. Govi's child can already count up to a hundred.

- Gli esperti si possono contare sulle dita.
  You can count experts on the fingers of one hand.

- La sua opinione conta poco (/molto).
  His opinion counts for little (/a lot).

- Questo non conta.
  This doesn't count (is not important).

- Tua madre conta i giorni (/le ore/i minuti) che mancano al tuo arrivo.
  Your mother is counting the days (/hours/minutes) until your arrival.

- Non hai contato sua moglie.
  You didn't take his wife into account.

- Contava almeno cinquant'anni.
  He was at least fifty years old.

- Ho il denaro contato.
  I have just the exact amount (or I don't have money to spare).

contare su (di) qc/qco   to count on sb/sth

- Potete contare sul nostro aiuto (/su Giovanni/su di lui).
  You can count on our help (/on John/on him).

contare di + *inf*   to intend to + *inf*

- Contavo di telefonarti (/andare al cinema/dirglielo/partire subito).
  I intended to call you (/go to the movies/tell her [him]/leave right away).

- Conto di farlo.
  I intend to do it.

contare che + *subj/past conditional*   to count on + *ger*

- Luca contava che venissi anche tu.
  Luke was counting on your coming also.

- Contavo che saresti andato.
  I counted on your going.

contarci   to count, depend on it

- Cercherò di venire, ma non contarci.
  I'll try to come, but don't count on it.

- Arriverai in tempo? —Puoi contarci.
  Will you arrive on time? —You can depend on it.

contarsi   to consider oneself

- Si contava tra i migliori della sua classe (/tra i possibili vincitori).
  He considered himself one of the best in his class (/possible winners).

contenere   to contain; to hold; to repress, hold back

- Il succo d'arancia contiene la vitamina C.
  Orange juice contains vitamin C.

■ Questa bottiglia contiene un litro e mezzo.
This bottle holds a liter and a half.

■ Quel ragazzo non poté più contenere l'emozione.
That boy could not hold back his emotion anymore.

continuare   (auxiliary *avere* if the verb can be followed by a direct object; otherwise *essere*) to continue; to extend; to carry on, go on

■ Ho paura che il cattivo tempo continuerà.
I am afraid the bad weather will continue.

■ Questa strada (/Questo programma) continua fino alla spiaggia (/alle tre).
This road extends to the beach. (/This program continues till three o'clock.)

■ Continua.
To be continued.

■ Il ragazzo ha continuato il lavoro del nonno.
The boy carried on his grandfather's work.

■ Continui, signor Bacigalupo.
Go on, Mr. Bacigalupo.

continuare a + *inf*   to keep on/go on + *ger*

■ Continuarono a interrompere (/telefonarci).
They kept on interrupting (/calling us).

contrarre   to contract; to twist; to catch; to form, take up

■ Non contragga i muscoli (/debiti/un prestito), signor Silva.
Don't contract your muscles (/debts/a loan), Mr. Silva.

■ Il malato contrasse la bocca in una smorfia di dolore.
The sick man twisted his mouth in a grimace of pain.

■ C'è il pericolo che molti altri possano contrarre quella malattia.
There is the danger that many others may catch that disease.

■ È molto facile contrarre quel vizio.
It is very easy to take up that (bad) habit.

contrarsi   to contract

■ Le sue pupille si contrassero.
His pupils contracted.

contravvenire a qco   to contravene sth, violate

■ Hanno contravvenuto alla legge.
They contravened (violated) the law.

contribuire   to contribute

- Tutti abbiamo contribuito al successo dell'impresa.
  We all contributed to the success of the undertaking.
- Avete contribuito alle spese?
  Did you share in the expenses?

1. convenire   (auxiliary *essere*) to be suitable; to suit; to gather

- Non gli conviene.
  It doesn't suit him.
- Una moltitudine di tifosi era convenuta nello stadio.
  A crowd of fans was gathered in the stadium.

   convenire che + *subj*   to be better that

- Conviene che partiate subito.
  It is better that you leave right away.

   convenire a qc + *inf*   to be better for sb to + *inf*

- Gli conviene partire subito (/restare fino a giovedì).
  It is better for him to leave at once (/stay till Thursday).

2. convenire   (auxiliary *avere*) to agree; to admit; to grant

- Tutti convengono che è un buon prezzo.
  Everyone agrees that it's a good price.
- Non è stato onesto con lei, ne conviene.
  He has not been honest with her; he admits it.
- Convengo che hai ragione.
  I grant that you are right.

convergere   to converge

- Le due strade convergevano in quel punto.
  The two roads converged at that point.

convertire qc a qco   to convert sb to sth

- Giorgio cerca sempre di convertire tutti alle sue idee.
  George always tries to convert everybody to his own way of thinking.

   convertire qco in qco   to turn sth into sth

- Bisogna che tu converta i tuoi titoli in contanti.
  You must turn your securities into cash.

convertirsi a qco   to convert to sth

■   Si è convertita all'islamismo (/al cattolicesimo/al marxismo).
She converted to Islam (/Catholicism/Marxism).

convertirsi in qco   to change into sth

■   A volte l'amore si converte in odio.
Sometimes love changes into hatred.

convincere   to convince

■   Le tue parole non l'hanno convinta.
Your words didn't convince her.

convincere qc di qco   to convince sb of sth

■   L'ho convinto del suo sbaglio (/dell'innocenza dell'imputato).
I convinced him of his mistake (/of the innocence of the defendant).

convincere qc a + *inf*   to convince sb to + *inf*

■   Li abbiamo convinti a non partire domani (/comprare quella casa/sposarsi).
We convinced them not to leave tomorrow (/buy that house/get married).

convincersi (di qco/a + *inf*)   to convince oneself

■   Ti devi convincere a smettere di fumare (/lavorare di meno).
You must convince yourself to quit smoking (/work less).

convocare   to summon

■   Si dovrà convocare il Parlamento (/una riunione/quel testimone).
Parliament (/A meeting/That witness) must be summoned.

coprire   to cover; to hold; to hide; to heap; to drown

■   Hanno fatto coprire il pavimento con la moquette.
They had the floor covered with wall-to-wall carpeting.

■   Lo coprirono di ridicolo (/vergogna).
They covered him with ridicule (/shame).

■   La mia assicurazione non copre questo danno.
My insurance doesn't cover this damage.

■   Questo non coprirà le spese (/il costo di produzione).
This won't cover expenses (/production costs).

■   Il padre di Marina copre una carica molto importante.
Marina's father holds a very important post.

■   Cercò di coprire il malfatto del figlio.
He tried to hide his son's misdeed.

- Improvvisamente una grossa nuvola coprì il sole.
  Suddenly a large cloud hid the sun.

- Lo coprirono di onori (/insulti).
  They heaped honors (/insults) on him.

- L'hanno coperta di regali (/cortesie).
  They overwhelmed her with gifts (/kindnesses).

- Il rumore coprì la voce del bambino.
  The noise drowned the baby's voice.

    coprirsi   to cover (oneself); to become overcast

- Copriti. Fa molto freddo.
  Bundle up. It is very cold.

- L'accusato si coprì gli occhi con le mani.
  The accused covered his eyes with his hands.

- Il cielo si coprì.
  The sky became overcast.

    coprirsi di qco   to get covered; to cover oneself with sth

- La città si coprì di neve.
  The town became covered with snow.

- Si coprirono di onore (/gloria).
  They covered themselves with honor (/glory).

correggere   to correct; to adjust; to improve

- L'insegnante corresse tutti gli esami (/gli errori).
  The teacher corrected all the examination papers (/the mistakes).

- Questi nuovi occhiali dovrebbero correggere la tua vista.
  These new glasses should correct your vision.

- Correggete il tiro!
  Adjust the fire!

- Lei deve cercare di correggere la sua pronunzia, signor Zanini.
  You must try to improve your pronunciation, Mr. Zanini.

- Le piace il caffè corretto con la grappa?
  Do you like coffee laced with grappa [an Italian brandy]?

    correggersi di/da qco   to correct oneself; to break oneself of sth, get rid of sth;
                 to mend one's way

- Quello studente ha pronunciato male la parola, ma si è corretto subito.
  That student mispronounced the word but corrected himself right away.

- Devi correggerti di quel difetto (/dal vizio del gioco).
  You must get rid of that bad habit (/the bad habit of gambling).

■   Se non ti correggi, finisci male.
If you do not mend your ways, you'll come to a bad end.

correre   (auxiliary *essere* if destination is mentioned; otherwise *avere*)   to run, run toward; to go fast; to hurry up, rush; to travel; to be; to spread, circulate; to read

■   La bambina è corsa a casa (/a scuola) attraverso i campi.
The little girl ran home (/to school) through the fields.

■   Il sentiero correva lungo la costa (/il fiume/il confine).
The path ran along the coast (/river/border).

■   Corsi a più non posso.
I ran for my life.

■   Corsero dietro al ladro.
They ran after the thief.

■   Un brivido gli corse lungo la schiena.
A shiver ran down (up) his spine.

■   Quel ragazzo corre come il fulmine (/come il vento/come una lepre).
That boy runs like lightning (/the wind/a hare).

■   Ti rendi conto che hai corso il rischio di morire?
Do you realize you ran the risk of dying?

■   Per favore, non correre, ho paura.
Please don't go too fast; I am afraid.

■   Corri, sono già le otto e mezzo.
Hurry up. It is already eight-thirty.

■   Quando il campanello suonò, sua moglie corse alla porta.
When the bell rang, his wife hurried to the door.

■   La macchina correva ad almeno 150 chilometri all'ora.
The car was traveling at least 150 kilometers an hour.

■   Correva l'anno 800.
It was the year 800.

■   Era da aspettarselo, coi tempi che corrono!
It was to be expected, with things the way they are these days!

■   Corrono voci allarmanti sul conto di quell'impiegato.
Alarming rumors are circulating about that employee.

■   Fra te e lui ci corre molto.
There is a big difference between you and him.

■   Lei quando correrà il Giro d'Italia (/la maratona di New York)?
When will you take part in the Giro d'Italia [bicycle race] (/New York City Marathon)?

■   Il suo pensiero corse ai suoi bambini.
His thoughts flew to his children.

■ Ti sembra che questo passo corra bene?
Do you think this passage reads well?

■ Sarà meglio lasciar correre.
It's better to let it go.

■ Dicono che da giovane corresse dietro alle gonnelle.
They say that when he was young, he was always after women.

correre a + *inf*   to run + *inf*

■ Corri ad avvisarlo (/a prendere il giornale/ad aprire).
Run to warn him (/buy the newspaper/open the door).

corrispondere (a)   to correspond (to/with); to tally; to give, pay; to be in conformity with; to return

■ I dati numerici delle due tabelle non corrispondono.
The numerical data in the two tables do not correspond.

■ Corrispondono da un anno ma non si sono mai incontrati.
They have been corresponding for a year, but they have never met.

■ I due conti corrispondono.
The two accounts tally.

■ La merce consegnata non corrisponde al campione.
The delivered goods are not in conformity with the sample.

■ Il suo ex marito le corrisponde una bella cifra in alimenti.
Her ex-husband pays her a large amount in alimony.

■ Gina non ha mai corrisposto all'amore di Vittorio.
Gina never returned Victor's love.

■ Quello che ti hanno detto non corrisponde alla verità.
What they told you isn't true.

costare   (auxiliary *essere*) to cost

■ Quanto costa? —Costa diecimila lire.
How much does it cost? —It costs ten thousand lire.

■ Questa casa mi è costata poco (/molto/troppo/un patrimonio).
This house cost me little (/a lot/too much/a fortune).

■ La sua negligenza (/inesperienza) gli è costata il lavoro (/la vita).
His negligence (/inexperience) cost him his job (/life).

■ Costi quel che costi, lo farò.
Cost what it may, I'll do it.

costare a qc + *inf*   to cost sb to + *inf*

■ Ti costerebbe molto essere gentile?
Would it cost you a lot to be kind?

■   Gli è costato lasciarla.
It cost him (dearly) to leave her.

costituire   to constitute; to establish, form, set up; to consist; to be; to appoint

■   Pensano di costituire un'associazione.
They are thinking of setting up an organization.

■   La spedizione archeologica è costituita da dieci persone.
The archaeological expedition consists of ten people.

■   Hanno già costituito una società (/un governo).
They have already formed a corporation (/a government).

■   Questo non costituisce un precedente (/reato).
This is not a precedent (/a criminal offense).

■   Il suo padrino lo costituì suo erede.
His godfather appointed him his heir.

costituirsi   to form; to give oneself up; to appear as

■   I vari stati si costituirono in federazione.
The various states formed a federation.

■   L'omicida si è costituito alla polizia.
The murderer gave himself up to the police.

■   Si costituiranno parte civile.
They will appear as plaintiffs.

costruire   to build (up); to construct

■   Stanno costruendo un ponte (/una casa/un muro/una nuova ala dell'albergo/
un garage/un grattacielo).
*They are building a bridge (/house/wall/new wing of the hotel/garage/
skyscraper).*

■   Il signor Formenti ha costruito la sua fortuna.
Mr. Formenti built up his fortune.

■   Costruiranno una nuova diga.
They will construct a new dam.

creare   to create; to form; to cause; to make; to establish

■   Dio (/Michelangelo) creò il mondo (/un capolavoro).
God (/Michelangelo) created the world (/a masterpiece).

■   Non createmi altre difficoltà (/altri problemi).
Don't create more difficulties (/problems) for me.

■   Hanno deciso di creare una nuova società.
They have decided to form a new company.

■   Le sue parole crearono un certo imbarazzo fra i presenti.
His words caused a certain embarrassment among those present.

- Fu creato capo del reparto (/presidente del club).
  He was made head of the department (/president of the club).

- Cercate di non creare un precedente.
  Try not to establish a precedent.

credere a/in qc/ a/in qco   to believe (in) sb/sth

- Non credo a quell'uomo (/alle tue promesse).
  I do not believe that man (/your promises).

- Perché pensi che io non ti creda?
  Why do you think I don't believe you?

- Vincenzo non crede in Dio (/negli uomini/nell'utilità di queste riunioni).
  Vincent doesn't believe in God (/man/in the usefulness of these meetings).

- Non potevo credere ai miei occhi!
  I could hardly believe my eyes!

- Lo credevano malato (/un genio/più furbo/all'estero).
  They believed him to be sick (/a genius/smarter/abroad).

    credere che + *subj/past conditional*   to believe, think (that)

    - Credevo che fossero già arrivati (/saresti venuto).
      I thought they had already arrived (/you would come).

    - Crede che tutto gli sia permesso.
      He thinks (that) he is allowed to do anything.

    credere di + *inf*   to think *or* believe (that)

    - Credo di avere ragione.
      I think I am right.

    - Simone credeva di riuscire.
      Simon believed (that) he would succeed.

    crederci   to believe it

    - Non ci credo!
      I don't believe it!

    credersi   to believe oneself to be

    - Si crede la donna più bella del mondo.
      She believes she is the most beautiful woman in the world.

crescere   (auxiliary *essere*) to grow (up); to rise, wax

- Sua figlia è cresciuta dall'anno scorso, signora Merlini.
  Your daughter has grown since last year, Mrs. Merlini.

- La mia amica è cresciuta in campagna.
  My friend grew up in the country.

- Siamo tutti preoccupati perché il livello del fiume continua a crescere.
  We are all worried because (the level of) the river keeps on rising.

- La luna cresce e cala.
  The moon waxes and wanes.

cucinare   to cook; to prepare, make

- Chi cucina in casa tua?
  Who cooks in your house?

- Tua madre cucina molto bene.
  Your mother is a good cook (or can cook very well).

- Hai già cucinato la cena?
  Have you already cooked dinner?

cuocere   to cook, grill, bake, boil, stew, roast, simmer; to fire; to be hot

- La carne può essere cotta alla griglia, al forno, a lesso, in umido, arrosto, a fuoco lento.
  The meat can be grilled, baked, boiled, stewed, roasted, simmered.

- La pasta va cotta al dente.
  Pasta should be cooked al dente (i.e., firm to the bite).

- Hai cotto la crema a bagnomaria?
  Did you cook the custard in a double boiler?

- Lascialo cuocere nel suo brodo. (*idiomatic*)
  Let him stew in his own juices. (idiomatic)

- Stanno cuocendo i vasi (/i mattoni).
  They are firing the vases (/bricks).

- Oggi il sole cuoce.
  Today the sun is really hot.

- Luigi è cotto di quella ragazza. (*idiomatic*)
  Louis has a crush on that girl. (idiomatic)

curare   to take care of; to see to sth; to treat

- Devi curare la tua salute (/le tue finanze).
  You must take care of your health (/your finances).

- Cureremo la spedizione della merce.
  We'll see to the shipment of the merchandise.

- Lo stanno curando con dosi massive di antibiotici.
  They are treating him with massive doses of antibiotics.

- Chi ti ha curato la ferita?
  Who dressed your wound?

curarsi   to take care of oneself; to follow a treatment

- ■   Curati.
    Take care of yourself.

- ■   Sara si cura con rimedi omeopatici.
    Sarah follows a treatment of homeopathic remedies.

curarsi di qco   to pay attention to sth, take notice of sth

- ■   Non mi curo di quello che dice la gente.
    I don't pay attention to what people say.

D

1. dare (qco a qc)   to give (sth to sb/sb sth); to set; to give off

- Dalle una sigaretta (/dei soldi/un foglio di carta/del pane e burro/quel lavoro/ da bere/la medicina).
  Give her a cigarette (/some money/a sheet of paper/some bread and butter/that job/something to drink/her medicine).

- Gli hanno dato tre anni di carcere.
  He was given three years in prison.

- Stefano diede il braccio (/un bacio) alla vecchia signora.
  Stephen gave the old lady his arm (/a kiss).

- Diedero un ricevimento (/una festa/un banchetto/un concerto).
  They gave a reception (/party/banquet/concert).

- Glielo ho dato per il suo compleanno.
  I gave it to her (him) for her (his) birthday.

- Gli diedero le chiavi della città (/uno schiaffo/un pugno/un calcio/dei consigli/ una mano/una spinta/aiuto/coraggio/il permesso di uscire).
  They gave him the keys to the city (/a slap/a punch/a kick/advice/a hand/ a push/help/courage/permission to go out).

- Diedero fuoco al negozio.
  They set fire to the store.

- Non so cosa darei per sapere dove sono adesso i miei amici.
  I would give anything to know where my friends are now.

- Questa stufa dà molto calore.
  This stove gives off a lot of heat.

- Non dare preoccupazioni ai tuoi genitori.
  Don't make your parents worry.

- Non gli danno mai ascolto.
  They never listen to him.

dare a + *inf*   to give + *inf*

- Gli hanno dato a intendere che sarebbero stati pronti a vendere.
  They gave him to understand that they would be ready to sell.

- Le si può dare a bere qualunque cosa. (*idiomatic*)
  One can make her believe anything.

dare alla luce   to give birth

- L'anno dopo diede alla luce un'altra coppia di gemelli.
  The following year she gave birth to another set of twins.

darsi (per) + *adj/ptp* to give (oneself) up; to pretend

- Non darti per vinto.
  Don't give up.

- Si diedero prigionieri.
  They gave themselves up (surrendered).

- Si dà sempre ammalato quando c'è molto da fare.
  He always pretends he is sick when there is a lot to do.

2. dare to pay; to award; to attach; to yield, produce; to let sb have sth; to lend sb sth/sth to sb; to hand; to make (math); to perform; to show

- Mi daranno centomila lire per quella traduzione.
  They'll pay me one hundred thousand lire for that translation.

- Gli hanno dato il primo premio.
  They awarded him the first prize.

- Non dare troppa importanza alle sue parole.
  Do not attach too much importance to his words.

- Questa terra dà molto grano (/un magro raccolto).
  This land yields a lot of wheat (/a meager harvest).

- Questo melo (/non) dà molte mele.
  This apple tree produces (/does not produce) many apples.

- Gli ho dato il mio biglietto per la rappresentazione di domani.
  I let him have my ticket for tomorrow's performance.

- Puoi darmi la tua penna (/la tua macchina)?
  Can you lend me your pen (/your car)?

- Non ho ancora dato la lettera al fattorino.
  I have not handed the letter to the messenger yet.

- La nostra segretaria ha dato le dimissioni.
  Our secretary handed in her resignation.

- Trenta più venti dà cinquanta. Tre per tre dà nove.
  Thirty plus twenty makes fifty. Three times three makes nine.

- La settimana prossima daranno una commedia del Goldoni.
  Next week they'll perform a play by Goldoni.

- Che cosa danno al cinema stasera?
  What are they showing at the movie theater tonight?

dare (un esame) to take (an exam)

- Ho dato il primo esame ieri.
  I took my first exam yesterday.

dare su qco to look onto, overlook sth

- Il nostro balcone (/la nostra finestra) dà sul giardino (/sul lago).
  Our balcony (/window) overlooks the garden (/lake).

dare qc/qco per + *adj/ptp*   to presume sb/sth to be; to take for (granted); to consider

- Fu dato per morto.
  He was presumed dead.

- Non darlo per scontato.
  Don't take it for granted.

- Ormai lo do per perso.
  I consider it to be lost by now.

darsi   to exchange

- Si diedero una stretta di mano.
  They exchanged a handshake.

darsi a qco/a + *inf*   to take to + *ger*

- Si è dato al bere (/gioco).
  He took to drinking (/gambling).

datare   to date

- La lettera era datata 9 maggio 1865.
  The letter was dated May 9, 1865.

- È quasi impossibile datare quel manoscritto (/documento/dipinto).
  It is almost impossible to date that manuscript (/document/painting).

- Questa lettera va datata.
  This letter must be dated.

- A datare dal primo di giugno questo ufficio sarà aperto dalle nove alle quattordici.
  Beginning June 1, this office will be open from nine A.M. to two P.M.

decidere   to decide

- Quel fatto decise la mia scelta (/il nostro futuro).
  That event decided my choice (/our future).

decidere di + *inf*   to decide, settle, resolve to + *inf*

- Abbiamo deciso di aiutare (/telefonargli/fare qualcosa//non fare niente).
  We decided to help (/call him/do something/do nothing).

- Si decise di rispettare la decisione del ministro.
  It was decided to respect the minister's decision.

- Bisogna decidere la questione adesso.
  The question must be settled now.

decidere dove (/quando) + *inf*   to decide where (/when) to + *inf*

- Hanno deciso dove andare in vacanza (/quando partire).
  They have decided on where to go on vacation (/when to leave).

decidersi   make up one's mind

■   Decidetevi!
Make up your minds!

decidersi a + *inf*   to make up one's mind to + *inf*

■   Non sa decidersi a ammetterlo (/parlargli/comprare un'altra macchina).
She can't make up her mind to admit it (/talk to him/buy a new car).

dedicare   to dedicate; to devote; to name

■   Hanno dedicato questa chiesa (/il loro libro) a San Marco (/ai giovani).
They have dedicated this church (/their book) to Saint Mark (/the young).

■   Il figlio di Anna dedica tutto il suo tempo libero alla musica (/alla ricerca scientifica/allo sport).
Ann's son devotes all his free time to music (/scientific research/sports).

■   Forse gli dedicheranno una scuola.
They may name a school after him.

dedicarsi a qc/qco   to dedicate oneself to sb/sth

■   La loro sorella si vuole dedicare a Dio (/ai poveri/all'insegnamento).
Their sister wants to dedicate herself to God (/the poor/teaching).

definire   to define; to settle

■   Dobbiamo definire la nostra posizione (/i confini della nostra proprietà), signor Galbiati.
We must define our position (/our property lines), Mr. Galbiati.

■   Questo termine (/concetto) va definito meglio.
This term (/concept) must be defined better.

■   Pensi che definiranno la lite?
Do you think they will settle the dispute?

demolire   to demolish

■   Hanno demolito quel vecchio edificio.
They demolished that old building.

■   Un filosofo francese ha tentato di demolire quella teoria.
A French philosopher tried to demolish that theory.

depositare   to deposit; to leave; to register

■   Ho depositato l'assegno in banca.
I deposited the check in the bank.

■   Il vino ha depositato un fondo.
Dregs have formed in the wine.

■ Ogni anno il fiume deposita molto fango.
Every year the river leaves a lot of silt.

■ Hanno depositato il marchio di fabbrica.
They registered the trademark.

deprimere to depress

■ Il brutto tempo (/Il caldo) lo deprime.
The bad weather (/The heat) depresses him.

■ Questa medicina deprime l'attività dei reni.
This medication depresses the activity of the kidneys.

> **deprimersi** to get discouraged
>
> ■ Tua nipote si deprime.
> *Your niece gets discouraged.*

derivare da qco to be due to; to derive from sth; to result; to base

■ Ciò deriva dal fatto che è un uomo così ambizioso.
This is due to the fact that (or This is because) he is such an ambitious man.

■ L'italiano (/La parola) deriva dal latino volgare.
Italian (/The word) derives from vulgar Latin.

■ Le materie plastiche derivano dal petrolio.
Plastic is derived from oil.

■ Questa scoperta è derivata da lunghi studi sperimentali.
This discovery resulted from long experimental studies.

■ L'autore ha derivato la trama del romanzo da un fatto di cronaca.
The author has based the plot of his novel on a newspaper story.

descrivere (qco a qc) to describe (sth to sb); to relate

■ La nostra amica ci descrisse il panorama.
Our friend described the view to us.

■ Tu lo descrivi come un furfante; lei lo descrive come un santo.
You describe him as a rascal; she describes him as a saint.

■ Mi descriva il ladro; me lo descriva.
Describe the thief to me; describe him to me.

■ Il giornalista descrisse le ultime battaglie.
The reporter related the latest battles.

desiderare to wish for, want, would like

■ C'è un signore che La desidera, signor Ferrari.
There is a gentleman who wishes to speak to you, Mr. Ferrari.

- Qualcuno La desidera al telefono, signor Fumagalli.
  Someone wants you on the phone, Mr. Fumagalli.

- Desidera qualcosa da bere?
  Would you like something to drink?

desiderare   to want, need (help) (in stores)

- Il signore (/La signora/La signorina) desidera?
  May I help you, Sir (/Madam/Miss)?

- Desidera (qualcosa d') altro?
  Is there anything else I can help you with?

desiderare + *inf*   to wish, want + *inf*

- Desiderava assaggiare un po' di tutto (/sapere la verità).
  He wanted to taste a bit of everything (/to know the truth).

- Desideriamo dichiarare la nostra posizione (/ascoltarlo).
  We want to declare our position (/to listen to him).

desiderare che + *subj.*   to want, wish sb/sth + *inf*

- Desideriamo che voi dichiariate la vostra posizione (/lo ascoltiate).
  We want you to declare your position (/listen to him).

- Quando desiderate che sia mandata la lettera?
  When do you wish the letter to be mailed?

farsi desiderare   to be late

- La sorella di Giovanni si fa sempre desiderare. (*idiomatic*)
  John's sister is always late.

desiderare (molto)   to long for; to crave

- Desideravano molto rivederla.
  They longed to see her again.

- Desiderano un figlio.
  They long for a child.

destinare   to decide, will

- Il cielo ha destinato così.
  Heaven has willed it so.

destinare qc/qco a qc/qco   to destine sb/sth for *or* to + *inf;* to set aside for (*or* apart for); to be assigned to; to be reserved for; to devote to; to intend for, mean for; to address to

- La commedia era destinata al successo.
  The play was destined to be successful.

- Il nonno aveva destinato questo regalo al tuo bambino.
  Grandfather had set aside this present for your child.

- Questo denaro è destinato alle spese impreviste.
  This money is set aside for unforeseen expenses.

- Il nuovo impiegato sarà destinato al reparto spedizioni.
  The new employee will be assigned to the shipping department.

- Il loro fratello fu destinato alla fanteria.
  Their brother was assigned to the infantry.

- Le prime file di posti sono destinate alla autorità.
  The front rows of seats are reserved for the authorities.

- Devo destinare tutta la giornata ai preparativi per la partenza.
  I must devote the entire day to preparations for my departure.

- Questo ruolo è destinato a un bravo attore.
  This role is meant for a very good actor.

- La lettera era destinata a te, ma i soldi erano destinati a lui.
  The letter was addressed to you, but the money was meant for him.

- È un libro destinato ai bambini.
  It is a book intended for children.

- L'avevano destinata in moglie a un uomo ricco.
  They had intended her to be a wife for a rich man.

destinare a + *inf*   to destine to, mean, be intended + *inf*

- Tu sei destinato a finire male (/rimanere scapolo).
  You are destined to meet a bad end (/remain a bachelor).

- Il piano è destinato a fallire.
  The plan is destined to fail.

- Era destinato a morire sul patibolo.
  He was destined to die on the scaffold.

- Il premio era destinato a onorare la loro memoria.
  The prize was meant to commemorate them.

determinare   to define; to fix; to settle; to determine; to bring about; to come about; to ascertain, locate

- Hanno determinato il suo potere.
  They defined his power.

- Prima di tutto si deve determinare il significato della parola.
  First of all, the meaning of the word must be defined.

- Non sono stati ancora determinati i confini del nuovo stato.
  The borders of the new state have not yet been fixed.

- Non penso che abbiano già determinato il prezzo della merce.
  I don't think they have already settled on the price of the merchandise.

■ Puoi determinare la durata della trasmissione?
Can you determine the length of the broadcast?

■ La tensione fra i due paesi ha determinato il conflitto.
The tension between the two countries has brought about the conflict.

■ Si è determinata una situazione spiacevole.
An unpleasant situation has come about.

■ Non hanno ancora determinato la posizione del nemico (/della nave).
They haven't yet ascertained the enemy's (/ship's) position.

dettare   to dictate; to tell; to suggest

■ Ho dettato un memorandum alla segretaria.
I dictated a memorandum to my secretary.

■ I vincitori hanno dettato delle condizioni molto dure.
The winners dictated very tough conditions.

■ Fate come vi detta la coscienza.
Do as your conscience tells you.

■ Queste sono norme dettate dal buon senso (/dall'esperienza).
These are rules suggested by common sense (/experience).

deviare (da)   to deviate (from), stray (from); to divert; to make a detour; to deflect

■ Quella stradina devia dalla strada principale.
That little road deviates from the main road.

■ Non deviare da questo tema.
Don't stray from this topic.

■ Credo che stiano deviando questo treno su un altro binario.
I think they are diverting this train onto another track.

■ Hanno deviato il corso di questo fiume (/il traffico).
They have diverted the course of this river (/the traffic).

■ Le due automobili deviarono verso est.
The two cars made a detour eastward.

■ La conversazione deviò su altri argomenti.
The conversation turned to different topics.

■ La palla deviò verso sinistra.
The ball deflected to the left.

dibattere   to debate; to flutter

■ Dibattevamo il pro e il contro della situazione.
We were debating the pros and cons of the situation.

■ Il comitato dibatté a lungo la proposta (/questione).
The committee debated the proposal (/the matter) for a long time.

■ L'uccellino si levò in volo dibattendo le ali.
Fluttering its wings, the little bird flew up.

dibattersi   to struggle; to flounder

- Il prigioniero si dibatteva per liberarsi.
  The prisoner was struggling to get free.

- Lo videro dibattersi nell'acqua.
  They saw him floundering in the water.

- Mi dibattevo nel dubbio (/nell'incertezza). (*fig*)
  I struggled with doubt (/uncertainty).

dichiarare   to declare; to certify; to find

- Avete qualcosa da dichiarare?
  Do you have anything to declare?

- È stato dichiarato lo sciopero generale.
  A general strike has been declared.

- Lo hanno dichiarato vincitore.
  They declared him the winner.

- Il loro matrimonio fu dichiarato nullo.
  Their marriage was declared invalid.

- Dobbiamo dichiarare guerra alla corruzione (/alla criminalità).
  We must declare war on corruption (/crime).

- Si dichiara che il signor Amato lavora da un anno alle nostre dipendenze.
  It is hereby certified that Mr. Amato has been working for us for a year.

- Fu dichiarato colpevole (/innocente).
  He was found guilty (/not guilty).

  dichiarare di + *inf*   to state (that)

  - Il testimone ha dichiarato di non aver mai visto l'accusato.
    The witness stated he had never seen the accused.

  dichiararsi   to declare oneself; to propose

  - Si è dichiarato vinto.
    He declared himself beaten.

  - Si dichiararono favorevoli (/contrari) alla proposta.
    They declared themselves against (/for) the proposal.

  - Si dichiarò dopo solo un mese di corteggiamento.
    After only one month of courtship, he proposed.

difendere   to plead; to stand up for sb; to hold one's own

- Daniele sa difendere la sua tesi.
  Daniel can plead his argument.

■ Molti di loro difesero la causa dei senza tetto.
Many of them pleaded the cause of the homeless.

■ Io difendo i miei amici.
I stand up for my friends.

■ Tu sai difendere la tua opinione.
You can hold your own.

difendere qc/qco da qc/qco   to defend sb/sth from or against sb/sth; to protect from sth

■ Difesero la città (/il ponte) dagli attacchi nemici (/dal nemico).
They defended the city (/the bridge) from the enemy attacks (/against the enemy).

■ Lo difesero dalle critiche.
They defended him against criticism.

■ La lana difende dal freddo.
Wool protects (one) from the cold.

difendersi   to defend oneself; to manage; to protect oneself

■ I soldati si difesero con valore.
The soldiers bravely defended themselves.

■ L'accusato non ha saputo difendersi.
The accused could not defend himself.

■ Non sono un grande tennista, ma mi difendo.
I am not a great tennis player, but I manage.

■ Difenditi dal freddo.
Protect yourself from the cold.

dimenticare   to forget

■ La nonna di Roberto dimentica facilmente i nomi (/i numeri di telefono/gli indi-rizzi/la fisionomia della gente).
Robert's grandmother easily forgets names (/telephone numbers/addresses/people's faces).

■ Ho dimenticato la valigia in macchina (/gli occhiali in ufficio).
I have forgotten my suitcase in the car (/my glasses at the office).

■ L'hanno già dimenticata. È stata dimenticata da tutti.
They have already forgotten her. She has been forgotten by everyone.

dimenticarsi di qc/qco/ *or inf*   to forget sb/sth/+ *inf*

■ Si è già dimenticata di noi (/della tua lettera).
She has already forgotten us (/your letter).

■ Non ti dimenticare di comprare il giornale (/telefonarmi).
Don't forget to buy the newspaper (/to call me).

dimenticarsi che   to forget (that)

- Mi sono dimenticato che giovedì era il compleanno di Maria (/oggi avevo lezione di piano/dovevo comprare i francobolli).
  I forgot that Thursday was Mary's birthday (/today I had a piano lesson/ I was supposed to buy stamps).

dimenticarsene   to forget about it

- Te ne sei dimenticato? —Come potrei dimenticarmene?
  Have you forgotten about it? —How could I forget about it?

dimostrare qco   to prove, show; to demonstrate; to look

- Come si può dimostrare l'esistenza di Dio (/la validità di questa teoria)?
  How can God's existence (/the truth of this theory) be proven?
- Voglio dimostrargli la mia stima (/la mia gratitudine).
  I want to show him my esteem (/gratitude).
- Questo dimostra la sua malafede (/la necessità di un serio provvedimento).
  This shows his bad faith (/the need for a serious measure).
- Da bambina aveva dimostrato una grande attitudine alla danza.
  As a child she had shown a great aptitude for dancing.
- Potete dimostrare questo teorema di geometria?
  Can you demonstrate this theorem of geometry?
- Tua madre non dimostra più di trent'anni.
  Your mother doesn't look older than thirty.

dimostrare di + *inf*   to show (that)

- Tu dimostri di non aver capito niente (/non conoscere la materia).
  You show that you didn't understand anything (/you do not know the topic).

dimostrare per qco   to demonstrate for sth

- Hanno dimostrato per la pace (/per la guerra).
  They demonstrated for peace (/war).

dimostrarsi   to prove (to be); to turn out to be

- I miei timori si sono dimostrati infondati.
  My fears proved to be groundless.
- Tuo figlio si è dimostrato un incosciente (/un egoista).
  Your son proved to be irresponsible (/selfish).

dipendere da qc/qco   (auxiliary *essere*) to depend on sb/sth; to result from, be caused by

- Verrai da noi stasera? —Dipende.
  Will you come to our house tonight? —It depends.

- Quel ragazzo non vuole dipendere da suo padre (/dalla sua famiglia).
  That boy does not want to depend on his father (/his family).

- Il nostro futuro (/La nostra vittoria) dipenderà dalla loro decisione (/dall'elemento sorpresa).
  Our future (/victory) will depend on their decision (/the surprise factor).

- L'incidente aereo è dipeso dal maltempo.
  The plane accident resulted from (or was caused by) the bad weather.

dipingere   to paint; to portray; to depict

- Quel pittore l'ha dipinto all'acquarello (/a olio/dal vero/di giallo/su tela).
  That painter painted it in watercolor (/in oil/from life/yellow/on canvas).

- Tu l'hai dipinto come un farabutto!
  You depicted him as a rascal!

dire   to tell, say, utter; to express; to bid; to speak (ill/well)

- Ti dirò quello che mi hanno detto.
  I'll tell you what they said to me.

- Giuseppe dice sempre bugie (/la verità).
  Joseph always tells lies (/the truth).

- Marco disse: "Questo è quello che mi hanno detto."
  Mark said, "This is what they told me."

- Come si dice "amore" in inglese?
  How do you say amore *in English (or What's the English for* amore*)?*

- Chi te lo disse? —Me lo disse suo padre.
  Who told you so? —His father told me so.

- Questo film dice molto sulla condizione della donna nella società moderna.
  This movie says a lot about the condition of women in modern society.

- È inutile dire che non hanno mantenuto la promessa.
  It goes without saying that they did not keep their promise.

- L'ho detto per scherzo (*or* per ridere).
  I said it as a joke.

- Dicono male (/bene) di lui.
  They speak ill (/well) of him.

  dire a qc che   to tell sb that

  - Le dissero che era ora di partire (/Marco non sarebbe venuto/la festa era finita/tutti l'avrebbero ammirata).
    They told her that it was time to leave (/Mark would not come/the party was over/everybody would admire her).

dire a qc di + *inf*   to tell sb to + *inf*

- Gli ho detto di tacere (/riposarsi/telefonarci/entrare).
  I told him to be quiet (/to rest/to call us/to go in).

dire buongiorno/buonasera/buonanotte/addio   to bid good morning/good evening/good night/good-bye

- Non gli avete detto buongiorno (/buonasera/buonanotte/addio).
  You did not bid him good morning (/good evening/good night/good-bye).

dire di + *inf*   to state, declare

- Il testimone disse di non aver visto la macchina parcheggiata vicino alla casa (/non conoscerli/non sapere niente).
  The witness declared that he hadn't seen the car parked near the house (/he didn't know them/he did not know anything).

dire di qc/qco   to say to, think of sb/sth

- Cosa ne diresti di uno spuntino (/un giro in macchina)?
  What would you say to a snack (/a drive)?

- Cosa dici della nuova segretaria (/di quel film francese)?
  What do you think of the new secretary (/that French movie)?

dire di sì/di no   to say yes, accept; to say no, refuse

- Spero che tu non abbia detto di sì (/no).
  I hope you did not say yes (/no).

dirsi   to tell each other; to call oneself

- Si dicono tutto.
  They tell each other everything.

- E ti dicevi mio amico!
  And you called yourself my friend!

dirigere   to direct; to turn; to address; to edit; to manage; to aim at; to conduct; to run

- Il vigile dirigeva il traffico.
  The (traffic) policeman was directing the traffic.

- Perché non dirigi i tuoi passi verso casa?
  Why don't you turn your steps toward home?

- Quella osservazione (/lettera) era diretta a Lei, signor Angelini.
  That remark (/letter) was addressed to you, Mr. Angelini.

- Il signor Parodi dirige quella fabbrica.
  Mr. Parodi manages that factory.

- Diressero il tiro sul nemico (/bersaglio).
  They aimed at the enemy (/target).

■ L'orchestra sarà diretta da un giovane direttore d'orchestra italiano.
The orchestra will be conducted by a young Italian conductor.

■ Non so chi diriga la casa (/la scuola) adesso.
I don't know who runs the house (/the school) now.

dirigersi (a/verso)   to go, make for, direct one's steps; to head; to fly

■ È possibile che si siano diretti verso casa.
It is possible that they made off for (or headed) home.

■ La nave si diresse a sud.
The ship headed south.

■ L'aereo si dirigeva verso l'aeroporto, quando improvvisamente scoppiò.
The plane was flying toward the airport when suddenly it blew up.

discendere   (auxiliary *essere;* if the verb is followed by a direct object, auxiliary *avere*)   to descend; to go down, fall

■ La principessa discese le scale lentamente.
The princess descended the stairs slowly.

■ La temperatura è già discesa.
The temperature has already fallen.

discendere verso qco   to descend; to slope down; to flow toward sth

■ Il fiume discende verso il mare.
The river flows toward the sea.

■ La loro proprietà discende verso il bosco.
Their property slopes down to the woods.

discendere da qco   to descend from sth; to get off sth

■ Il pallone discese dal cielo.
The balloon descended from the sky.

■ Dicono che lei discenda da una nobile famiglia spagnola.
They say she is descended from a noble Spanish family.

■ I passeggeri discesero dall'autobus (/treno).
The passengers got off the bus (/train).

discendere in qco   to descend, go down into sth

■ I bambini discesero nel pozzo.
The children went down into the well.

discendere su qc/qco   to descend on sb/sth

■ Una densa nebbia è discesa sulla valle.
A thick fog has descended on the valley.

discolpare qc   to clear sb

- Cercheranno di discolparla.
  They'll try to clear her.

discutere   to discuss, debate, argue

- Prima di decidere, discutiamo.
  Before deciding, let's discuss.
- Discutemmo la loro proposta.
  We debated their proposal.
- Smettetela di discutere!
  Stop arguing!

  discutersi   to be questioned

  - Gli ordini non si discutono.
    Orders cannot be questioned.

  discutere qco/su qco/intorno a qco/di qco   to discuss sth, debate about sth; to question

  - Abbiamo discusso un problema tecnico (/un progetto di legge).
    We've discussed a technical problem (/a bill).
  - Da tempo si discute su questo accordo (/sul prezzo della benzina).
    They have been discussing this agreement (/the price of gas) for some time.
  - Non voglio discutere con te dei miei sentimenti (/di politica).
    I don't want to discuss my feelings (/politics) with you.
  - Dobbiamo discutere sul da farsi.
    We have to discuss what is to be done.
  - La causa sarà discussa il mese prossimo.
    The lawsuit will be debated next month.
  - Su questo non si discute.
    This is beyond question.

disertare   to desert

- Hanno disertato dall'esercito (/dal partito).
  They deserted from the army (/the party).
- Tutti disertarono il paese.
  Everyone abandoned the village.

disfare   to undo; to unmake; to melt; to defeat; to unravel; to unpack; to unwrap; to strip; to take out (stitches)

- Non riesco a disfare questo nodo.
  I can't undo this knot.
- Il nemico fu disfatto.
  The enemy was defeated.
- Sua nonna ha disfatto il golf.
  Her grandmother unraveled the sweater.
- Hai già disfatto le valigie?
  Have you already unpacked?
- Il bambino non vedeva l'ora di disfare il pacchetto.
  The child could not wait to unwrap the package.
- Perché avete disfatto il letto?
  Why did you strip your bed?
- Ho dovuto disfare tutte le cuciture.
  I had to take out all the seams.

disfarsi   to melt; to come undone

- La neve si è disfatta appena è apparso il sole.
  The snow melted as soon as the sun came out.
- Quei cioccolatini si disfano in bocca.
  Those chocolates melt in your mouth.
- Il nodo dei capelli le si disfa sempre.
  The bun in her hair always comes undone.
- Il nodo della sua cravatta si era disfatto.
  The knot of his tie was undone.

disfarsi di qc (*idiomatic*)   to get rid of sb

- Non puoi disfarti di quell'attaccabottoni (/quel pacco)?
  Can't you get rid of that buttonholer (/that package)?

disgustare   to disgust; to make sick

- Il sapore di quel cibo (/Quel lavoro/La carne) lo disgusta.
  The taste of that food (/That job/Meat) disgusts him.

disgustare   to shock

- Le loro opinioni (/La mia indifferenza) la disgustarono.
  She was shocked by their opinions (/my indifference).

disgustarsi di/per qco   to get disgusted with sth; to get sick of sth

- Mi sono disgustato dei cibi grassi (/della sua ipocrisia).
  I got disgusted with fatty foods (/his hypocrisy).

- Si è già disgustata del suo lavoro.
  She has already gotten sick of her job.

dispensare   to dispense; to exempt; to bestow; to deal out, dole out

- Dispensarono favori.
  They dispensed favors.

- L'hanno dispensata da quell'obbligo.
  They have exempted her from that obligation.

- Quegli studenti sono dispensati dalle tasse scolastiche.
  Those students are exempt from tuition.

- Il vecchio sacerdote fu dispensato dal digiuno.
  The old priest was exempted from fasting.

- L'attrice dispensava sorrisi a tutti.
  The actress was bestowing smiles on everyone.

- Dispensarono viveri agli alluvionati.
  They doled out provisions to the victims of the flood.

disperare   to give up, lose hope

- Anche quando tutto va male, non bisogna disperare.
  Even when everything goes wrong, we must not give up hope.

- Sono stati molto coraggiosi, ma adesso cominciano a disperare.
  They have been very brave, but now they're beginning to lose hope.

disperare di + *inf*   to give up hope of + *ger*

- Disperavano di salvarlo (/riuscire nell'esperimento/vincere/trovarlo in vita).
  They had given up hope of saving him (/succeeding in the experiment/ winning/finding him alive).

disperare di qco   to lose hope of sth

- Disperano della buona riuscita dell'impresa (/della guarigione del bambino).
  They have lost hope of the successful outcome of the undertaking (the child's recovery).

disperarsi   to give oneself to despair; to lose hope

■   Non disperarti.
    Don't give yourself to despair.

■   Se penso a tutti i problemi che devo risolvere, mi dispero.
    If I think of all the problems I have to solve, I lose hope.

dispiacere + *inf*   (auxiliary *essere*) to mind, regret + *ger*

■   Ti dispiacerebbe passarmi il sale (/darmi il loro numero di telefono)?
    Would you mind passing me the salt (/giving me their phone number)?

■   Mi dispiace dover rifiutare il tuo invito (/dovertelo dire).
    I regret having to refuse your invitation (/having to tell you).

dispiacere a qc/qco   to displease sb; to upset; to be sorry; to mind; to be disagreeable to sb/sth

■   La sua decisione è dispiaciuta a tutti.
    His decision displeased (or upset) everyone.

■   La tua assenza è dispiaciuta molto alla mamma.
    Your absence upset Mother a lot.

■   Mi (/gli/le) dispiace moltissimo (/infinitamente).
    I am (He is/She is) very (/extremely) sorry.

■   Se non Le (/ti/vi) dispiace, io vorrei andare a casa.
    If you don't mind, I'd like to go home.

dispiacere che + *subj*   to be sorry, to mind

■   Mi dispiace che tua sorella non sia potuta venire.
    I am sorry your sister could not come.

■   Ci dispiace che abbiate dovuto rifarlo.
    We are sorry you had to redo it.

■   Le dispiacerebbe se venissero con Lei?
    Would you mind if they came with you?

dispiacersi di/per qco   to be offended by sth

■   Si è dispiaciuto del (per il) tuo rifiuto.
    He was offended by your refusal.

disporre   to arrange, place; to prepare; to dispose

■   La mia segretaria ha disposto le cartelle (/i nomi in ordine alfabetico).
    My secretary arranged the folders (/the names in alphabetical order).

■ Devo disporre tutto per il pranzo.
   I have to prepare everything for the luncheon.

■ L'uomo propone e Dio dispone. (*proverb*)
   Man proposes, and God disposes. (proverb)

disporre che/di + *inf*   to provide that; to be provided for; to order; to decide on sth/to + *inf;* to state

■ La legge dispone che gli evasori fiscali siano perseguiti.
   The law provides that tax dodgers be prosecuted.

■ Il comandante dispose che le truppe si ritirassero.
   The commander ordered the troops to retreat.

■ Il direttore disporrà nel modo che riterrà opportuno.
   The manager will decide in a way that he considers appropriate.

■ Avevano disposto di vendere la casa.
   They had decided to sell the house.

■ Il contratto dispone che il pagamento sia effettuato alla fine di ogni mese.
   The contract states that payments must be effected at the end of each month.

disporre di qc/qco   to have at one's disposal; to depend on; to hold; to decide on sth

■ Disponete pure di me.
   Consider me at your disposal.

■ Se hai bisogno di qualcosa, disponi di me.
   If you need something, you can depend on me.

■ Non ho una persona di fiducia di cui disporre.
   I don't have a reliable person I can depend on.

■ Quella società dispone di grossi capitali.
   That company has a great deal of capital at its disposal.

■ Lo stadio dispone di trentamila posti.
   The stadium holds thirty thousand seats.

■ Ognuno dispone della propria vita.
   Everybody decides on his own life.

disporsi a qco/inf   to get ready for sth/inf

■ Mi disponevo ad uscire di casa (/partire) quando hai chiamato.
   I was getting ready to leave the house (/to leave) when you called.

disporsi in fila, in cerchio   to line up; to form a circle

■ Si disposero in fila (/cerchio).
   They formed a line (/circle).

dissimulare   to hide, conceal

- Credo che quel ragazzo abbia imparato a dissimulare i suoi sentimenti.
  I think that boy learned to hide his feelings.

- Le due ragazze cercavano di dissimulare la loro gioia.
  The two girls were trying to conceal their joy.

- Non seppero dissimulare il loro disappunto.
  They could not conceal their disappointment.

dissolvere   to dissolve; to dispel; to break up, shatter

- Questa polvere va disciolta nell'acqua.
  This powder must be dissolved in water.

- Le sue parole, signor Perrini, hanno dissolto tutti i miei dubbi (/sospetti).
  Your words, Mr. Perrini, have dispelled all my doubts (/suspicions).

- Questo ha dissolto l'unità nazionale.
  This shattered (or broke up) national unity.

  dissolversi   to dissolve; to vanish

  - La neve (/La nebbia) si è dissolta in poco tempo.
    The snow vanished (/fog dissolved) in a short time.

  - La società (/Quel partito) si è dissolta (/dissolto).
    The company (/That party) dissolved.

  - Credo che le tue ansie si dissolveranno presto.
    I believe your anxieties will soon vanish.

dissuadere qc da + *inf*   to dissuade, deter sb from + *ger*

- Lo dissuademmo dal comprarlo
  We dissuaded him from buying it.

- Niente potrà dissuaderlo dal farlo.
  Nothing can deter him from doing it.

distendere   to stretch (out); to spread; to knock sb down/out; to relax

- Il ragazzo distese le gambe (/le braccia).
  The boy stretched his legs (/arms).

- L'uccellino distese le ali e volò via.
  The little bird spread its wings and flew away.

- Il pugile distese l'avversario alla seconda ripresa.
  The boxer knocked his opponent out in the second round.

- Il loro fratello lo distese con un pugno ben assestato.
  Their brother knocked him flat with a well-aimed punch.

- Questa musica (/tisana) distende i nervi.
  This music (/herbal tea) relaxes the nerves.

■ Lei deve imparare a distendere i muscoli, signor Ruggero.
You need to learn to relax your muscles, Mr. Ruggero.

■ L'avvocato distese l'atto di vendita.
The attorney drew up the sales contract.

distendere qc/qco su qco   to lay sb/sth on sth

■ La cameriera distese la coperta (/tovaglia) sul letto (/sulla tavola).
The maid laid the bedspread (/tablecloth) on the bed (/table).

■ Hanno disteso il ferito sulla lettiga.
They laid the wounded man on the stretcher.

distendere qco a + *inf*   to hang sth out to + *inf*

■ Le donne (/I pescatori) distesero il bucato (/le reti) ad asciugare.
The women (/fishermen) hung the laundry (/nets) out to dry.

distendersi (su qco)   to extend; to stretch; to lie down on sth; to relax

■ La pianura si distendeva a perdita d'occhio.
The plain extended as far as the eye could see.

■ La valle si distende verso sud.
The valley stretches southward.

■ Non distendetevi sull'erba: è bagnata.
Don't lie down on the grass; it's wet.

■ Io mi distendo leggendo libri gialli.
I relax reading detective stories.

distinguere   to divide; to mark; to characterize; to make out

■ L'abbiamo distinto con la lettera D.
We have marked it with the letter D.

■ Con la grazia che lo distingue, mi ha urtato.
With the (lack of) gracefulness that is typical of him (or characterizes him), he bumped into me.

■ Non potevo distinguere le persone nel buio.
I could not make out the people in the darkness.

distinguere (qc/qco da qc/qco)   to distinguish, tell (sb from sb/sth from sth)

■ L'etichetta distingue questa bottiglia dall'altra.
The label distinguishes this bottle from the other.

■ Bisogna distinguere il vero dal falso, il bene dal male.
One must distinguish true from false, good from evil.

■ Non riesco a distinguere la sua voce da quella di sua madre.
I can't tell her voice from her mother's.

■   Non sanno distinguere l'originale dalla imitazione.
     They cannot tell the original from the imitation.

distinguersi   to distinguish oneself; to stand out

■   Si è sempre distinto per capacità organizzativa.
     He has always distinguished himself with his organizational ability.

■   Quella casa si distingue dalle altre perché è dipinta di giallo.
     That house stands out from the others because it is painted yellow.

distribuire   to distribute; to hand out, to deliver; to arrange; to spread out; to deal (out); to award; to station; to assign

■   Hanno distribuito i soldi (/i dividendi) alle vittime dell'uragano (/agli azionisti).
     They distributed the money (/dividends) among the victims of the hurricane (/the shareholders).

■   Hanno già distribuito le paghe agli operai?
     Have they already handed out the wages to the workers?

■   Non hanno ancora distribuito la posta.
     They haven't delivered the mail yet.

■   Abbiamo distribuito le medicine negli armadi.
     We arranged the medicines in the cupboards.

■   Il carico dovrebbe essere distribuito in modo più uniforme.
     The load should be spread out more evenly.

■   Il croupier distribuì cinque carte a ciascun giocatore.
     The croupier dealt each player five cards.

■   L'uomo distribuiva colpi a destra e a sinistra.
     The man was dealing out blows right and left.

■   I premi saranno distribuiti durante la cerimonia.
     The prizes will be awarded during the ceremony.

■   I soldati furono distribuiti lungo la riva del fiume.
     Soldiers were stationed along the riverbanks.

■   Perché non cominci a distribuire i posti a tavola?
     Why don't you start assigning seats at the table?

distribuirsi   to distribute themselves

■   I poliziotti in borghese si distribuirono nello stadio.
     Plainclothes detectives distributed themselves (or spread out) around the stadium.

distruggere   to destroy: to be consumed by

■   I bombardamenti hanno distrutto l'intero paese.
     The bombings destroyed the whole country.

■ Temono che la grandine abbia distrutto il raccolto.
They fear the hail may have destroyed the crops.

■ Le tue parole hanno distrutto tutta la nostra fede.
Your words destroyed all our faith.

■ Chicago fu distrutta da un incendio.
Chicago was destroyed by a fire.

■ Fu distrutta dal dolore.
She was consumed by grief.

■ Il bere l'ha distrutto.
Drinking ruined him.

disturbare   to disturb; to bother; to trouble; to jam

■ Non volevamo disturbarla mentre lavorava, signor Neri!
We did not want to disturb you while you were working, Mr. Neri!

■ Mi scusi se La disturbo, signora Marini.
Excuse my disturbing you, Mrs. Marini.

■ Non mi disturbare.
Don't bother me.

■ Sono spiacente di disturbarvi.
I am sorry to trouble you.

■ Queste interferenze disturbano la trasmissione.
This interference jams the transmission.

disturbarsi (a + *inf*)   to trouble oneself; to take the trouble

■ Non disturbatevi!
Don't trouble yourselves!

■ Perché ti sei disturbato a venire qui (/riportarmi il libro)?
Why did you take the trouble to come here (/to bring me back the book)?

diventare   (auxiliary *essere*) to become; to get; to grow (into); to change; to turn (into); to make

■ Sono sicuro che diventerà sindaco (/presidente).
I am sure he'll become (or he'll be elected) mayor (/president).

■ Diventò famoso (/il loro peggior nemico/sospettoso di tutti).
He became famous (/their worst enemy/suspicious of everyone).

■ Diventerà medico (/avvocato/elettricista/dentista/architetto).
He will become a doctor (/a lawyer/an electrician/a dentist/an architect).

■ Susanna è diventata una bella donna.
Susan has grown into a beautiful woman.

■ Come sei diventato alto, Antonio!
How tall you have grown, Anthony!

- I loro figli stanno diventando insopportabili.
  Their children are getting (growing) unbearable.

- L'amore è diventato odio.
  Their love changed to hatred.

- Il latte è diventato acido. Il vino è diventato aceto.
  The milk turned sour. The wine turned into vinegar.

- Quando lo vide il ragazzo diventò pallido.
  When he saw him, the boy turned pale.

- Giovanna è diventata la loro amica.
  Joan made friends with them.

- La farai diventare pazza!
  You'll drive her insane!

divertire   to amuse, entertain

- La conversazione dei bambini la divertiva.
  The children's conversation amused her.

- I pagliacci divertono i bambini.
  Clowns entertain children.

- Quell'attore sa divertire il pubblico.
  That actor knows how to entertain the public.

  divertirsi   to amuse, enjoy oneself; to have fun

  - Divertiti!
    Enjoy yourself!

  - Vi siete divertiti a Roma?
    Did you enjoy yourselves in Rome?

  - Dopo tanto lavoro avete bisogno di divertirvi.
    After so much work, you need to have fun.

  - Gli piace divertirsi alle spalle di tutti.
    He likes laughing behind everyone's back.

  divertirsi a + *inf*   to enjoy + *ger*

  - Quel bambino (/Suo marito) si diverte a costruire castelli di sabbia
    (/prendermi in giro).
    That child (/Her husband) enjoys building sand castles (/teasing me).

  - Non sai quanto mi diverta a farla arrabbiare.
    You don't know how much I enjoy driving her crazy.

dividere   to divide; to part (separate)

- Dividete questo numero per quattro.
  Divide this number by four.

■ Solo la morte potrà dividerci.
Only death can separate us.

dividere qco in qco   to divide sth into sth

■ Perché non dividiamo questo foglio in due (/questo terreno in lotti)?
Why don't we divide this sheet of paper in two (/parcel of land in lots)?

■ Divisero gli operai in varie squadre.
They divided the workers into various teams.

■ Devi dividere questa parola in sillabe (/la torta in cinque porzioni).
You must divide this word into syllables (/the pie into five portions).

dividere qco fra qc   to divide sth among sb

■ Gli utili furono divisi fra gli azionisti.
The profits were divided among the shareholders.

■ L'eredità sarà divisa tra i figli.
The inheritance will be divided among the children.

dividere qco con qc   to share sth with sb

■ Carlo divise il panino con l'amico.
Charles shared the sandwich with his friend.

■ Non ho nulla da dividere con loro.
I have nothing to share with them.

dividere da qco   to divide by sth, separate

■ I due paesi sono divisi da un fiume.
The two countries are divided by a river.

■ Perché non dividi il bene dal male (/la ragione dal torto).
Why don't you separate good from evil (/right from wrong)?

dividersi (in)   to split up; to divide (into)

■ I ladri si divisero il bottino.
The thieves split up the loot.

■ Il gruppo si divise poi in varie sette (/fazioni).
The group later divided into various sects (/factions).

■ La strada si divideva in due sentieri.
The road divided (branched off) into two paths.

dividersi da qc   to separate from sb; to part from sb

■ Si è diviso dalla moglie parecchi anni fa.
He separated from his wife several years ago.

■ Si divisero con dolore dai loro amici.
They parted from their friends with sorrow.

dividersi fra   to divide one's time between

■   La sorella di quel mio amico si divide fra l'insegnamento e la famiglia (/lo studio e il lavoro).
The sister of that friend of mine divides her time between teaching and her family (/study and work).

domandare (qco a qc)   to ask (sb for sth)

■   Perché lo domandi?
Why do you ask?

■   Gli ho domandato il tuo indirizzo (/delle informazioni/l'ora/il permesso di uscire/un consiglio/se sapeva quando saresti tornato).
I asked him for your address (/some information/the time/permission to go out/a piece of advice/if he knew when you would come back).

■   Le hanno domandato perdono (/aiuto/la sua opinione/il prezzo/notizie dei suoi genitori/un favore).
They asked her for forgiveness (/help/her opinion/the price/news of her parents/a favor).

domandare di qc   to inquire after sb; to ask about or for sb/sth

■   Gli amici ci hanno domandato di te.
Our friends inquired after you.

■   Gli ho domandato del suo lavoro.
I asked him about his job.

■   Al telefono c'è qualcuno che domanda di Lei, signor Bianchi.
There's someone on the phone asking for you, Mr. Bianchi.

domandarsi   to wonder

■   Mi domando che cosa sia successo (/perché non abbiano ancora telefonato/dove siano andati).
I wonder what happened (/why they have not phoned yet/where they went).

dominare   to dominate; to master; to control

■   Gli amici lo dominano.
His friends dominate him.

■   Tuo nipote domina quella lingua (/materia) perfettamente.
Your nephew has mastered that language (/topic) completely.

■   Federico non sa dominare le sue passioni.
Frederick can't control his passions.

■   Un buon cavaliere sa come dominare il suo cavallo.
A good rider knows how to control his horse.

dominare (su)   to rule (over)

■   Il re dominò il paese per pochi anni.
The king ruled (over) the country for a few years.

■   La metà del mondo era dominata dall'impero.
Half the world was ruled by the empire.

■   Non lasciarti dominare dai tuoi sentimenti.
Don't let yourself be ruled by your feelings.

dominarsi   to control oneself

■   Per favore, signor Masi, cerchi di dominarsi!
Mr. Masi, try to control yourself, please!

■   Tu non ti sai dominare.
You have no self-control.

dormire   to sleep; to spend the night

■   Il bambino dorme da due ore.
The baby has been sleeping for two hours.

■   Il bambino dorme supino (/bocconi/su un fianco/tutta la notte).
The child is sleeping on his back (/on his stomach/on his side/all through the night).

■   Dovresti prendere qualcosa che ti faccia dormire.
You should take something that will make you sleep.

■   Questa conferenza fa dormire.
This lecture is boring.

■   La mamma lo sta mettendo a dormire.
Mother is putting him to bed.

■   Devo dormirci su. (*fig*)
I have to sleep on it. (fig)

■   Dormirò in quell'albergo (/fuori) domani sera.
I'll spend the night in that hotel (/out) tomorrow.

■   Quel bambino parla dormendo.
That child talks in his sleep.

■   Non dormire sugli allori. (*idiomatic*)
Don't rest on your laurels. (idiomatic)

dovere (*Note:* In compound tenses, if *dovere* is followed by a verb requiring *essere,* the auxiliary *avere* or *essere* can be used—see the first example.)   must, need, should, ought to, have to; to be likely; to be supposed; to be due, bound; to owe

■   Hanno dovuto (*or* Sono dovuti) andare in banca stamattina.
They had to go to the bank this morning.

■   Devi farlo subito (/fermarti al semaforo/studiare).
You must do it at once (/stop at the traffic light/study).

■   Quelle devono essere le Alpi.
Those must be the Alps.

■   Non devi farlo oggi.
You needn't do it today.

■   Avrei dovuto ascoltarti!
I should have listened to you!

■   Doveva diventare un grande scienziato.
He was to become a great scientist.

■   Cosa devo fare?
What am I to do?

■   Non devono essere ancora a casa.
They are not likely to be at home yet.

■   Deve piovere oggi.
It is likely to rain today.

■   Non dovrei dirlo.
I am not supposed to say it.

■   A che cosa è dovuto questo incidente? —Credono che sia dovuto alla negligenza di un operaio.
What is this accident due to? —They think it is due to a worker's negligence.

■   Il treno (/L'aereo) deve arrivare alle 11:30.
The train (/The plane) is due to arrive at 11:30.

■   Presto o tardi questo doveva capitare.
Sooner or later this was bound to happen.

■   Tuo nipote deve la sua promozione a te.
Your nephew owes his promotion to you.

■   Gli devono circa un milione (/la vita).
They owe him about a million (/their lives).

■   Riccardo deve tutto a se stesso.
Richard is a self-made man.

dubitare di qc/qco   to doubt sb/sth

■   Carlo dubita dei fatti (/della verità delle tue asserzioni/dell'immortalità dell'anima/del successo di questo prodotto/dell'esistenza di Dio/di sé/della vostra onestà/di tutto/di tutti).
Charles doubts the facts (/the truth of your statements/the immortality of the soul/the success of this product/the existence of God/himself/your honesty/everything/everybody).

dubitare che + subj   to doubt (that)

■   Dubito che vengano (/le loro intenzioni siano buone).
I doubt they are coming (/their intentions are good).

■   Dubitavo che tu vincessi.
I doubted you would win.

non dubitare   to be sure; to not worry; to depend (on it)

■ Non dubito che riuscirai a farlo (/che lei lo abbia detto).
I am sure you can do it (/she said it).

■ Sarò puntuale, non dubitare.
I'll be on time; don't worry.

■ Manterrò il segreto, non dubitare!
I'll keep the secret; (you can) depend on it!

durare   (auxiliary *essere*) to last; to persist; to remain in office; to keep; to wear

■ La guerra è durata molti anni.
The war lasted many years.

■ Sono sicuro che la loro relazione non durerà molto.
I am sure that their relationship will not last long.

■ Dottore, quanti giorni può durare la febbre?
Doctor, how many days could the fever last?

■ Il presidente durò in carica otto anni.
The president remained in office for eight years.

■ Qesto pesce non dura se non lo metti nel congelatore.
This fish won't keep if you don't put it in the refrigerator.

■ Ho paura che questo rayon non duri molto.
I am afraid this rayon does not wear well.

E

eccedere in qco   to drink, eat, do sth to excess

- Il loro padre eccede nel bere (/nel mangiare).
  Their father drinks (/eats) too much.

- Tu eccedi in tutto.
  You do everything to excess.

eccellere   to excel, be superior to

- Suo figlio eccelle sui suoi coetanei.
  Her son excels over (or is superior to) other children of his age.

   eccellere in qco   to excel in sth

   - Quel pittore (/Questo studente) eccelle nei paesaggi (/in matematica).
     That painter (/This student) excels in landscapes (/mathematics).

eccitare qc/qco   to excite sb/sth; to provoke; to arouse, whet

- Quei bambini hanno bisogno di letture che eccitino la fantasia.
  Those children need readings that will excite their imagination.

- Tutti erano eccitati dalla notizia del suo arrivo.
  Everybody was excited by the news of his arrival.

- Le sue azioni eccitarono l'ira (/l'odio/la gelosia) di molti.
  His actions provoked the wrath (/the hatred/the jealousy) of many.

- Le sue parole eccitarono il riso.
  His words provoked laughter.

- Quella condanna eccitò la folla (/l'indignazione di tutti).
  That sentence aroused the crowd (/everybody's indignation).

- Bisogna eccitare il suo appetito.
  It is necessary to whet his appetite.

   eccitarsi   to get excited

   - Non eccitarti per così poco (/niente/ogni novità).
     Don't get excited over so little (/nothing/anything new).

eclissare   to eclipse, overshadow

- La luna eclissò il sole.
  The moon eclipsed the sun.

eclissarsi   to eclipse; to vanish

- Il sole si è eclissato.
  There was an eclipse of the sun.

- Il signor Vanni si eclissò senza salutare.
  Mr. Vanni vanished without saying goodbye.

elaborare   to draw up, devise; to process; to secrete

- Hanno elaborato un piano.
  They have devised a plan.

- Il computer elaborerà i risultati della ricerca.
  The computer will process the results of the research.

- Il pancreas elabora l'insulina.
  The pancreas secretes insulin.

eleggere   to elect

- Lo hanno eletto (/sindaco/deputato).
  They elected him (/mayor/a member of Parliament).

- Chi eleggeresti?
  Whom would you elect?

elevare   to elevate; to raise; to erect; to square/cube a number *(math)*

- Era un sermone che elevava lo spirito.
  It was a sermon that elevated the spirit.

- Devono elevare il piano stradale.
  They must raise the roadway.

- Fu elevato alla dignità cardinalizia (/alla carica di prefetto di polizia).
  He was raised to the station of cardinal (/office of prefect of police).

- Hanno elevato il loro tenore di vita.
  They have improved their standard of living.

- Hanno elevato un monumento ai caduti.
  They erected a memorial to the fallen.

- Dobbiamo elevare questi numeri al quadrato e al cubo.
  We must square and cube these numbers.

elevarsi   to rise, improve

- Hanno saputo elevarsi a una condizione economica invidiabile.
  They managed to reach an enviable financial condition (or level).

- Il loro tenore di vita (/La temperatura) si è elevato (/elevata).
  Their standard of living (/The temperature) has risen.

elevarsi (su qco)   to rise; to tower over sth, overlook

■ Quella montagna si eleva oltre i duemila metri.
That mountain rises above two thousand meters.

■ Il nostro palazzo si eleva sulle case attorno.
Our building towers over the surrounding houses.

■ La montagna si eleva sul lago.
The mountain overlooks the lake.

eliminare   to eliminate, eradicate, abolish

■ Hanno eliminato questa clausola (/teoria/tutti gli altri concorrenti).
They eliminated this clause (/theory/all the other competitors).

■ Si devono eliminare la povertà e l'ignoranza.
Poverty and ignorance must be eliminated (or eradicated).

■ In molti stati la pena di morte è stata eliminata.
In many states capital punishment has been abolished.

eliminare qc   to knock sb out; to kill sb

■ Il pugile è stato eliminato alla seconda ripresa.
The boxer was knocked out in the second round.

■ L'hanno eliminato perché era un testimone pericoloso.
They killed him because he was a dangerous witness.

eliminare qco   to get rid of sth; to remove, eliminate, suppress sth

■ Perché non elimini tutta questa roba inutile?
Why don't you get rid of all this useless stuff?

■ Sono stati eliminati tutti i sospetti (/i dubbi/gli ostacoli).
All suspicions (/doubts/obstacles) have been removed.

■ Questa medicina elimina il dolore.
This medicine suppresses (or eliminates) the pain.

emettere   to emit; to deliver; to pass; to issue; to utter

■ Questa stufa non emette calore, soltanto fumo.
This stove does not emit heat, only smoke.

■ La giuria ha emesso un giudizio (/un verdetto).
The jury delivered a judgment (/a verdict).

■ Hanno emesso una sentenza.
They passed a sentence.

■ Lo stato ha emesso nuovi biglietti di banca (/buoni del Tesoro).
The state has issued new money bills (/Treasury bonds).

■ La ragazza emise un grido (/un sospiro/un gemito).
The girl uttered a cry (/sigh/moan).

entrare   (auxiliary *essere*) to go *or* come in/into, enter; to march into; to fit; to go into (*math*)

■   Entri, signora Campana!
Come in, Mrs. Campana!

■   Li vidi entrare in un cinema.
I saw them enter a movie theater.

■   Entra Edipo (/Re Lear).
Enter Oedipus (/King Lear).

■   Il ladro entrò nella stanza dove il bambino stava dormendo.
The thief went into the room where the child was sleeping.

■   I bambini entrarono correndo.
The children ran in.

■   Le truppe entrarono nella città.
The troops marched into the city.

■   Questa chiave non entra nel buco della serratura.
This key does not fit the lock.

■   Non entrava più nell'abito da sposa.
The wedding dress didn't fit her anymore.

■   Il tre nel nove entra tre volte.
Three goes into nine three times.

entrare a + *inf*   to go/come in + *inf*

■   È entrata a prendere il suo libro.
She came (went) in to get her book.

entrarci   to get into sth; to be contained; to have anything to do with it

■   In questa macchina non ci si entra in più di tre.
No more than three people can get in this car.

■   In questa bottiglia non ci può entrare tutto.
That bottle can't contain it all.

■   Tu non c'entri.
You have nothing to do with it.

ereditare   to inherit

■   Speriamo che il bambino erediti la bellezza della madre e l'intelligenza del padre.
Let's hope the child inherits his mother's beauty and his father's intelligence.

■   Iacopo ha ereditato dal nonno una collezione di quadri (/la passione per il gioco/due appartamenti).
Jacob inherited a collection of paintings (/the passion for gambling/two apartments) from his grandfather.

esagerare   to exaggerate

■   Come esageri!
You do exaggerate! (or How you exaggerate!)

- Paolo esagera sempre le difficoltà del suo lavoro (/la sua importanza).
  Paul always exaggerates the difficulties of his job (/his importance).

- Alla mostra ci saranno state dieci persone in tutto, non esagero.
  At the exhibit there must have been ten people in all; I am not exaggerating.

esagerare (in qco)   to go too far (with sth)

- Non ti sembra che Beniamino esageri nelle spese (/nei complimenti)?
  Don't you think Benjamin goes too far with his expenses (/compliments)?

esagerare nel/nell'/nello + *inf*   to overdo sth

- Tu esageri nel mangiare (/nel bere/nello spendere).
  You overeat (/overdrink/overspend).

esaminare   to examine; to take into consideration

- Non hanno ancora esaminato i testimoni.
  They have not examined the witnesses yet.

- La nostra proposta verrà esaminata presto.
  Soon our proposal will be taken into consideration.

- Devi esaminare la tua coscienza.
  You must examine your conscience.

escludere qc/qco (da qco)   to exclude sb/sth (from sth)

- La folla (/La donna) fu esclusa dalla aula (/dalla sala).
  The public (/The woman) was excluded from the courtroom (/hall).

- Hanno escluso due candidate dal concorso per Miss Italia.
  They have excluded two contestants from the Miss Italy pageant.

escludere che + *subj*   to refuse to admit (that)

- Escludo che siano colpevoli (/questo sia vero).
  I refuse to admit that they are guilty (/this is true).

non escludere che + *subj*   it is possible (that)

- Non escludo che siano colpevoli (/questo sia vero).
  It is possible that they are guilty (/this is true).

escludersi   to exclude each other

- I contrari si escludono.
  Opposites exclude each other.

eseguire   to execute, carry out; to perform; to enforce

- Hanno eseguito il piano.
  They executed the plan.

- Gli ordini vanno eseguiti.
  Orders must be carried out.

- Eseguirono un quartetto di Paganini (/un concerto di musica elettronica).
  They performed a Paganini quartet (/a concert of electronic music).

■   La legge va eseguita.
   The law must be enforced.

esercitare (qco su qc)   to exert (sth on sb); to exercise; to practice (a profession)

■   Esercitò tutta la sua influenza per riuscire.
   He exerted all his influence in order to be successful.

■   Dovremmo esercitare pressione sui candidati.
   We should exert pressure on the candidates.

■   Dovresti esercitare la tua autorità (/le tue facoltà mentali/i tuoi diritti).
   You should exercise your authority (/your mental faculties/your rights).

■   Quel dottore non esercita più? —No, esercita ancora.
   Has that doctor given up his practice? —No, he still practices.

   esercitarsi a/in qco   to practice sth

   ■   Ugo si esercita in inglese (/al piano/alla lotta) un'ora al giorno.
      Hugh practices his English (/piano/wrestling) an hour a day.

   esercitarsi a + *inf*   to practice + *ger*

   ■   Dovresti esercitarti a parlare in pubblico (/scrivere/usare il computer).
      You should practice speaking in public (/writing /using the computer).

esigere   to exact; to collect; to require, demand

■   Esigono il ripagamento del prestito entro il 10.
   They require (or exact) repayment of the loan by the tenth.

■   Si devono esigere le imposte.
   Taxes must be collected.

■   La situazione esige molta attenzione (/dei provvedimenti drastici).
   The situation requires a lot of attention (/drastic measures).

   esigere qco (da qc)   to demand sth (of/from sb)

   ■   Esigevi troppo da lui.
      You demanded too much of (or from) him.

   ■   Io esigo una risposta (/una spiegazione/rispetto/delle scuse).
      I demand an answer (/an explanation/respect/some apologies).

esistere   (auxiliary *essere*) to exist; to be; to be in existence; to live

■   Tu credi che esistano le sirene (/i fantasmi)?
   Do you believe that mermaids (/ghosts) exist?

■   Non esistono prove della sua colpevolezza.
   There is no proof of his guilt.

■   Non esiste dubbio che l'abbiano fatto.
   There is no doubt that they did it.

■ Esistono ancora alcuni suoi manoscritti.
Some manuscripts of his are still in existence.

■ Esiste ancora qualcuno che si ricordi quella guerra?
Is there anyone still alive who remembers that war?

■ È la più grande bugiarda che sia mai esistita.
She's the biggest liar who ever lived.

esitare   to hesitate; to waver; to falter

■ Lo studente esitò prima di rispondere (/decidersi).
The student hesitated before answering (/making up his mind).

■ Lo facemmo senza esitare.
We did it unhesitatingly (or without a moment's hesitation).

■ Esitavano fra le varie proposte (/soluzioni).
They were wavering among the various proposals (/solutions).

■ Il giovane scalò la rupe senza esitare.
The young man scaled the cliff without faltering.

esitare a + *inf*   to hesitate to + *inf*

■ Quel mio amico non esitò ad aiutarmi (/a rispondere).
That friend of mine did not hesitate to help me (/to answer).

esonerare qc da qco   to exempt sb from sth; to excuse sb from sth; to relieve sb from sth

■ Lo esonerarono dal lavoro (/dal servizio militare/dalle tasse/dagli esami).
They exempted him from work (/military service/payment of taxes/exams).

■ L'hanno esonerata dalle lezioni di educazione fisica.
She was excused from PE (or gym) classes.

■ Il generale è stato esonerato dal comando (/dall'incarico).
The general was relieved of his command (/charge).

esortare qc a qco   to exhort sb to sth

■ Lo avevano sempre esortato allo studio (/al rispetto dei genitori).
They had always exhorted him to study (/respect his parents).

esortare qc a + *inf*   to urge sb to + *inf*

■ Ti esorto a dire la verità (/essere paziente con lei).
I urge you to tell the truth (/to be patient with her).

esporre   to expose; to display; to put (up); to exhibit; to hang sth out; to explain; to state

■ Lo hanno esposto a un grande pericolo.
They exposed him to great danger.

■ L'avviso era esposto alla vista di tutti.
The notice was exposed to public view.

■ La commessa non ha ancora esposto i nuovi capi in vetrina.
The shop assistant hasn't yet displayed the new articles (of clothing) in the window.

- Domani esporranno un avviso.
  Tomorrow they'll put up a notice.

- È un pittore che ha esposto nelle più importanti gallerie d'Europa.
  He's a painter who has exhibited in the most important European galleries.

- Ieri hanno esposto la bandiera perché era giorno di festa nazionale.
  Yesterday they hung out the flag because it was a national holiday.

- Vi ho esposto i fatti.
  I explained the facts to you.

- Il professore ci ha esposto il testo.
  The professor explained the text to us.

- Esporrò la mia opinione (/le mie idee).
  I'll state my opinion (/my ideas).

esporsi   to expose oneself; to compromise oneself

- Non esporti alle correnti d'aria (/al sole/ai rischi/alle critiche)!
  Don't expose yourself to drafts (/the sun/risks/criticism)!

- Si espone troppo coi suoi scritti.
  He compromises himself too much in his writings.

esprimere   to express; to word; to voice

- Ho solo espresso le mie idee (/il mio punto di vista/i miei sentimenti).
  I only expressed my ideas (/my viewpoint/my feelings).

- Desideriamo esprimere le nostre condoglianze (/i nostri ringraziamenti).
  We wish to express our sympathy (/thanks).

- La clausola era espressa nel modo più vago possibile.
  The clause was worded in the vaguest way possible.

- Perché non esprimete la vostra opinione (/il vostro malcontento)?
  Why don't you voice your opinion (/discontent)?

esprimersi   to express oneself

- Quella mia studentessa non riesce a esprimersi in modo chiaro (/in inglese).
  That student of mine cannot express herself clearly (/in English).

1. essere   (auxiliary *essere*) to be; to exist; to happen; to become; to be like

- Penso, dunque sono.
  I think, therefore I am.

- Lei è italiana?
  Are you Italian?

- Chi è? —Siamo noi.
  Who is it? —It's us.

- Che ore sono? —È tardi, è l'una.
  What time is it? —It is late. It is one o'clock.

- Siamo quasi a Milano.
  We are nearly in Milan.

- Francesco non è a casa.
  Francis is not at home.

- E la luce fu.
  And then there was light.

- Quello che sarà, sarà.
  What will be, will be.

- Dio è.
  God exists.

- Quel bambino ha detto che quando sarà grande, farà l'astronauta.
  That little boy said that when he grows up, he'll be an astronaut.

- Sono due ore (/È un'ora) che li aspetto.
  I have been waiting for them for two hours (/an hour).

- Che è stato? —Niente.
  What happened? —Nothing.

- Che sarà di me?
  What will become of me?

- Com'è la ragazza di tuo nipote?
  What's your nephew's girlfriend like?

esserci   there is, are

- Non ci sono uomini perfetti.
  There are no perfect men.

- Non c'è nessuno che sia così ingenuo.
  There is nobody who is so naïve.

- C'era una volta un re.
  Once upon a time there was a king.

essere + *adj* + *inf*/che+ *subj*   to be + *adj* + *inf*/(that) + *subject* + *verb*/for + *noun* + *inf*

- È difficile vederli.
  It is difficult to see them.

- Non è possibile che vengano.
  It is not possible that they'll come (for them to come).

essere a + *inf*   to be, go to + *inf*

- Sono stati a trovarlo.
  They have been (/gone) to see him.

essere da qc   to be worthy of sb

- Quest'azione non è da persona intelligente.
  This action isn't worthy of an intelligent person.

essere da qc   to be at sb's home/at the office of a professional (doctor, dentist, etc.)/at a restaurant

■   Ero da Marco (/dal signor Bosi/dalla signora Dini/dal dottore/dall'avvocato).
I was at Mark's (/Mr. Bosi's/Mrs. Dini's/the doctor's/the lawyer's).

essere da/di qc/qco   to be on sb's side

■   Sei dalla loro parte o sei dei nostri?
Are you on their side or ours (or are you one of ours)?

essere di qco   to be made of; to be of sth

■   Questo anello (/Questa collana) è d'oro (/d'argento).
This ring (/necklace) is made of gold (/silver).

■   Loro sono di famiglia nobile.
They are of a noble family.

■   Sono stati di conforto (/aiuto) ai miei figli.
They have been of comfort (/help) to my children.

■   Siamo d'avviso (/d'opinione) che voi non dobbiate accettarlo.
We are of a mind (/an opinion) that you shouldn't accept it.

essere di qc   to belong to sb

■   Questa casa è dei miei genitori.
This house belongs to my parents.

essere in qco   to be in/at sth

■   La signora Anselmi è in buona (/cattiva) salute.
Mrs. Anselmi is in good (/bad) health.

■   Quella mia amica è in lutto (/nei pasticci/nei guai).
That friend of mine is in mourning (/in a mess/in trouble).

■   Il signor Redaelli è in città (/in viaggio/negli Stati Uniti).
Mr. Redaelli is in town (/traveling/in the United States).

■   Sono in pace (/guerra).
They are at peace (/at war).

■   Se fossi in te (/nei tuoi panni/nei panni di Giovanni), non partirei. *(idiomatic)*
If I were you (/in your shoes/in John's shoes), I wouldn't leave. (idiomatic)

essere per/contro qc/qco   to be for/against sb/sth

■   Quella era una dimostrazione per (/contro) il diritto all'aborto.
That was a demonstration for (/against) the right to abortion.

2. essere   (auxiliary for the passive form and certain classes of verbs)

■   È (Era/È stata/Fu/Sarà/Sarebbe/Sarebbe stata) ammirata da tutti.
She is (/was/has been/was/will be/would be/would have been) admired by everyone.

■ Ieri è piovuto.
Yesterday it rained.

■ Penso (/Pensavo) che siano partiti (/fossero partiti) ieri.
I think (/thought) they left (/had left) yesterday.

■ Ho paura che a loro non sia piaciuto quel regalo.
I am afraid they did not like that present.

■ Ha detto che sarebbe restata a casa.
She said she would stay at home.

■ Mia sorella è molto invecchiata.
My sister has aged a lot.

■ Penso di essere andato in Italia almeno venti volte.
I think I've gone to Italy at least twenty times.

■ Quando siete passati dalla biblioteca?
When did you stop by the library?

■ Si sono sposati l'anno scorso.
They got married last year.

■ La loro bambina è nata (/morta) in ottobre.
Their little girl was born (died) in October.

■ La lezione è cominciata (/finita) alle dodici.
The class started (ended) at twelve.

■ La conferenza è durata un'ora.
The lecture lasted an hour.

■ La mia vita non è cambiata.
My life has not changed.

3. essere   to be, taste like; to cost

■ Come'è la carne? —È molto buona.
What is the meat like? —It is very good.

■ Quanto sono queste mele?
How much are these apples?

estrarre   to draw

■ Hanno estratto il numero 25 (/il tuo nome/il nome del vincitore).
They have drawn number 25 (/your name/the name of the winner).

estrarre qco da qco   to extract sth from sth; to mine; to quarry sth (from sth)

■ Estraggono il sale dall'acqua di mare (/l'olio dalle olive).
They extract salt from seawater (/oil from olives).

■ Devo estrarre la radice quadrata di questo numero.
I have to find (/extract) the square root of this number.

■   Il dentista gli ha estratto la radice di quel dente.
The dentist extracted the root of that tooth.

■   Quel marmo viene estratto a Carrara.
That marble is quarried in Carrara.

■   Da quella miniera non estraggono più il carbone (/i diamanti).
They don't mine coal (/diamonds) from that mine anymore.

evitare   to avoid; to escape; to dodge (around); to steer clear of

■   Cerca di evitare i cibi piccanti (/i pericoli/quel seccatore).
Try to avoid spicy food (/danger/that bore).

■   Il conducente riuscì ad evitare il pedone.
The driver managed to avoid the pedestrian.

■   Evitarono a malapena la morte (/il meritato castigo).
They barely escaped death (/the deserved punishment).

■   Il direttore ha evitato la domanda (/il problema).
The manager dodged the question (/the problem).

■   Dobbiamo evitare quella barca a vela (/camion).
We must steer clear of that sailboat (/truck).

evitare qco a qc   to save sb sth; to spare sb sth

■   Gli ho potuto evitare un viaggio inutile.
I was able to save him a useless trip.

■   Farò il possibile per evitarti questa noia.
I'll do my best to spare you this trouble.

evitare di + *inf*   to avoid + *ger;* to escape + *ger*

■   Dovresti evitare di toccare quell'argomento (/bere).
You should avoid mentioning that topic (/drinking).

■   Tu dovresti evitare di farti vedere con lei.
You should avoid being seen with her.

evitarsi   to avoid each other, one another

■   Dopo l'incidente i due si evitano.
After the accident, the two avoid each other.

F

fabbricare   to build; to make, produce; to fabricate

- Hanno fabbricato un nuovo grattacielo (/nuovi palazzi) in centro.
  They have built a new skyscraper (/new buildings) downtown.

- Quell'industria fabbrica sapone (/mobili).
  That company makes soap (/furniture).

- La merce deve essere fabbricata su campione (/ordinazione).
  The merchandise must be made according to the sample (/to order).

- Hanno fabbricato false accuse (/notizie false).
  They fabricated accusations (/rumors).

   fabbricarsi   to build for oneself

   - Si sono fabbricati una casetta in montagna.
     They built themselves a little house in the mountains.

facilitare   to make (sth) easier; to help

- Queste informazioni faciliteranno l'indagine.
  This information will make the investigation easier.

- La tua esperienza in Africa dovrebbe facilitarti il compito.
  Your experience in Africa should make the task easier for you.

- Il tuo aiuto mi facilitò la soluzione del problema.
  Your support helped me in solving the problem.

fallire (in qco)   (auxiliary *essere;* if the verb has a direct object, auxiliary *avere*) to fail (in sth); to go under; to go bankrupt; to miss

- I piani (/Tutti i tentativi/Gli esperimenti) sono falliti.
  The plans (/All the efforts/The experiments) have failed.

- Le negoziazioni di pace sono fallite di nuovo.
  The peace negotiations have failed again.

- La vecchia ditta è fallita malgrado le sovvenzioni.
  The old company went under despite the subsidies.

- Quel commerciante è fallito.
  That merchant has gone bankrupt.

- Tirò molti colpi senza fallirne uno.
  He fired a number of shots without missing one.

- Hai fallito il bersaglio (/la palla).
  You missed the target (/the ball).

familiarizzare qc con qco   to familiarize sb with sth

- Devi familiarizzare i tuoi figli all'idea del trasferimento in Europa.
  You must familiarize your children with the idea of moving to Europe.

  familiarizzarsi con qc/qco   to familiarize oneself with sb/sth

  - Mio figlio si è subito familiarizzato con gli altri bambini (/col nuovo sistema/coll'inglese).
    My son familiarized himself right away with the other children (/the new system/English).

1. fare   to do, make; to act (as), perform, play the part of

- Che cosa fate stasera?
  What are you doing tonight?

- Cosa posso fare per te?
  What can I do for you?

- Lei ha fatto i piatti, ma non ha ancora fatto i letti.
  She did the dishes, but she has not made the beds yet.

- Questa cura (/La villeggiatura) non gli ha fatto bene.
  This treatment (/The vacation) has not done him any good.

- Dobbiamo fare il nostro dovere (/un piacere al signor Grimaldi).
  We must do our duty (/a favor for Mr. Grimaldi).

- Avevano paura che lo facessero sindaco (/vicepresidente).
  They were afraid they would make him mayor (/vice-president).

- La regina l'ha fatto baronetto.
  The queen made him a knight.

- Perché non gli fai posto?
  Why don't you make room for him?

- La camomilla mi fa da calmante.
  Chamomile acts as a sedative for me.

- Non fare lo stupido.
  Don't act like a fool.

- Hanno fatto l'*Otello*. Quell'attrice faceva la parte di Desdemona.
  They performed Othello. *That actress played the part of Desdemona.*

  fare qc   to make sb feel sth

  - Questo gli farà piacere (/dispiacere/disgusto/impressione/paura).
    This will please (/displease/disgust/impress/frighten) him.

  fare + *adj*   to make sb + *adj*

  - Quello che mi dici mi fa felice.
    What you're telling me makes me happy.

fare + *inf* + **qc/qco**   to make sb/sth + *inf*

- Fa'cantare (/mangiare/dormire/studiare) i bambini.
  Make the children sing (/eat/sleep/study).

fare + *inf* + **qco**   to have sth + *ptp*

- Farò spedire la lettera (/tradurre l'articolo/costruire una piscina).
  I'll have the letter mailed (/the article translated/a swimming pool built).

2. **fare**   to be (*profession*); to be suitable; to be (*math*); to say; to show; to be (*weather*); to be on, be shown

- Quando sarò grande, farò l'astronauta (/il dottore/lo scultore).
  When I grow up, I'll be an astronaut (/a doctor/a sculptor).

- Questa vita (/Questo lavoro) non fa per lei.
  This life (/job) is not suitable for her.

- Sei più sette fa tredici. Quattro per due fa otto. Sedici meno cinque fa undici. Ventisette diviso nove fa tre.
  Six and seven are thirteen. Two times four is eight. Sixteen minus five is eleven. Twenty-seven divided by nine is three.

- Il mio orologio fa le tre e dieci.
  My watch says ten past three.

- Il termometro fa 20 gradi (68°F).
  The thermometer shows 20 degrees C (68°F).

- Che tempo fa?
  What's the weather like?

- Ieri faceva freddo (/caldo/fresco/bello/brutto/bel tempo/brutto tempo).
  Yesterday it was cold (warm/cool/nice/bad/nice weather/bad weather).

- Cosa fanno al cinema (/a teatro/alla televisione) stasera?
  What's on at the movies (/at the theater/on TV) tonight?

3. **fare**   to have; to deliver; to decide

- Quanti abitanti fa questa città?
  How many inhabitants does this city have?

- La loro gatta ha fatto cinque gattini. Posso averne uno, Mamma?
  Their cat has had five kittens. Can I have one, Mom?

- Il presidente ha fatto un bel discorso.
  The president delivered a good speech.

- Quanto dobbiamo dare al cameriere? —Non so, faccia Lei.
  How much should we give the waiter? —I don't know. You decide.

4. fare   to paint; to sculpt, carve; to write; to create; to build

- Ho fatto una natura morta (/un paesaggio/un ritratto).
  I painted a still life (/a landscape/a portrait).

- Ho fatto una statua (/un mosaico).
  I made a statue (/a mosaic).

- Quel giornalista ha fatto un articolo sui pigmei (/un bel libro).
  That journalist wrote an article on Pygmies (/a fine book).

- Dio fece la donna (/il mondo in sette giorni).
  God created woman (/the world in seven days).

- Stanno facendo una nuova autostrada.
  They are building a new highway.

5. fare   to cook, roast, boil, grill, stew, bake

- Piero faceva sempre da mangiare (/pranzo/cena).
  Peter always cooked a meal (/lunch/dinner).

- Mia cugina fa dei piatti prelibati.
  My cousin cooks some delicious dishes.

- Perché non fai questa carne arrosto (/lessa/ai ferri/in umido)?
  Why don't you roast (/boil/grill/stew) this meat?

- La mamma ha fatto una torta di mele.
  Mother baked an apple pie.

6. fare   to walk, drive, go; to climb

- Hanno fatto un chilometro a piedi, dieci chilometri in macchina.
  They walked one kilometer and drove ten.

- Noi facciamo la stessa strada (/le scale).
  We go the same way (/climb the stairs).

7. fare a + *inf*   can, to be able to + *inf*

- Come fai a dire (/fare/promettere) cose di questo genere?
  How can you say (/do/promise) things like this?

8. fare qc + *adj*   to think sb + *adj*

- Lo facevo più intelligente (/ormai morto).
  I thought he was smarter (/dead by now).

9. fare da   to be like, behave like

- Le aveva fatto da padre.
  He had been like a father to her.

10. fare acqua   to leak

- La pentola fa acqua.
  The pot is leaking.

■   Il tuo ragionamento fa acqua. (*idiomatic*)
Your argument is shaky.

11. fare causa a qc   to sue sb

■   Gli faranno causa.
They will sue him.

12. fare colazione   to have breakfast

■   A che ora ha fatto colazione, signora Sordelli?
At what time did you have breakfast, Mrs. Sordelli?

13. fare il pieno (di benzina)   to fill up (with gas)

■   Devo fare il pieno.
I have to fill up (the tank).

farsi   to get (*weather/time*); to buy for oneself

■   Si fa buio (/tardi).
It is getting dark (/late).

■   Si sono già fatti la macchina (/l'appartamento al mare)?
Have they already bought a car (/an apartment at the seaside)?

■   Si è fatto la ragazza. (*idiomatic*)
He has gotten himself a girlfriend.

farsi + *adj*   to grow, become, turn

■   Come ti sei fatto grande! Come si è fatta bella!
How tall you have grown! How beautiful she has become!

■   Si sono fatti più gentili.
They have become more amiable.

■   Si è fatto buddista.
He became a Buddhist.

■   Si fece rossa in viso.
She turned red in the face.

farsi + *inf*   to make oneself + *ptp*

■   Loro si fanno amare (/odiare/capire/ammirare) da tutti.
They make themselves loved (/hated/understood/admired) by everyone.

farsi + *inf* + qco   to have sth + *ptp*

■   La signora Giudici si fa tagliare i capelli dal mio parrucchiere.
Mrs. Giudici has her hair cut by my hairdresser.

farcela   to be able to do it, make it; to manage

■   Sono sicuro che (non) puoi farcela.
I am sure you can (not) do it.

■ Non credo di farcela per le tre.
I don't think I can make it by three.

■ Non ce la faccio più.
I can't go on.

felicitarsi (con qc per qco/di qco)   to congratulate (sb on sth)

■ Ci felicitammo con lui per il matrimonio (/la promozione).
We congratulated him on his marriage (/promotion).

ferire   to hurt; to be a blow to sb

■ Improvvisamente una luce violenta ferì i miei occhi.
Suddenly a violent light hurt my eyes.

■ La tua indifferenza (/ingratitudine) l'ha ferita.
Your indifference (/ingratitude) hurt her.

■ Questo ferirebbe il suo amor proprio (*or* Questo lo ferirebbe nel suo amor proprio).
This would be a blow to his self-respect.

ferire (qc a/in)   to wound

■ La pallottola lo ferì al collo.
The bullet wounded him in the neck.

■ Lo hanno ferito nell'amor proprio.
They wounded his self-esteem.

■ Due soldati furono uccisi e cinque feriti.
Two soldiers were killed and five wounded.

ferirsi (a qco)   to wound, hurt oneself (in/at sth)

■ Il bambino cadde e si ferì gravemente.
The child fell and seriously hurt himself.

■ La ragazza si è ferita alla spalla nell'incidente.
The girl hurt her shoulder in the accident.

fermare   to stop; to stunt; to interrupt; to take into custody; to sew securely; to secure

■ Niente (/Nessuno) lo può fermare.
Nothing (/Nobody) can stop him.

■ Hanno fermato una macchina (/un tassì/un cavallo imbizzarrito/il pagamento di un assegno/il motore/la palla/il traffico).
They stopped a car (/a taxi/a runaway horse/a check/the engine/the ball/traffic).

■ L'autobus 60 ferma qui?
Does bus number 60 stop here?

■ Giovanni voleva andarsene ma io l'ho fermato.
John wanted to leave, but I stopped him.

■ Il dottore non riuscì a fermare l'emorragia (/il sangue).
The doctor could not stop the hemorrhage (/the flow of blood).

■ Quel prodotto ferma la crescita delle erbacce.
That product stunts the growth of weeds.

■ Il lavoro non va fermato per nessuna ragione.
Work must not be interrupted for any reason.

■ Tutti i dimostranti (/gli scioperanti) sono stati fermati.
All the demonstrators (/strikers) were taken into custody.

■ La polizia ha fermato due individui sospetti.
The police have taken two suspicious persons into custody.

■ Se non fermerai quel bottone, lo perderai.
If you do not sew that button securely, you'll lose it.

■ Puoi fermare la porta che continua a sbattere?
Can you secure the door that keeps on banging?

fermarsi (a/in)   to stop oneself (at/in); to stay

■ Fermatevi!
Stop (yourselves)!

■ Il mio orologio (/Il tempo) si è fermato.
My watch (/Time) has stopped.

■ Tua nipote parla senza mai fermarsi.
Your niece speaks without stopping.

■ Ci fermeremo a casa vostra (/pagina dodici).
We'll stop at your house (/page twelve).

■ Mio zio si ferma sempre da noi fino a tardi.
My uncle always stays at our house till late.

fermarsi a + *inf*   to stop to + *inf*

■ Si fermano sempre là a prendere un caffè (/comprare il giornale/parlare).
They always stop there to have coffee (/buy the newspaper/talk).

fidare (in qc/qco)   to trust in; to rely on

■ Fidate in Dio.
Trust in God.

■ Non fidare soltanto nelle tue forze.
Don't rely only on your own resources.

fidarsi di qc/qco   to trust sb; to believe

■ Non ci fidiamo di quella banca.
We don't trust that bank.

■ Il loro amico è una persona di cui non ci si può fidare.
Their friend is an untrustworthy person.

■   Se fossi in te, non mi fiderei delle sue promesse.
   If I were you, I would not believe his promises.

fidarsi a + *inf*   to trust oneself to do sth, feel up to + *ger*

■   Dopo l'incidente non mi fido a guidare da solo.
   After my accident, I don't feel up to driving by myself.

figurare   to symbolize, stand for; to feign, pretend; to appear; to be; to look good, smart; to dress well

■   La colomba figura la pace.
   A dove symbolizes peace.

■   Il cane figura la fedeltà.
   The dog stands for faithfulness.

■   È inutile che figuri di non capire (/non conoscerla).
   There is no point in your pretending not to understand (/not to know her).

■   L'indirizzo di quel dottore (/La mia commissione) non figura nell'elenco (/nel conto).
   The address of that doctor (/My commission) does not appear in the list (/on the bill).

■   Il signor Segni deve figurare come debitore, non come creditore!
   Mr. Segni has to appear as a debtor, not as a creditor!

■   Tra i partecipanti figuravano alcune stelle del cinema.
   There were some movie stars among the participants.

■   Sua moglie si preoccupa solo di figurare bene.
   His wife cares only about looking smart (or dressing well).

figurarsi qc/qco   to imagine, picture, just think

■   Te lo figuravi grasso e brutto?
   Did you imagine him to be fat and ugly?

■   Non me la sarei mai figurata così.
   I would never have imagined her like this.

■   Figurati il mio stato d'animo!
   Imagine my state of mind!

■   Te la figuri la mia faccia?
   Can you picture my face?

■   Figurati!
   Just think!

■   La disturbo? —Si figuri!
   Do I disturb you? —Not in the least.

figurarsi di + *inf*   to imagine

■   Mi figuravo di volare.
    I imagined I was flying.

figurarsi che   just think (that)

■   Si figuri che non ne sapevo proprio nulla (/l'avevo preso per suo marito).
    Just think. I knew absolutely nothing about it (/I had mistaken him for her husband).

fingere   to pretend, feign

■   Carla non sa fingere con suo marito.
    Carla cannot pretend to her husband.

■   Il bambino non dorme ancora: finge soltanto.
    The child isn't asleep; he is only pretending.

■   La ragazza finse uno svenimento (/la pazzia/gioia/amore/ammirazione).
    The girl feigned a fainting spell (/madness/joy/love/admiration).

fingere che   to assume that

■   Fingiamo che le cose stiano così.
    Let's assume that things remain this way.

fingere di + *inf*   to imagine + *ger;* to pretend to + *inf*

■   Fingi per un momento di essere un assassino (/un attore).
    Imagine for a moment being a murderer (/an actor).

■   Il suo ragazzo fingeva di non conoscermi (/essere ubriaco).
    Her boyfriend pretended not to know me (/to be drunk).

fingersi   to pretend to be

■   Si finse un ricco industriale (/cieco/morto/malato).
    He pretended to be a rich industrialist (/blind/dead/sick).

finire   (auxiliary *avere* when the subject is a person/animal or devices operated by people; otherwise *essere*) to end, finish, be done with; to stop; to spend (*money*); to lead to; to finish off, kill

■   So già come finisce il film (/il libro/la commedia).
    I already know how the movie (/the book/the play) ends.

■   La conferenza (/La seconda guerra mondiale) è finita alle tre (/nel 1945).
    The lecture (/The Second World War) ended at three (/in 1945).

■   Il professor Augusti ha appena finito il suo primo libro (/il suo lavoro).
    Professor Augusti has just finished his first book (/his work).

■   Hai finito?
    Are you done?

■ Finalmente il temporale finì.
At long last the storm stopped.

■ Hai finito tutti i soldi in due giorni?
Did you spend all the money in two days?

■ La birra (/La Coca-Cola) è finita.
The beer (/Coke) is all gone (or There is no beer [/Coke] left).

■ Lo finirono con un colpo alla testa.
They killed him with a blow to the head.

finire col/coll'/con lo *or* **per** + *inf*   to finish, end up + *ger*

■ Finii col comperare tutti i libri (/coll'accettare la loro proposta).
I ended up buying all the books (/accepting their proposal).

■ Finirai col pagare tutti i conti di tuo figlio (/coll'ammalarti).
You'll end up paying all your son's bills (/falling ill).

finire di + *inf*   to finish, be done with + *ger,* be over

■ Avete finito di mangiare (/lamentarvi/guardare la tv/lavare la macchina)?
Have you finished eating (/complaining/watching TV/washing the car)?

■ Ha finito di soffrire. (*fig*)
His sufferings are over.

finirla (di) + **inf.**   to stop it; to stop doing sth

■ È ora di finirla! È ora di finirla con queste chiacchiere.
It's time to stop it! It's time to stop this idle talk!

■ Finiscila!
Stop it! (or Cut it out!)

■ Non la finivano più di parlare.
They wouldn't stop talking.

■ Quando la finirai di gridare così?
When will you stop yelling like that?

finire in   to end (up) in; to lead to

■ Questa strada finisce nella piazza del paese.
This street leads to the village square.

■ Dove è finito il mio portafoglio?
Where has my wallet ended up (or What happened to my wallet)?

finire in qco   to turn into sth; to end (up) in sth

■ Un'impresa di questo genere può finire in un disastro.
An undertaking of this kind can turn into disaster.

■ Tutti i miei progetti sono finiti in fumo.
All my plans ended (up) in smoke.

■   Suo fratello è finito in un brutto posto (/in carcere/in un fossato).
     His brother ended up in a bad spot (/prison/a ditch).

andare a finire (con)   to end, lead; to mean (by)

■   Non so dove vada a finire questo sentiero.
     I do not know where this path ends (or leads to).

■   Non so dove Lei voglia andare a finire con questo discorso.
     I don't know what you mean by these words.

firmare   to sign

■   Ho appena firmato il contratto (/l'assegno/la petizione/il cartellino).
     I have just signed the contract (/the check/the petition/my timecard).

■   Il vecchio firmò facendo una croce.
     The old man signed with an X.

■   Non si resero conto di firmare la loro condanna.
     They did not realize they were sealing their own fate.

fissare qco (a/in/su)   to fasten, to fix sth (to/in/on); to book; to reserve; to gaze, stare

■   Dobbiamo fissare quella persiana (/la finestra/la porta).
     We have to fix that shutter (/the window/the door).

■   Hanno fissato due specchi (/un gancio) alla parete.
     They affixed two mirrors (/a hook) to the wall.

■   Va fissato con chiodi o con viti?
     Is it to be nailed or screwed?

■   Lui fissò lo sguardo sui gioielli (/sulla ragazza).
     He fixed his eyes on the jewels (/girl).

■   Ho fissato una camera a due letti in quell'albergo (/una macchina per domani/tre
     posti a teatro).
     I booked a double room in that hotel (/a car for tomorrow/three seats at the theater).

fissare qco   to establish, fix

■   Non hanno ancora fissato la data del loro matrimonio (/il prezzo della
     macchina/il giorno della riunione/le condizioni del contratto).
     *They have not yet fixed the date of their wedding (/the price of the car/the
     day of the meeting/the terms of the contract).*

fissare di + *inf*   to agree to + *inf*

■   Fissarono di partire il giorno dopo (/andare alla partita).
     They agreed to leave the next day (/to go to the soccer game).

fissarsi   to fix; to settle

■   I suoi occhi si fissarono sulla porta aperta (/su di lei).
     He fixed his eyes on the open door (/her).

■   Decisero di fissarsi in quel paesino (/a Roma).
They decided to settle in that little village (/in Rome).

fissarsi di + *inf*   to get it into one's head

■   Si è fissato di essere perseguitato.
He has got it into his head that he is being persecuted.

fondare   to found; to establish; to start

■   Fondarono una città modello.
They founded a model city.

■   La chiesa (/La colonia/La biblioteca) fu fondata cinquant'anni fa.
The church (/colony/library) was founded fifty years ago.

■   Il loro padre voleva fondare un giornale (/una rivista).
Their father wanted to start a newspaper (/a magazine).

fondare su qco   to base on sth

■   L'accusa (/La difesa) è fondata su dati sicuri (/prove inconfutabili).
The accusation (/defense) is based on facts (/irrefutable arguments).

fondarsi su qc/qco   to rely on sb/sth

■   Non dovete fondarvi su vaghe promesse (/sul suo aiuto)!
You should not rely on vague promises (/his help)!

fondere   to melt; to cast; to merge

■   Il ghiaccio fonde a 0 gradi centigradi.
Ice melts at 0 degrees centigrade (32 degrees F).

■   Hanno fuso un'enorme statua di bronzo (/una campana).
They cast a huge bronze statue (/a bell).

fondersi   to melt; to blend; to blow; to unite

■   Il ghiaccio (/La cera) si fondeva durante il giorno (/al calore).
The ice (/Wax) melted during the day (/in the heat).

■   La ragazza si fondeva in lacrime. (*fig*)
The girl dissolved into tears. (fig)

■   L'azzurro del cielo si fondeva col verde del mare.
The blue of the sky blended with the green of the sea.

■   I suoni si fondevano.
The sounds blended.

■   Le società si sono fuse.
The companies merged.

■   I partiti si fonderanno.
The parties will unite.

■   Si è fusa una valvola.
      A fuse has blown.

formare   to form

■   Come si forma il plurale dei nomi in italiano?
     How is the plural of nouns formed in Italian?

■   Sulle strade si era già formata una lamina di ghiaccio.
     A sheet of ice had already formed on the roads.

■   Si deve formare un nuovo governo (/comitato/partito).
     A new government (/committee/party) must be formed.

■   Che numero si deve formare per avere l'ora esatta?
     Which number must one dial to get the time (of day)?

formarsi   to form; to be trained; to develop

■   Non mi sono ancora formata un'opinione chiara sull'argomento.
      I have not yet formed a clear opinion on the subject.

■   Gli si è formato un bernoccolo sulla fronte.
      A bump formed on his forehead.

■   Si è formato alla scuola dei Gesuiti (/alla scuola del dolore).
      He was trained at the Jesuit school (/in the school of grief).

■   Mio nipote si sta ancora formando.
      My nephew is still developing.

■   Il suo corpo non si è ancora formato completamente.
      His body is not yet fully developed.

fornire   to furnish; to provide

■   Non credo che possano fornirne la prova.
     I don't think they can furnish proof of it.

■   L'accusato non ha potuto fornire un alibi.
     The defendant could not provide an alibi.

■   Dovrebbero fornire ulteriori chiarimenti (/i dati necessari).
     They should supply a further explanation (/the necessary data).

fornire qco a qc *or* qc/qco di qco   to supply sb with sth; to provide sb/sth with sth

■   Gli hanno fornito vino (/pane/generi di prima necessità/combustibile).
      They supplied him with wine (/bread/basic commodities/fuel).

■   La natura ha fornito di artigli quegli uccelli.
      Nature provided those birds with claws.

fornire qco di qco   to equip sth with sth

■ Questo stabilimento va fornito di nuovi macchinari (/nuovi impianti tecnici/ferro).
This factory must be equipped with new machinery (/new technical installations/iron).

fornirsi   to provide oneself with; to buy from

■ Prima di partire i ragazzi si fornirono di tutto il necessario.
Before leaving, the boys provided themselves with everything necessary.

■ Non credo che si forniscano più da quella ditta.
I don't believe they buy from that company anymore.

forzare   to force; to break sth open; to quicken; to twist, distort

■ Ho dovuto forzare il coperchio della scatola.
I had to force the lid on the box.

■ Non gli forzare la mano!
Don't force his hand!

■ Dovranno forzare la serratura (/la porta).
They will have to break the lock (/the door) open.

■ I soldati forzarono il passo (/la marcia).
The soldiers quickened their step (/pace).

■ Lei ha forzato il significato delle mie parole.
You twisted the meaning of my words.

forzare qc a + *inf*   to force, compel sb to + *inf*

■ Lo forzarono a firmare il contratto (/mangiare/fare quello che non voleva/accettare/confessare).
They forced him to sign the contract (/eat/do what he didn't want to do/accept/confess).

fuggire   (auxiliary *essere;* if the verb is followed by a direct object, auxiliary *avere*)   to run away; to elope; to escape; to flee

■ Il ragazzo lanciò un sasso contro la loro finestra e fuggì.
The boy threw a stone at their window and ran away.

■ La loro figlia è fuggita di casa.
Their daughter ran away from home.

■ La figlia del sindaco fuggì col suo ragazzo, un ladro.
The mayor's daughter eloped with her boyfriend, a thief.

■ Quel prigioniero ha già cercato di fuggire dal carcere.
That prisoner has already tried to escape from jail.

■ Quell'industriale è fuggito in Svizzera per non pagare le tasse.
That industrialist fled to Switzerland in order not to pay taxes.

■ Devi fuggire le tentazioni (/il pericolo).
You must avoid temptations (/danger).

fulminare   to strike down (by lightning); to strike dead; to electrocute; to shatter

■ Due ragazzi sono stati fulminati durante il temporale.
Two boys were struck by lightning in the storm.

■ Il mio avvocato è stato fulminato da un infarto.
My attorney was struck down by a heart attack.

■ Il gangster lo fulminò a rivoltellate.
The gangster shot him dead with a revolver.

■ Il nostro insegnante ci fulminò con lo sguardo. (*fig*)
Our teacher crushed us with a glare. (fig)

■ Fu fulminato dalla corrente.
He was electrocuted.

■ La notizia ci ha fulminati.
We were shattered by the news.

fumare   to smoke

■ Quel mio professore fuma come un turco. (*idiomatic*)
That professor of mine smokes like a chimney. (idiomatic)

■ Dovresti smettere di fumare.
You should quit smoking.

■ Tuo nonno fumava la pipa?
Did your grandfather smoke a pipe?

fungere da   to act as

■ Fungevo da giudice nelle loro discussioni.
I used to act as a judge in their arguments.

■ Funge da segretario.
He acts as secretary.

funzionare   to work; to run; to be on; to go, work; to function

■ Questo telefono funziona?
Does this telephone work?

■ I freni della tua macchina funzionano male.
The brakes in your car work badly.

■ Il motore della mia macchina non funziona più.
My engine doesn't run anymore.

■ Il riscaldamento funziona dalle sette alle ventidue.
The heat is on from seven A.M. to ten P.M.

■ La loro ditta funziona bene.
Their business is going well.

■ I reni non le funzionano bene.
Her kidneys don't function well.

far funzionare qco   to make sth work

■ Non sono riusciti a farlo funzionare.
They could not make it work.

G

garantire   to guarantee, warrant

■   Hanno garantito il rimborso dei soldi.
They guaranteed the refund of the money.

■   Questo zaino è garantito per cinque anni.
This backpack is guaranteed for five years.

> **garantire qc (che)**   to assure sb (that)
>
> ■   Posso garantirti che le cose stanno così.
> *I can assure you that things are this way.*
>
> ■   Ve lo garantiamo!
> *We assure you!*

gareggiare con qc (per qco)   to compete with sb, vie with sb (for sth)

■   Nessuno può gareggiare con lui.
Nobody can compete with him.

■   Gareggiarono con lui per il primo posto.
They vied (or competed) with him for first place.

■   Atleti provenienti da molti paesi gareggiavano per il titolo.
Athletes from many countries were vying for the title.

gelare (qco) (auxiliary *essere;* if the verb has a direct object, auxiliary *avere;* when referring to weather, auxiliary *essere* or *avere*)   to freeze sth (over); to kill (plants)

■   Due giorni fa è (ha) gelato.
Two days ago it froze.

■   L'inverno scorso tutte le condutture gelarono.
Last winter all the pipes froze.

■   Io gelo.
I am freezing.

■   Il freddo ha gelato le mie piante (/le gemme).
The cold has killed all my plants (/the buds).

gettare   to spout, gush; to cast; to flow; to let out; to bud, sprout, shoot; to yield

■   La ferita gettò sangue.
Blood gushed from the wound.

■   Gettammo le reti (/l'ancora/l'amo/i dadi).
We cast the nets (/anchor/the line/the dice).

■ La fontana nella piazza del paese non gettava più.
The fountain in the village square had stopped flowing.

■ La ragazza gettò un urlo.
The girl let out a shout.

■ In marzo le piante cominciano a gettare.
In March the plants start budding.

■ Le tasse gettano molti miliardi allo stato.
Taxes yield billions to the state.

gettare qco a qc   to throw, toss sb sth/sth to sb

■ Ho gettato le chiavi al vicino di casa (/il giornale a te/un bacio alla mamma).
I threw the keys to the neighbor (/the newspaper to you/a kiss to Mom).

■ Gli gettarono un pacchetto di sigarette.
They tossed him a pack of cigarettes.

gettare qco contro qc   to throw sth at sb

■ I ragazzi cominciarono a gettare pietre contro i poliziotti.
The kids started throwing stones at the policemen.

gettare qc/qco (da qco/in qco)   to throw sb/sth (from *or* out of sth/into sth)

■ Lo gettarono nell'acqua (/nel fiume/nel lago).
They threw him (/it) into the water (/river/lake).

■ Credono che il marito l'abbia gettata dalla finestra.
They believe her husband threw her out of the window.

■ Non gettare i soldi dalla finestra. (*fig*)
Don't throw money down the drain. (fig)

gettare qco su qc/qco   to throw (cast) sth on sb/sth

■ Perché getti la colpa su di lui?
Why do you throw (or cast) the blame on him?

■ Gettarono luce sul fatto (/uno sguardo sulla merce).
They threw light on the event (/a glance at the merchandise).

■ Questo fatto ha gettato un'ombra sulla sua reputazione. (*fig*)
This fact cast a shadow on his reputation. (fig)

gettare via qco   to throw sth away

■ Non gettare via queste cose (/la tua ultima occasione).
Don't throw these things (/your last chance) away.

gettarsi (da qco/in qco)   to throw oneself (from sth/into sth)

- I ragazzi si gettarono dal tetto.
  The boys threw themselves from the roof.

- La ragazza si gettò in piscina.
  The girl threw herself into the pool.

- Alla loro figlia non piace gettarsi dal trampolino.
  Their daughter does not like to dive from the diving board.

gettarsi a qco   to throw oneself

- Il pellegrino si gettò a terra.
  The pilgrim threw himself on the ground.

- I prigionieri si gettarono contro le sbarre.
  The prisoners threw themselves against the bars.

gettarsi in qco   to flow into sth

- Dove si getta questo ruscello?
  Where does this stream flow?

gettarsi sotto qco/su qco   to throw oneself under sth/(down) on sth

- La ragazza si è gettata sotto il treno.
  The girl threw herself under the train.

- I bambini si gettarono sull'erba (/sul letto).
  The children threw themselves down on the grass (/bed).

giocare   to play; to deceive; to stake, bet

- Giocano in casa perché piove fuori.
  They're playing in the house because it's raining outside.

- Domenica il Milan gioca contro la Juventus.
  Sunday Milan plays Juventus (soccer teams).

- Tocca a me giocare.
  It's my turn to play.

- Gli hanno giocato un brutto tiro. (*idiomatic*)
  They played a bad trick on him.

- Il loro cugino gioca nella Fiorentina (/ala destra/in Nazionale).
  Their cousin plays soccer on the Fiorentina team (/right wing/on the national team).

- Lo hanno giocato.
  They deceived him.

- Quanto hai giocato?
  How much did you bet?

giocare qco/a qco   to bet on sth

■   Tutte le settimane gioca un ambo (/lo stesso numero/alle corse).
Every week he bets on a double (/the same number/the horses).

giocare a qco   to play sth

■   Staranno giocando a carte (/scacchi/dama/tennis/pallacanestro).
They are probably playing cards (/chess/checkers/tennis/basketball).

■   A che gioco giochiamo? (*idiomatic*)
What's your game? (or What do you think you're doing?)

giocare con qco   to play with sth

■   Tuo nonno giocava sempre con la catena dell'orologio.
Your grandfather used to play with his watch chain all the time.

giocare per qco   to play for sth

■   Noi non giochiamo per interesse, giochiamo per divertimento.
We do not play for money; we play for fun.

giocare su qco   to exploit sth

■   Tu giochi sulla loro ingenuità (/buona fede).
You exploit their naïveté (/good faith).

giocare (in borsa)   to play the market; to speculate

■   Suo padre cominciò a giocare in borsa quando era molto giovane.
Her father started to play the market when he was very young.

■   Giocano al ribasso (/rialzo).
They are speculating on a fall (/rise).

giocarsi   to bet; to lose; to risk

■   Si è giocato tutto quello che aveva (/la camicia).
He bet everything he had (/his shirt).

■   Perchè non ci giochiamo una bottiglia (/diecimila lire)?
Why don't we bet a bottle (/ten thousand lire)?

■   Si è giocato l'impiego (/l'eredità/una fortuna/la reputazione).
He lost his job (/his inheritance/a fortune/his reputation).

■   Potresti giocarti la vita (/l'avvenire)!
You could risk your life (/your future)!

girare   to turn (over); to spin; to change; to tour; to avoid, get around; to endorse; to feel like

■   Lei deve girare a destra e poi a sinistra.
You have to turn (to the) right and then (to the) left.

■   Prova a girare il rubinetto (/la maniglia/la ruota/la chiave nella toppa).
Try turning the faucet (/handle/wheel/key in the lock).

■ La donna girò il capo.
The woman turned her head.

■ Gira la pagina.
Turn the page.

■ La trottola (/Il mio frullatore) non gira.
The top (/My blender) does not spin.

■ Mi girava la testa.
My head was spinning (or I was dizzy).

■ Non girare il discorso!
Don't change the subject!

■ Hanno girato il mondo (/tutta l'Italia/tutti i musei di Firenze).
They toured the world (/the whole of Italy/all the museums in Florence).

■ Dovete imparare a girare le difficoltà.
You must learn to avoid (or get around) difficulties.

■ Signor Angelini, si è ricordato di girare l'assegno?
Mr. Angelini, did you remember to endorse the check?

■ Se mi gira, parto oggi pomeriggio.
If I feel like it, I'll leave this afternoon.

girare intorno/per/su   to go (drive/ride/turn/revolve) around; to wander (about)

■ Un muro gira intorno alla loro proprietà.
A wall goes around their property.

■ Girano cattive notizie su di lui.
Nasty rumors are going around about him.

■ Gli piace girare per le vie della città.
He likes to wander the streets of the city.

girare un film/una scena   to shoot a movie/a scene

■ Stanno girando un film vicino a casa mia.
They are shooting a movie near my house.

girare a vuoto/in folle   to idle

■ Il motore gira a vuoto.
The motor is idling.

far girare qco   make sth turn (spin)

■ Non riesco a far girare la ruota.
I can't make the wheel turn.

■ Il vino mi fa girare la testa.
Wine makes my head spin (or makes me dizzy).

■ Il denaro (/Il successo/Elena) gli ha fatto girare la testa. (*fig*)
Money (/Success/Helen) made his head turn. (fig)

girarsi   to turn (oneself), turn around; to toss

- Quando mi girai per salutarla, la signora Guarini non c'era più.
  When I turned to greet her, Mrs. Guarini was not there anymore.

- Non sapevo da che parte girarmi. (*fig*)
  I did not know which way to turn. (fig)

- Girati.
  Turn around.

- La mamma si girava e rigirava senza poter dormire.
  Mom was tossing and turning, unable to sleep.

giudicare   to consider; to decide, deem

- Tutti lo giudicavano una persona onesta (/normale).
  Everyone considered him an honest person (/normal).

- Giudica tu se questo è possibile.
  You decide if this is possible.

- Giudicarono pericoloso procedere nel buio.
  They deemed it unsafe to proceed in the dark.

giudicare qc (da qco)   to judge sb (by sth)

- Non giudicatela troppo severamente!
  Don't judge her too severely!

- Non si dovrebbe mai giudicare dalle apparenze.
  One should never judge by appearances.

- A giudicare dalle sue parole sembrerebbe sincera.
  Judging by what she says, one would think she is sincere.

giudicare bene (male) qc   to think well (ill) of sb

- Lo giudicano molto bene (/male).
  They think very well (/badly, ill) of him.

giudicare (una causa)   to try (a case)

- Giudicheranno la causa il mese prossimo.
  They will try the case next month.

giudicare qc colpevole/innocente   to find sb guilty/not guilty

- L'imputato fu giudicato colpevole.
  The defendant was found guilty.

giungere (a)   (auxiliary *essere*)   to arrive; to reach

- Il ministro giungerà all'aeroporto di Fiumicino alle nove e trenta.
  The minister will arrive at Fiumicino airport at nine-thirty.

- I componenti della spedizione sono giunti sani e salvi.
  The members of the expedition arrived safe and sound.

■ La musica non giungeva alle loro orecchie.
The music did not reach their ears.

■ Siamo finalmente giunti in porto! (*fig*)
We have finally reached our goal!

■ Come possono essere giunti a una conclusione di questo genere?
How can they have reached a conclusion of this kind?

giungere a + *inf*   to succeed in + *ger;* to go so far as + *inf*

■ Sua moglie non giunse mai a farglielo capire.
His wife never succeeded in making him understand.

■ Suo marito giunse a minacciarmi.
Her husband went so far as to threaten me.

giurare   to swear

■ Ho giurato la verità.
I swore to (tell) the truth.

■ Credo che il testimone abbia giurato il falso.
I believe the witness committed perjury.

■ È inutile che tu giuri e spergiuri: non ti credo.
It's useless for you to swear till you're black and blue; I don't believe you.

■ Giureresti che è vero?
Would you swear to it?

giurare di + *inf*   to swear (+ *inf/subject* + *vb*)

■ Potrei giurare di averlo visto.
I could swear I saw him.

■ Ha giurato di dire quello che ha fatto ieri sera.
He swore to tell what he did last night.

■ L'imputato giurò di essere innocente.
The defendant swore he was innocent.

giurare di + *inf*   to swear off + *ger*

■ Quel mio amico ha giurato di smettere di fumare (/bere).
That friend of mine swore off smoking (/drinking).

giurare qco a qc   to vow sth to sb

■ Romeo le giurò amore eterno (/fedeltà).
Romeo vowed to her (his) eternal love (/fidelity).

giurare su qc/qco   to swear by sb/on sth

■ L'uomo giurò sulla croce (/sulla Bibbia/sulla tomba del padre.)
The man swore on the cross (/the Bible/his father's grave).

godere   to enjoy; to have

■ Bisogna godere la vita quando si è giovani.
One must enjoy life when one is young.

■ Nonostante la sua età, il loro padre godeva un'ottima salute.
Despite his age, their father enjoyed excellent health.

■ L'albergo (/La città) gode di una magnifica vista sul lago.
The hotel (/city) has a marvelous view of the lake.

godere a + *inf*   to enjoy + *ger*

■ Tu sembri godere a dirgli cose spiacevoli.
You seem to enjoy telling him unpleasant things.

■ Quella ragazza gode a starsene a letto.
That girl enjoys staying in bed.

godere di qco   to enjoy sth; to take pleasure in sth

■ Godevano della completa fiducia del padrone.
They enjoyed their master's complete trust.

■ Il loro erede gode di quel privilegio (/quel diritto/quella rendita) da molti anni.
Their heir has been enjoying that privilege (/right/income) for many years.

■ Tu godi delle disgrazie degli altri (/dei successi di tuo figlio).
You take pleasure in other people's misfortunes (/your son's achievements).

godersi qco   to enjoy sth

■ I bambini si sono veramente goduti lo spettacolo dei burattini.
The children really enjoyed the puppet show.

■ Adesso voglio godermi la famiglia (/gli amici/i miei nipotini).
Now I want to enjoy my family (/my friends/my grandchildren).

gridare   to shout; to cry, call for; to yell

■ Non gridare, non sono sordo!
Don't shout; I'm not deaf!

■ Si misero a gridare per richiamare l'attenzione dei passanti.
They started shouting to attract the attention of the passersby.

■ I bambini gridavano a gran voce (/a squarciagola/a più non posso).
The children were shouting aloud (/at the top of their voices/as loud as they could).

■ Gridai: "Evviva!" (/"Al fuoco!"/"Abbasso i dittatori!"/"Al ladro!"/"Aiuto!")
I shouted "Hurrah!" (/"Fire!"/"Down with the dictators!"/"Stop, thief!"/ "Help!")

■ Il ragazzo gridava aiuto.
The boy was crying (calling) for help.

■ Gli scioperanti gridarono le loro proteste.
The strikers screamed their protests.

■ Questo è un delitto che grida vendetta.
This is a crime that cries out for vengeance.

■ Sfogò la sua rabbia gridando.
He yelled out (in) his rage.

■ Ugo gridò il mio nome.
Hugh yelled my name.

gridare da qco/di qco   to scream with/in sth

■ La bambina gridava dal dolore (/di paura).
The little girl was screaming with pain (/in fear).

guadagnare   to earn, make money; to gain; to make a profit; to win; to reach

■ Guadagnavo soltanto duecentomila lire al mese.
I used to earn only two hundred thousand lire a month.

■ Tu pensi solo a guadagnare?
Are you interested only in making money?

■ Suo marito guadagna molto (/bene/male).
Her husband makes a lot of money (/a lot/very little).

■ Il ciclista cileno guadagnava terreno sugli altri.
The Chilean cyclist was gaining on the others.

■ L'apparecchio (/Il nemico) guadagnò quota (/terreno).
The airplane (/The enemy) gained altitude (/ground).

■ Cerchiamo di guadagnare tempo.
Let's try to gain time.

■ Non c'è niente da guadagnare.
There's nothing to be gained.

■ In quell'affare (/quella vendita) hanno guadagnato una notevole somma.
In that business transaction (/On that sale), they made a remarkable profit.

■ Il signor Castaldi ha guadagnato due milioni alla roulette.
Mr. Castaldi won two million playing roulette.

■ Finalmente guadagnarono la cima del monte.
Finally they reached the top of the mountain.

guadagnarci   to look better; to get out of sth

■ Con la barba Pietro ci guadagna.
Peter looks better with a beard.

■ Visto di giorno questo posto ci guadagna.
By day this place looks better.

■ Che cosa ci guadagno in questo affare?
What do I get out of this deal?

guadagnarsi   to earn; to win

■   La zia di Lucia si guadagnava la vita dando lezioni di piano.
Lucy's aunt used to earn a living by giving piano lessons.

■   Quello sciatore si guadagnò la medaglia d'oro alle Olimpiadi.
That skier earned a gold medal at the Olympics.

■   Andrea si guadagnò la confidenza (/la stima/l'amicizia) di tutti.
Andrew won everyone's confidence (/esteem/friendship).

1. guardare   to look (at/down/back/forward/out/up/over/after); to face; to watch; to peep; to stare; to guard

■   Guarda cosa mi va a capitare!
Look what's happening to me!

■   Ci guardano increduli.
They look at us in disbelief.

■   Lo guardò in faccia.
He looked at him straight in the face.

■   Perché mi guardi come se mi vedessi per la prima volta?
Why are you looking at me as if you were seeing me for the first time?

■   Le piaceva fermarsi a guardare le vetrine.
She liked to stop and look at the shop windows.

■   Non guardare indietro, guarda avanti.
Don't look back; look forward.

■   Non so perché lei guardi tutti dall'alto in basso.
I don't know why she looks down on everybody.

■   Guardavo dalla finestra quando l'ho visto.
I was looking out of the window when I saw him.

■   Hai guardato il compito di tuo figlio?
Did you look over your son's homework?

■   Tutti lo guardavano come un esempio da imitare.
Everyone looked up to him as an example to be followed.

■   Tutti gli anni passavano l'estate guardando le pecore.
Every year they would spend the summer looking after sheep.

■   La finestra guardava sul lago (/sul giardino/sulla strada).
The window looked out onto the lake (/garden/street).

■   La mia camera da letto è sempre fredda (/calda) perché guarda a nord (/sud).
My bedroom is always cold (/warm) because it faces north (/south).

■   Quei bambini non fanno altro che guardare la tv tutto il giorno.
Those children do nothing but watch TV all day long.

■   Lo vidi guardare dal buco della serratura.
I saw him peeping through the keyhole.

- Lui la guardava fisso.
  He was staring at her.

- Guardavano a bocca aperta tutto quel denaro.
  They were staring openmouthed at all that money.

- Non l'ho vista bene. L'ho guardata di sfuggita.
  I didn't see her well. I just glanced at her.

- Le sentinelle guardavano il ponte.
  The sentries were guarding the bridge.

guardare se   to look and see, go and see, check

- Guarda se il conto è giusto.
  Look and see if the bill is right.

- Hai già guardato se il pane è cotto?
  Have you already checked whether the bread is baked?

guardarsi   to look at oneself, look at each other/one another; to look around; to protect oneself

- Guardati, sei tutto sporco!
  Look at yourself! You're all dirty!

- Maria passa delle ore a guardarsi allo specchio.
  Maria spends hours looking at herself in the mirror.

- Guardati intorno.
  Look around you.

- Ci guardiamo negli occhi quando parliamo.
  We look into each other's eyes when we talk.

- I soldati avrebbero dovuto guardarsi alle spalle.
  The soldiers should have protected their rear.

2. guardare   to mind; to care; to favor; to be interested; to consider

- Guarda ai fatti tuoi.
  Mind your own business.

- Antonio non guarda in faccia nessuno quando si tratta del suo interesse.
  Anthony doesn't care about anybody when his interests are at stake.

- Guardavano di buon occhio la sua amicizia con una persona così importante.
  They favored her friendship with such an important person.

- Per favore, non guardiamo tanto per il sottile! *(idiomatic)*
  Please, let's not split hairs! (idiomatic)

- Vostro zio guarda solo al denaro.
  Your uncle is interested only in money.

- Cercate di guardare le cose dal nostro punto di vista.
  Try to consider things from our viewpoint.

guardare di + *inf*   to take care, be sure to + *inf*

- Guarda di convincerla a venire (/non sporcarti/non farlo più).
  Take care to convince her to come (/not to get dirty/not to do it anymore).

- Guarda di farti rispettare (/farti amare da tutti).
  Be sure to make yourself respected (/well liked by all).

guardarsi da + *inf*   to abstain from + *ger*

- Faresti meglio a guardarti dal bere (/fumare).
  You'd better abstain from drinking (/smoking).

guardarsi da qc/qco   to beware of sb/sth

- Guardati da tipi come lui.
  Beware of people like him.

guardarsi bene dal/dallo/dalli + *inf*   to take good care not to + *inf*

- Naturalmente ti sei ben guardato dal farlo (/dallo scriverle/dal comprarlo).
  Of course you took good care not to do it (/write to her/buy it).

guarire (da qco)   (auxiliary *essere*) to recover (from sth); to heal; to get rid of

- Il bambino è guarito in pochi giorni.
  The child recovered in a few days.

- La ferita non è ancora guarita.
  The wound hasn't healed yet.

- Devi guarire da quella cattiva abitudine. (*fig*)
  You must get rid of that bad habit.

guarire qc da/di qco   (auxiliary *avere*) to cure sb of sth

- Il dottore l'ha guarita dalla scarlattina.
  The doctor cured her of scarlet fever.

- Ti guarirò del vizio del fumo.
  I'll cure you of the smoking habit.

guidare   to lead; to guide; to manage; to drive

- Il comandante guidò i soldati all'assalto.
  The commander led the soldiers in the attack.

- L'ho visto che guidava a Firenze un gruppo di turisti.
  I saw him leading a group of tourists in Florence.

- La madre guidava i primi passi del bambino.
  The mother guided the first steps of her child.

- Il figlio guida l'azienda di famiglia da più di quindici anni.
  The son has been managing the family business for more than fifteen years.

- Il primo ministro guida gli affari di stato.
  The prime minister manages the affairs of state.

■   Carlo guidava una macchina sportiva (/un trattore/un autobus).
Charles was driving a sports car (/a tractor/a bus).

■   Tu non sai guidare?
Can't you drive?

gustare   to taste; to enjoy; to like

■   Questo raffreddore mi impedisce di gustare qualsiasi cosa.
This cold prevents me from tasting anything.

■   Per gustare meglio i cibi è necessario assaporarli lentamente.
(In order) to taste food better, it is necessary to savor it slowly.

■   Hanno sempre gustato i piaceri della vita.
They have always enjoyed life's pleasures.

I

identificare   to identify

- Non hanno ancora potuto identificare l'assassino (/il colpevole/le impronte digitali).
  They haven't been able yet to identify the murderer (/culprit/fingerprints).

   identificarsi con qc   to identify (oneself) with sb

   - La figlia si identifica con la madre.
     The daughter identifies with her mother.

ignorare   to not know, ignore, overlook

- Quello studente ignora le cose più semplici.
  That student does not know the simplest things.

- Non si possono ignorare le voci dei cittadini.
  The voices of the citizens cannot be ignored (overlooked).

illudere   to delude, deceive

- Mi hai deluso.
  You deluded me.

   illudersi   to delude, deceive oneself

   - Non illuderti; non hai vinto.
     Don't deceive yourself; you didn't win.

   illudersi di + *inf*   to fool oneself (into thinking that)

   - Il signor Zanoli si illudeva di essere promosso.
     Mr. Zanoli fooled himself that he was intelligent.

   illudersi che   to fool oneself, deceive oneself (into thinking that)

   - Ci eravamo illusi che tua sorella fosse cambiata.
     We fooled ourselves into thinking your sister had changed.

   - Noi ci illudevamo che lui fosse sano e salvo.
     We deceived ourselves into thinking he was safe and sound.

illuminare   to illuminate; to light (up)

- Il palazzo (/La scena) era illuminato (/illuminata) da riflettori.
  The building (/scene) was lit by floodlights.

- Le vie, scarsamente illuminate, erano pericolose di notte.
  The badly lit streets were dangerous at night.

illuminarsi   to lighten; to be lit up

- Il volto del ragazzo si illuminò di ottimismo.
  The boy's face lit up with optimism.

- Improvvisamente il cielo (/la stanza) si illuminò.
  Suddenly the sky (/room) lit up.

imbarazzare   to embarrass, puzzle, bewilder; to hamper

- Le loro domande lo imbarazzarono.
  Their questions embarrassed (or puzzled) him.

- Il vestito le imbarazzava i movimenti.
  The dress hampered her movements.

imbarcare   to carry, embark; to take on board; to board; to load; to leak

- Quella nave non imbarca passeggeri.
  That ship does not carry passengers.

- Non hanno ancora imbarcato i soldati (/i passeggeri).
  They have not yet taken the soldiers (/passengers) on board.

- Tutte le macchine saranno imbarcate domani.
  All the cars will be loaded on board the ship tomorrow.

- La barca imbarca acqua!
  The boat is leaking!

imbarcarsi   to go on board; to sign on

- I passeggeri si stanno imbarcando.
  The passengers are going on board.

- Il nipote del signor Parodi si imbarcherà come mozzo.
  Mr. Parodi's nephew will sign on as a ship's boy.

imbarcarsi (per/su)   to embark (for); to take a ship

- S'imbarcarono per l'America (/in un brutto affare).
  They embarked for America (/on a bad business venture).

- Si imbarcheranno sulla prima nave in partenza da Napoli.
  They will take the first ship sailing from Naples.

immaginare   to imagine, suppose; to guess; to conceive

- È facile immaginare la gioia di quei bambini.
  It is easy to imagine how happy those children were.

- Lo immagino.
  I suppose so.

- Non se lo sarebbe mai immaginato (*or* Non l'avrebbe mai immaginato).
  He would have never thought so.

■   Appena lo vidi, immaginai cosa pensava.
    As soon as I saw him, I guessed what he was thinking.

■   Non riesco a immaginarlo.
    I can't guess it.

■   Dobbiamo immaginare nuovi metodi (/una trama diversa).
    We must conceive new methods (/a different plot).

   immaginare che   to think, imagine, suppose (that)

   ■   Immagini che sia stato molto triste?
       Do you imagine it was very sad?

   ■   Non immaginavo che fossero ancora qui.
       I didn't think they were still here.

   immaginare di + *inf*   to think, imagine, suppose (that)

   ■   Adesso immagina di essere sulla luna (/milionario).
       Now imagine that you are on the moon (/a millionaire).

   immaginarsi   to picture (to oneself); to expect; "don't mention it," "not at all"

   ■   C'era da immaginarselo. Avrebbero dovuto immaginarselo.
       It was to be expected. They should have expected it.

   ■   Grazie mille. —S'immagini.
       Thanks a lot. —Don't mention it.

   ■   Disturbo? —S'immagini!
       Am I disturbing (you)? —Not at all.

impadronirsi   to seize; to get hold of; to take possession of

■   Il ladro si era già impadronito delle pellicce.
    The thief had already seized the furs.

■   La gelosia (/Il panico) si impadronì di lei.
    Jealousy (/Panic) got hold of her.

imparare qco (da qc)/come/a memoria   to learn sth (from sb)/by heart

■   Dovresti imparare la grammatica (/le buone maniere/una lingua straniera).
    You should learn grammar (/good manners/a foreign language).

■   Quella ragazza ha molto da imparare da te.
    That girl has a lot to learn from you.

■   A scuola ci facevano imparare a memoria molte poesie.
    At school they used to make us learn many poems by heart.

■   Così impari!
    This will teach you a lesson! (or This way you'll learn a thing or two!)

imparare a + *inf*   to learn to + *inf*

■   Dovresti imparare a tacere (/usare il computer/fare qualcosa).
You should learn to keep quiet (/to use the computer/to do something).

impedire   to prevent; to block, obstruct

■   Hanno impedito un delitto.
They prevented a crime.

■   Una frana impedì il traffico per parecchi giorni.
A landslide blocked traffic for several days.

■   Un edificio molto alto impedisce la vista del lago.
A very high building obstructs the view of the lake.

impedire a qc di + *inf*   to prevent, keep, stop sb from + *ger*

■   Gli impedirono di parlare.
They prevented him from speaking.

■   La pioggia ha impedito ai bambini di giocare in giardino.
The rain kept the children from playing in the yard.

■   Chi t'impedisce di telefonarle?
Who's stopping you from calling her?

impedire a qc che + *subj*   to prevent sb from + *ger*

■   Hanno impedito che la partita si svolgesse regolarmente.
They prevented the game from being played as usual.

impedire qco a qc   to hamper sb/sth

■   L'ingessatura (/La gonna lunga) le impediva certi movimenti.
Her cast (/long skirt) hampered her movements.

impegnare   to pawn; to pledge; to book; to bind; to keep sb busy; to keep pressure on sb

■   Ha impegnato i gioielli della moglie.
He pawned his wife's jewels.

■   Hanno impegnato due stanze.
They booked two rooms.

■   Questa lettera non t'impegna.
This letter doesn't bind you.

■   Questa è una risposta che non impegna.
This is a noncommittal answer.

■   Il lavoro lo impegna molto.
His work keeps him very busy.

■ Il tennista italiano impegnò l'avversario.
The Italian tennis player kept the pressure on his opponent.

impegnare qc a qco   to oblige sb to sth

■ La sua carica lo impegna a una vita sociale molto attiva.
His position obliges him to have a very active social life.

impegnarsi a + *inf*   to undertake to + *inf*

■ Mi sono impegnato a finire oggi (/farlo da solo).
I have undertaken to finish it today (/do it by myself).

impegnarsi in qco   to devote oneself to sth; to become engaged, involved in sth

■ Quello studente si impegna molto nello studio.
That student devotes himself to his studies.

■ Non vogliono impegnarsi in un affare rischioso.
They don't want to get involved (or engaged) in a risky business.

implicare   to entail; to imply

■ Quel corso (/Il successo) implica molte ore di laboratorio (/duro lavoro).
That course (/Success) entails many hours in the lab (/hard work).

■ Il progetto implica una grande spesa.
The plan implies a big expense.

implicare che + *subj*   to imply (that)

■ Questo non implica che suo marito sia un farabutto.
This does not imply that her husband is a crook.

implicare qc (in qco)   to implicate sb (in sth)

■ Quei due ragazzi furono implicati nell'assassinio di un vecchio.
Those two boys were implicated in the murder of an old man.

imporre   to entail

■ La vita in comune impone sacrifici.
Life together entails sacrifices.

imporre qco a qc   to impose sth on sb; to command

■ Gli hanno imposto la loro presenza.
They have imposed their presence on him.

■ Gli imposero l'ubbidienza.
They commanded obedience from him. (or They commanded him to be obedient.)

■ La delicatezza dell'argomento gli imponeva il massimo riserbo.
The sensitivity of the subject commanded his utmost discretion.

imporre qco su qco   to impose sth on sth

- È stata imposta una tassa sul tabacco.
  A tax on tobacco has been imposed (or levied).

imporre a qc di + *inf*   to order sb to + *inf;* to force sb to + *inf*

- Il nostro comandante ci impose di andare (/restare/non dire una parola).
  Our commander ordered us to go (/stay/not to say a word).

- Le sue condizioni di salute gli impongono di condurre una vita tranquilla.
  His (health) condition forces him to lead a quiet life.

imporre (nome)   to give (a name)

- Al figlio (/Allo zio) imposero il nome Sebastiano (/un soprannome).
  The son (/The uncle) was given the name Sebastian (/a nickname).

imporsi   to impose (oneself); to attract attention; to become popular/a success; to become necessary

- Lo designer s'impose subito all'attenzione generale.
  The designer attracted everyone's attention right away.

- È una moda che si è imposta in poco tempo.
  It is a fashion that has become popular in a short time.

- Le sue teorie s'imposero.
  His theories became a success.

- A quel punto si impose un cambiamento drastico (/una revisione del processo).
  At that point a drastic change (/a rehearing of the trial) became necessary.

imporsi (su qc)   to make oneself respected; to assert one's authority on sb

- Quegli insegnanti non sanno imporsi.
  Those teachers can't make themselves respected.

- Il nuovo direttore si è subito imposto sui dipendenti.
  The new director immediately asserted his authority on his employees.

importare a qc (+ *inf*)   to be important to sb, matter to sb

- Quello che gli importa di più è la sicurezza.
  Security is what matters most to him.

- Non importa. Importa molto (poco).
  It doesn't matter. It matters a lot (/a little).

- Non me ne importa niente.
  It doesn't matter at all to me. (or I don't care about it in the least.)

- Ai tuoi genitori importa sapere dove vuoi andare (/vederti felice).
  It is important to your parents to know where you want to go (/to see you happy).

importare a qc che + *subj*   to matter to sb (that)

- A noi importa che voi siate felici.
  It matters to us that you're happy.

importare a qc di qc   to matter to sb about sb

- Non gli importa molto della squadra.
  His team doesn't matter much to him.

importare che + *subj*   to be necessary for sb + *inf*

- Non importa che tu lo faccia adesso.
  It is not necessary for you to do it now.

importare qco da   to import sth from

- L'Italia importa caffè dal Brasile.
  Italy imports coffee from Brazil.

impregnare (di)   to soak, impregnate (with); to fill (with)

- La camicia del ragazzo era impregnata di sudore.
  The boy's shirt was soaked with sweat.
- Il fazzoletto della ragazza era impregnato di profumo scadente.
  The girl's handkerchief was soaked (or impregnated) with cheap perfume.
- Questa stanza è impregnata di fumo.
  This room is filled with smoke.

imputare qco a qc/qco   to impute, attribute sth to sb/sth

- Hanno imputato al caso (/a negligenza) la causa della sciagura.
  They attributed the accident to chance (/carelessness).
- Io imputo il fallimento dell'impresa alla cattiva organizzazione.
  I attribute the failure of the business to the bad organization.

imputare qc di qco   to charge sb with sth

- Fu imputato di omicidio premeditato.
  He was charged with premeditated murder.

incaricare qc di qc/ + *inf*   to charge, entrust sb with sth/+ ger

- L'ex-presidente americano fu incaricato di una missione di pace.
  The former American president was charged with a peace mission.
- Mi hanno incaricato di seguire tutte le pratiche d'ufficio.
  They have charged (or entrusted) me with all the office business.
- La signorina Andreini sarà incaricata d'insegnare francese in questa scuola.
  Miss Andreini will be entrusted with the teaching of French in this school.

incaricarsi di qco   to take care of sth; to attend to sth

■   Mi incarico io di questa faccenda.
I will take care of (or attend to) this matter.

incaricarsi di + *inf*   to take it upon oneself to + *inf*

■   Mio figlio si incaricherà di parlargli (/d'informarli).
My son will take it upon himself to speak to him (/inform them).

incaricarsene   to take care of it

■   Non preoccuparti, me ne incarico io.
Don't worry. I'll take care of it.

incendiare qco   to set sth on fire, set fire to sth, inflame

■   Hanno incendiato l'ambasciata (/la scuola/l'appartamento).
They set the embassy (/the school/the apartment) on fire.

incendiarsi   to catch fire

■   Il pollaio (/Il bosco) si è incendiato.
The henhouse (/The woods) caught fire.

incidere   to fix; to record, tape

■   Il viso della ragazza è inciso nella mia memoria.
The girl's face is fixed in my memory.

■   L'opera è stata incisa da quella orchestra con gli interpreti originali.
The opera was recorded by that orchestra with the original cast.

■   Hai inciso quel discorso?
Did you tape that speech?

incidere qco (su qco)   to cut sth into sth, carve sth on sth; to etch; to tap; to weigh heavily on sth; to affect

■   Avevano inciso le loro iniziali sul tronco di un albero (/su una panchina).
They had carved (or cut) their initials into a tree trunk (/on a bench).

■   Mio cugino passava ore a incidere all'acquaforte.
My cousin would spend hours etching.

■   Incidono gli alberi per estrarre il lattice.
They tap the trees to extract the sap.

■   Questa spesa inciderà sul loro bilancio.
This expense will weigh heavily on their budget.

■   Le esperienze dell'infanzia incidono sul carattere.
Childhood experiences affect the temperament.

incidersi in qco   to be engraved in, on sth

■   Quelle parole si sono incise nel mio cuore.
Those words are engraved on my heart.

inclinare   to bend; to lean

■   Suo nonno inclinò la testa e s'addormentò.
Her grandfather bent his head and fell asleep.

■   La torre (/Il quadro) inclina a destra (/a sinistra).
The tower (/picture) leans to the right (/left).

inclinare a + *inf*/**a qco**   to be inclined to, tend to + *inf*

■   Inclino a crederti (/pensare così).
I am inclined to believe you (/think so).

■   Suo figlio inclina alla solitudine.
His son tends to keep to himself.

inclinarsi   to tilt; to lean

■   La tavola s'inclinò mentre mangiavamo.
The table tilted while we were eating.

■   La torre di Pisa s'inclina sempre di più.
The Tower of Pisa is leaning more and more.

includere   to include; to enclose

■   In quel dizionario sono state incluse molte parole straniere.
Many foreign words have been included in that dictionary.

■   Le spese di trasporto sono incluse nel prezzo.
The price includes freight.

■   Mi sono dimenticato di includere il listino prezzi (/l'elenco degli invitati).
I forgot to enclose the price list (/the guest list).

incontrare   to meet (with); to play; to be popular, be a success; to sell well; to appeal to, find favor with

■   Carlo ha incontrato quel mio amico a teatro (/al supermercato).
Charles met that friend of mine at the theater (/supermarket).

■   Ieri sera il pugile inglese ha incontrato quello americano.
Last night the English boxer met the American one.

■   Quell'uomo ha incontrato molte difficoltà (/molti pericoli/molti ostacoli).
That man has met with many difficulties (/dangers/obstacles).

■   Domenica l'Inter incontrerà il Napoli.
Next Sunday Inter will play Napoli (soccer team).

■   Questa bicicletta incontra molto.
This bicycle is very popular (or sells well).

■   Questo è un prodotto che incontrerà il gusto dei clienti più raffinati.
This is a product that will appeal to the most refined customers.

■   Quella nuova rivista ha incontrato il favore dei giovani.
That new magazine found favor with young people.

incontrarsi   to meet each other/one another; to meet up with sb

■   Si sono incontrati in vacanza.
They met while they were on vacation.

■   Finalmente mi sono incontrato in una persona onesta.
At long last I met up with an honest person.

incontrarsi (in/su qco)   to correspond; to agree on sth

■   I loro gusti (/Le loro idee) s'incontrano.
Their likes and dislikes (/ideas) correspond.

■   Non s'incontrano mai su niente.
They never agree on anything.

incoraggiare   to boost

■   Bisogna incoraggiare la produzione.
Production should be boosted.

incoraggiare qc a + *inf*   encourage sb to + *inf*

■   Noi tutti li incoraggiammo a continuare (/provare/studiare).
We all encouraged them to continue (/try/study).

incorrere in qco   (auxiliary *essere*) to incur sth

■   Sono incorsi in un grave pericolo (/una multa/una pena/un errore).
They incurred serious danger (/a fine/a penalty/a mistake).

incrociare   to cross

■   Incrocia le dita! (*idiomatic*)
Cross your fingers! (idiomatic)

■   Vogliono provare a incrociare un bracco con un boxer (/due tipi di rose).
They want to try to cross a bloodhound with a boxer (/two kinds of roses).

■   Gli operai hanno incrociato le braccia. (*fig*)
The workers refused to work.

incrociarsi   to cross; to intersect; to meet; to exchange

■   Le due strade si incrociano vicino alla piazza.
The two roads cross near the square.

■   Due rette parallele non si incrociano mai.
Two parallel lines never intersect.

■   I loro sguardi si incrociarono.
Their eyes met.

- Fra i due gruppi si incrociavano battute.
  Witty remarks were exchanged between the two groups.

indicare qc/qco   to indicate, show sb/sth; to point at sb/sth

- Il barometro (/L'orologio) indica cattivo tempo (/l'ora).
  The barometer (/clock) indicates bad weather (/time).

- Per favore, può indicarmi l'entrata (/l'uscita)?
  Can you please show me the entrance (/exit)?

- La bambina indicò il venditore di palloni.
  The little girl pointed at the balloon vendor.

  indicare qco   to denote, mean sth; to suggest, prescribe sth

  - Questi sono sintomi che possono indicare una grave malattia.
    These are symptoms that may denote a serious disease.

  - Non so che cosa indichino questi simboli matematici.
    I don't know what these mathematical symbols mean.

  - Puoi indicarmi un buon ristorante?
    Can you suggest a good restaurant to me?

  - Dottore, può indicarmi un buon rimedio per il mal di testa?
    Doctor, can you suggest a good remedy to me for headaches?

  - Questa è la cura che mi è stata indicata.
    This is the treatment that was prescribed for me.

indignare   to make indignant; to fill with indignation

- Quel discorso (/Quella proposta) ha indignato tutti.
  That speech (/proposal) made everyone indignant.

  indignarsi per qco   to get indignant at sth

  - Si sono indignati per l'ingiustizia (/l'offesa/il vostro atteggiamento).
    They got indignant at the injustice (/offense/at your attitude).

indirizzare qco a qc   to address sth to sb

- Gli ho indirizzato diverse lettere ma non ho ricevuto risposta.
  I addressed several letters to him, but I didn't get any answers.

  indirizzare qc a qc/qco   to direct sb to sb/sth

  - Lo indirizzarono al pronto soccorso.
    They directed him to the emergency room.

  - Hanno indirizzato tutti i loro sforzi per la realizzazione del progetto.
    They directed all their energies to the realization of the plan.

indovinare   to guess; to (fore)tell

■   Hai indovinato.
You guessed right.

■   Indovina chi viene a cena (/come mi chiamo/che cosa ha detto Maria).
Guess who's coming to dinner (/what my name is/what Mary said).

   indovinarla   to hit the nail on the head

   ■   L'hai proprio indovinata!
   You certainly hit the nail on the head! (fig)

indurre   to induce

■   Questo induce magnetismo (/elettricità).
This induces magnetism (/electricity).

■   Questa è corrente indotta.
This is induced current.

   indurre qc a + *inf*   induce sb to + *inf*

   ■   Niente può indurmi a farlo.
   Nothing can induce me to do it.

   indurre qc a qco   to drive sb to sth

   ■   La morte dei figli lo indusse a una profonda depressione (/una dolorosa
       decisione).
   *The death of his sons drove him into a deep depression (/a painful
   decision).*

   indurre qc in qco   to lead sb into sth

   ■   Non indurci in tentazione.
   Lead us not into temptation.

   ■   Lo indussero in errore.
   They misled him.

influire su qc/qco   to influence sb/sth, have influence on sb/sth, affect sb/sth

■   Fattori esterni (/Queste circostanze) hanno influito sul risultato dell'impresa.
Outside factors (/These circumstances) influenced the result of the enterprise.

■   Questo non influisce sulla mia opinione.
This has no influence on my opinion.

■   La situazione economica influirà sui tassi d'interesse.
The economic situation will affect interest rates.

informare qc di/su qco   to inform sb about sth; to report sth to sb

■   Lo informammo dell'accaduto (/dello svolgimento degli eventi).
We informed him about what happened (/the course of the events).

- Abbiamo informato subito le autorità dell'accaduto.
  We immediately reported to the authorities what happened.

  informarsi   to inquire; to obtain information, find out

  - Quel mio amico s'informa sempre della tua salute.
    That friend of mine always inquires about your health.

  - Ci siamo informati sul costo della vita in quel paese.
    We got information about living costs in that country.

  - Da chi potrei informarmi? —Potresti informarti all'agenzia di viaggi.
    Where could I get information? —You could get information from the travel agency.

  - Informati se è vero.
    Find out if it is true.

ingannare   to deceive, cheat (on); to evade; to alleviate

- Tu hai cercato d'ingannarmi ma io sono più furba di te.
  You tried to deceive me, but I'm more clever than you.

- Era il mese di dicembre, se la memoria non mi inganna.
  It was the month of December, if (my) memory does not deceive me.

- Tutti sanno che inganna la moglie.
  Everyone knows that he cheats on his wife.

- Il prigioniero ha ingannato la sorveglianza dei poliziotti ed è fuggito.
  The prisoner evaded police supervision and escaped.

- Puoi darmi qualcosa per ingannare la fame?
  Can you give me something to alleviate my hunger?

  ingannarsi (su qc/qco)   to be mistaken (about sb/sth)

  - Era un giovedì, se non m'inganno.
    It was a Thursday, if I am not mistaken.

  - Mi sono ingannato sul loro conto (/su di lei).
    I was mistaken about them (/about her).

inghiottire   to swallow (up)

- Devi inghiottire una pillola amara. (*idiomatic*)
  You must swallow a bitter pill. (idiomatic)

- La bambina (/La barca) è stata inghiottita dalla folla (/dalle onde).
  The little girl (/The boat) was swallowed up by the crowd (/the waves).

iniettare (qco a qc/in qco)   to inject (sth into sb/sth)

- L'anestesista comiciò a iniettare l'anestetico nella vena del paziente.
  The anesthesiologist started injecting the anesthetic into the patient's vein.

- Certi rettili iniettano il veleno coi denti.
  Some reptiles inject poison with their fangs.

iniettarsi   to inject oneself

■   Li ho visti iniettarsi qualcosa nel braccio.
I saw them injecting something into their arms.

innamorarsi di   to fall in love with

■   Si è innamorata di lui quando aveva sedici anni.
She fell in love with him when she was sixteen.

inquinare   to pollute

■   Gli scarichi industriali possono inquinare il mare.
Industrial waste can pollute the sea.

insegnare (qco a qc)   to teach (sb sth); to be a teacher; to show sb sth

■   Il loro padre insegna scienze politiche da molti anni.
Their father has been teaching political science for many years.

■   La nonna di Amelia le ha insegnato quella preghiera (/lo spagnolo).
Amelia's grandmother taught her that prayer (/Spanish).

■   La storia (/L'esperienza) insegna che tutti facciamo errori.
History (/Experience) teaches (or shows) that we all make mistakes.

■   Tua zia insegna qui?
Is your aunt a teacher here?

■   Chi Le ha insegnato l'educazione?
Where did you learn your manners? (literally: Who taught you manners?)

insegnare a qc a + *inf*   to teach sb (how) to + *inf*

■   Le insegnerò a guidare (/leggere/scrivere/dipingere/fare la maglia).
I'll teach her to drive (/read/write/paint/knit).

inserire qco in qco   to insert sth in(to) sth; to put, fit sth into sth

■   Devo inserire una vite nel foro.
I must insert a screw into the hole.

■   Inserisci la chiave nella serratura (/i loro nomi nella lista degli invitati).
Put the key in the lock (/their names on the guest list).

■   Si deve inserire quel tubo nell'altro.
That pipe must be fitted into the other.

■   Questo apparecchio deve essere inserito nel circuito.
This apparatus must be put in the circuit.

inserirsi in qco   to become part of, get into

■   Si sono inseriti nel nuovo partito.
They became part of (or got into) the new party.

insistere (su/in qco)   to insist (on sth); to subtend

■   Il mio insegnante insiste molto sulla puntualità (/ortografia).
My teacher insists a lot on punctuality (/spelling).

■ Va bene, se proprio insisti, accetto.
All right. If you really insist, I'll accept.

■ La prego di non insistere, signor Martini.
Please do not insist, Mr. Martini.

■ Disegni un angolo che insiste su un arco.
Draw an angle subtending an arc.

insistere a + *inf*   to keep on, insist + *ger*

■ Tu insisti a fare lo stesso errore (/comprare lo stesso prodotto).
You keep on making the same mistake (/buying the same product).

■ L'accusato insiste a dirsi innocente.
The accused insists on saying he is not guilty.

insistere con qc perché + *subj*   to urge sb to + *inf*

■ Insisterò col preside perché prenda dei provvedimenti disciplinari.
I'll urge the principal to take disciplinary measures.

insistere in qco   to persist in sth

■ Se insisterai nelle tue ricerche, riuscirai.
If you persist in your research, you will succeed.

insistere per + *inf*   to insist on + *ger*

■ Abbiamo insistito per essere ricevuti (/per sapere la verità).
We insisted on being received (/knowing the truth).

intendere   to intend, mean

■ Questi prodotti sono intesi solo per l'esportazione.
These products are intended only for export.

■ Non intendevo fare del male.
I intended no harm.

■ Io non intendevo questo.
I didn't mean this.

intendere + *inf*   to intend, mean + *inf/ger*

■ Le autorità intendono aprire un'inchiesta.
The authorities intend opening (or to open) an inquiry.

■ Intendevano andare a letto subito (/partire domani/sposarsi).
They intended to go to bed right away (/leave tomorrow/get married).

■ Cosa intendete dire alla conferenza?
What do you intend to say at the lecture (conference)?

■ Che cosa intende dire con queste parole, signor Damiani?
What do you mean with these words, Mr. Damiani?

intendersi (su qco)   to agree on sth; to understand each other

- Ci siamo intesi?
  *Is it clear? (*literally: *Do we understand each other?)*

- Posso venire anch'io? —S'intende!
  Can I come, too? —Of course!

- Intendiamoci bene.
  Let this be quite clear.

- Questo s'intende.
  This goes without saying.

- Ci siamo già intesi sulle condizioni di consegna.
  We have already agreed on the terms of delivery.

- Penso che cominciamo a intenderci.
  I think we are beginning to understand each other.

interessare qc/qco   to interest sb; to be of interest to sb; to get sb interested in sth; to affect sth; to be concerned with

- È un argomento che interessa tutti.
  It is a topic that interests everyone.

- Questo argomento non interessa i nostri lettori.
  This topic is of no interest to our readers.

- Interesserò il ministro al tuo caso.
  I'll get the minister interested in your case.

- Il signor Giacomoni ha interessato i figli nell'azienda.
  Mr. Giacomoni gave an interest in his business to his sons.

- Questa legge interessa in particolare i professionisti.
  This law affects professional people in particular.

- È una malattia che interessa il cervello.
  It is a disease that affects the brain.

- La sorte dei passeggeri di quell'aereo interessa noi tutti.
  We are all concerned with the fate of the passengers on that plane.

interessarsi a/di qc/qco   to be interested in sth; to take an interest in sb/sth; to take care of; to interfere; to mind

- Il dottore si interessò molto alla mia storia.
  The doctor was very interested in my story.

- Suo marito si interessava di filatelia.
  Her husband was interested in stamp collecting.

- Mi interessai molto del suo caso.
  I took a great interest in his case.

- Si è sempre interessata di lui.
  She has always taken an interest in him.

■ La Croce Rossa si sta interessando dei feriti (/dei bambini).
The Red Cross is taking care of the wounded (/children).

■ Non devi interessarti degli affari degli altri.
You should not interfere in other people's affairs.

■ Interessati dei fatti tuoi.
Mind your own business.

interessarsi che + *subj*   to see (that)

■ Potresti interessarti che abbiano tutto quello di cui hanno bisogno?
Could you see that they have everything they need?

interpretare   to interpret; to explain, expound; to play; to star; to read

■ Come interpreti il discorso del presidente (/questo testo/il mio sogno)?
How do you interpret the president's speech (/this text/my dream)?

■ Interpretano sempre male le mie parole.
They always misinterpret my words.

■ Come possiamo interpretare questo fenomeno (/il loro strano comportamento)?
How can we explain this phenomenon (/their strange behavior)?

■ Il sacerdote interpreta la Bibbia.
The priest expounds on the Bible.

■ Chi interpreterà la parte di Giulietta?
Who will play (the part of) Juliet?

■ L'anno scorso quell'attore ha interpretato cinque film.
Last year that actor starred in five movies.

■ Io non so interpretare quei segnali.
I cannot read those signs.

interrogare   to examine; to consult

■ Si dovrebbe sempre interrogare la propria coscienza.
One should always sound out (or examine) one's own conscience.

■ I romani interrogavano l'oracolo di Delfi.
The Romans used to consult the oracle at Delphi.

interrogare qc (su/in qco)   to interrogate sb (about sth), question sb (about sth), ask sb (about sth); to quiz or examine sb (in sth)

■ Il poliziotto interrogò due persone sospette.
The policeman interrogated two suspects.

■ L'imputato fu interrogato dal pubblico ministero.
The defendant was questioned by the public prosecutor.

■ L'hanno interrogato a lungo sull'incidente.
They asked him a lot of questions about the accident.

■   Stamattina sono stato interrogato in francese.
This morning I was tested in French.

interrompere   to interrupt sb/sth; to break off/up sth; to cut off

■   Lo squillo del telefono interruppe la nostra conversazione.
The ring of the phone interrupted our conversation.

■   Non interrompere papà quando parla.
Don't interrupt your dad when he is talking.

■   Le trattative per il cessate il fuoco sono state interrotte.
The negotiations for the cease-fire have broken off.

■   Quella linea elettrica (/telefonica) sarà interrotta per una settimana.
That electrical (/telephone) line will be cut off for a week.

    interrompersi   to interrupt oneself; to break off, stop

    ■   Il nonno s'interruppe nel pieno del racconto.
    Grandfather stopped (or broke off) in the middle of his story.

intervenire (a/in qco)   (auxiliary *essere*) to intervene; to interfere; to step in sth; to
stand up; to attend sth; to operate

■   Sono intervenuti nella discussione (/nel dibattito).
They intervened in the dispute (/debate).

■   Penso che il padre della ragazza non voglia intervenire nei suoi affari.
I think the girl's father doesn't want to interfere in her business.

■   Ieri sera c'è stata una rissa e la polizia ha dovuto intervenire.
Last night there was a brawl and the police had to step in.

■   Il signor Rosati è intervenuto a favore del ragazzo.
Mr. Rosati stood up for the boy.

■   Il console è intervenuto al ricevimento in onore di quello scrittore.
The consul attended the reception in honor of that writer.

■   Abbiamo dovuto far intervenire la polizia.
We had to bring the police on the scene.

■   Il chirurgo ha deciso di intervenire immediatamente.
The surgeon has decided to operate right away.

intervistare qc   to interview sb (politician, celebrity)

■   I giornalisti hanno intervistato il ministro degli affari esteri (/l'autore di quel best
seller/quella famosa attrice).
*The journalists interviewed the foreign minister (/the author of that bestseller
/that famous actress).*

intrattenere to entertain; to engage in conversation

- La signora Marini sa intrattenere i suoi ospiti.
  Mrs. Marini knows how to entertain her guests.

- Mio padre lo intrattenne sulla politica dei paesi del Medioriente.
  My father engaged in a conversation with him on the politics of Middle Eastern countries.

    intrattenersi a + *inf* to stop + *inf*

- Si intrattennero al bar con gli amici.
  They stopped at the bar with their friends.

    intrattenersi su qco to dwell on sth

- Il professor Giannini si intrattenne a lungo su quel tema.
  Professor Giannini dwelled on that subject for a long time.

introdurre qc/qco in/da to introduce sb/sth in(to)/to; to show sb into, usher sb into; to slip sb in; to insert sth in; to smuggle sth into; to bring (in/up)

- Sembra che sia stato Marco Polo a introdurre le spezie in Europa.
  It seems that it was Marco Polo who introduced spices to Europe.

- Bisogna introdurre prodotti italiani nei paesi stranieri.
  It is necessary to introduce Italian products into foreign countries.

- La introdussero in casa di nascosto.
  They slipped her into the house.

- La domestica li introdusse in una splendida sala.
  The maid ushered them into a marvelous hall.

- Il segretario mi introdusse dal ministro.
  The secretary showed me into the minister's office.

- Se vuoi aprire la porta, devi introdurre la chiave nella toppa.
  If you want to open the door, you must insert the key in the lock.

- Quella merce è stata introdotta in Italia di contrabbando.
  That merchandise was smuggled into Italy.

- Gli stranieri introdussero nuove usanze nella società.
  Foreigners brought new customs into society.

    introdursi in to get into, slip into

- I ragazzi si sono introdotti nella scuola durante la notte.
  The children got into school during the night.

- Mio nipote si introdusse furtivamente in camera di sua madre.
  My nephew slipped into his mother's room.

invadere to invade; to burst into, swarm onto sth; to flood; to spread, trespass upon sth

- L'Italia fu invasa dagli Ostrogoti nel 489.
  Italy was invaded by the Ostrogoths in 489.

- Le cavallette invasero i campi.
  Grasshoppers invaded the fields.

- Una folla invase il teatro.
  A crowd burst into the theater.

- I teppisti invasero il campo.
  The hooligans swarmed onto the playing field.

- Il colera aveva invaso tutta la regione.
  Cholera had spread into the whole region.

- Il mercato fu invaso da prodotti fatti a Hong Kong.
  The market was flooded by products made in Hong Kong.

- Non invadere il mio campo.
  Don't trespass on my territory.

investire   to hit, collide with; to run over; to ply; to invest

- L'automobile investì il ciclista.
  The car hit the cyclist.

- Il figlio della signora Sandrini è stato investito da un treno ieri sera.
  Mrs. Sandrini's son was run over by a train last night.

- Hanno investito di domande il segretario di stato.
  They plied the secretary of state with questions.

- Penso che tuo padre abbia investito tutti i suoi soldi in titoli.
  I think your father invested all his money in stocks.

- Fu investito di pieni poteri.
  He was given (or invested with) full power.

  investirsi   to live (one's part)

  - L'attore s'investì della parte.
    The actor lived his part.

invitare qc a qco   to invite sb to sth

- L'hanno invitata a pranzo (/a cena/a teatro/a casa loro/al cinema).
  They invited her to dinner (/supper/the theater/their house/the movies).

  invitare qc a + *inf*   to invite sb to + *inf;* to request sb to + *inf*

  - La inviterei a riflettere sulle possibili conseguenze, signor Parini.
    I would invite you to think about the possible consequences, Mr. Parini.

  - Il ragazzo li invitò a bere alla salute di Vittorio.
    The boy invited them to drink to Victor's health.

  - Si invitano i passeggeri a scendere subito.
    Passengers are requested to get off immediately.

irritare   to irritate, vex

- Il tuo comportamento l'ha veramente irritata.
  Your behavior really irritated her.

■ Le lamentele continue di sua moglie lo irritano.
His wife's endless complaining vexes him.

irritarsi to get nervous; to get irritated, inflamed

■ In questi giorni tua figlia si irrita per un nonnulla.
These days your daughter is getting nervous over the slightest thing.

■ Gli occhi di quel bambino si irritano in piscina.
That child's eyes get inflamed in the pool.

ispirare qc to inspire sb

■ La brevità della vita ispira i poeti.
The brevity of life inspires poets.

ispirare qco a qc to inspire sb with sth

■ Ho bisogno di una persona che ispiri fiducia (/timore/rispetto) a tutti.
I need a person who inspires everyone with confidence (/fear/respect).

ispirarsi a qco to get inspiration from sth; to be inspired by, imbued with sth

■ Si ispirarono agli esempi degli uomini illustri.
They got inspiration from the examples of famous men.

■ Quello scrittore si ispirava alle idee del romanticismo.
That writer was inspired by the ideas of romanticism.

■ Queste leggi si ispirano ai principi della costituzione.
These laws are imbued with the principles of the constitution.

istruire qc (in/su/di qco) to instruct sb (in sth); to teach sb (sth), inform sb (about sth); to train sb; to institute

■ L'avvocato ha istruito il testimone sulle risposte da dare.
The attorney instructed the witness about the answers to give.

■ Vi hanno istruito dell'accaduto?
Did they inform you about what happened?

■ Hanno già istruito le reclute.
They already trained the recruits.

■ Non hanno ancora istruito il processo.
They have not prepared the (legal) case yet.

istruirsi to educate oneself; to improve one's mind

■ Ci si può istruire seguendo dei corsi serali (/leggendo).
One can educate oneself by taking night courses (/reading).

L

lacerare to lacerate; to break; to tear; to rend, pierce

- Il filo spinato gli lacerò la carne.
  The barbed wire lacerated his flesh.

- Sono lacerati dal senso di colpa (/sospetto).
  They are torn by a sense of guilt (/suspicion).

- I gridi dei prigionieri laceravano l'aria.
  The screams of the prisoners pierced the air.

- Era un suono che lacerava gli orecchi.
  It was an ear-splitting sound.

  ### lacerarsi to tear

  - Le donne si laceravano le vesti dalla disperazione.
    The women were tearing their clothes in desperation.

lagnarsi di qc/qco to complain of/about sb/sth; to moan about sth

- Il figlio di Alberto da una settimana si lagna di dolori alla schiena.
  Albert's son has been complaining of back pains for a week.

- Tutti si lagnano delle nuove tasse.
  Everyone is complaining about the new taxes.

- Tua sorella si lagna sempre di tutto.
  Your sister is always moaning about everything.

  ### lagnarsi di + *inf* to complain (that)

  - Si è lagnata di non essere stata invitata.
    She complained she had not been invited.

lamentare to lament, mourn

- Si lamentano molte vittime. (*idiomatic*)
  There were many deaths.

  ### lamentarsi di qco to complain of/about sth

  - Di che cosa ti lamenti? —Ho buone ragioni per lamentarmi.
    What are you complaining about? —I have good cause for complaining.

  - Il paziente si lamentava di un forte dolore di testa.
    The patient was complaining of a bad headache.

  - Come vanno le cose? —Non mi lamento.
    How are things going? —I can't complain.

lampeggiare (auxiliary *avere;* when referring to weather, auxiliary *avere* or *essere*)   to be lightning; to flash; to sparkle

■   Lampeggia e tuona da dieci minuti.
    It has been lightning and thundering for ten minutes.

■   Ha (È) lampeggiato tutta la sera.
    It was lightning the whole night.

■   Una luce rossa lampeggiava sul cruscotto.
    A red light was flashing on the dashboard.

lanciare qco (in qco)   to throw (out) sth, fling sth (into/up); to toss; to raise, utter; to launch; to speed up; to cast

■   Il tuo amico ha lanciato un'ottima idea (/una proposta interessante).
    Your friend threw (tossed) out a very good idea (/an interesting proposal).

■   Il bambino lanciò il libro nell'acqua.
    The child flung the book into the water.

■   Dobbiamo lanciare in aria una moneta?
    Shall we toss a coin?

■   La donna lanciò un urlo.
    The woman gave a shout.

■   Pensano di lanciare a una nuovo dentifricio (/il cantate/un siluro).
    They are planning to launch the new toothpaste (/the singer/a torpedo).

■   Gli piace lanciare la macchina a tutta velocità.
    He likes to speed up his car.

■   Il pescatore lanciò la lenza.
    The fisherman cast his line.

lanciare qco contro qc   to throw sth at sb; to hurl

■   I ragazzi cominciarono a lanciare palle di neve contro i passanti.
    The kids started throwing snowballs at passersby.

■   I componenti di quella tribù lanciavano frecce con la punta avvelenata.
    The members of that tribe were hurling arrows with poisoned tips.

■   Lanciarono insulti contro di lui.
    They hurled insults at him.

lanciarsi in qco   to hurl oneself into sth; to throw oneself into sth

■   I soldati si lanciarono contro il nemico.
    The soldiers hurled themselves against the enemy.

■   Credo che tu ti sia lanciato in un affare rischioso.
    I believe you threw yourself into a risky business.

lanciarsi da qco   to throw oneself from sth

- ■ Mia nipote si è lanciata dall'aereo con il paracadute.
  My niece parachuted from the plane.

- ■ Il ragazzo si lanciò dall'auto in corsa.
  The boy threw himself from the moving car.

languire   to languish; to fade

- ■ Il detenuto fu lasciato languire in carcere per mesi.
  The prisoner was left languishing for months.

- ■ La luce languiva.
  The light was fading.

lasciare   to leave (behind); to abandon; to quit; to give up; to desert; to break off

- ■ Il loro padre lasciò la scuola (/la casa/Roma) quando era molto giovane.
  Their father left school (/home/Rome) when he was very young.

- ■ Lasciami in pace.
  Leave me in peace.

- ■ Ho lasciato le chiavi (/il pacco) in macchina (/a casa).
  I left my keys (/the package) in the car (/at home).

- ■ Il gatto lasciò (andare) l'uccellino.
  The cat let the bird go.

- ■ Lasciate ogni speranza!
  Abandon all hope!

- ■ Se non starò meglio presto, dovrò lasciare il mio lavoro.
  If I'm not better soon, I'll have to quit my job.

- ■ Quella ragazza ha lasciato una carriera promettente per sposarlo.
  That girl gave up a promising career to marry him.

- ■ Antonio lasciò gli amici per entrare in una setta religiosa.
  Anthony deserted his friends to join a religious sect.

- ■ Il fratello di Giovanni ha lasciato la sua ragazza.
  John's brother broke off with his girlfriend.

  lasciare + *inf*   to leave, let + *inf*

  - ■ Lascialo stare.
    Leave him alone.

  - ■ Lascia fare a lui.
    Leave it to him.

  - ■ Lasciate passare qualche giorno.
    Let a few days go by.

  - ■ Lascia perdere. (*idiomatic*)
    Never mind (or *Forget it* or *Drop it*). (idiomatic)

lasciare + *inf* + **qc**   let sb + *inf*

- Lasciammo mangiare (/dormire/giocare) i bambini.
  We let the children eat (/sleep/play).

- Lascia entrare (/uscire) il gatto.
  Let the cat in (/out).

lasciare che qc + *subj*   to allow sb + *inf*

- Non lasciai che lui lo facesse (/dicesse una parola).
  I didn't allow him to do it (/to say a word).

lasciare qco + *adj/ptp*   to leave sth + *adj/ptp*

- Perché hai lasciato la finestra aperta (chiusa)?
  Why did you leave the window open (/closed)?

- Il loro nonno ha lasciato scritto le sue volontà?
  Did their grandfather leave a will?

- Hanno lasciato la luce accesa (/spenta)
  They left the light on (/off).

lasciarci qco   to lose sth

- In quell'incidente Francesco ci ha lasciato una gamba (/la pelle).
  In that accident Francis lost a leg (/his life).

lasciarsi   to part; to break up

- Si lasciarono senza dirsi addio.
  They parted without saying good-bye.

- Si sono lasciati un anno fa.
  They broke up a year ago.

lasciarsi + *inf*   to let oneself + be + *ptp*

- Si sono lasciati trasportare dall'ira (/convincere/ingannare).
  They let themselves be carried away by anger (/convinced/swindled).

laurearsi   to get an advanced degree (master's or Ph.D.)

- Il figlio del signor Tassoni si laureà in fisica (/ingegneria) quest'anno.
  Mr. Tassoni's son will get a Ph.D. in physics (/engineering) this year.

lavare qco (da qco)   to wash sth; to cleanse sth (of sth)

- Ho lavato la macchina (/tutti i bicchieri/la mia camicetta/i panni).
  I washed my car (/all the glasses/my blouse/the clothes).

- La confessione lava l'anima dalle colpe.
  Confession cleanses the soul of its sins.

- Questo vestito va lavato a secco.
  This dress must be dry cleaned.

■ La madre gli ha lavato la testa. (*fig*)
His mother told him off.

lavarsi   to wash oneself; to brush (teeth)

■ Anna si lava i capelli (/le mani).
Anna washes her hair (/hands).

■ Me ne lavo le mani. (*fig*)
I wash my hands of it. (fig)

■ Questa stoffa si lava facilmente.
This fabric washes easily.

■ Tu non ti sei lavato i denti.
You did not brush your teeth.

lavorare   to work, till; to operate; to knead; to knit

■ Dopo le ferie estive abbiamo ripreso a lavorare.
After the summer break we resumed work.

■ Lo zio di Vincenzo lavora il metallo (/il ferro/il rame/il legno).
Vincent's uncle works in metal (/iron/copper/wood).

■ Tu lavori molto (/troppo/poco/otto ore al giorno).
You work hard (/too much/very little/eight hours a day).

■ Lavorano la terra.
They work (or till) the land.

■ Quella povera donna lavora giorno e notte.
That poor woman works night and day.

■ Non si deve lavorare troppo la pasta.
You shouldn't knead dough too much.

■ A mia zia piace lavorare a maglia.
My aunt likes to knit.

■ La nuova parrucchiera lavora molto.
The new hairdresser does a good business.

■ Il padre di Pietro lavora in proprio.
Peter's father is self-employed.

lavorare a   to work on/by/against

■ Lavorate a contratto (/a giornata)?—No, lavoriamo a cottimo.
Do you work on contract (/by the day)?—No, we do piecework.

lavorare per qc/qco   to work for sb/sth

■ Lavorano per il loro padre (/una ditta americana/la gloria).
They work for their father (/an American company/nothing).

far lavorare qc   to make sb work, work sb

- Credo che il signor Pietri li faccia lavorare troppo.
  I think Mr. Pietri works them too much.

leccare   to lick, lap

- Il bambino leccava il gelato.
  The child was licking his ice cream.

- Voi tutti gli leccate i piedi. (*idiomatic*)
  You all lick his boots. (idiomatic)

- Il gato leccava il latte.
  The cat lapped up the milk.

  leccarsi   to lick

  - Il bambino (/Il gattino) si leccava le labbra (/la coda).
    The child (/The kitten) was licking his lips (/tail).

legare (qc/qco con qco)   to tie (up) (sb/sth with sth); to fasten (sth to sth); to connect; to link up; to bind; to set; to thicken

- Legarono tutti i vecchi giornali (/i prigionieri).
  They tied up all the old newspapers (/prisoners).

- Il chirurgo ha dovuto legare quell'arteria (/le sue tube).
  The surgeon had to tie that artery (/her tubes).

- Ho legato l'aquilone (/il cane all'albero).
  I fastened the kite (/tied the dog to the tree).

- Sono legati da una profonda amicizia.
  They are bound by a deep friendship.

- Devi legare le parti del discorso (/un'idea all'altra).
  You must connect the parts of speech (/one idea with another).

- Hanno legato il loro nome a quella impresa.
  They linked their name with that enterprise.

- Questa maionese non lega.
  This mayonnaise doesn't thicken.

  legarsi (qco con qco)   to tie (sth with sth)

  - La ragazza si era legata i capelli con un nastro rosso.
    The girl had tied her hair with a red ribbon.

leggere   to read

- Quel bambino ha imparato a leggere quando aveva tre anni.
  That child learned to read when he was three.

- Maria leggeva una storia (/poesia/fiaba) ai bambini.
  Maria was reading a story (/poem/fairy tale) to the children.

■　Ho letto il tuo libro da cima a fondo.
I read your book from cover to cover.

■　Quando avevo diciotto anni, una zingara mi ha letto la mano.
When I was eighteen, a gypsy read my palm.

leggere di qco　to read about sth

■　Avete letto di quell'incidente?
Did you read about that accident?

levare　to lift

■　Quelle macchine possono levare un peso enorme.
Those machines can lift an enormous weight.

■　È ora di levare le tende. (*fig*)
It is time to leave.

levare qco da qco　to take sth away/off/out; to abolish; to remove

■　Devo levare tutte quelle carte dal mio tavolo (/l'anitra dal forno).
I have to take all those papers off my desk (/the duck out of the oven).

■　Gli hanno levato le tonsille.
They took out his tonsils.

■　Lo hanno levato da quella scuola.
They took him out from that school.

■　Forse leveranno quella tassa.
They may abolish that tax.

levare qc/qco di qco　to take off/out sb/sth

■　Levale le mani di dosso.
Take your hands off her.

■　Me l'hai levato di bocca. (*idomatic*)
You have taken the words right out of my mouth. (idiomatic)

■　Bisognerebbe levarlo di mezzo.
It would be necessary to get rid of (or kill) him.

levarsi (qco *or* di *or* da qco)　to rise; to get up; to appease; to take off/out; to stand up

■　Oggi il sole si leva alle sei.
Today the sun rises at six.

■　Ti sei levato di cattivo umore stamattina?
Did you get up on the wrong side of the bed this morning?

■　Il poveretto non riusciva a levarsi la fame (/la sete).
The poor fellow could not appease his hunger (/quench his thirst).

■　Levati l'impermeabile (/le scarpe/il cappello).
Take off your raincoat (/shoes/hat).

- Levati il dito di bocca.
  Take your finger out of your mouth.

- Levati di torno (/dai piedi).
  Get out of here (/Clear off).

liberare qc (da qco)   to set sb free; to release; to vacate; to rescue

- Tutti gli ostaggi furono liberati.
  All the hostages were set free.

- L'omicida è stato liberato.
  The murderer was released.

- Devono liberare l'appartamento per la fine del mese.
  They have to vacate the apartment by the end of the month.

- Li abbiamo liberati da un grave pericolo.
  We rescued them from serious danger.

liberarsi da qco/di qc   to rid oneself of sth/sb; to free oneself from sth

- Mi sono liberata da quell'idea (/quell'onere).
  I rid myself of that idea (/burden).

- Spero di potermi liberare dalle mie responsabilità.
  I hope I can free myself from my commitments.

- Mi sono liberato di quel seccatore (/lei).
  I got rid of that bore (/her).

licenziare   to discharge; to dismiss, get fired; to graduate

- Abbiamo licenziato il commesso del piano superiore.
  We fired the salesclerk on the upper floor.

- La nostra amica è stata licenziata in tronco.
  Our friend was discharged without notice.

- Il presidente lo licenziò con parole gentili.
  The president dismissed him with kind words.

- L'istituto ha licenziato duecento ragazzi l'anno scorso.
  The school graduated two hundred boys last year.

licenziarsi   to give up one's job, resign

- Mi licenzierò alla fine di febbraio.
  I'll resign at the end of February.

limitare   to limit, restrict, surround, bound

- Dobbiamo limitare il numero dei candidati (/le spese/la velocità).
  We must limit the number of the candidates (/expenditures/our speed).

- La vista è limitata da quell'edificio.
  The view is restricted by that building.

- Hanno limitato l'orto con una siepe.
  They surrounded their vegetable garden with a hedge.

■   Una catena di montagne limita la regione a nord.
A mountain range bounds the region to the north.

limitarsi a qco   to limit oneself to sth

■   Pietro deve limitarsi a una caramella (/due bicchieri di vino) al giorno.
Peter has to limit himself to one candy (/two glasses of wine) a day.

limitarsi nel/nello/nelli + *inf*   to limit oneself to + *ger*

■   Devo limitarmi nel fumare (/nello spendere/nel mangiare/nel bere).
I must limit my smoking (/spending/eating/drinking).

litigare (con qc per qco)   to fight, quarrel (with sb over sth)

■   Antonio ha litigato con tutti.
Anthony fought with everybody.

■   Hanno litigato per niente.
They quarreled over nothing.

lottare contro qco   to fight against sth, battle with/against sth, struggle with sb/sth; to strive

■   Vogliono lottare contro la povertà (/la criminalità).
They want to fight against poverty (/crime).

■   Cercammo di lottare contro il sonno, ma ci addormentammo.
We tried to fight it off, but we fell asleep.

■   Abbiamo lottato contro le onde.
We battled against the waves.

■   I loro genitori hanno dovuto lottare contro le avversità.
Their parents had to struggle with adversity.

■   È inutile lottare contro il destino.
It is useless to strive against fate.

lottare per qco   to fight, struggle, strive for sth

■   Lottarono per l'indipendenza del loro paese (/un avvenire migliore).
They struggled for the independence of their country (/a better future).

■   Lottavamo per la pace (/la supremazia).
We were striving for peace (/supremacy).

lottare per + *inf*   to struggle to + *inf*

■   Lottavano per sopravvivere.
They were struggling to survive.

M

maledire   to curse

- Luisa maledì il giorno in cui lo aveva conosciuto (/era nato).
  Louise cursed the day she had met him (/he was born).

- Maledissi la sorte.
  I cursed my fate.

mancare   (auxiliary *avere* with verbs meaning "miss" in the sense of "not to hit/get"; otherwise *essere*) to miss, lack; to be missing; to not have; to need; to die

- Mancano le mie scarpe (/cento dollari).
  My shoes (/A hundred dollars) are missing.

- L'attaccante ha mancato il gol.
  The forward missed the goal.

- Hai mancato il bersaglio (/un'ottima occasione).
  You missed the target (/a very good opportunity).

- Hai mancato il treno (/l'autobus) delle dieci.
  You missed the ten-o'clock train (/bus).

- Sul documento mancano la data e la firma.
  The date and signature are missing on the document.

- Gli mancano i suoi amici.
  He misses his friends.

- Gli manca la ragione.
  He lacks reason.

- Ci manca il tempo (/il coraggio) di farlo.
  We lack the time (/the courage) to do it.

- Tutti i piatti mancavano di sale.
  All the dishes needed salt.

- Mi manca un cappotto pesante.
  I need a heavy coat.

- Questa proprio ci mancava!
  That was the last straw!

- Mi manca l'energia (/la pazienza) per farlo. Mi mancano i mezzi per farlo.
  I don't have the energy (/the patience) to do it. I don't have the means to do it.

- Gli mancarono le forze.
  He felt his strength failing.

- È mancata la corrente.
  There was a power failure.

- Il loro padre mancò all'improvviso.
Their father died suddenly.

- Mancano da casa (/dall'Italia/dal loro paese/da qui) da molti anni.
They have been away from home (/Italy/their village/here) for many years.

non mancare di + *inf*   (auxiliary *avere*) not to fail to + *inf*

- Non mancherò di ringraziarli.
I won't fail to thank them.

- Non ho mai mancato di far fronte ai miei impegni (/mantenere la parola).
I've never failed to face my responsibilities (/keep my word).

mancare poco che + *subj*   (auxiliary *essere*) nearly/almost + *verb*

- Mancò poco che cadessi.
I nearly fell.

- Mancò poco che venissero alle mani.
They almost came to blows.

mancare poco a   to be almost

- Mancava poco alla fine dell'inverno (/dell'anno accademico) quando decisero di andare a sciare per l'ultima volta.
It was almost the end of winter (/the academic year) when they decided to go skiing for the last time.

- Credo che manchi poco alla fine del primo atto.
I think the first act is almost finished.

mancare + *length of time* **+ a qco**   to be + *length of time* + until sth

- Mancano solo pochi giorni a Pasqua.
It is only a few days to Easter.

- Mancano dieci minuti alle otto.
It's ten to eight.

mandare qc/qco   to send sb/sth (in/off/out/down/back); to banish; to broadcast

- Le mandarono una lettera (/un pacchetto/gli auguri di Natale/due fax).
They sent her a letter (/a package/their Christmas greetings/two faxes).

- Li abbiamo mandati a casa (/a letto/a scuola/al cinema/alla mostra).
We sent them home (/to bed/to school/to the movie theater/to the exhibit).

- Il signor Graziani ha già mandato le sue dimissioni.
Mr. Graziani has already sent in his resignation.

- La merce va mandata per ferrovia, non per via aerea.
The merchandise must be sent by rail, not by air.

- Fu mandato ambasciatore a Washington.
He was sent as ambassador to Washington.

- La mamma lo manda sempre in ordine e ben vestito.
  His mother always sends him off neat and well dressed.

- L'hanno mandato via.
  They sent him away (or They fired him).

- Tu devi mandarlo indietro.
  You must send it back.

- Ti manderò giù la mia segretaria.
  I'll send my secretary down to you.

- Ordinate al bar (di mandare su) dell'acqua minerale.
  Ask the bar to send up some mineral water.

- L'hanno mandata fuori.
  They sent her out.

- La signora Ferrari non glielo mandò a dire. *(idiomatic)*
  Mrs. Ferrari told him so to his face.

- Manda un bacio alla nonna.
  Blow Grandma a kiss.

mandare qc a + *inf*   to send sb to + *inf*

- L'hanno mandata a informarsi della mia salute (/comprare il giornale/fare una commissione/studiare in Svizzera).
  They sent her to inquire about my health (/to buy the newspaper/on an errand/to study in Switzerland).

- Potrebbe mandarmi qualcuno a dare un'occhiata alla mia tv?
  Could you send somebody around to have a look at my TV?

mandare a chiamare qc   to send for sb

- Hanno mandato a chiamare il dottore (/la polizia).
  They sent for the doctor (/the police).

mandare a prendere qco   to send for sth

- Mandate a prendere quattro caffè (/dei panini).
  Send for four coffees (/some sandwiches).

mandare in onda   to broadcast

- Lo spettacolo è stato mandato in onda alle dieci.
  The show was broadcast at ten o'clock.

maneggiare   to handle; to wield

- Quell'artista sa maneggiare il pennello (/lo scalpello) molto bene.
  That artist can handle his brush (/chisel) skillfully.

- Il chirurgo maneggiava il bisturi con mano sicura.
  The surgeon handled the scalpel with a steady hand.

- Quello scrittore sa maneggiare la penna.
  That writer knows how to wield his pen.

- Suo marito è un tipo difficile da maneggiare.
  Her husband is a difficult person to deal with.

- Questo registratore è facile da maneggiare.
  This tape recorder is easy to use.

mangiare   to eat (away/into/out/up); to feed

- Loro non mangiano mai pesce (/carne/verdura).
  They never eat fish (/meat/vegetables).

- Marco mangia in fretta (/adagio/molto/poco/con appetito/come un lupo).
  Mark eats fast (/slowly/a lot/little/heartily/like a horse).

- Non è ancora ora di mangiare.
  It isn't time to eat yet.

- In questo ristorante si può mangiare alla carta o a prezzo fisso.
  In this restaurant one can eat à la carte or at a fixed price.

- Il giovedì sera mangiano sempre fuori (/al ristorante).
  Thursday nights they always eat out (/at the restaurant).

- L'acido (/La ruggine) ha mangiato il metallo.
  Acid (/Rust) has eaten into the metal.

- Hai dato da mangiare ai bambini (/al gatto)?
  Did you feed the children (/cat)?

- Ti mangio la pedina (/la regina). (*chess*)
  I take your pawn (/queen).

  mangiarsi   to eat up; to squander; to bite (one's fingernails)

  - Si è mangiato tutta la minestra.
    He ate up all the soup.

  - Si è mangiato tutti i soldi che aveva.
    He squandered all the money he had.

  - Dovresti smettere di mangiarti le unghie.
    You should stop biting your nails.

manifestare   to manifest; to show; to reveal; to express; to demonstrate

- Il suo sguardo manifestava tristezza (/il suo proposito/il suo segreto).
  His eyes revealed sadness (/his purpose/his secret).

- La signora Guglielmi manifestò la sua volontà.
  Mrs. Guglielmi expressed her will.

- I lavoratori manifestarono contro i licenziamenti in massa.
  The workers demonstrated against the mass layoffs.

manomettere   to tamper with; to open illegally

■ Ho paura che il pacco (/il documento) sia stato manomesso.
I am afraid the parcel (/the document) has been tampered with.

■ Qualcuno ha manomesso i sigilli della lettera.
Somebody broke the seals of the letter.

mantenere   to maintain; to support; to keep

■ Io mantengo la mia opinione.
I maintain my opinion.

■ Deve mantenere la moglie e due figli.
He has a wife and two children to support.

■ Quell'insegnante non sa mantenere la disciplina.
That teacher does not know how to maintain discipline.

■ Tu non hai mantenuto la parola (/il giuramento)
You did not keep your word (/oath).

■ Lo hanno mantenuto in vita.
They kept him alive.

■ Dovreste mantenere i rapporti con loro.
You should keep up relations with them.

 mantenersi   to last; to earn one's living

 ■ Il bel tempo non si manterrà a lungo.
 The good weather will not last long.

 ■ Nostro figlio lavora molto per mantenersi.
 Our son works hard to earn his living.

marcare   to mark; to brand; to score; to accentuate

■ Tutti i prodotti sono stati marcati con il marchio della ditta.
All the products were marked with the company seal.

■ Il giocatore marcava l'avversario.
The player marked (or guarded) his opponent.

■ Non avevano ancora marcato tutto il loro bestiame.
They had not yet branded all their cattle.

■ Il calciatore argentino ha marcato un gol (/due volte).
The Argentinian soccer player scored a goal (/twice).

■ Devi marcare di più quelle linee.
You must accentuate those lines.

marciare   to march; to go

■ Marciarono sul nemico (/sulla capitale).
They marched on the enemy (/the capital).

- I dimostranti marciavano in colonna.
  The demonstrators were marching in rows.

- Gli studenti entrarono (/uscirono) marciando.
  The students marched in (/out).

- Credo che il treno marci a cento chilometri all'ora.
  I believe the train is going at a hundred kilometers an hour.

- Il gruppo marciava verso il confine, quando si sentì uno sparo.
  The group was going toward the border when a shot was heard.

mascherare   to mask, disguise; to hide

- Quell'uomo ha saputo mascherare molto bene i suoi veri sentimenti.
  That man managed to mask (or disguise) his true feelings very well.

- L'ospite era mascherato da donna.
  The host was disguised as a woman.

- Hanno mascherato la trappoca con dei rami.
  They hid the trap with some branches.

  mascherarsi   to dress up as, disguise oneself as; to hide

  - Mio figlio si è mascherato da pirata.
    My son dressed up as a pirate.

  - Il ladro si mascherò il viso con una calza.
    The thief hid his face with a stocking.

masticare   to chew; to mutter

- Mastica bene quella carne.
  Chew that meat well.

- Masticano sempre il chewing gum (/il tabacco).
  They are always chewing gum (/tobacco).

maturare   to ripen; to mature; to mellow; to come to a head

- Quando maturano le olive?
  When do olives ripen?

- I tempi per un cambiamento politico stanno maturando.
  The times are ripening for a political change.

- Il vino viene lasciato a maturare.
  Wine is left to mellow.

- Dobbiamo aspettare che la situazione maturi.
  We must wait for the situation to come to a head.

menare   to lead; to take

- Sai dove mena quella via? —Mena alla stazione.
  Do you know where that street leads? —It leads to the station.

- Lo menano alla rovina.
  They are leading him to ruin.

- Sono sempre pronti a menar le mani.
  They are always ready to fight.

- Dove ci meni?
  Where are you taking us?

- Non menare il can per l'aia. (*idiom*)
  Don't beat around the bush. (idiom)

mentire   to (tell a) lie

- Elvira è incapace di (/incline a) mentire.
  Elvira can't (/is inclined to) lie.

- Perché dovrei mentirle, signor Francioni?
  Why should I lie to you, Mr. Francioni?

- Tu hai mentito sapendo di mentire.
  You told a deliberate lie.

menzionare   to mention

- Non hanno nemmeno menzionato il tuo nome in quell'articolo.
  They didn't even mention your name in that article.

- Il professore ha menzionato quello scrittore (/quello studio) molte volte.
  Our professor has mentioned that writer (/study) many times.

- Non avresti dovuto menzionarlo.
  You shouldn't have mentioned it.

meravigliare   to surprise

- Questo non mi meraviglia.
  This does not surprise me.

- Ti meraviglia il fatto che si siano sposati?
  Are you surprised by the fact that they got married?

  meravigliarsi di qc/qco   to be surprised at sb, amazed at sth

  - Si meravigliava del comportamento del fratello.
    She was surprised at her brother's behavior.

  - Mi meraviglio del tuo coraggio (/del tuo successo).
    I am amazed at your courage (/success).

  - Non c'è da meravigliarsi che si sia comportata così (/sia andata con lui).
    No wonder she behaved like that (/went with him).

meritare   to deserve sth; to earn; to be worthwhile; to need

- Gualtiero merita il primo premio (/una ricompensa).
  Walter deserves the first prize (/a reward).

■ L'avvenimento gli meritò grande fama.
The event earned him great fame.

■ È questo che gli meritò la promozione.
This is what earned him his promotion.

■ Questo non merita conto.
This is not worthwhile.

■ La notizia merita conferma.
The news item needs confirmation.

meritare di + *inf*   to deserve to + *inf*

■ La squadra italiana di calcio meritava di vincere.
The Italian soccer team deserved to win.

■ Non merita di essere trattato così (/andare in prigione).
He does not deserve to be treated like that (/to be sent to prison).

meritare che + *subj*   to deserve + *inf;* to be worth + *ger*

■ Merita che lo si inviti.
He deserves to be invited.

■ Non merita che se ne parli.
It isn't worth talking about.

meritarsi   to deserve

■ Quello studente si merita un premio (/un castigo).
That student deserves a prize (/a punishment).

meritarselo   to thoroughly deserve it; to serve sb right

■ Te lo sei meritato.
You thoroughly deserved it (or It served you right).

mescolare   to mix; to mingle; to shuffle

■ Avevo già mescolato i vari ingredienti (/i colori/l'insalata).
I had already mixed the various ingredients (/the colors/the salad).

■ Gli piace mescolare vari stili (/prosa e poesia).
He likes to mingle different styles (/prose and poetry).

■ Le carte non sono state mescolate.
The cards haven't been shuffled.

mescolarsi a/fra qc   to mingle with sb

■ La padrona di casa si mescolò agli ospiti.
The hostess mingled with her guests.

■ Gli piaceva mescolarsi fra la folla.
He liked to mingle with the crowd.

mettere qco (su/a/in)   to put, place (on/at/in); to stick; to hang; to make; to cut

- Guarda dove metti i piedi!
  Look where you put your feet!

- Ho messo la bottiglia sul tavolo (/il libro sulla scrivania).
  I put the bottle on the table (/the book on the desk).

- L'ho messo nell'armadietto (/nel cassetto/nella valigia/in cucina).
  I have put it in the cabinet (/drawer/suitcase/kitchen).

- Abbiamo messo tutto quello che avevamo sul numero 5 (/su quel cavallo).
  We put (bet) everything we had on number 5 (/that horse).

- Pensano di mettere una nuova tassa sui liquori.
  They are planning to place a new tax on liquor.

- Ha già messo il bambino a letto, signora Carlini?
  Have you already put the baby to bed, Mrs. Carlini?

- Hai messo i numeri in colonna (/gli scolari in fila/la museruola al cane/le valigie
  nel ripostiglio/il sale nella minestra/una toppa ai tuoi jeans)?
  *Have you put the numbers in columns (/the schoolboys in line/the muzzle on the
  dog/the suitcases in the storage room/salt in the soup/a patch on your jeans)?*

- Devono mettere una nuova conduttura per l'acqua.
  They must put in a new water pipe.

- Non mettere le dita (/il dito) in bocca (/nel naso).
  Don't stick your fingers (/finger) in your mouth (/up your nose).

- Abbiamo messo il quadro alla parete (/le tende alle finestre).
  We have hung the picture on the wall (/curtains on the windows).

- Questo odore mette fame. Il sale mette sete. Questa noiosa conferenza mette
  sonno. L'idea di (non) vederli mi mette gioia (/tristezza).
  *This smell makes you hungry. Salt makes you thirsty. This boring lecture makes
  you sleepy. The idea of (not) seeing them makes me (un)happy.*

- La sua bambina ha già messo due denti.
  Her little girl has already cut two teeth.

mettere (il caso) che + *subj*   to suppose (that), assume (that)

- Mettiamo che io vada via (/che piova).
  Suppose I leave (/it rains).

- Mettiamo il caso che il treno non arrivi (/che lui abbia ragione).
  Let's assume that the train does not arrive (/he is right).

metterci   to take (time)

- Ci ha messo tre ore a finire il compito.
  It took him three hours to finish his homework.

mettersi   to place, put oneself; to put on; to get into; to turn fine (nasty); to take a turn for; to set to do sth

- Si mise vicino al suo ragazzo.
  She placed herself near her boyfriend.

- Mettiti nei miei panni.
  Put yourself in my shoes (or in my place).

- Si è messa in abito da sera (/costume da bagno).
  She put on an evening dress (/bathing suit).

- Perché non ti metti il cappello (/la giacca/gli stivali)?
  Why don't you put on your hat (/jacket/boots)?

- Si è messo in una situazione imbarazzante (/nei pasticci).
  He has gotten into an awkward position (/trouble).

- Il tempo si mette al bello (/al brutto).
  The weather is turning nice (/nasty).

- La situazione si mette male (/bene).
  The situation is taking a turn for the worse (/good).

- Mettiti a sedere.
  Sit down.

- Mettetevi a tavola.
  Sit down at the table.

mettersi a + *inf*   to begin, start + *inf*

- Si misero a lavorare (/studiare/leggere).
  They started to work (/study/read).

- Si mise a piovere.
  It began to rain.

mettersi in mente di + *inf*   to get it into one's head + *inf*

- Il suo fidanzato si mise in mente che la colpa fosse mia.
  Her fiancé got it into his head that it was my fault.

- Lucia si è messa in mente di farlo.
  Lucy got it into her head to do it.

migliorare   to improve; to increase; to make progress; to better

- Le condizioni di quel paziente sono molto migliorate.
  The condition of that patient has greatly improved.

- Il gusto migliora dopo qualche giorno.
  The taste improves after a few days.

- Saranno migliorate le condizioni di lavoro.
  Work conditions will be improved.

- I salari vanno migliorati.
  Salaries must be increased.

- Quei miei due studenti sono migliorati.
  Those two students of mine have made progress.

- Bisogna migliorare la propria posizione.
  One must better one's position.

minacciare   to threaten

- Il mancato accordo minacciava le trattative per la pace.
  The lack of an agreement was threatening the peace negotiations.

minacciare qc con qco   to threaten sb with sth

- Lo minacciarono con un coltello.
  They threatened him with a knife.

minacciare di + *inf*   to threaten to + *inf*

- L'uomo minacciò di ucciderci (/tenerci in ostaggio/denunciarci).
  The man threatened to kill us (/keep us as hostages/denounce us).

- La malattia minaccia di diffondersi.
  The disease threatens to spread.

misurare   to measure, gauge; to estimate; to fit for; to try; to limit

- Dovresti misurare la distanza (/l'intensità del suono).
  You should measure the distance (/the intensity of the sound).

- Dobbiamo misurare le difficoltà (/gli ostacoli/la gravità della situazione).
  We must estimate the difficulties (/obstacles/gravity of the situation).

- La sarta mi ha misurato il cappotto.
  The dressmaker fitted me for the coat.

- Quell'atleta deve misurare le sue forze.
  That athlete must try his strength.

- Dobbiamo cercare di misurare le spese.
  We must try to limit our expenses.

- Hai misurato la temperatura al bambino?
  Did you take the child's temperature?

- Questa stanza misura tre metri per cinque.
  This room is three meters by five.

misurarsi qco/con qc   to try sth on; to compete (with sb)

- Ti sei misurato quelle scarpe?
  Did you try those shoes on?

- La squadra italiana si misurerà con quella americana.
  The Italian team will compete with the American one.

montare   to mount; to rise, to ride; to climb; to assemble

- Ho fatto montare il mio smeraldo.
  I had my emerald mounted.

- Quando monta la marea?
  When does the tide rise?

- L'acqua è montata durante la notte.
  The water has risen overnight.

- Il principe (/Il fantino) montava un cavallo bianco.
  The prince (/jockey) was riding a white horse.

- Abbiamo montato cinquecento scalini.
  We climbed five hundred steps.

- Devono ancora montare la macchina (/il trenino per mio figlio).
  They still have to assemble the machine (/the little train for my son).

- Il trionfo gli ha montato la testa (*or* Il trionfo lo ha montato).
  Success has gone to his head.

- Perché non fai montare la fotografia di tua madre (/quel dipinto)?
  Why don't you have your mother's picture (/that painting) framed?

montare su/a/in qco   to mount (on); to get (/on/into) sth; to whip

- Sofia montò a cavallo e sparì nel bosco.
  Sophia mounted her horse and disappeared into the woods.

- Se non ci arrivi, monta su una sedia.
  If you cannot reach up there, get on a chair.

- Monta in bicicletta (/treno/automobile) e vai.
  Get on your bike (/on the train/into your car) and go.

- Non hai ancora montato la panna (/il bianco d'uovo)?
  Haven't you whipped the cream (/the egg white) yet?

- Montare in vettura!
  All aboard!

montarsi   to get swell-headed

- Si è montata per tutti i complimenti che ha ricevuto.
  She has gotten swell-headed because of all the compliments she received.

mordere   to bite (into); to hold; to corrode

- La bambina morse la pera (/un pezzo di pane).
  The little girl bit into a pear (/a piece of bread).

- Il cane del signor Valenti l'ha morsa di nuovo. Le ha morso la gamba.
  Mr. Valenti's dog has bitten her again. He has bitten her on the leg.

mordersi   to bite (one's tongue, lips, etc.); to kick oneself

- Appena detto questo, si sarebbe morsa le labbra (/la lingua).
  As soon as she said it, she could have bitten her lips (/her tongue).

morire (di/in/da)   (auxiliary *essere*) to die (off)/(in/of); to end

■ Credono che sia morto a casa (/in mare).
They believe he died at home (/at sea).

■ È morto di inedia (/sete/paura/vecchiaia).
He died of starvation (/thirst/fright/old age).

■ Sua moglie è morta di parto.
His wife died in childbirth.

■ Muoiono come mosche.
They die like flies.

■ Muoio di noia (/stanchezza)
I'm bored to death (/dead tired).

■ Morirono in una rissa (/in esilio/in carcere/in miseria/in un incidente).
They died in a brawl (/in exile/in jail/in poverty/in an accident).

■ Morì ammazzato (/impiccato).
He was killed (/hanged).

■ Il freddo fa morire le rose.
The cold weather kills the roses.

morire dalla voglia (dal desiderio) di + *inf*   to be longing/dying to + *inf*

■ Muoio dalla voglia di ballare (/bere/fumare un sigaretta/rivederti).
I am longing (dying) to dance (/drink/smoke a cigarette/see you again).

morire per + *inf*   to die (in order) to + *inf*

■ Sono morti per difendere la patria.
They died to defend their country.

mormorare   to murmur; to be rumored; to speak ill of sb; to mutter; to grumble

■ La vecchia mormorò una preghiera.
The old woman murmured a prayer.

■ Si mormora che abbia accettato una grossa tangente.
It is rumored that he accepted a large kickback.

■ Si mormora molto sul conto di quell'attore.
There is a lot of talk about that actor.

■ La gente mormora alle tue spalle.
People speak ill of you behind your back.

■ Lo studente mormorò qualcosa fra i denti.
The student muttered something between his teeth.

■ Tutti mormoravano contro il decreto del governo.
Everyone was grumbling about the government decree.

mostrare qco a qc   to show sb sth; to point out

■ Gli ho mostrato la strada (/la patente/come funziona la macchina).
I showed him the way (/my driver's license/how the machine works).

■ L'avvocato difensore mostrò l'infondatezza dell'accusa.
The counsel for the defense showed that the accusation was baseless.

mostrare di + *inf*   to show; to be evident (that); to pretend

■ La loro figlia mostrò di ignorare i fatti (/non accorgersi di quello che stava succedendo/avere poco giudizio).
Their daughter showed she did not know the facts (/did not notice what was happening/had little judgment).

■ Perché mostri di non curartene?
Why do you pretend not to care?

mostrarsi   to show oneself; to seem; to prove; to appear

■ Si mostrò molto ingiusto (/crudele/egoista/degno del premio).
He showed himself to be unfair (/cruel/selfish/worthy of the award).

■ Si mostrò soddisfatto (/entusiasta/felice).
He showed his satisfaction (/enthusiasm/happiness).

■ Quell'attrice non si mostra più in pubblico.
That actress no longer appears in public.

muovere   to move; to advance on; to start; to stretch

■ Il bambino continuò a muovere le mani (/i piedi/le braccia/gli occhi).
The little boy kept moving his hands (/feet/arms/eyes).

■ Tocca a te muovere. (*chess/checkers*)
It is your turn to move.

■ Le truppe nemiche muovono verso la capitale.
The enemy troops are advancing on the capital.

■ Loro muovono da posizioni opposte.
They start from opposite positions.

■ Devo muovere le gambe.
I have to stretch my legs.

■ Lui non mosse un dito per aiutarli. (*fig*)
He did not lift a finger to help them. (fig)

■ Il bambino cominciava a muovere i primi passi.
The toddler was starting to take his first steps.

muoversi   to move, hurry up; to stir; to rise against

■ Nessuno si muova.
Nobody move.

■ La terra si muove attorno al sole.
The earth moves around the sun.

■ L'ammalato non poteva muoversi dal letto.
The sick man could not move from his bed.

■   Si mossero a pietà (/a compassione).
They were moved to pity (/compassion).

■   Il mulo non si mosse.
The mule did not budge.

■   Muoviti!
Hurry up!

■   Non si muoveva una foglia.
Not a leaf was stirring.

■   I contadini si mossero contro il proprietario terriero.
The peasants rose up against the landowner.

mutare (in)   to change; to molt

■   Fareste meglio a mutare registro *or* tono (/opinione/partito/argomento).
You'd better change your tone of voice (/mind/party/subject).

■   In quel paese mutavano governo molto spesso.
They changed governments so often in that country.

■   Sono mutati in meglio (/peggio).
They have changed for the better (/worse).

■   E l'acqua fu mutata in vino.
And water was changed into wine.

■   I rettili mutano la pelle (/Gli uccelli mutano le penne).
Reptiles molt their skin (/Birds molt their feathers).

mutarsi   to change

■   Il brutto anatroccolo si mutò in un cigno (/La pioggia si mutò in neve).
The ugly duckling changed into a swan (/The rain changed into snow).

N

1. nascere (auxiliary *essere*) to be born; to be hatched; to have one's source

- Mia figlia è nata il 29 aprile.
  My daughter was born on April 29.

- Credi proprio che Grazia sia nata ieri? (*fig*)
  Do you really think that Grace was born yesterday? (fig)

- È nato povero (/ricco/nobile/cieco/muto/sordo).
  He was born poor (/rich/noble/blind/mute/deaf).

- Siamo nati per soffrire.
  We were born to suffer.

- Questi quattro pulcini sono appena nati.
  These four chicks are newly hatched.

- Il Mississippi nasce nel (nello stato del) Minnesota.
  The Mississippi River has its source in Minnesota.

nascere a/in (+ *art*) to be born in

- La tua sorellina è nata a Venezia (/in Italia/negli Stati Uniti)?
  Was your little sister born in Venice (/Italy/the United States)?

- Dante nacque nel 1265 e morì nel 1321.
  Dante was born in 1265 and died in 1321.

- La sorella di Alessandra è nata in settembre.
  Alexandra's sister was born in September.

nascere da to be born from

- Giovanna è nata da padre italiano e madre norvegese.
  Joan was born of an Italian father and a Norwegian mother.

nascere per qco to be cut out for sth

- Non è nato per questo mestiere (/questo tipo di vita/queste cose).
  He isn't cut out for this job (/this kind of life/these things).

2. nascere to rise; to sprout; to start to grow

- Il sole nasce a est (/alle cinque/presto/tardi).
  The sun rises in the east (/at five/early/late).

- Nascono come funghi.
  They sprout like mushrooms.

- Questi fiori nascono tra la neve.
  These flowers grow in the snow.

far nascere qco　to bring sth about/forth; to give (an idea)

- Questo le fece nascere l'idea di aprire una scuola di lingue.
  This gave her the idea of opening a language school.

nascondere　to hide, conceal

- Non si sa dove il ladro (/il loro cane) abbia nascosto il malloppo (l'osso).
  No one knows where the thief (/their dog) hid the loot (/the bone).

- È inutile che tu cerchi di nascondere quello che senti (/il tuo odio).
  It is useless for you to try to hide the way you feel (/your hatred).

nascondersi　to hide oneself

- L'uccellino si nascondeva fra i rami.
  The little bird was hiding in the branches.

- Il bambino si nascose dietro di lei (/dietro la porta/in cucina).
  The child hid behind her (/behind the door/in the kitchen).

- I bambini giocavano a nascondersi.
  The children were playing hide-and-seek.

navigare　to sail (against /along/at/down/on); to be at sea

- Il padre di Anna ha navigato tanti anni fa (/l'oceano/i mari del sud).
  Ann's father sailed many years ago (/the ocean/the southern seas).

- Navigammo lungo la costa (/lungo il fiume/controvento).
  We sailed along the coast (/down the river/against the wind).

- Mio zio era un vecchio lupo di mare, che navigava da anni.
  My uncle was an old salt, who had been at sea for years.

- Credo che navighino in cattive acque. (*fig*)
  I think they are hard up. (fig)

negare　to deny; to refuse

- Gli fu negata la grazia.
  His petition for mercy was denied.

- Non puoi negare la realtà (/questa possibilità).
  You cannot deny reality (/this possibility).

- Non potete negare a un cittadino i suoi diritti (/la libertà).
  You cannot deny a citizen his rights (/freedom).

- I genitori non le hanno mai negato nulla.
  Her parents have never refused her anything.

negare di + *inf*　to deny + *ger*

- Perché hai negato di averlo visto (/aver firmato/averlo detto)?
  Why did you deny having seen him (/having signed/having said it)?

negarsi qco   to deny oneself sth

- Non posso negarmi il piacere di una sigaretta.
  I cannot deny myself the pleasure of a cigarette.

notare   to note, make a note of; to write down; to notice; to mind; to mark

- Ho notato il loro nome e il loro numero di telefono.
  I made a note of their name and telephone number.

- Il vigile notò il numero di targa.
  The traffic police wrote down the license plate number.

- Hai notato la sua espressione (/come era stanca Angela)?
  Did you notice her expression (/how tired Angela was)?

- Non mi è antipatica, nota bene, ma preferirei che non venisse con noi.
  I don't find her unpleasant, mind you, but I would rather she not come with us.

- Ho notato in rosso gli errori.
  I marked the mistakes in red.

  far notare qco a qc   to point out sth to sb

  - Devo farle notare, signor Galli, che questo non era l'accordo.
    I have to point out to you, Mr. Galli, that this wasn't the agreement.

  farsi notare   to draw attention; to distinguish oneself

  - Vestita così si farà notare da tutti.
    Dressed that way, she'll draw everybody's attention.

nuocere a qc/qco   to harm sb/sth; to injure sb/sth; to damage

- È un vizio che nuoce alla salute.
  It's a habit that harms one's health.

- Avevo paura che il brutto tempo nuocesse a queste piante.
  I was afraid the bad weather would damage these plants.

- Credo che l'affare delle tangenti abbia nuociuto alla sua carriera politica
  (/al suo prestigio).
  I think the kickback affair damaged his political career (/prestige).

nutrire qc/qco   to feed sb/sth; to nourish

- Il signor Traversa deve nutrire una numerosa famiglia.
  Mr. Traversa has a large family to feed.

- L'olio nutriva le fiamme, rendendo più difficile l'opera dei pompieri.
  The oil fed the flames, making the firefighters' job more difficult.

- Questa terra ha bisogno di essere nutrita con concime.
  This soil needs to be nourished with manure.

- Non nutrire brutti pensieri (/rancore contro di lui/sospetti)!
  Don't harbor ugly thoughts (/a grudge against him/suspicions)!

nutrirsi   to feed on, live on

- Le mucche si nutrono di erba.
  Cows feed on grass.

- Si nutrono di frutta e verdura.
  They live on fruit and vegetables.

- Tu ti nutri di libri gialli! (*fig*)
  You feed on mystery stories! (fig)

O

obbligare qc a + *inf* to force sb to + *inf;* to require; to confine

- Il cattivo tempo ci obbligò a restare là un altro giorno.
  The bad weather forced us to stay there an extra day.
- La legge obbliga il cittadino a pagare le tasse.
  The law requires citizens to pay taxes.
- La malattia lo obbliga a stare a letto.
  His disease confines him to bed.

obbligare qc/qco a + *inf* to force sb/sth

- Il gas lacrimogeno li obbligò a uscire da dove si erano nascosti.
  The tear gas forced them out of their hiding place.

occorrere (auxiliary *essere*) to be necessary

- Che cosa le occorre, signor Bucci?
  What do you need, Mr. Bucci?
- A tuo figlio occorre una buona macchina (/aiuto/un computer/del denaro).
  Your son needs a good car (/help/a computer/some money).
- Non occorre, grazie.
  It isn't necessary, thank you.

occorrere che + *subj* to be necessary (to) + *inf*

- Non occorre che tu lo faccia (/venga/gli telefoni) immediatamente.
  You don't need to do it (/come/call him) right away.
- Non occorreva che lo aspettassimo.
  We didn't need to wait for him.

occorrere + *inf* to be necessary + *inf*

- Occorre parlare al medico (/ascoltare la radio/aprire la finestra).
  It is necessary to talk to the doctor (/listen to the radio/open the window).

occupare to occupy; to take up; to spend (time); to hold, be busy; to employ

- I ferrovieri (/Gli studenti) hanno occupato la stazione (/la scuola).
  The railway workers (/students) have occupied the station (/school).
- Questo tavolo occupa troppo posto.
  This table takes up too much room.
- Tutti i posti erano occupati.
  All the seats were taken.
- Molti dubbi occupavano la mente della mamma.
  Mother's mind was full of doubts.

■ Una mia amica occupa il tempo libero facendo la volontaria in un ospedale.
   A friend of mine spends her free time doing volunteer work in a hospital.

■ Sono molti anni che mio cognato occupa questo posto (/quella carica).
   My brother-in-law has held this job (/that office) for many years.

■ Il loro telefono era sempre occupato.
   Their phone was always busy.

■ Quella fabbrica occupa duecento operai.
   That factory employs two hundred workers.

   occuparsi di   to occupy oneself with; to look after; to see to; to get involved; to
   mind

   ■ Io mi occupo di giardinaggio (/opere di carità)
      I occupy myself with gardening (/charities).

   ■ Puoi occuparti dei bambini domani?
      Can you look after the children tomorrow?

   ■ Mi occuperò io di questo. Tu non occupartene.
      I'll see to this matter. Don't you get involved.

   ■ Si occupi dei fatti suoi, signor Gatti.
      Mind your own business, Mr. Gatti.

odiare   to hate; to loathe; to detest

■ Lo odiano. Lo odiano a morte.
   They hate him. They loathe him.

■ Si è fatta odiare.
   She made herself hated (i.e., *She made everyone hate her*).

   odiarsi   to hate oneself, each other/one another

   ■ Il signor Sassoli si odiò per averlo fatto.
      Mr. Sassoli hated himself for doing so.

   ■ Penso che i due cugini si odino.
      I think the two cousins hate each other.

odorare   to smell; to scent

■ Il nonno sta odorando le rose in giardino.
   Grandfather is smelling the roses in the garden.

■ Il lupo aveva odorato la preda.
   The wolf had scented its prey.

   odorare di qco   to smell of sth

   ■ La salsa odora di basilico.
      The sauce smells of basil.

■   Questa faccenda odora d'imbroglio. (*fig*)
This matter smells fishy to me. (fig)

offendere   to offend, insult

■   Mi dispiace, non intendevo offenderti.
I'm sorry. I didn't mean to offend you.

■   Hai offeso la sua memoria.
You insulted his memory.

offendersi   to be offended, take offense

■   Suo marito si è offeso per le tue osservazioni.
Her husband was offended by your remarks.

■   Si è offesa perché non l'hanno invitata alla festa (/non glielo hanno detto).
She took offense because they did not invite her to the party (/tell her).

offrire   to offer; to sponsor; to tender/bid

■   Gli offrirono una tazza di caffè (/un bicchiere di vino/un whiskey/aiuto).
They offered him a cup of coffee (/a glass of wine/a whiskey/help).

■   Perché non hai offerto a loro qualcosa da mangiare (/bere)?
Why didn't you offer them something to eat (/drink)?

■   Le hanno offerto un nuovo contratto (/una splendida occasione).
She was offered a new contract (/a splendid opportunity).

■   Ti posso offrire ospitalità per questa notte.
I can put you up for the night.

■   Questo programma è offerto dalla ditta Gemelli.
This program is sponsored by the Gemelli company.

■   Quanto offre per questo tavolo Chippendale?
How much do you bid for this Chippendale table?

offrirsi   to come up

■   Ogni volta che se ne offre l'occasione, Laura fa un viaggio.
Whenever the occasion comes up, Laura takes a trip.

offrirsi di + *inf*   to offer (oneself) to + *inf*

■   Ci siamo offerti di aiutarla (/portarla al cinema/prestarle la macchina).
We offered to help her (/take her to the movies/lend her our car).

onorare   to honor; to fulfill

■   Onora il padre e la madre (/la memoria dei caduti).
Honor thy father and thy mother (/the memory of the fallen).

■   Si devono onorare i propri obblighi.
One must fulfill one's obligations.

operare   to work, operate; to perform, carry out; to act

- Quel diuretico (/medicinale) opera velocemente.
  That diuretic (/drug) works rapidly.

- Il tempo ha operato cambiamenti radicali in lui.
  Time worked radical changes in him.

- L'hanno operato a caldo (/freddo).
  They operated on him in the acute stage (/between attacks).

- Operarono una grande riforma (/una ritirata).
  They carried out a great reform (/a withdrawal).

- Non credo che operino nel nostro interesse.
  I don't think they are acting in our interest.

  operarsi   to undergo surgery; to occur

  - Il fratello di Annamaria si operò allo stomaco qualche anno fa.
    Annamaria's brother underwent surgery on his stomach a few years ago.

  - Si operò uno strano mutamento in lui.
    A strange change occurred in him.

opporre   to oppose; to refuse

- Si deve opporre pace a guerra.
  One should oppose war with peace.

- Mio padre oppose un rifiuto alla proposta.
  My father refused the proposal.

  opporsi a qco   to oppose sth; to be opposed to, against sth; to object to sth

  - Molti si opposero alla sua candidatura (/alla proposta di legge).
    Many opposed his candidacy (/the bill).

  - I genitori si opposero alla decisione del figlio.
    The parents were opposed to their son's decision.

  - Mi oppongo!
    I object!

ordinare (a/da)   to order (from); to put/set in order; to ordain

- Hai già ordinato? —Sì, ho ordinato il pesce al forno.
  Have you already ordered? —Yes, I ordered the baked fish.

- Questa è la fattura per la merce che avete ordinato a loro.
  This is the bill for the merchandise you ordered from them.

- Devo ordinare i miei appunti (/la mia scrivania/le mie idee).
  I must put my notes (/desk/ideas) in order.

- Il nipote del signor Arnaldi è stato ordinato (sacerdote) un mese fa.
  Mr. Arnaldi's nephew was ordained (a priest) a month ago.

ordinare a qc di + *inf*   to order sb to + *inf*

- Il dottore gli ha ordinato di riposare per un paio di giorni.
  The doctor ordered him to rest for a couple of days.

organizzare   to organize

- Hanno organizzato una partita di caccia (/un nuovo partito politico).
  They have organized a hunting party (/a new political party).
- I ribelli stanno organizzando un movimento di resistenza.
  The rebels are organizing a resistance movement.

organizzarsi   to organize oneself

- Si organizzano in gruppi di protesta contro la guerra.
  They're organizing in groups protesting the war.

osare (qco)   to be daring; to attempt, risk (sth)

- Hai osato tanto?
  Were you so daring?
- Non osare troppo!
  Don't go too far!
- Osarono un'impresa che tutti giudicavano impossibile.
  They attempted an enterprise everybody deemed impossible.
- Dobbiamo osare il tutto per tutto.
  We must risk our all.

osare + *inf*   to dare (to) + *inf*

- Il suo ragazzo non osò telefonarle (/venire/parlare/dircelo/muoversi).
  Her boyfriend did not dare call her (/come/speak/tell us/move).

osservare   to observe, look at, watch, notice; to object; to keep (to)

- Si deve osservare la legge (/il comandamento/la parola data).
  The law (/commandment/One's word) must be observed.
- Osserva il frammento di roccia (/la struttura di questa cellula).
  Look at the rock fragment (/the structure of this cell).
- Si sentiva osservata da tutti.
  She felt everybody was watching her.
- Non hai osservato qualcosa di strano in lei?
  Haven't you noticed something strange about her?
- L'avvocato ha osservato che il contratto era scaduto.
  The lawyer objected that the contract had expired.
- Quel paziente deve osservare una dieta molto rigorosa.
  That patient must keep to a very strict diet.

far osservare   to point out

- Voglio farle osservare tutti gli errori che ha fatto, signorina.
  I want to point out to you all the mistakes you made, Miss.

ottenere   to obtain, get; to gain

- Penso di avere ottenuto un buon risultato (/il loro consenso).
  I think I obtained a good result (/their consent).

- Antonio non ottiene mai ciò che desidera.
  Anthony never gets his wish.

- Il figlio dell'avvocato ha ottenuto un prestito dalla banca (/quel premio).
  The lawyer's son got a loan from the bank (/that award).

ottenere di + *inf*   to get permission to + *inf*

- Abbiamo ottenuto di farlo il mese prossimo.
  We got permission to do it next month.

P

pagare   to pay (for)

- Quanto hai pagato questa cravatta? —L'ho pagata venti dollari.
  How much did you pay for this tie? —I paid twenty dollars for it.

- Me la pagheranno! (*fig*)
  They'll pay for that! (fig)

- Pagheremo il computer a rate (/in contanti/con la carta di credito).
  We'll pay for the computer in installments (/in cash/with our credit card).

- Pago io da bere!
  I'm buying drinks (or Drinks are on me)!

  far pagare   to charge

  - Quanto ti hanno fatto pagare quella valigia (/quella stanza)?
    How much did they charge you for that suitcase (/room)?

paragonare qc/qco con qc/qco   to compare sb/sth with sb/sth

- Non si può paragonare il mio lavoro col tuo.
  One cannot compare my work with yours.

  paragonare qc/qco a qc/qco   compare sb/sth to sb/sth

  - Paragoniamo la terra a una palla.
    Let's compare the earth to a ball.

  paragonarsi a qc   to compare oneself to sb

  - Tu vuoi sempre paragonarti a lui.
    You always want to compare yourself to him.

parare   to keep off/out; to parry; to save

- C'è una persiana per parare il sole.
  There is a shutter to keep out the sun.

- Il pugile riuscì a parare il colpo.
  The boxer managed to parry (or ward off) the blow.

- Il portiere non è riuscito a parare.
  The goalie could not save (the ball).

  parare da qco   to shield, protect from sth

  - Come la possiamo parare dalla pioggia (/dal freddo/dalla neve)?
    How can we shield her from the rain (/cold/snow)?

pararsi (da qco)   to shield oneself (from sth); to appear (suddenly); to present itself

- Come potremmo pararci dal sole (/dal freddo/dai pericoli)?
  How could we shield ourselves from the sun (/cold/danger)?

- Giorgio mi si parò dinnanzi (/sull'uscio).
  George suddenly appeared before me (/at the door).

- Sono sicuro che saprai superare qualunque ostacolo ti si pari davanti.
  I am sure you'll be able to overcome any difficulty that presents itself.

parere   (auxiliary *essere*) to seem, appear; to look, sound, taste, feel like; to think

- Guido pareva una persona onesta (/sana), ma non lo era.
  Guy seemed (or appeared) to be an honest (/healthy) person, but he wasn't.

- Vestita in quel modo pareva un pagliaccio.
  Dressed that way, she looked like a clown.

- Questo pare un concerto di Vivaldi.
  This sounds like a concerto by Vivaldi.

- Pare aceto.
  It tastes like vinegar.

- Quella stoffa pareva velluto.
  That fabric felt like velvet.

- Che gliene pare di questo vino, signor Bianchi?
  What do you think of this wine, Mr. Bianchi?

- Non mi pare vero.
  I can't believe it (i.e., It does not seem true to me).

- Faccia come le pare, signor Golino.
  Do as you like (i.e., Do as seems right to you), Mr. Golino.

- Pare (im)possibile (/facile/difficile), ma non lo è.
  It seems (im)possible (/easy/difficult), but it isn't.

- Franco ha avuto la promozione? —Pare di sì (/Pare di no).
  Did Frank get the promotion? —It seems so (/It doesn't seem so).

parere a qc che + *subj*   to seem to sb

- A lei pareva che fosse ora di andare.
  She thought (i.e., It seemed to her) it was time to go.

parere di + *inf*   to think

- Le pare di sognare.
  She thinks (i.e., It seems to her that) she is dreaming.

- Mi pare di averlo già letto.
  I think (i.e., It seems to me that) I've read it already.

parlare (con/a qc, di qc/qco)   to speak, talk (with/to sb, about sb/sth); to address; to refer to

■ Cinzia non parla mai.
Cynthia never speaks.

■ Sai parlare il cinese?
Can you speak Chinese?

■ Loro parlano bene (/male) di lui.
They speak well (/badly, ill) of him.

■ Di che partita parlavate?
What game were you talking about (or referring to)?

■ Pronto, chi parla?
Hello, who's speaking?

■ Vorrei parlare con l'avvocato a quattrocchi.
I would like to talk to the lawyer privately.

■ Il presidente parlerà al Consiglio dei Ministri.
The president will address the Cabinet.

■ Parliamo d'altro.
Let's change the subject.

■ Parlai chiaro al signor Gardini.
I spoke frankly to Mr. Gardini (or I spoke my mind to Mr. Gardini).

■ Non parlare a voce bassa (/così in fretta/così piano).
Don't speak in a low voice (/so quickly/so slowly).

■ E non parliamo di quello che hanno fatto loro!
And let's not mention what they did!

parlare di + *inf*   to talk about + *ger*

■ Parlano di trasferirsi in un'altra città (/lanciare un nuovo prodotto).
They are talking of moving to another town (/launching a new product).

■ Si parla di licenziare cinquemila persone.
There is talk of dismissing five thousand people.

parlarne   to talk about it; to mention it

■ Non voglio parlarne più. Non parlarmene.
I don't want to talk about it anymore. Don't talk to me about it.

■ Non se ne parli più (*or* Non parliamone più).
Let's forget about it.

■ L'articolo non ne parla.
The article doesn't mention it.

far parlare   to make sb talk; to say more

■ Non sono riusciti a farlo parlare.
They could not make him talk.

- Non mi faccia parlare!
  Don't make me say any more!

parlarsi   to speak to each other/one another

- Ci parliamo al telefono tutti i giorni.
  We speak on the phone every day.

partecipare   to announce; to inform

- Il signore e la signora Galletto partecipano la nascita di Laura.
  Mr. and Mrs. Galletto announce the birth of Laura.

- Giacomo e Flavia partecipano il loro matrimonio.
  James and Flavia announce their marriage.

  partecipare a   to participate, take part in; to share; to attend

  - La moglie del dottor Trani non ha partecipato alla festa (/alla riunione).
    Doctor Trani's wife did not participate in the party (/meeting).

  - Tutti parteciperanno alle spese (/agli utili).
    Everybody will share the expenses (/in the profits).

  - Il mese scorso ho partecipato a un convegno (/a un corso d'aggiornamento).
    Last month I attended a conference (/a refresher course).

partire   (auxiliary *essere*) to depart, leave; to take off; to start (from); to go flat (as a tire)

- Sono partiti in treno (/in macchina/in aereo) per Napoli.
  They departed by train (/car/plane) for Naples.

- La signora Mazzotta partì di sera (/presto/per il mare/per la Sicilia).
  Mrs. Mazzotta left in the evening (/early/for the beach/for Sicily).

- La nave partirà stasera alle sei diretta a New York.
  The ship will leave tonight at six, bound for New York.

- A partire da domani le lezioni cominceranno alle nove.
  As of tomorrow, classes will start at nine.

- Tu parti da un presupposto sbagliato (/un concetto diverso).
  You're starting from a wrong presupposition (/a different concept).

- Mi è partita una gomma.
  One of my tires went flat.

passare (a/da/in/per/tra)   (auxiliary *essere;* if the verb has a direct object, auxiliary *avere*)   to pass (by); to be passed; to go (by, in, through); to get in; to cease, stop; to cross; to move, transfer; to spend (time); to be promoted; to strain, filter

- Potrebbe passargli lo zucchero, per piacere?
  Could you pass him the sugar, please?

- Una volta passata la chiesa, volti a sinistra.
  Once past the church, turn (or go) to the left.

■ Li ho visti passare.
I saw them pass by (go by).

■ Hai letto la targa di quella macchina che è appena passata?
Did you read the license plate of that car that just passed by?

■ Se passi in biblioteca, prendimi questo libro, per favore.
If you pass by the library, please get me this book.

■ Il gatto (/Il ladro) deve essere passato per la finestra.
The cat (/thief) must have gone in through the window.

■ Passeranno anche per Milano (/il centro della città).
They will also pass through Milan (/the center of town).

■ Dobbiamo ancora passare la dogana.
We still have to go through customs.

■ La signora Vanni ne ha passate tante.
Mrs. Vanni went through a lot.

■ Quel ragazzo crede di poter passare senza biglietto.
That boy thinks he can get in without a ticket.

■ L'uragano (/Il dolore) è passato.
The hurricane (/pain) has stopped.

■ Passeranno il confine (/il fiume) domani all'alba.
They will cross the border (/the river) tomorrow at dawn.

■ Non mi era neanche passato per la mente.
It hadn't even crossed my mind.

■ Quella signora deve aver passato i cinquant'anni.
That lady must be over fifty.

■ Suo marito è stato passato all'agenzia di Napoli.
Her husband has been transferred to the branch in Naples.

■ Abbiamo passato insieme le vacanze (/il Natale/il fine settimana/l'estate/un paio d'ore).
We spent our vacation (/Christmas/the weekend/the summer/a couple of hours) together.

■ Quel vino va passato.
That wine must be filtered.

■ È passato capitano.
He was promoted to captain.

passare per + *adj/noun*   to pass for, be considered + *adj/noun*

■ La vuole far passare per sua moglie (/stupida).
He wants to pass her off as his wife (/[being] stupid).

■ Quella ragazza passa per bella (/furba/ricca/un buon partito).
That girl is considered beautiful (/clever/rich/a good catch).

passare a + *inf*   to stop by to + *inf*

■ Quando passi a ritirare il pacchetto (/pagare il conto)?
When are you going to stop by to collect the package (/pay the bill)?

patire   to suffer

■ Avevano patito molti torti (/molte offese/le pene dell'inferno).
They had suffered many wrongs (/many insults/the pains of hell).

■ Pativano la sete (/il freddo). Pativano la fame.
They were suffering from thirst (/cold). They were starving.

■ Ha finito di patire.
His sufferings are over.

■ La popolarità di quel cantante non ne ha patito.
The popularity of that singer did not suffer from it.

pendere (da/su/verso)   to hang (from/down/on/over); to lean; to tip

■ Una corda pendeva dal soffitto della cella.
A rope was hanging from the ceiling of the cell.

■ L'edificio pende da questo lato.
The building leans to this side.

■ La bilancia pendeva dalla parte del nemico.
The scales tipped in the enemy's favor.

■ Alla maestra pende sempre la sottoveste.
The teacher's slip is always showing.

penetrare   (auxiliary *essere*) to penetrate

■ Il freddo (/L'umidità) ci penetrava le ossa.
The cold (/dampness) penetrated our bones.

penetrare in qco   to penetrate sth/into sth; to pierce; to break in

■ Gli esploratori penetrarono nella giungla (/nell'interno del paese).
The explorers penetrated into the jungle (/into the heart of the country).

■ La lama (/Una spina) gli penetrò nella carne.
The blade (/A thorn) pierced his flesh.

■ I ladri sono penetrati nel nostro appartamento ieri sera.
Thieves broke into our apartment last night.

pensare   to think; to imagine; to guess; to consider; to worry

■ Penso, dunque sono.
I think, therefore I am.

■ Puoi venire al concerto? —Penso di sì (/Penso di no).
Can you come to the concert? —I think so (/I don't think so).

■ Vi lascio pensare la mia paura (/sorpresa).
Just imagine my fear (/surprise).

■ Pensa chi viene a cena (/chi ho visto l'altro giorno)?
Guess who's coming for dinner (/who I saw the other day)?

■ Avrebbero dovuto pensare che era molto tardi.
They should have considered (the fact) that it was very late.

■ Pensano bene (/male) di lui.
They have a good (/bad) opinion of him.

■ Il suo avvenire ci dava da pensare.
His future worried us.

pensare a qc/qco   to think of sb/sth; to take care of sb/sth; to mind

■ Non pensare a me (/al domani/a Stefano).
Don't think of me (/tomorrow/Stephen).

■ Chi penserebbe a lui, se sua moglie morisse?
Who would take care of him if his wife should die?

■ Teresa pensa ai bambini; Giorgio pensa al negozio.
Theresa takes care of the children; George minds the shop.

■ Pensate agli affari vostri.
Mind your own business.

pensare che + *subj*   to think (that)

■ Penso che sia ora di andare (/siano già partiti/si sia sposata).
I think it is time to go (/they already left/she got married).

pensare di + *inf*   to think (that)/of + *ger*

■ Penso di aver ragione (/averla già conosciuta in qualche posto).
I think I am right (/I already met her somewhere).

pensare di + *inf*   to plan

■ Pensano di fare un viaggio (/ritornare/comprare un condominio).
They are planning to take a trip (/come back/buy a condominium).

pensarci   to think of it

■ Dovevano pensarci mesi fa.
They should have thought of it months ago.

pentirsi (di qco)   to regret (sth)

■ Se non lo farai, te ne pentirai amaramente.
If you don't do it, you'll regret it bitterly.

pentirsi di + *inf*   to regret + *ger*

■ Mi pento di non aver studiato il piano (/avertelo dato).
I regret not having studied the piano (/having given it to you).

■ Quell'avvocato si è pentito di aver preso il suo caso.
That lawyer regretted taking on his case.

perdere   to lose; to miss; to waste

- Il loro cugino ha perso un dito (/i capelli/la testa/la bussola/tutti i soldi che aveva ereditato/il portafoglio/una partita a carte/la pazienza).
  Their cousin lost a finger (/his hair/his head/his bearings/all the money he had inherited/his wallet/a game of cards/his patience).

- Michele (/non) sa perdere.
  Michael is a good (/poor) loser.

- Credo che abbiano perso l'aereo (/il concerto/questa occasione).
  I think they missed the plane (/the concert/this opportunity).

- Non perdere tempo!
  Don't waste time!

- Sai cosa fa Rosa? —Non so, l'ho persa di vista.
  Do you know what Rosa is doing? —I don't know. I've lost sight of her.

- Lascia perdere!
  Forget it (or Never mind)!

  perdere   to leak

  - Questo contenitore (/serbatoio) perde.
    This container (/tank) is leaking.

  perdersi   to get lost

  - Ho paura che la tua lettera si sia persa.
    I am afraid your letter got lost.

perdonare   to forgive, excuse; to spare

- Non le perdonerò mai quello che ha scritto.
  I'll never forgive her (for) what she wrote.

- Mi hai perdonato?
  Am I forgiven?

- Perdoni se la contraddico, signor Bini.
  Forgive (or excuse) me for contradicting you, Mr. Bini.

- La morte non perdona nessuno.
  Death does not spare anybody.

  perdonare qc di/per + *inf*   to forgive sb for + *ger*

  - Perdonami di non averti scritto (/averti mentito/non averti risposto prima).
    Forgive me for not writing to you (/having lied to you/not replying earlier).

  perdonare a qc   to forgive sb for sth

  - Non glielo perdono.
    I cannot forgive him/her for it.

  perdonarsi   to forgive oneself

  - Non mi perdono di essere stato così stupido.
    I can't forgive myself for having been so stupid.

permettere   to allow; to permit; to afford

- Permette?
  May I?

- È permesso?
  May I come in?

- Lo faremo domani, tempo permettendo (/Dio permettendo).
  We'll do it tomorrow, weather permitting (/God willing).

- Non è permesso camminare sull'erba.
  Walking on the grass is not allowed.

- Fortunatamente i suoi mezzi glielo permettono.
  Luckily he/she can afford it.

  permettere a qc di + *inf*   to let, allow sb to + *inf*

  - Mi permette di entrare (/usarlo/fare una telefonata)?
    Will you allow me to come in (/use it/make a call)?

  - Signora De Angelis, mi permetta di presentarle mio figlio.
    Mrs. De Angelis, allow me to introduce my son to you.

  permettere che + *subj*   to bear + *ger*

  - Come permetti che il capo ti tratti così?
    How can you bear the boss's treating you that way?

  permettersi   to allow oneself; to dare

  - Si sono permessi una vacanza (/una crociera).
    They allowed themselves a vacation (/a cruise).

  - Come ti permetti!
    How dare you!

  permettersi di + *inf*   to take the liberty of + *ger*

  - Mi permetto di farle notare che Lei si sbaglia, signor Beraldi.
    I am taking the liberty of telling you that you're mistaken, Mr. Beraldi.

  permettersi il lusso di + *inf*   to afford + *inf*

  - Non possiamo permetterci il lusso di comprare un altro televisore!
    We can't afford to buy another TV set!

persistere (in qco)   to persist (in sth)

- L'ondata di caldo (/Il cattivo tempo) persiste.
  The heat wave (/bad weather) persists.

- Puoi dirgli quello che vuoi, ma Antonio persiste nel suo rifiuto.
  You can tell him what you want, but Anthony will persist in his refusal.

  persistere a + *inf*   to persist in + *ger*

  - Persisto a credere che il buco dell'ozono non stia diventando più grande.
    I persist in believing that the hole in the ozone is not getting any bigger.

persuadere (qc di qco) to persuade, convince (sb of sth)

■ Non sono persuasi di quel fatto.
They are not persuaded by that fact.

■ Non riuscii a persuaderlo.
I couldn't convince him.

    persuadere qc che to persuade sb (that)

    ■ Li ho persuasi che avevano torto (/non dovevano farlo).
    I persuaded them that they were wrong (/should not do it).

    persuadere qc a + *inf* to persuade, convince sb to + *inf*

    ■ Nessuno ha potuto persuaderla a vendere la casa (/partire).
    Nobody could persuade her to sell the house (/leave).

    persuadersi to convince, persuade oneself

    ■ Si è persuasa che questo è il miglior modo di farlo (/Giovanni ha ragione).
    She has convinced herself that this is the best way to do it (/John is right).

pesare to weigh

■ Quanto pesa? —Pesa molto (/poco/un quintale).
How much does it weigh? —It weighs a lot (/a little/a hundred kilos).

■ Dobbiamo pesare le parole (/i pro e i contro della situazione). (*fig*)
We must weigh our words (/the pros and cons of the situation). (fig)

    pesare a/su to weigh, lie heavily on; to be, seem; to be a burden to; to hang on

    ■ Quella responsabilità le pesava molto.
    That responsibility weighed heavily on her.

    ■ L'aglio mi pesa sullo stomaco.
    Garlic lies heavy on my stomach.

    ■ Quel lavoro (/Quel tipo di vita) gli pesa molto.
    He finds that job (/that kind of life) very hard (i.e., That job seems very hard to him).

    ■ Quella tassa pesa sui poveri.
    That tax is a burden to the poor.

    ■ Un silenzio pesava sull'assemblea.
    A silence hung on the assembly.

    ■ Gli pesa dover lavorare (/scrivere).
    It is hard for him to work (/to write).

    pesarsi to weigh oneself

    ■ Non mi peso da molto tempo.
    I haven't weighed myself for a long time.

piacere   (auxiliary *essere*) to please

■ Fai come ti piace.
   Do as you like.

■ A lei piace Giovanni (/il balletto/quel libro), a lui no.
   She likes John (/ballet/that book); he doesn't.

■ Gli piacciono le albicocche. Gli piacciono molto.
   He likes apricots. He likes them a lot.

■ Vi è piaciuta la torta di mele che ha fatto Giovanna? —No, non ci è piaciuta.
   Did you like the apple pie Joan baked? —No, we did not like it.

■ Piaccia o non piaccia, dobbiamo farlo.
   Whether we like it or not, we must do it.

   piacere che + *subj*   to be pleasing (that); to like

   ■ Gli piaceva che le cose fossero in ordine (/l'idea che tu gli telefonassi).
      He liked things to be in order (/the idea that you would call him).

   ■ Mi piacerebbe che Lei fosse mio ospite (/che loro tornassero).
      I would like for you to be my guest (/them to come back).

   piacere + *inf*   to like + *ger or inf*

   ■ A loro piace viaggiare (/sciare/leggere).
      They like traveling (/skiing/reading).

   ■ Mi sarebbe piaciuto vedervi (/esserci/comprarlo).
      I would have liked to see you (/be there/buy it).

piangere   to cry, weep; to grieve; to mourn; to water

■ Bambino, perché piangi? Su, non piangere più.
   Child, why are you crying? Come on, don't cry anymore.

■ Piansero lacrime di coccodrillo. (idiomatic)
   They wept crocodile tears. (idiomatic)

■ Piangevano la morte del loro padre.
   They were mourning their father's death.

■ L'allergia le fa piangere gli occhi.
   The allergy makes her eyes water.

■ Mi piange il cuore a sentire quello che hai dovuto affrontare.
   It breaks my heart to hear what you had to go through.

   piangere (di/per/su qco)   to cry; to water

   ■ La donna piangeva di gioia (/dolore/paura/rabbia).
      The woman was crying for joy (/from pain/out of fear/in rage).

   ■ Ci piangevano gli occhi per l'inquinamento (/fumo).
      Our eyes were watering from the pollution (/smoke).

far piangere qc   to make sb cry

■   Non far piangere il bambino.
Don't make the baby cry.

piantare (a)   to plant (with): to thrust, drive; to pitch; to desert, jilt; to cut it out

■   Ho piantato molti fiori in giardino.
I planted many flowers in the garden.

■   Hanno piantato quel terreno a ulivi (/patate/viti).
They planted that land with olive trees (/potatoes/vines).

■   Gli piantò il pugnale nel cuore.
He thrust the dagger into his heart.

■   Devo piantare due chiodi qui.
I have to drive two nails here.

■   Non hanno ancora piantato le tende.
They haven't pitched the tents yet.

■   Luisa l'ha piantato.
Luisa jilted him.

■   Piantala!
Cut it out!

piantarsi   to plant oneself

■   Non piantarti davanti alla finestra.
Don't plant yourself in front of the window.

piegare   to fold (up), bend; to turn, bow

■   Il professor Tagliani piegò il foglio in due e se lo mise in tasca.
Professor Tagliani folded the sheet in two and put it into his pocket.

■   La ragazza (/L'operaio) piegò le ginocchia (/la sbarra di ferro).
The girl (/worker) bent her knees (/the iron bar).

■   Dopo il ponte la strada piega a sud.
The road turns south after the bridge.

■   Il nonno piegò il capo e s'addormentò.
Grandfather bowed his head and fell asleep.

piegarsi   to bend

■   I rami si piegavano a terra per la neve.
The branches bent down from the snow.

piovere   to rain, pour (auxiliary *essere;* when referring to weather, auxiliary *essere* or *avere*)

■   Ieri ha (è) piovuto tutto il giorno.
Yesterday it rained all day long.

■ Oggi vuol piovere.
It looks like rain today.

■ Il mese scorso sono piovuti a Firenze molti stranieri.
Last month many foreigners poured into Florence.

■ Ci piovevano colpi (/inviti/fiori/proiettili) da tutte le parti.
Blows (/Invitations/Flowers/Bullets) poured in on us from all sides.

plasmare   to mold

■ Susanna passa ore a plasmare la creta.
Susan spends hours molding clay.

■ Suo nonno ha plasmato la sua natura. (*fig*)
His grandfather molded his nature.

portare (a/in qc/qco)   to bring; to take; to carry; to wear; to get; to drive; to lead; to have; to blow off or away

■ Portami il giornale di oggi (/una birra), per favore.
Bring me today's newspaper (/a beer), please.

■ Dove ci porti?
Where are you taking us?

■ Non porto mai con me gli assegni.
I never carry checks on me.

■ Dopo la partita i tifosi li portarono in trionfo.
The fans carried them in triumph after the game.

■ Scrivo 5 e porto 2. (*math*)
I put down 5 and carry 2. (math)

■ Mi ricordo che tu portavi un cappotto blu (/i capelli lunghi/gli occhiali).
I remember you were wearing a blue coat (/your hair long/glasses).

■ Signorina, può portarmi un programma?
Can you get me a program, Miss?

■ La porto all'aeroporto (/a casa/a scuola) in macchina.
I am going to drive her to the airport (/home/to school).

■ Tutte le strade portano a Roma. (*proverb*)
All roads lead to Rome. (proverb)

■ Sua moglie porta il nome della nonna.
His wife has her grandmother's name.

■ Il vento ha portato via il giornale.
The wind blew the newspaper.

portare + *inf*   to take to + *inf*

■ Il signor Botti ci ha portato a mangiare in un ristorante cinese.
Mr. Botti took us to a Chinese restaurant to eat.

portarsi   to move, go, reach; to take with, carry

- La macchina si portò sulla destra (/sul ciglio della strada).
  The car moved (or went) to the right (/the edge of the road).

- Un gruppo di soldati si portò sul luogo del disastro.
  A group of soldiers reached the site of the disaster.

- Non mi porto mai la borsa.
  I never carry my purse.

potere   (*Note:* In compound tenses, if *potere* is followed by a verb requiring *essere*, the auxiliary *avere* or *essere* can be used. See the first example.)   can/could; may/might; to be able; to be allowed

- Non hanno potuto andare (*or* Non sono potuti andare).
  They could not go.

- Se non potrò andare, scriverò.
  If I can't go, I'll write.

- Potresti andarci, se fosse necessario?
  Could you go there if it were necessary?

- Cenerentola avrebbe potuto ballare tutta la notte.
  Cinderella could have danced all night long.

- Prometto di fare tutto quello che posso.
  I promise I'll do all I can (or my best or my utmost).

- Non ne posso più.
  I am exhausted (or I am at the end of my rope).

- Posso vederla?
  May I see her?

- Vincenzo potrebbe telefonare domani.
  Vincent might call tomorrow.

- Sono sicuro che non potrai entrare.
  I am sure that you will not be allowed to go in.

  può darsi che + *subj*   it may be (that); perhaps

  - Può darsi che arrivino più tardi (/che ti abbiano già scritto).
    They may (or Perhaps they will) arrive later (/may have written to you already).

praticare   to practice, be in practice; to employ; to make; to frequent; to give; to engage in; to charge

- Il suo sogno era di praticare la professione di avvocato a Roma.
  His dream was to practice as a lawyer in Rome.

- Praticano il sacrificio umano (/il cannibalismo)?
  Do they practice human sacrifice (/cannibalism)?

■ Quell'avvocato non pratica più.
That lawyer is no longer in practice.

■ Che metodo pratichi?
Which method do you employ?

■ Devi praticare un'apertura (/un buco/un taglio/un'incisione).
You have to make an opening (/a hole/a cut/an incision).

■ Una volta praticavo quel caffè.
Once I used to go to that café.

■ Gli hanno praticato la respirazione artificiale.
They have given him artificial respiration.

■ Raffaele pratica molti sport.
Raphael engages in many sports.

■ In quel negozio praticano prezzi troppo alti.
In that store they charge too high prices.

predicare   to preach

■ Il sacerdote predicava la parola di Dio (/le virtù cardinali).
The priest was preaching the word of God (/the cardinal virtues).

preferire   to prefer, like (sb/sth); to like better, best

■ Fanno come preferiscono.
They do as they like.

■ Preferiscono il caffè al tè.
They like coffee better than tea.

preferire + *inf*   to prefer + *ger/inf*

■ A tua sorella piace sciare? —Sì, ma preferisce pattinare.
Does your sister like skiing? —Yes, but she prefers skating.

■ Preferirei andare al cinema stasera (/bere qualcosa di caldo).
I would rather go to the movies tonight (/drink something hot).

■ Avremmo preferito restare a casa a guardare la partita (di calcio) alla tv.
We would have preferred to stay home and watch the soccer game on TV.

preferire che + *subj*   to prefer (that)

■ Preferisco che tu non venga (/che i bambini vadano a letto presto).
I prefer that you not come (/that the children go to bed early).

pregare (per qc/qco)   to say prayers; to pray (for sb/sth)

■ I bambini pregano prima di andare a letto.
The children say prayers before going to bed.

■ La ragazza pregava in silenzio (/per la guarigione del padre/per la pace).
The girl was praying in silence (/for her father's recovery/for peace).

pregare qc di + *inf*   to ask sb to + *inf;* to request sb to + *inf*

■ L'ho pregata di non farlo (/farmi sapere quando arriva/aiutarmi).
I asked her not to do it (/to let me know when she's coming/to help me).

■ I membri della giuria sono pregati di riunirsi nell'altra sala.
The members of the jury are requested to assemble in the other room.

(ti/La/vi) prego   please

■ Non disturbarti, ti prego. Non si disturbi, La prego. (/Non disturbatevi, vi prego).
Please don't trouble yourself (/Please don't trouble yourselves or Please don't bother).

prego + *command*   please + *command*

■ Prego, si accomodi.
Please, come on in.

prego   you're welcome

■ Grazie. —Prego.
Thank you. —You're welcome.

Prego?   I didn't understand. Can you repeat it, please?

prendere   to catch, seize; to take; to get, win; to handle; to have

■ Il falco ha preso la sua preda.
The hawk caught its prey.

■ Questo brano è preso da un romanzo di Calvino.
This passage is taken from a novel by Calvino.

■ Pietro ha preso il primo premio.
Peter won first prize.

■ La loro figlia ha preso la laurea in filosofia.
Their daughter got a Ph.D. in philosophy.

■ La devi prendere con le buone.
You have to handle her tactfully.

■ Che cosa prende, signora Brancati? —Un cappuccino, grazie.
What are you having, Mrs. Brancati? —A cappuccino, thank you.

prendere qc per   to seize sb by (*part of the body*)

■ Lo presero per il collo (/il braccio).
They seized him by his neck (/arm).

prendere qc per   to take sb for

■ Mi prende per un ladro, signor Franchi?
Do you take me for a thief, Mr. Franchi?

preoccupare to worry

■ L'avvenire di suo figlio (/L'esame) lo preoccupava molto.
His son's future (/The exam) worried him greatly.

preoccuparsi (di/per) to worry, be worried, concerned (about)

■ Non ti preoccupare, non c'è nessun pericolo.
Don't worry; there is no danger.

■ La nonna si preoccupa per tutti noi (/della nostra salute).
Grandmother worries about all of us (/our health).

preoccuparsi di + *inf* to make sure, take the trouble

■ Mi sono preoccupato di spedirgli subito il biglietto.
I made sure I sent him the ticket right away.

■ Non ti sei preoccupato di darmi il resto.
You haven't taken the trouble to give me the change.

preoccuparsene to worry (about it)

■ Non preoccupartene. —Ma io non me ne preoccupo affatto.
Don't worry about it. —But I'm not worrying at all (about it).

preparare to prepare, get ready; to coach; to have in store

■ Stanno preparando una spedizione in Africa (/un saggio critico).
They are preparing an expedition to Africa (/a critical essay).

■ Devo preparare il pranzo (/la cena/la camera per gli ospiti).
I have to get lunch (/supper/the room for the guests) ready.

■ Luisa, prepara la tavola, per favore.
Louise, set the table, please.

■ Lo stanno preparando per i 100 metri a ostacoli.
They are coaching him for the 100 meter hurdles.

■ Chissà cosa ci prepara il futuro!
Who knows what the future has in store for us!

prepararsi (a) to get ready; to study; to be about to happen

■ Preparatevi.
Get ready.

■ Si preparano agli esami.
They are studying for their exams.

■ Si prepara qualcosa di grave.
Something serious is about to happen.

■ Si stava preparando una burrasca.
A storm was brewing.

prepararsi a + *inf* to get ready to + *inf;* to be about to + *inf*

■ Mi sto preparando a partire.
I am getting ready to leave (or I am about to leave).

- Preparatevi ad atterrare.
  Get ready to land.

presentare   to present; to show; to introduce; to propose; to submit; to describe

- I delegati furono presentati al ministro.
  The delegates were presented to the minister.

- La soluzione del problema presenta qualche difficoltà.
  The solution of the problem presents some difficulties.

- L'estratto conto presenta un saldo a tuo favore.
  The bank statement shows a balance in your favor.

- Si deve presentare il passaporto (/la patente di guida).
  You must show your passport (/driver's license).

- Gli presentò suo marito (/il nuovo direttore).
  She introduced her husband (/the new manager) to him.

- Presentarono un nuovo piano di risanamento.
  They introduced a new reclamation plan.

- Presentarono la candidatura di un giovane.
  They proposed a young man as a candidate.

- Vogliono presentare un reclamo (/una domanda/un'istanza).
  They want to register a complaint (/submit an application/a petition).

- Così come la presenti, la cosa sembra molto facile.
  The way you describe it, the matter seems very easy.

presentarsi   to present oneself; to introduce oneself; to appear; to look; to run; to offer; to seem; to occur

- L'imputato si è presentato alla giuria.
  The defendant presented himself to the jury.

- Il ragazzo di Silvia si è presentato ai suoi genitori.
  Sylvia's boyfriend introduced himself to her parents.

- La loro figlia si presentò alla porta col bambino in braccio.
  Their daughter appeared at the door with her child in her arms.

- Devono presentarsi in tribunale la settimana prossima.
  They must appear in court next week.

- La damigelle d'onore si presentavano molto bene.
  The bridesmaids looked very nice.

- Si presenterà candidata, o ha capito che non sarà eletta?
  Will she run, or has she understood that she won't be elected?

- Non è la prima occasione che si presenti.
  It is not the first opportunity that has offered itself.

- Il compito non si presenta così difficile dopotutto.
  The task doesn't seem that hard after all.

- Ho paura che un caso del genere possa presentarsi anche qui.
  I am afraid a case of this kind may occur here too.

■ Come hai il coraggio di presentarti qui!
How dare you show your face here!

prestare   to lend; to loan

■ Puoi prestarle diecimila lire (/la tua macchina/il tuo dizionario)?
Can you lend her ten thousand lire (/your car/your dictionary)?

■ Nicola presta denaro a interesse (/al dieci per cento/senza interesse).
Nicolas lends money with interest (/at ten percent interest/without interest).

■ Presta attenzione a quello che dico.
Pay attention to what I am saying.

■ Qui prestano la loro opera molti disabili.
Many handicapped (people) work here.

■ Non prestargli fede.
Don't believe (trust) him.

farsi prestare qco da qc   to borrow sth from sb

■ Mi farò prestare dei soldi da mia madre.
I'll borrow some money from my mother.

prestarsi   to lend oneself; to help; to be fit

■ Quella signora si presta molto per i poveri.
That lady helps the poor a lot.

■ Questo teatro non si presta per opere come l'*Aida*.
This theater is not fit for operas like Aida.

pretendere   to expect; to ask

■ Che cosa pretendi? Non pretendere l'impossibile!
What do you expect? Don't expect the impossible!

■ Questo è pretendere troppo!
This is asking for too much!

pretendere che qc + *subj*   to expect sb to + *inf*

■ Pretendeva che andassimo da lui (/lo pagassimo subito).
He expected us to go to his house (/to pay him right away).

pretendere di + *inf*   to think oneself capable of + *ger*

■ Pretendeva di impararlo in pochissimo tempo.
He thought himself capable of learning it in a very short time.

pretendere di + *inf*   to think (that); to claim, profess, pretend to + *inf*

■ Il professor Giannini pretende di essere un esperto (/un grande studioso).
Professor Giannini claims to be an expert (/a great scholar).

■ Il mio collega pretende di saperlo fare.
My colleague thinks he can do it.

prevalere (auxiliary *essere*)   to prevail

■ Questa è l'opinione che è prevalsa.
This is the opinion that prevailed.

prevedere   to foresee; to forecast; to expect; to provide

■ Non si poteva prevedere l'esito.
The outcome could not be foreseen.

■ Per la settimana prossima si prevede neve (/sole).
They are forecasting snow (/sunshine) for next week.

■ Prevedo che arriverà col treno delle dieci.
I expect him to arrive on the ten-o'clock train.

■ Lo statuto della società non prevede aumenti di capitale.
The company statute does not provide for capital increases.

■ Il contratto prevede l'arbitrato internazionale.
The contract provides for international arbitration.

prevenire   to prevent; to anticipate; to forestall; to warn; to forewarn; to be prejudiced against

■ La polizia intervenne per prevenire uno spargimento di sangue.
The police intervened to prevent bloodshed.

■ Stava per dirglielo, ma lui l'ha prevenuta.
She was about to tell him, but he forestalled her.

■ Il conferenziere prevenne le domande (/le obiezioni) del pubblico.
The lecturer anticipated the questions (/objections) of his audience.

■ Vi prevengo che non potrete entrare (/vederlo).
I warn you that you won't be allowed to go in (/to see him).

■ Potevate prevenirci, no?
You could have forewarned us, couldn't you?

■ Perché sono prevenuti contro di lui?
Why are they prejudiced against him?

privare   to deprive; to divest

■ Non si può privare un cittadino della sua libertà (/dei suoi diritti).
A citizen cannot be deprived of his freedom (/rights).

■ La guerra la privò della sua casa (/di un figlio).
The war deprived her of her house (/of a son).

■ Fu privata della sua autorità.
She was divested of her position.

privarsi   to deprive, do without

■ Sua madre si privava di tutto per lui.
His mother deprived herself of everything for him.

■ Sono così poveri che devono privarsi anche del necessario.
They are so poor that they even have to do without necessities.

procedere (auxiliary *essere* for a physical movement, otherwise *avere*) to proceed; to take legal steps; to go on, continue; to start

■ Le ricerche (/Gli affari) procedono bene.
The research (/Business) is proceeding well.

■ Procederanno per vie legali contro di lui.
They will take legal steps against him.

■ Avvocato, proceda, questo non è così importante.
Counselor, go on. This isn't so important.

■ L'ingegnere dette l'ordine di procedere alla distruzione del muro.
The engineer gave the order to start destroying the wall.

procurare to get, procure; to cause

■ Il signor Bruno mi ha procurato un impiego.
Mr. Bruno got me a job.

■ Ho paura che questo mi procurerà dei problemi (/delle grane).
I am afraid this will cause me some problems (/troubles).

■ Quella frattura gli procura molto dolore.
That fracture causes him a lot of pain.

procurare di + *inf*   to try, make sure to + *inf*

■ Procura di arrivare puntuale (/comportarti bene/ottenere i documenti).
Make sure to be punctual (/behave well/get the documents).

procurare che + *subj*   to make sure (that)

■ Procura che vengano tutti.
Make sure that everybody comes.

procurarsi   to get; to cause

■ Dobbiamo procurarci i soldi per l'affitto.
We must get the money for the rent.

produrre to produce, yield; to cause; to bear

■ Questa pianta non produce fiori.
This plant does not produce flowers.

■ Quest'articolo sarà prodotto in serie.
This article will be mass produced.

■ L'avvocato difensore ha prodotto prove della sua innocenza.
The attorney for the defense produced evidence of his innocence.

■ La siccità (/Il suo discorso) ha prodotto gravi danni (/grande emozione).
The drought (/His speech) caused great damage (/great emotion).

- Quest'ulivo non produce frutti ancora.
  This olive tree does not bear fruit yet.

  prodursi   to inflict on oneself; to play; to occur

  - Il prigioniero si è prodotto una ferita al collo.
    The prisoner inflicted a neck wound on himself.

  - Quell'attore si produrrà in un musical.
    That actor will play in a musical.

  - Molti cambiamenti si sono prodotti recentemente.
    Many changes have occurred recently.

progettare   to plan; to design

- Stiamo progettando un viaggio in Sardegna.
  We are planning a trip to Sardinia.

- Questa casa è stata progettata da Frank Lloyd Wright.
  This house was designed by Frank Lloyd Wright.

  progettare di + *inf*   to plan to + *inf*

  - Progettano di andarci in barca (/di fare un viaggio in Tibet).
    They plan to go there by boat (/to travel to Tibet).

proibire   to forbid; to prohibit

- Il dottore ti ha proibito i latticini?
  Has the doctor forbidden you dairy products?

- Solo in quella sala di questo ristorante è proibito fumare.
  Smoking is prohibited only in that room of this restaurant.

- Questo è proibito dalla legge.
  This is prohibited by law.

  proibire di + *inf*   to prohibit; to forbid to + *inf*

  - Vi proibisco di farlo (/uscire/comprarlo).
    I forbid you to do it (/go out/buy it).

  - Gli è stato proibito di bere (/vederla).
    He was forbidden to drink (/see her).

promettere   to promise

- Non ve lo posso promettere.
  I can't promise (you).

- È un pittore (/uno studente/un musicista) che promette bene.
  He is a promising painter (/student/musician).

- Il tempo promette pioggia (/un temporale).
  It looks like rain (/a storm).

promettere di + *inf*   to promise to + *inf*

- ■   Ugo ha promesso di non mangiarsi le unghie (/studiare di più/aiutarla).
  Hugh promised not to bite his nails (/to study more/to help her).

promuovere   to promote; to pass

- ■   Dobbiamo promuovere la causa dei senzatetto (/l'agricoltura).
  We must promote the cause of the homeless (/agriculture).

- ■   Lo zio di Maria fu promosso tenente colonello.
  Mary's uncle was promoted to lieutenant colonel.

- ■   Il nipote del signor Nannini non è stato promosso.
  Mr. Nannini's grandson (or nephew) did not pass.

pronunciare   to pronounce, utter

- ■   Quello studente non riesce a pronunciare bene certe consonanti.
  That student cannot pronounce certain consonants well.

- ■   Non hanno pronunciato una parola per tutta la sera.
  They haven't uttered a word the whole evening.

  pronunciarsi   to pronounce; to give one's opinion; to declare oneself

  - ■   Il dottore non ha voluto pronunciarsi.
    The doctor didn't want to give his opinion.

  - ■   Si sono pronunciati contro il progetto (/a favore del progetto).
    They pronounced (or declared) themselves against (/in favor of) the plan.

proporre   to propose

- ■   Proponiamolo tesoriere (/presidente).
  Let's propose him as treasurer (/president).

- ■   Hanno proposto al signor Ravasi un buon affare.
  They proposed a good deal to Mr. Ravasi.

  proporre che + *subj*   to propose, suggest (that)

  - ■   Propongo che sia assunto.
    I suggest that he be hired.

  proporre di + *inf*   to suggest to + *inf*

  - ■   Propongo di bere qualcosa (/tornare a casa/visitare Siena).
    I suggest we drink something (/go back home/visit Siena).

  proporsi   to propose; to plan

  - ■   Mi propongo questo obiettivo (/questa meta).
    I propose this aim (/goal) for myself.

  - ■   Mi proponevo di andare al cinema (/telefonarti/cambiare casa).
    I planned to go to the movies (/call you/move).

proseguire   (auxiliary *avere* if referring to people; *essere* if referring to things) to go on/further; to carry on, go on, continue; to forward

■ Loro non sono scesi qui, hanno proseguito per Venezia.
They did not get off here. They went on to Venice.

■ Si avvisano i viaggiatori che questo treno non prosegue.
We inform the passengers that this train does not go any farther.

■ Vorremmo proseguire nelle nostre ricerche (/nei nostri studi).
We would like to go on with our research (/studies).

■ Voglia proseguire la lettura.
Please continue reading.

■ Si prega di far proseguire al nuovo indirizzo.
Please forward to the new address.

proteggere   to protect, shelter; to favor; to guard; to promote, encourage

■ Volevano proteggere i loro figli dal pericolo (/questa pianta dal freddo).
They wanted to protect their children from harm (this plant from the cold).

■ Una pesante tenda proteggeva dal sole e dal caldo.
A heavy curtain protected one from the sun and the heat.

■ Sono protetti dalla polizia.
They are guarded by the police.

■ Si devono proteggere le arti e le scienze.
One must promote the arts and sciences.

■ I piccoli commercianti vanno protetti.
Owners of small businesses must be encouraged.

proteggersi   to protect oneself

■ Costruirono una capanna per proteggersi.
They built a hut to protect themselves.

protestare   to protest; to declare; to state

■ I dimostranti protestavano contro il licenziamento di mille operai.
The demonstrators were protesting against the laying off of a thousand workers.

■ Tutti protestarono contro l'aumento del prezzo della benzina.
Everybody protested the increase in the price of gas.

■ La cambiale è stata protestata.
The bill (of exchange) was protested.

■ Protestarono la loro fiducia (/stima/lealtà/devozione) per lui.
They declared (or stated) their trust in (/esteem for/loyalty for) him.

protestarsi   to protest oneself

■ L'accusato si protesta innocente.
The accused protests his innocence.

■ Si protesta mio amico, ma io non mi fido di lui.
   He professes himself (to be) a friend of mine, but I don't trust him.

provare   to prove; to demonstrate, show; to try; to try on, have a fitting; to debilitate; to test; to rehearse

■ Non possiamo provarlo.
   We cannot prove it.

■ Quel fatto proverà che avevano ragione.
   That fact will show they were right.

■ Fammi provare la tua macchina.
   Let me try your car.

■ Prova quel vestito prima di comprarlo.
   Try that dress on before you buy it.

■ Domani devi andare a provare il vestito.
   Tomorrow you have to go for a fitting.

■ Era chiaro che la grave malattia l'aveva provata.
   It was evident that her serious illness had debilitated her.

■ Tutte le macchine sono provate prima di essere vendute.
   All the cars are tested before being sold.

■ Non si può entrare nel teatro adesso perché stanno provando.
   One cannot enter the theater now, because they are rehearsing.

   provare (qco)   to feel + *adj*

   ■ Io provai stupore (/rabbia/gioia/piacere/una grande delusione).
      I felt amazed (/furious/happy/pleased/very disappointed).

   provare a + *inf*   to try + *ger/inf*

   ■ Provarono a suonare il campanello (/bussare), ma nessuno rispose.
      They tried ringing the bell (/knocking), but no one answered.

   ■ Prova ad alzarti (/a farlo).
      Try to get up (/to do it).

   provarsi (a + *inf*)   to try (+ *inf/ger*)

   ■ Provati e vedrai. —Mi proverò.
      Just try and see. —I'll try.

   ■ Si provi a farlo! —Mi proverò a farlo.
      Try to do it! —I'll try to do it.

provocare   to provoke, cause; to excite; to induce

■ Quella battuta provocò una risata generale.
   That witty remark provoked general laughter.

■ La mareggiata ha provocato enormi danni.
   The storm at sea has caused enormous damage.

- Questo provocò la nostra curiosità.
  This excited our curiosity.

- Quella ragazza si diverte a provocare gli uomini.
  That girl enjoys provoking men.

- Gli hanno dovuto dare qualcosa per provocare il vomito.
  They had to give him something to induce vomiting.

provvedere   to provide, supply; to see to it; to take care

- Ricordati che tu hai moglie e figli a cui provvedere.
  Remember that you have a wife and children to provide for.

- Il signor Agostini ci provvede di legna tutti gli anni.
  Mr. Agostini supplies us with wood every year.

- A questo provvediamo noi.
  We'll see to it.

- Se dovessero morire, lo stato provvederà ai figli.
  If they die, the state will take care of their children.

  provvedersi   to provide oneself

  - Si sono provveduti di cibo, acqua e medicine.
    They have provided themselves with food, water, and medicine.

pulire   to clean; to wash

- Devo pulire la casa (/il mio appartamento/le finestre).
  I have to clean the house (/my apartment/the windows).

- Attento: ho appena pulito il pavimento.
  Careful! I just washed the floor.

- Puliscigli le mani (/la faccia).
  Wash his hands (/face).

  pulirsi   to clean, wash oneself; to brush; to wipe

  - Pulisciti il naso.
    Wipe your nose (or Blow your nose).

  - Pulisciti le scarpe.
    Brush your shoes.

Q

quadrare   to make square; to square; to tally; to please; to balance; to fit in

- Prima di tutto dovete quadrare il foglio.
  First of all, you must make the sheet of paper square.

- Devi quadrare il numero. (*math*)
  You must square the number.

- Questa teoria non quadra coi fatti. (*fig*)
  This theory does not square with the facts. (fig)

- Non mi preoccupo: i conti quadrano.
  I'm not worried: the accounts tally.

- Quell'uomo (/Il loro comportamento) non mi quadra.
  I do not like that man (/their behavior) (literally: *That man does not please me*).

- Dovete far quadrare il bilancio.
  You must balance the account.

- Le mie idee non quadrano con le tue.
  My ideas do not fit in with yours.

qualificare   to qualify; to call; to make of

- Lo qualificano un genio (/un buon a niente).
  They call him a genius (/a good-for-nothing).

- Non so come qualificare il loro modo di agire.
  I don't know what to make of their behavior.

   qualificarsi   to present oneself as; to qualify (*sports*)

   - Si era qualificato come architetto (/medico).
     He described himself as an architect (/a doctor).

   - Si sono qualificati per il campionato europeo (/le semifinali).
     They qualified for the world championship (/semifinals).

querelare   to sue; to take action against

- Lo hanno querelato per diffamazione.
  They sued him for libel.

quotare   to quote; to appreciate

- Questo titolo non è quotato in borsa.
  This security is not quoted on the stock exchange.

- Il padre di Martino è molto quotato nel suo campo.
  Martin's father is highly esteemed in his field.

quotarsi per qco   to subscribe for sth

- Ci quotammo per diecimila lire ciascuno.
  We subscribed for ten thousand lire each.

R

raccogliere   to pick (up); to assemble; to collect; to reap, harvest; to gather; to receive

- Per piacere, raccogli le schede.
  Please pick up the ballots.

- Gli schiavi raccoglievano tabacco e cotone.
  The slaves picked tobacco and cotton.

- L'autobus si è fermato a raccogliere i turisti.
  The bus stopped to pick up the tourists.

- Gli insegnanti si devono raccogliere in biblioteca.
  The teachers must assemble in the library.

- Quell'amico di Pietro raccoglie francobolli (/monete).
  That friend of Peter's collects stamps (/coins).

- Abbiamo raccolto in un volume tutti i suoi saggi (/centomila dollari per quella opera di carità).
  We collected all his essays in one volume (/a hundred thousand dollars for that charity).

- I contadini sperano di raccogliere molto quest'anno.
  The farmers hope to harvest a lot this year.

- La Croce Rossa raccolse i feriti (/i sopravvissuti al naufragio).
  The Red Cross gathered the wounded (/survivors of the shipwreck).

  raccogliersi in qco/attorno a qc   to be absorbed in sth; to gather around sb

  - Tutti erano raccolti in preghiera.
    They all were absorbed in prayer.

  - Tutti i nipoti (/i partecipanti alla conferenza/i giocatori) si sono raccolti attorno al vecchio (/all'oratore/all'allenatore).
    All his grandchildren (/the conference participants/the players) gathered around the old man (/the speaker/the coach).

raccomandare   to recommend; to entrust

- Potresti raccomandare Marco (/quel candidato) al direttore della scuola?
  Could you recommend Mark (/that candidate) to the principal of the school?

- Ci puoi raccomandare un buon ristorante (/un buon film)?
  Can you recommend a good restaurant (/a good movie)?

- Ti raccomando i più piccini.
  I entrust the littlest ones to you.

raccomandarsi (a qc)   "please" + *command*; to commend oneself (to sb)

- Stai attento (/Non dirlo a nessuno), mi raccomando.
  Please be careful (/don't tell anybody).

- Il ragazzo si raccomandò a Dio e si tuffò.
  The boy commended himself to God and dived.

- Si raccomandarono alle proprie gambe. (*idiom*)
  They took to their heels. (idiom)

raccontare   to recount; to tell

- Mamma, raccontami una storia.
  Mom, tell me a story.

- Quella mia amica vuol sempre raccontarmi la trama dei film.
  That friend of mine always wants to tell me the plot of movies.

- Devi raccontami per filo e per segno quello che è successo.
  You must tell me in detail what happened.

- Raccontatemi la verità.
  Tell me the truth.

- Ne raccontano delle belle (/di tutti i colori) sul conto di Carla. (*idiom*)
  They tell tales (/all sorts of things) about Carla. (idiom)

radere   to shave (off); to raze

- Il barbiere gli ha raso i baffi (/la barba) col rasoio.
  The barber shaved off his mustache (/beard) with a razor.

- Hanno raso il bosco (/la città) a terra (*or* al suolo).
  They razed the woods (/the city) to the ground.

  radersi   to shave

  - Mio padre si taglia spesso quando si rade.
    My father often cuts himself when he shaves.

raggiungere   to reach; to catch up with; to attain

- Credo che ieri la temperatura abbia raggiunto i 35 gradi centigradi.
  I think that yesterday the temperature reached 35 degrees centigrade.

- Domani le truppe (/gli scalatori) raggiungeranno la città (/la vetta).
  Tomorrow the troops (/the climbers) will reach the city (/the top).

- Non sono riusciti a raggiungerlo.
  They could not catch up with him.

- Ti raggiungo al ristorante.
  I'll join you in the restaurant.

- Hai raggiunto la perfezione!
  You attained perfection!

rallegrare   to cheer up; to make happy; to brighten

- La vostra visita (/telefonata/decisione) l'ha rallegrata molto.
  Your visit (/call/decision) cheered her up a lot.

- Quello che mi hai detto mi rallegra molto.
  What you told me makes me very happy.

- Le nuove tende rallegrano la stanza.
  The new drapes brighten the room.

  rallegrarsi che   to be glad (that)

  - Mi rallegro che tu ti sia rimesso (/Giovanni abbia potuto venire).
    I'm glad you recovered (/John could come).

  rallegrarsi di + *inf*   to be glad to + *inf*

  - Mi rallegro di sapere che stanno meglio.
    I'm glad to hear that they're better.

  rallegrarsi (con qc per qco)   to congratulate (sb on sth)

  - Mi rallegro (con te) per la tua promozione.
    I congratulate you on your promotion.

rappresentare   to represent, portray, depict; to describe; to show; to stage; to act for; to be an agent for

- È una statua che rappresenta i caduti.
  It is a statue that represents the fallen.

- Il suo avvocato la rappresenterà all'udienza.
  Her lawyer will represent her at the hearing.

- Il disegno rappresentava una partita a scacchi.
  The drawing depicted a game of chess.

- È un libro che rappresenta bene quel periodo storico (/quel mondo).
  It is a book that describes that historical period (/that world) well.

- La scena rappresenta la camera da letto della contessa.
  The scene shows the countess's bedroom.

- Il mese prossimo rappresenteranno *Re Lear*.
  Next month they will stage King Lear.

- Tu hai rappresentato un ruolo importante in quelle trattative.
  You played an important role in those dealings.

- Rappresento mio fratello nella conclusione del contratto.
  I am acting for my brother in drawing up the contract.

- Il signor Damiani rappresenta la ditta Ferri.
  Mr. Damiani is an agent for the Ferri company.

rappresentarsi (qco)   to imagine (sth)

- Non riesco a rappresentarmi la scena.
  I can't imagine the scene.

rassegnare (le dimissioni)   to resign; to hand in one's resignation

- Mio padre ha rassegnato le dimissioni dal consiglio d'amministrazione.
  My father resigned from the board of directors.

- Tutti hanno rassegnato le dimissioni.
  They all handed in their resignations.

rassegnarsi a qco/a + *inf*   to resign oneself to sth/ to + *ger*

- Dobbiamo rassegnarci a questa tragica perdita.
  We have to resign ourselves to this tragic loss.

- Si sono dovuti rassegnare a pagare.
  They had to resign themselves to paying.

realizzare   to realize; to make; to carry out; to score

- Credevo di poter realizzare le mie speranze (/i miei sogni/il mio progetto).
  I thought I could realize my hopes (/dreams/project).

- Hanno realizzato un film di fantascienza due anni fa.
  They made a science fiction film two years ago.

- Vogliono realizzare il loro piano.
  They want to carry out their plan.

- La squadra italiana ha realizzato un gol nel primo tempo.
  The Italian team scored a goal in the first half.

realizzarsi   to come true; to feel fulfilled

- Il loro sogno di andare in Indonesia si è realizzato.
  Their dream of going to Indonesia has come true.

- Carolina si sente realizzata nel suo ruolo di madre.
  Caroline feels fulfilled in her role as a mother.

reclamare   to claim; to demand; to complain

- Dopo la sua morte il figlio naturale reclamò una parte dell'eredità.
  Upon his death his illegitimate son claimed part of the inheritance.

- Sei sicuro che non vogliano reclamare il risarcimento dei danni?
  Are you sure that they do not want to claim damages?

- Reclamano da tempo il ripagamento del prestito.
  They have been demanding the repayment of the loan for some time.

- Non sono stato l'unico a reclamare.
  I was not the only one to complain.

regalare   to give as a gift; to sell cheap

- Gli regalerò un libro d'arte (/una cravatta).
  I'll give him an art book (/a tie) as a gift.

- Questo te l'hanno regalato!
  They sold this to you cheap!

rendere   to give back, return; to yield; to produce; to make; to portray; to translate

- Te lo renderò domani.
  I'll give it back to you tomorrow.

- Quell'investimento ha reso un bel profitto.
  That investment has returned a nice profit.

- Questi certificati di deposito rendono il cinque per cento d'interesse.
  These certificates of deposit yield five percent interest.

- La loro terra rende tanto.
  Their land produces a lot.

- La pioggia rese inutili i nostri preparativi.
  The rain made our preparations useless.

- Il denaro da solo non rende felici.
  Money by itself does not make one happy.

- Quel romanzo rende bene il mondo dei giovani.
  That novel portrays (or describes) well the world of young people.

- È quasi impossibile rendere quei versi in italiano.
  It is almost impossible to translate those verses into Italian.

- Ti renderò pan per focaccia. (*idiom*)
  I'll give you tit for tat. (idiom)

  rendersi   to become

  - L'operazione si è resa assolutamente indispensabile.
    Surgery has become absolutely necessary.

  - Non si deve rendere schiava delle abitudini, signora Vanini.
    You should not become a slave to your habits, Mrs. Vanini.

  rendersi + *adj*   to make oneself + *adj*

  - Si è resa utile (/antipatica) a tutti.
    She made herself useful to (/disliked by) everybody.

  rendersi conto (di/che)   to realize

  - Spero che tu ti renda conto di quello che hai fatto.
    I hope you realize what you did.

  - Non si sono ancora resi conto che noi siamo qui.
    They have not realized yet that we are here.

resistere (a qco)   to resist (sth); to withstand (sth); to hold out (against sth); to endure (sth)

■ Tu devi resistere alle tentazioni.
You must resist temptation.

■ La barca non resistette all'impeto del vento.
The boat did not withstand the strength of the wind.

■ Non potranno resistere a lungo.
They won't be able to hold out for long.

■ Ti ammiro perché hai saputo resistere alla tortura (/alla fatica).
I admire you because you managed to endure torture (/fatigue).

respingere   to drive, push back, repel; to reject; to fail; to return

■ La polizia respinse i dimostranti.
The police drove (or pushed) back the demonstrators.

■ Lottarono per respingere l'invasore.
They fought to repel the invader.

■ Ho paura che respingano la nostra offerta (/la nostra proposta).
I am afraid they may reject our offer (/proposal).

■ Molti candidati sono stati respinti all'esame di matematica.
Many candidates failed the math examination.

■ Questa lettera va respinta al mittente.
This letter must be returned to the sender.

   respingersi   to repel each other

   ■ Le due cariche elettriche si respingono.
   The two electric charges repel each other.

restare   (auxiliary *essere*) to stay, remain; to be left

■ Quanto tempo resteranno qui?
How long will they stay here?

■ È restata in ufficio fino a tardi (/al mare un mese).
She stayed at the office late (/beach one month).

■ I bambini vogliono restare alzati stasera.
The children want to stay up tonight.

■ La galleria d'arte resterà chiusa per un mese.
The art gallery will be (remain) closed for a month.

■ In questo paese non restano che i vecchi.
Only the old people are left in this village.

■ Resta solo una settimana a Natale.
There is only a week left until Christmas.

■ Gli restano pochi giorni di vita.
He has only a few days left (to live).

■ Le restano dieci pagine da leggere per finire l'ultimo capitolo.
   She has ten pages left (in order) to finish the last chapter.

■ Non vi resta altro da dire (/fare/aggiungere).
   There is nothing left for you to say (/do/add).

■ Togli due da cinque e resta tre.
   Two from five leaves three.

■ Non mi resta che mettermi il cappotto.
   All I have (left) to do is put on my coat.

restituire   to return, give back; to restore

■ Devo restituire questi due libri alla mia insegnante.
   I have to return these two books to my teacher.

■ Restituitemi i soldi che vi ho prestato.
   Give me back the money I lent you.

■ Quella medicina la restituì alla vita.
   That medication restored her to life.

■ Sono riusciti a restituire i colori a quell'affresco.
   They managed to restore the colors to that mural.

ribellarsi a/contro qc/qco   to rebel against sb/sth

■ Si ribellarono contro il governo militare.
   They rebelled against the military government.

■ Antonio si è ribellato contro i genitori.
   Anthony rebelled against his parents.

ricadere   (auxiliary *essere*) to fall (down) again; to hang down; to relapse

■ Il malato tentò di alzarsi ma ricadde sul letto.
   The sick man tried to raise himself but fell back on the bed.

■ Sono ricaduti nelle mani del diavolo.
   They fell into the devil's hands again.

■ I capelli gli ricadevano sulle spalle.
   His hair hung down on his shoulders.

■ Il giovane ricadde nel vizio (/in uno stato di depressione).
   The young man relapsed into vice (/into a state of depression).

ricevere   to receive; to get; to admit, accept; to welcome

■ Ho ricevuto la tua lettera (/una bella notizia/molte visite) ieri.
   I received your letter (/a good piece of news/many visits) yesterday.

■ Il dentista riceve solo di pomeriggio.
   The dentist receives patients only in the afternoon.

■ Quel cespuglio di rose non riceve abbastanza sole.
   That rosebush does not get enough sunshine.

■ Il ragazzo ha ricevuto un pugno sul naso (/un calcio negli stinchi).
The boy received a punch in the nose (/a kick in the shins).

■ Fu ricevuto dal nostro gruppo.
He was admitted to our group.

■ Ti riceveremo a braccia aperte.
We will welcome you with open arms.

riconoscere (qc da/qco)   to recognize (sb by sth); to see; to admit; to acknowledge

■ La riconobbero subito dall'accento.
They recognized her right away by her accent.

■ Ti riconoscerei fra mille!
I could recognize you in a crowd!

■ Si riconosce subito in lui lo studioso (/il grande artista).
You can see immediately that he is a scholar (/a great artist).

■ Devi riconoscere il tuo sbaglio.
You must admit your mistake.

■ I ribelli lo hanno riconosciuto come loro comandante.
The rebels acknowledged him as their leader.

riconoscersi   to recognize oneself, each other; to admit; to acknowledge

■ Non mi riconosco più.
I don't recognize myself anymore.

■ I due fratelli non si riconobbero.
The two brothers did not recognize each other.

■ L'accusata rifiutò di riconoscersi colpevole.
The accused refused to admit her guilt.

■ Mi sono riconosciuto vinto.
I acknowledged defeat.

farsi riconoscere   to identify oneself; to make oneself known

■ Non ho modo di farmi riconoscere.
I have no way to identify myself.

ricordare   to remember, recall; to remind

■ Non ricordo le sue parole (/quello che è successo).
I don't remember his words (/what happened).

■ Non ricordo il titolo di quell'opera (/l'indirizzo di Marta).
I can't recall the title of that opera (/Martha's address).

■ Devo ricordarti chi comanda in questa casa?
Do I have to remind you who is the boss in this house?

ricordare di + *inf*   to remember + *ger*

■ Ricordo di averglielo detto (/d'averla vista/d'averli già conosciuti).
I remember having told him/her (/having seen her/having met them already).

ricordare che + *indicative*; **(non) ricordare che** + *subj*   (not) to remember that/it + *ger*

- Ricordo che tu me l'hai detto.
  I remember your telling me (or that you told me).

- Non ricordo che tu me l'abbia detto.
  I don't remember your telling me.

ricordare qc a qc   to remind sb of sb

- La tua bambina mi ricorda molto la nonna.
  Your little girl reminds me of Grandmother.

ricordare qc di + *inf*   to remind sub to + *inf*

- Ricordami di telefonare alla signora Ariatti (/comprare il giornale).
  Remind me to call Mrs. Ariatti (/to buy the newspaper).

ricordarsi   to remember; to commemorate

- Mi ricordo che Maria era molto magra.
  I remember that Mary was very thin.

- Il ragazzo non si ricordava più del delitto.
  The boy didn't remember the crime anymore.

- Hanno messo una lapide che ricorda i caduti della seconda guerra mondiale.
  They have put up a plaque commemorating the fallen in the Second World War.

- Tu non ti ricordi dal naso alla bocca. (*idiomatic*)
  You would forget your own name.

ridere (di/per)   to laugh (at); to make fun (of); to sparkle

- Tutti rideranno di te.
  Everybody will make fun of (or laugh at) you.

- Beppe rise di cuore (/sotto i baffi/in faccia a loro/alle loro spalle).
  Joe laughed heartily (/up his sleeve/in their face/behind their backs).

- C'è poco da ridere.
  It is no laughing matter.

- Non c'è niente da ridere.
  There is nothing to laugh about.

- Le ridevano gli occhi.
  Her eyes were sparkling.

- Si faceva per ridere!
  It was only a joke!

far ridere   to be ridiculous, funny

- Queste scuse fanno ridere.
  These excuses are ridiculous.

■   Questo comportamento fa ridere i polli. (*fig*)
This behavior is absolutely ridiculous.

far ridere qc   to make sb laugh

■   Non farlo ridere.
Don't make him laugh.

ridurre   to reduce, cut down, curtail, bring down; to abridge; to turn; to adapt

■   Si deve ridurre il personale.
The staff must be reduced (or cut back or downsized).

■   Hanno già ridotto i prezzi (/le spese/gli stipendi/gli sprechi).
They have already reduced prices (/expenses/salaries/waste).

■   Appena hanno visto la macchina della polizia, i ragazzi hanno ridotto la velocità.
As soon as they saw the police car, the kids reduced their speed.

■   Sono sicuro che lo ridurranno al silenzio (/all'obbedienza/alla disperazione).
I am sure they will reduce him to silence (/obedience/despair).

■   Non c'è modo di ridurlo alla ragione.
There is no way to make him see reason.

■   Tu riduci sempre la tua stanza in un campo di battaglia.
You always turn your room into a battlefield.

■   Hanno ridotto quell'albergo (/quella villa/quel convento) in appartamenti (/in un letamaio).
They have turned that hotel (/villa/convent) into apartments (/into a dungheap).

■   Questa è la versione ridotta dell'originale.
This is the abridged version of the original.

■   Quel best seller (/Quella commedia) sarà certamente ridotto per lo schermo (/ridotta per la televisione).
That bestseller (/play) will certainly be adapted for the screen (/television).

ridursi   to reduce oneself; to dwindle; to break (to pieces)

■   Il prigioniero si era ridotto a pelle e ossa.
The prisoner was reduced to skin and bones.

■   I nostri risparmi si sono ridotti a poche migliaia di dollari.
Our savings have dwindled to a few thousand dollars.

■   Quel vaso di porcellana è caduto per terra e si è ridotto a pezzi.
That china vase fell to the floor and broke into pieces.

ridursi a + *inf*   to lower oneself to + *ger*

■   Non si ridurranno mai a chiedere l'elemosina (/accettare compromessi).
They will never lower themselves to begging (/accepting compromises).

riempire (di qco)   to fill, stuff (with sth); to fill out

■   Le vostre parole mi riempiono di gioia (/speranza/dolore/tristezza).
Your words fill me with joy (/hope/sorrow/sadness).

■ Riempimi il bicchiere d'acqua (/di vino/di succo d'arancia/di latte), per favore.
Fill my glass with water (/wine/orange juice/milk), please.

■ Ho già riempito una valigia di vestiti (/uno scaffale di libri).
I have already filled a suitcase with dresses (/a shelf with books).

■ Lei deve riempire questo modulo.
You have to fill out this form.

■ Devi riempire il tacchino adesso.
You have to stuff the turkey now.

riempirsi (di)   to fill (with); to stuff oneself (with)

■ La bambina si è riempita di cioccolatini.
The little girl stuffed herself with chocolates.

■ Si sono riempiti la testa di idee pazze.
They stuffed their heads with crazy ideas.

■ Il teatro (/Lo stadio) si è riempito subito.
The theater (/The stadium) filled right away.

riferire   to tell; to report, relate

■ Non so cosa gli abbiano riferito.
I don't know what they told him.

■ Quel mio collega ha riferito tutto (/le tue parole) al direttore.
That colleague of mine reported everything (/your words) to the director.

■ Bisogna sempre riferire l'effetto alla causa.
One should always relate the effect to its cause.

riferirsi (a)   to refer (to); to concern

■ Mi riferisco alla vostra lettera del 10 febbraio.
I am referring to your letter of February 10.

■ Non capisco a che cosa si riferisca il signor Bassi.
I do not understand what Mr. Bassi is referring to.

■ Quello che ti ho detto si riferisce solo a te.
What I told you concerns only you.

rifiutare   to refuse; to deny; to decline; to reject

■ Hanno rifiutato la nostra offerta (/la tua proposta/quel lavoro).
They refused our offer (/your proposal/that job).

■ Rifiutano di dare il loro consenso.
They refuse to give their consent.

■ Il loro candidato ha rifiutato la nomina.
Their candidate refused the nomination.

■ Gli hanno rifiutato quel favore (/aiuto/la libertà).
They denied him that favor (/help/freedom).

- Il cliente ha rifiutato la merce in quanto difettosa.
  The customer rejected the merchandise as defective.

- Hanno rifiutato il nostro invito.
  They declined our invitation.

rifiutarsi di + *inf*   to refuse to + *inf*

- Si è rifiutata di farlo (/parlargli/mangiare/testimoniare contro di lui).
  She refused to do it (/speak to him/eat/testify against him).

riflettere (su)   to reflect; to think (about); to think over

- La piscina rifletteva il palazzo.
  The pool reflected the building.

- I tuoi occhi riflettono i tuoi sentimenti.
  Your eyes reflect your feelings.

- Ho riflettuto prima di parlargli.
  I thought it over before speaking to him.

- L'ho fatto senza riflettere.
  I did it without thinking.

riflettersi   to be reflected; to reflect

- La luna si rifletteva nel mare.
  The moon was reflected on the sea.

- I suoi crimini si riflettevano su tutti loro.
  His crimes reflected on all of them.

rimproverare qc (di/per qco)   to rebuke sb (for sth); to reproach; to scold; to blame; to begrudge

- L'insegnante rimproverò lo studente per la sua negligenza (/la sua pigrizia).
  The teacher rebuked the student for his carelessness (/laziness).

- Furono rimproverati per il loro ritardo.
  They were reproached for being late.

- La madre lo rimproverò per i suoi errori.
  His mother scolded him for his mistakes.

- Gli rimproverarono il suo comportamento.
  He was blamed for his behavior.

- Il padre gli rimprovera anche il poco che gli dà (/il pane che mangia).
  His father begrudges him even the little bit he gives him (/the bread he eats).

rimproverare qc per + *inf*/**perché**   to reproach sb for + *ger*

- Lo rimproverarono per non averlo detto subito (*or* perché non l'aveva detto subito).
  They reproached him for not saying it right away.

rimproverarsi to reproach, blame oneself for sth

- Tu non hai niente da rimproverarti.
  You have nothing to reproach yourself for (or blame yourself for).

ringraziare qc (di qco) to thank sb (for sth)

- Non so chi ringraziare.
  I don't know whom to thank.

- Vi ringrazio di cuore (/di tutto cuore).
  I thank you sincerely (/with all my heart).

- L'ho ringraziata del regalo (/dell'invito/per iscritto).
  I thanked her for the present (/invitation/in writing).

  ringraziare qc di + *inf* to thank sb for + *ger*

  - Ti ringrazio di avermi telefonato (/essere venuto).
    I thank you for calling me (/coming).

rinunciare to give up, renounce

- Ho rinunciato al piacere di vederli (/fare quel viaggio).
  I gave up the pleasure of seeing them (/taking that trip).

- Io ci rinuncio.
  I give up.

- Mio cugino ha rinunciato al suo sogno.
  My cousin renounced his dream.

  rinunciare a + *inf* to give up + *ger*

  - Rinunciai a comprarlo (/parlargli/vedere quel film/imparare il cinese).
    I gave up buying it (/speaking to him/seeing that movie/learning Chinese)

riparare to protect; to repair; to make up for; to rectify

- Un giubbotto di pelle lo riparava dal vento. Il casco gli riparava la testa.
  A leather jacket protected him from the wind. The helmet protected his head.

- Devo far riparare la macchina (/la televisione/le scarpe/l'orologio).
  I have to have my car (/television/shoes/watch) repaired.

- Devono riparare quei torti.
  They have to make up for those wrongs.

- Dobbiamo riparare quell'ingiustizia.
  We have to rectify that injustice.

  riparare in to take refuge in, escape to

  - I partigiani ripararono in montagna.
    The partisans took refuge in the mountains.

  - Sono riparati in Svizzera.
    They took refuge in (or escaped to) Switzerland.

ripararsi   to protect oneself; to take shelter

- Cercarono di ripararsi dai colpi.
  They tried to protect themselves from the blows.

- Si ripararono dalla pioggia sotto la tettoia della stazione.
  They took shelter from the rain under the station awning.

ripetere   to repeat, tell over and over; to go over; to take again

- Hanno ripetuto lo stesso sbaglio (/lo stesso esame).
  They repeated the same error (/test).

- Te l'ho ripetuto tante volte!
  I told you over and over again!

- Per favore, non ripeta a nessuno quello che le ho detto.
  Please don't tell anybody what I told you.

- Dovresti ripetere la lezione ancora una volta.
  You should go over your lesson once again.

- Quante volte lo devo ripetere?
  How many times must I say it?

- Quello studente deve ripetere l'esame.
  That student has to take the exam again.

ripetersi   to repeat oneself; to happen again

- Gli errori si ripetono.
  Mistakes repeat themselves.

- Questi incidenti non si devono ripetere più.
  These accidents must not happen anymore.

riposare   to rest

- Il paziente riposa da due ore.
  The patient has been resting for two hours.

- Le fondamenta della tua casa riposano sulla sabbia.
  The foundations of your house rest on sand.

riposarsi   to rest (oneself)

- Sei stanco. Riposati un po'.
  You are tired. Rest a little.

- Dopo tante ore di lavoro al computer dovrei riposarmi la vista.
  After many hours of work at the computer, I should rest my eyes.

risalire (auxiliary *essere;* if the verb is followed by a direct object, auxiliary *avere*)
to go up again; to go, date back; to go upstream

- Scendo e risalgo subito.
  I am going downstairs, but I'll be back right away.

- Dobbiamo risalire alle cause di questo problema.
  We have to go back to the causes of this problem.

- Il signor Visconti risalì in macchina e partì.
  Mr. Visconti got back into his car and left.

- La loro casa (/Questo campanile) risale al Settecento.
  Their house (/This steeple) dates back to the eighteenth century.

- Hanno risalito il corso del fiume su un gommone.
  They went upstream on a rubber raft.

- Il delitto risale a un anno fa.
  The crime occurred a year ago.

rischiare (qco/di + *inf*)   to risk (sth); to run the risk (of + *ger*)

- Hai rischiato la vita (/la salute).
  You risked your life (/health).

- Ho rischiato di perdere la vista (/essere licenziato).
  I ran the risk of losing my sight (/being fired).

risentire   to hear again; to feel again; to suffer; to feel the effect of; to show traces of

- Vorrei risentire la voce di quel famoso cantante (/quel notturno di Chopin).
  I'd like to hear the voice of that famous singer (/that nocturne by Chopin) again.

- Non ho più risentito quel prurito al ginocchio.
  I haven't felt that tingling in my knee anymore.

- Risentono molto la morte del padre.
  They feel (i.e., suffer) the loss of their father a lot.

- Quello sciatore (/Quell'impiegato/Quel ragazzo) risente ancora della sua caduta (/della sua disonestà/della severità dell'educazione ricevuta).
  That skier (/employee/boy) is still feeling the consequences of his fall (/his dishonesty/the strict education he received).

- Il romanzo di quello scrittore risente della sua infanzia infelice.
  That writer's novel shows traces of his unhappy childhood.

  risentirsi   to talk to each other again; to take offense

  - Ci risentiamo fra una settimana.
    We are going to speak to each other again in a week.

  - Il figlio del signor Marino si risente per niente.
    Mr. Marino's son takes offense at nothing.

risolvere   to solve, resolve; to break down

- È molto brava a risolvere gli indovinelli (/le equazioni/i problemi).
  She is very good at solving riddles (/equations/problems).

- Puoi risolvermi una difficoltà?
  Can you resolve a difficulty for me?

- Dovevano risolvere i composti nei loro elementi.
  They had to break down the compounds into their elements.

  risolvere di + *inf*   to decide to + *inf*

  - Abbiamo risolto di partire la settimana prossima (/comprare la casa).
    We have decided to leave next week (/buy the house).

  risolversi   to turn (out); to clear up

  - Tutto si risolverà bene, sono sicuro.
    Everything will turn out well, I am sure.

  - La tua influenza si risolverà presto.
    Your flu will soon clear up.

  risolversi a + *inf*   to decide to + *inf*

  - Mi sono risolto a farlo (/dirglielo).
    I decided to do it (/tell him).

risparmiare   to save, spare; to economize

- Risparmia il fiato! (*fig*)
  Save your breath! (fig)

- Dobbiamo risparmiare centomila lire al mese.
  We must save a hundred thousand lire every month.

- Potresti risparmiare tempo e energia.
  You could save time and energy.

- Risparmiami i tuoi commenti (/consigli).
  Spare me your comments (/advice).

- Non hanno risparmiato fatiche per farlo.
  They spared no effort to do it.

- Cerchiamo di risparmiare il gas (/la luce).
  Let's try to economize on gas (/electricity).

  risparmiarsi   to take care of oneself

  - Risparmiati.
    Take care of yourself.

  risparmiarsi di + *inf*   to need not + *inf*

  - Per me, puoi risparmiarti di farlo.
    As far as I am concerned, you needn't do it.

rispondere (a qc/qco)   to reply, answer, respond; to open onto; to meet; to pay

- Rispondimi.
  Answer me.

- Perché non hai risposto alla mia domanda (/alla lettera del signor Sassoli)?
  Why didn't you answer my question (/Mr. Sassoli's letter)?

- Il signor Zolla ha risposto di sì (/con una risata).
  Mr. Zolla answered yes (/with a laugh).

- Perché non rispondete al telefono?
  Why don't you answer the phone?

- Non puoi rispondere al professore (/al babbo).
  You cannot talk back to your professor (/father).

- Mio zio mi ha risposto poche righe (/poche parole).
  My uncle wrote a few lines (/said a few words) in reply.

- Il motore (/L'aereo) non risponde (ai comandi).
  The motor (/The plane) does not respond (to the controls).

- Questo non risponde ai requisiti.
  This does not meet the requirements.

- Devi rispondere del danno.
  You have to pay for the damage.

  rispondere di qc/qco   to be responsible for sth; to vouch for sb

  - Non rispondo delle loro azioni (/di quello che potrà succedere).
    I'm not responsible for their actions (/what may happen).

  - La direzione non risponde degli articoli non depositati.
    The management cannot be held responsible for unchecked items.

  - Rispondo io di lui.
    I'll vouch for him.

  - Pagheranno: ne rispondo io.
    They will pay: take my word for it.

risultare   (auxiliary *essere*) to occur to; to turn out to be, result; to be; to understand

- Mi risulta che vi siete già accordati.
  I understand (i.e., It occurs to me) that you have already come to an agreement.

- Dall'autopsia risultò che erano morti di cause naturali.
  It turned out from the autopsy that they died of natural causes.

- La loro testimonianza è risultata falsa.
  Their testimony turned out to be false.

- Il corridore francese è risultato vincitore.
  The French runner was the winner.

- Questo non mi risulta.
  I don't know anything about this.

ritornare   (auxiliary *essere*) to go, come back, return

- Sono sicuro che ritorneranno a casa (/a Roma/in Italia) presto.
  I am sure they will come back home (/to Rome/to Italy) soon.

- Ritornano sempre sullo stesso argomento.
  They always come back to the same topic.

■ L'ho comprato ritornando da scuola.
I bought it on my way back from school.

■ Marta è ritornata in sé.
Martha has come to her senses.

ritornare a + *inf* to start sth again

■ È ritornata a lavorare.
She started work again.

riunire to put, gather, get together; to call, summon; to bring together again

■ Devo riunire i pezzi del trenino di Fabio.
I have to put the pieces of Fabio's little train together.

■ La ragazza riunì le sue cose e se ne andò.
The girl gathered her things and left.

■ Stasera riunisco degli amici per una festicciola. Vuoi venire?
Tonight I am getting some friends together for a little party. Do you want to come?

■ Il dolore li ha riuniti.
Grief has brought them together again.

■ Il direttore vuole riunire il consiglio dei professori.
The principal wants to call a teachers' meeting.

riunirsi to meet, gather; to be combined; to get back together

■ Dove ci riuniamo? —A casa di Pietro.
Where are we going to meet? —At Peter's.

■ I membri del Parlamento (/del consiglio di amministrazione) si riuniscono oggi pomeriggio.
The members of Parliament (/board of trustees) will meet this afternoon.

■ Si riunirono dopo anni di separazione.
They got back together after years of separation.

riuscire (auxiliary *essere*) to be successful; to get ahead

■ La missione (/L'operazione) è riuscita.
The mission (/The operation) was successful.

■ La festa (/non) è riuscita bene.
The party was (/was not) a success.

■ Sono sicuro che Alberto riuscirà nella vita.
I am sure that Albert will get ahead in life.

riuscire + *adj/adv* to be + *adj/adv*

■ Tutto questo gli riusciva assolutamente nuovo.
All this was absolutely new to him.

■ Enrico riesce molto bene in italiano.
Henry is very good at Italian.

■   Questo gli riesce difficile (/facile/insopportabile).
This is difficult (/easy/unbearable) for him.

riuscire a + *inf*   to succeed, manage, be able to + *inf*/in + *ger*

■   Non sono riuscito ad aprire la lattina (/a parlare con il signor Galbiati).
I was not able to open the can (/speak with Mr. Galbiati).

■   Sei riuscito solo a stancarmi.
You succeeded only in tiring (or managed only to tire) me.

■   Non credo di poterci riuscire.
I don't think I can manage (it).

■   Non sono riusciti a passare l'esame di guida.
They failed to pass their driving test.

rompere   to break (off), smash; to burst

■   Hai rotto il finestrino (/il bicchiere/la tazza/il digiuno)?
Did you break the car window (/the glass/the cup/your fast)?

■   Hanno paura che il fiume possa rompere gli argini stasera.
They are afraid the river may overflow its banks tonight.

■   Hanno rotto il loro fidanzamento (/le relazioni diplomatiche/le trattative).
They broke off their engagement (/diplomatic relations/negotiations).

■   Gli hanno rotto la testa (/la faccia/il naso).
They smashed his head (/face/nose).

■   Non rompermi i timpani.
Don't burst my eardrums.

■   La bambina ruppe in lacrime.
The little girl burst into tears.

rompersi   to break

■   Il vaso di cristallo è caduto e si è rotto.
The crystal vase fell and broke.

■   Si è rotta una spalla (/una gamba/la schiena/l'osso del collo) sciando.
She broke her shoulder (/leg/back/neck) skiing.

■   Mi sto rompendo la testa per cercare di ricordarmi quella formula.
I am racking my brains to try to remember that formula.

rovesciare   to spill; to turn up, upset, knock over; to overturn, overthrow; to empty; to reverse

■   Giorgio ha rovesciato l'acqua (/il caffè/il vino) sulla tavola.
George spilled the water (/coffee/wine) on the table.

■   Ho rovesciato l'olio sul pavimento.
I spilled oil on the floor.

■   Il contadino rovesciava le zolle con la vanga.
The farmer was turning up the sod with his spade.

■ Il gatto ha rovesciato la brocca.
The cat knocked over the pitcher.

■ Le onde rovesciarono la scialuppa dei naufraghi.
The waves overturned the lifeboat with the shipwrecked passengers on it.

■ Ho sentito che hanno rovesciato il governo. (*fig*)
I heard they have overthrown the government.

■ Ho rovesciato la borsetta (/le tasche) per vedere se trovavo le chiavi.
I emptied my handbag (/my pockets) to see if I could find my keys.

■ L'intervento del presidente potrebbe rovesciare la situazione.
The president's intervention could reverse the situation.

rovesciarsi   to capsize; to turn over; to spill

■ Pensano che il gommone si sia rovesciato a causa dei forti venti.
They think the rubber raft capsized because of high winds.

■ Il guidatore perse controllo della macchina, che si rovesciò in un fossato.
The driver lost control of the car, which turned over into a ditch.

■ Il caffè le si è rovesciato sulla camicetta bianca.
The coffee spilled on her white blouse.

rubare   to steal

■ Le hanno rubato la valigia (/i gioielli/tutto il denaro che aveva).
They stole her suitcase (/her jewels/all the money she had).

■ L'hanno sorpreso a rubare.
They caught him stealing.

■ Non voglio rubarle del tempo prezioso, signor Gesualdi.
I don't want to take up your precious time, Mr. Gesualdi.

■ Mi hai rubato la parola di bocca. (*fig*)
You took the words right out of my mouth. (fig)

S

sacrificare (qc/qco a/per qc/qco)   to sacrifice (sb/sth to/for sb/sth); to waste

- Sacrificavano agnelli (/vittime umane) agli dei.
  They used to sacrifice lambs (/human victims) to the gods.

- Hanno sacrificato la vita per la libertà del loro paese (/il loro interesse per il benessere generale).
  They sacrificed their lives for the freedom of their country (/their own interest for the general welfare).

- Quel mobile è sacrificato in quell'angolo.
  That piece of furniture is wasted in that corner.

- Non sacrificare la tua intelligenza in un'esistenza mediocre.
  Don't waste your intelligence on a mediocre life.

  sacrificare qco per + *inf*   to sacrifice, give up sth to + *inf*

  - Martino ha sacrificato molto per finire i suoi studi.
    Martin has given up a lot in order to finish his studies.

  sacrificarsi   to sacrifice one's life, make sacrifices

  - I martiri cristiani si sacrificarono per la fede.
    Christian martyrs sacrificed their lives for their faith.

  - I genitori si sacrificano per i figli.
    Parents make sacrifices for their children.

salire   (auxiliary *essere*; if the verb is followed by a direct object, auxiliary *avere*) to rise; to go, come up(stairs); to climb; to get on; to mount; to ascend

- L'elicottero saliva troppo velocemente.
  The helicopter was rising too fast.

- Il barometro (/La marea/Il livello del fiume) continua a salire.
  The barometer (/tide/river) keeps rising.

- Il sangue gli salì al viso.
  Blood rose to his head.

- Il pallone salì in cielo e poi scoppiò.
  The balloon went up in the sky and then burst.

- Il prezzo delle sigarette è salito di nuovo.
  The price of cigarettes went up again.

- Giovanni non salì, perché Maria non voleva vederlo.
  John did not go upstairs, because Mary did not want to see him.

- Non salire sugli alberi, potresti farti male.
  Don't climb the trees. You could hurt yourself.

■ Era salito sulle montagne più alte delle Dolomiti.
He had climbed the highest mountains in the Dolomites.

■ Abbiamo dovuto salire cinquecento gradini.
We had to climb five hundred steps.

■ Salga sul treno (/sull'autobus): sta per partire!
Get on the train (/bus). It's about to leave!

■ Sali in macchina!
Get into the car!

■ Perchè non sali su una sedia (/scala)?
Why don't you get on a chair (/ladder)?

■ L'uomo salì sul suo cavallo e s'allontanò.
The man mounted his horse and went away.

■ I passeggeri devono salire a bordo della nave.
Passengers are requested to board the ship.

■ Salì al trono nel 1912.
She/He ascended the throne in 1912.

salire a + *inf*   to go, come up(stairs) + *inf*

■ Dov'è tua figlia? —È salita a prendere le chiavi.
Where is your daughter? —She went upstairs to get her keys.

■ Perché non salite da noi a prendere un caffè?
Why don't you come up to our apartment to have a cup of coffee?

saltare   (auxiliary *essere*; if the verb is followed by a direct object, auxiliary *avere*)   to jump (over), hop; to skip, leave off/out; to come off; to leap

■ Il cavallo (/Il campione) ha saltato la siepe (sette metri).
The horse (/The champion) jumped the hedge (/seven meters).

■ La bambina saltava su un piede solo.
The little girl was hopping.

■ Dobbiamo saltare il primo capitolo (/due righe/mezza pagina/colazione).
We must skip the first chapter (/two lines/half a page/breakfast).

■ Nell'elenco hanno saltato il suo nome.
His name was left off the list.

■ Salterò questo brano che è molto difficile.
I'll skip this passage, which is very difficult.

■ Mi è saltato un bottone.
One of my buttons came off.

■ Il cane le è saltato addosso.
The dog leaped at her.

saltare da/di/in/giù/giù da qco   to jump from/with/into/down/out of sth/
off sth/over/across

■   Saltarono dalla finestra (/dal ponte/dal trampolino).
They jumped from the window (/bridge/diving board).

■   Il bambino saltava di gioia.
The child was jumping with joy.

■   Il ragazzo saltò nell'acqua.
The boy jumped into the water.

■   Appena vide il direttore, il fattorino saltò in piedi.
As soon as he saw the director, the errand boy jumped to his feet.

■   I bambini sono saltati giù (/giù dal letto/giù dal muro).
The children jumped down (/out of bed/off the wall).

■   Dobbiamo saltare il muro (/oltre il ruscello).
We have to jump over the wall (across the brook).

■   Quel ragazzo salta sempre di palo in frasca. (*idiomatic*)
That boy always jumps from one subject to another.

saltare (in aria)   to blow (up); to explode

■   Se accendi lì, salteranno le valvole.
If you turn on the switch there, the fuses will blow.

■   Il deposito di munizioni è saltato in aria.
The ammunition dump has exploded.

far saltare   to explode, blow up; to bring down; to break; to sauté

■   Hanno fatto saltare il ponte.
They blew up the bridge.

■   Hanno fatto saltare la nuova amministrazione.
They brought down the new administration.

■   Hanno fatto saltare la banca (/la serratura).
They broke the bank (/the lock).

■   Fate saltare la carne in un po' d'olio.
Sauté the meat in a little oil.

salutare   to greet; to say hello, give one's regards; to wave; to give a nod; to salute

■   Al suo arrivo il presidente fu salutato da una folla entusiasta.
On his arrival the president was greeted by an enthusiastic crowd.

■   Ti ho salutato due volte stamattina.
I said hello to you twice this morning.

■   Saluti sua moglie per me.
Give my regards to your wife.

- Silvia (/Il nostro professore) ci salutò con la mano (/con un cenno).
  Sylvia (/Our professor) waved to us (/gave us a nod).

- I soldati salutarono la bandiera.
  The soldiers saluted the flag.

  salutarsi   to greet each other; to say hello, good-bye to each other

  - Non si sono neanche salutati.
    They did not even say hello.

  - Ci siamo salutati per telefono.
    We said good-bye on the phone.

salvare   to save; to protect

- Il dottore spera di poterla salvare con una nuova terapia.
  The doctor hopes to be able to save her with a new therapy.

- Lo hanno salvato dal pericolo.
  They have saved him from danger.

- Gli hanno salvato la vita.
  They saved his life.

- Dobbiamo salvare la faccia (/la situazione/le apparenze/la pelle).
  We must save face (/the situation/appearances/our skin).

- Stanno cercando di salvare almeno una parte del loro patrimonio.
  They are trying to save at least a part of their patrimony.

- Tu devi salvare la tua reputazione (/il tuo nome/il tuo onore).
  You must protect your reputation (/name/honor).

  salvarsi   to save oneself; to survive; to escape

  - Solo poche persone si sono salvate in quell'incidente (/da quell'incendio).
    Only a few people survived that accident (/fire).

  - Maria si è salvata per miracolo.
    Mary escaped by a miracle.

  - Si sono salvati per il rotto della cuffia. (*idiomatic*)
    They escaped by the skin of their teeth. (idiomatic)

sanguinare   to bleed

- La ferita sanguina molto.
  The wound bleeds a lot.

- Gli sanguina ancora il naso. Le sanguinano spesso le gengive.
  His nose is still bleeding. Her gums often bleed.

sapere   to know; to be able; to be aware of; to hear; to taste; to smell

- Giovanni sa quello che vuole.
  John knows what he wants.

■ Non credo che quell'uomo sappia il suo mestiere.
I don't think that man knows his business.

■ Quel vecchio sa molte poesie a memoria.
That old man knows many poems by heart.

■ Non sapete più niente di vostro nipote?
Do you know anything more about your nephew?

■ Sai dirmi che ore sono (/dove abita Maria/chi sono quelle persone)?
Can you tell me the time (/where Maria lives/who those people are)?

■ Lei sa giocare a scacchi (/a tennis), signor Albani?
Do you know how to play chess (/tennis), Mr. Albani?

■ Tu conosci Giovanni? —No, ma so cosa fa (/dove vive/chi è).
Do you know John? —No, but I know what he does (/where he lives/who he is).

■ Sa il rischio che corre, signor Fagotti?
Are you aware of the risk you are running, Mr. Fagotti?

■ Ho saputo di una lite fra di loro.
I heard of a fight between them.

■ Questo è quello che abbiamo saputo.
That's what we heard.

■ Questo pomodoro non sa di niente.
This tomato has no taste.

■ La sua giacca sapeva di fumo.
His jacket smelled of smoke.

sbagliare   to make a mistake; to misspell; to mispronounce; to miss; to miscalculate

■ Tutti possono sbagliare.
Everyone can make a mistake.

■ Quel mio studente sbaglia sempre l'ortografia (/la pronuncia) di quella parola.
That student of mine always spells (/pronounces) that word incorrectly.

■ Il cestista (/Il cacciatore) ha sbagliato il tiro.
The basketball player (/hunter) missed his shot.

■ Io sbaglio sempre l'accento di quella parola.
I always put the wrong stress on that word.

■ Ho paura che abbiano sbagliato treno (/strada).
I am afraid they took the wrong train (/road).

■ Scusi, ho sbagliato numero.
Sorry. I dialed the wrong number.

■ Ho paura di aver sbagliato mestiere.
I'm afraid I chose the wrong job.

■ Ho sbagliato i calcoli e non ho più soldi.
I miscalculated my expenses, and I don't have any more money.

■ Sbagliando s'impara. (*proverb*)
You learn from your mistakes.

sbagliare nel/nell'/nello + *inf*   to make a mistake in + *ger*

■   Hai sbagliato nel prendere le misure (/nell'applicare la regola).
You made a mistake in taking the measurements (/in applying the rule).

sbagliare a + *inf*   to be wrong in + *ger*

■   Hai sbagliato a comportarti così (/tradurre tutto il capitolo).
You were wrong in behaving that way (/translating the whole chapter).

sbagliarsi   to be mistaken, be wrong; to go wrong, miss (sth)

■   Se non mi sbaglio, ci siamo già conosciuti.
If I am not mistaken, we have met before.

■   Credo che si sbaglino a non accettare quell'offerta.
I think they are wrong in not accepting that offer.

■   Credo che tu ti sbagli sul conto di quella persona.
I think you are wrong about that person.

■   Ti sbagli, non è quella.
You are wrong. It isn't that one.

■   La mia macchina è una vecchia Volkswagen blu, non puoi sbagliarti.
My car is an old blue Volkswagen. You cannot miss it.

sbalordire   to amaze; to stun

■   Quella notizia (/Quella vista/Quello spettacolo) ci ha sbalorditi.
That piece of news (/That sight/That show) amazed us.

■   Queste sono cose da sbalordire.
These are amazing things.

■   Il colpo lo sbalordì.
The blow stunned him.

sbattere   to beat; to whip; to knock (sth against/down); to throw (away/down/sb out); to slam; to bang; to flap; to waste; to hurl

■   Sbattere solo il bianco delle uova.
Beat the egg whites only.

■   Sbatterei la testa contro il muro. (*fig*)
I would beat my head against a wall. (fig)

■   Sbattere la panna.
Whip the cream.

■   Ho sbattuto la testa contro il muro.
I knocked my head against the wall.

■   Il giocatore sbatté giù le carte.
The player threw the cards down.

■   Vorrei che tu sbattessi via questi libri usati.
I'd like for you to throw away these used books.

■   L'hanno sbattuto fuori.
    They threw him out.

■   Speriamo che lo sbattano in galera.
    Let's hope they'll throw him in jail.

■   Potresti uscire senza sbattere la porta?
    Could you go out without slamming the door?

■   Gli hanno sbattuto la porta in faccia. (*also fig*)
    They slammed the door in his face.

■   Ci deve essere una persiana che sbatte.
    There must be a shutter banging.

■   Il passero sbatte le ali.
    The sparrow is flapping its wings.

■   Tu stai sbattendo via i soldi (/il tempo).
    You are wasting money (/time).

■   La nave fu sbattuta contro gli scogli.
    The ship was hurled against the rocks.

sbrigare   to get done/through; to settle; to handle

■   Devi sbrigare le faccende domestiche.
    You must get the housework done.

■   Puoi sbrigare questa pratica?
    Can you settle this matter?

■   Hai già sbrigato la corrispondenza?
    Have you already handled the correspondence?

   sbrigarsi (a + *inf*)   to get/be through; to hurry up (+ *ger*)

   ■   Mi sbrigherò in un minuto.
       I'll be through in a minute.

   ■   Sbrigati! Sbrigatevi! Si sbrighi!
       Hurry up!

   ■   Sbrigati a vestirti, è tardi.
       Hurry up getting dressed. It's late.

scaldare   to heat; warm (up)

■   L'acqua va scaldata.
    The water must be heated.

■   La mattina devi scaldare il motore per cinque minuti.
    In the morning you must warm up the engine for five minutes.

   scaldarsi   to warm oneself, warm up; to get angry

   ■   Se hai freddo vieni a scaldarti vicino alla stufa.
       If you are cold, come warm up at the stove (heater).

■ La minestra non si è ancora scaldata.
The soup has not warmed up yet.

■ Dopo il secondo gol, gli spettatori cominciarono a scaldarsi.
After the second goal the spectators began to warm up.

■ Scaldati le mani.
Warm up your hands.

■ Tu ti scaldi per niente.
You get angry over nothing.

■ A Cristina piace scaldarsi al sole come le lucertole.
Christina likes to bask in the sun like a lizard.

scambiare (qc/qco) to exchange (sb/sth)

■ Scambiarono saluti (/poche parole).
They exchanged greetings (/a few words).

■ È arrivato l'ordine di scambiare gli ostaggi.
The order arrived to exchange hostages.

scambiare qc/qco per to mistake sb/sth for

■ Lo avevano scambiato per quel celebre attore (/il ladro).
They had mistaken him for that famous actor (/the thief).

scambiarsi to exchange; to swap

■ Dovete scambiarvi le informazioni su questo argomento.
You must exchange information on this subject.

■ Simone e Andrea si sono scambiati il cappello (/regali/insulti/una visita).
Simon and Andrew exchanged hats (/gifts/insults/visits).

■ Si scambiarono le scarpe.
They swapped shoes.

scappare (auxiliary *essere*) to escape; to run away/off; to slip; to miss; to lose

■ I ladri sono scappati in Svizzera coi gioielli.
The thieves escaped to Switzerland with the jewels.

■ Due prigionieri sono scappati di prigione.
Two prisoners escaped from prison.

■ Devo scappare a casa (/in ufficio).
I must run home (/to the office).

■ Mi dispiace, devo scappare.
I am sorry. I have to run off.

■ Quel ragazzo è scappato di casa (/dal collegio).
That boy ran away from home (/the boarding school).

■ La caraffa mi è scappata di mano.
The carafe slipped from my hand.

■ Vi sono scappati parecchi errori.
Many mistakes slipped your attention.

■ Mi è scappato di mente il nome di quel ragazzo. (*fig*)
The name of that boy has slipped my mind. (fig)

■ Ti sei lasciato scappare un'ottima occasione.
You missed a very good opportunity (or You let a very good chance go by).

■ Al nostro insegnante scappa spesso la pazienza.
Our teacher often loses his patience.

scappare da + *inf*   could not help + *ger*

■ Ai bambini scappò da ridere (/piangere).
The children could not help laughing (/crying).

scaricare   to discharge, let off; to unload; to fire; to free; to get rid of; to shift; to deduct; to hit

■ Queste condutture della fognatura scaricano l'acqua nel lago.
These sewer pipes discharge their water into the lake.

■ Tutti i passeggeri sono stati scaricati.
All the passengers have been let off.

■ Non hanno ancora finito di scaricare il camion (/la nave).
They haven't finished unloading the truck yet (/the ship).

■ Il poliziotto ha scaricato il revolver.
The policeman unloaded (or fired) the revolver.

■ Mi hanno scaricato di quella responsabilità.
I have been freed from that responsibility.

■ Suo marito ha scaricato tutta la responsabilità (/la colpa) su di lei.
Her husband shifted all the responsibility (/the blame) on her.

■ Non puoi scaricare quel seccatore?
Can't you get rid of that bore?

■ Quando faccio le tasse, debbo ricordarmi di scaricare le spese.
When I do my taxes, I must remember to deduct my expenses.

■ Francesco gli scaricò addosso una gragnola di pugni.
Francis showered (or hit) him with (a number of) blows.

scaricarsi   to run down, to flow (into sth); to relieve (stress)

■ Se lasci le luci accese, si scarica la batteria.
If you leave the lights on, the battery will run down.

■ Quel fiume si scarica nel Mediterraneo.
That river flows into the Mediterranean Sea.

■ Mi sono scaricato di un segreto (/una responsabilità/un grosso peso).
I relieved myself of a secret (/a responsibility/a big burden).

■   Per scaricarmi faccio lunghe passeggiate.
To relieve stress, I take long walks.

scattare   (auxiliary *essere*) to spring; to go off; to release; to misfire; (auxiliary *avere*)
to snap

■   All'arrivo del cantante (/del generale) tutti (/i soldati) scattarono in piedi
(/sull'attenti).
*On the singer's (/general's) arrival, everybody (/the soldiers) sprang to his (/their)
feet (/attention).*

■   La trappola non è scattata.
The trap did not go off.

■   Attento a non far scattare la molla.
(Be) careful not to release the spring.

■   Il fucile non scattò.
The gun misfired.

■   I corridori sono scattati sul rettilineo d'arrivo.
The runners spurted on the home stretch.

■   Se gli dici qualcosa, scatta. (*fig*)
If you say something to him, he flies into a rage. (fig)

■   Penso che abbiano scattato almeno trenta fotografie al battesimo.
I think they snapped at least thirty pictures at the christening.

scegliere   to choose; to sort out; to pick (out)

■   Non so che cosa scegliere.
I don't know what to choose.

■   Non c'è da scegliere.
There's no choice.

■   Devi scegliere una carriera che ti piaccia (/la persona più adatta per questo
lavoro/le parole giuste).
*You must choose a career that you like (/the person most suitable for this job/
the right words).*

■   Scegli i libri (/la frutta) che preferisci.
Sort out the books (/the fruit) you prefer.

■   Tua sorella sceglie con cura.
Your sister picks and chooses.

■   Le ho scelte una a una.
I picked them out one by one.

scegliere qc per   to choose sb as

■   Massimiliano l'ha scelta per moglie (/segretaria/guida/infermiera).
Maximilian chose her as his bride (/secretary/guide/nurse).

scegliere qc per qco   to choose sb because of sth/on the basis of sth

- L'hanno scelto per la sua conoscenza dell'argomento (/la sua condizione sociale/la sua onestà).
  They chose him because of his knowledge of the topic (/status/honesty).

scegliere fra   to choose between

- Tra la carriera e l'amore, Silvia ha scelto l'amore.
  Between a career and love, Sylvia chose love.

- Devi scegliere fra lei e me.
  You must choose between her and me.

- Piuttosto che vivere con te, scelgo la solitudine.
  Rather than live with you, I choose to live alone.

- Si deve scegliere il minore dei mali. (*idiomatic*)
  One must choose the lesser of two evils. (idiomatic)

far/lasciar scegliere (a qc)   to let (sb) choose

- Lasciaglielo scegliere.
  Let him/her choose it.

scendere   (auxiliary *essere;* if the verb is followed by a direct object, auxiliary *avere*) to go or come down, descend; to get out, get off; to fall

- Scendevano la collina tutte le mattine.
  They would go down the hill every morning.

- Tutti speravano che i prezzi scendessero.
  Everybody hoped the prices would go down.

- La luna (/Il sole) sta scendendo.
  The moon (/sun) is going down.

- I capelli le scendevano fino alla vita.
  Her hair went down to her waist.

- Il vestito le scendeva alle caviglie.
  Her dress went down to her ankles.

- Aspetta—scendo fra qualche minuto.
  Wait—I'm coming down in a few minutes.

- Credo che la ragazza sia scesa da una macchina bianca.
  I think that the girl got out of a white car.

- Scendi (dalla macchina) prima che il semaforo diventi verde.
  Get out (of the car) before the light turns green.

- Scusi, Lei scende alla prossima fermata?
  Excuse me. Are you getting off at the next stop?

- La pioggia scende dal cielo.
  Rain falls from the sky.

- La temperatura era scesa di dieci gradi.
  The temperature had fallen ten degrees.

- Scendeva già la sera.
  Evening was already falling.

- Come siete scesi in basso!
  How low you stooped!

scendere da + *store*   to go down to + *store*

- È scesa dal panettiere (dal tabaccaio/dal macellaio).
  She went down to the bakery (/tobacco shop/butcher's).

scendere a + *inf*   to go down to + *inf*

- Perché non scendi a prendere il giornale (/a comprare qualcosa)?
  Why don't you go down to buy the newspaper (/to buy something)?

far scendere qc   to make sb get off

- Fallo scendere subito da quella scala (/quella sedia/quell'albero).
  Make him get off that ladder (/chair/tree) right away.

scherzare   to joke; to kid: to make fun of; to play with; to tease

- Non si deve scherzare su queste cose.
  One must not joke about these things.

- Non so mai se scherzi o dici sul serio.
  I can never tell if you are joking or serious.

- Non c'è niente da scherzare.
  It is no joke (or It is no laughing matter).

- Scherzi?
  Are you kidding?

- Alessandro scherza su tutto.
  Alexander makes fun of everything.

- Non scherzare col fuoco. (*fig*)
  Don't play with fire.

- Gli amici lo scherzavano per il suo accento (/perché era timido con le ragazze).
  His friends teased him because of his accent (/he was shy with the girls).

sciogliere   to untie; to let down; to cancel; to dissolve; to break up; to solve; to thaw; to disperse; to limber up; to fulfill

- Devi sciogliere il nodo (/i lacci).
  You have to untie the knot (/the laces).

- Mi piaci quando ti sciogli i capelli.
  I like you when you let your hair down.

- Hanno sciolto il contratto.
  They have canceled the contract.

- Hanno sciolto la società per azioni (/l'associazione/le Camere).
  They have dissolved the corporation (/the association/both chambers).

- Sciogliere due cucchiai di zucchero nell'acqua.
  Dissolve two spoonfuls of sugar in water.

- La seduta va sciolta.
  The meeting must be broken up.

- Sai sciogliere l'enigma (/il problema)?
  Can you solve the puzzle (/the problem)?

- Il sole scioglie il ghiaccio (/la neve).
  The sun melts the ice (/snow).

- La polizia sciolse l'assembramento.
  The police dispersed the crowd.

- L'aerobica scioglie i muscoli (/le gambe/le braccia).
  Aerobics limbers up the muscles (/legs/arms).

- La madre di Antonio ha sciolto il voto (/la promessa).
  Anthony's mother fulfilled her vow (/promise).

sciogliere qc da qco   to free sb of sth; to release sb from sth

- Hanno sciolto il prigioniero dalle catene.
  They freed the prisoner from his chains.

- L'hanno sciolta dal voto (/dalla promessa/dall'obbligo).
  They released her from her vow (/promise/obligation).

sciogliersi (da qco)   to free oneself (from sth); to melt

- Mi sciolsi dai lacci.
  I freed myself from my bonds.

- Il burro si scioglie. (/La caramella si scioglie in bocca).
  The butter is melting. (/The candy melts in your mouth).

- La ragazza si sciolse in lacrime. (*fig*)
  The girl dissolved into tears. (fig)

scivolare (su/giù/in/fuori/dentro)   (auxiliary *essere*) to slide (down/into/on); to glide away; to slip (out/into)

- I bambini scivolavano sul ghiaccio.
  The children were sliding on the ice.

- È facile scivolare nel vizio (/nelle cattive abitudini).
  It is easy to slide into vice (/bad habits).

- La barca si allontanò scivolando sull'acqua.
  The boat glided away on the water.

- Maddalena è scivolata sul pavimento e si è rotta il braccio.
  Madeleine slipped on the floor and broke her arm.

■ La tazza (/La rivista/La saponetta) gli è scivolata dalle mani.
The cup (/magazine/bar of soap) slipped out of his hands.

■ Il ladro scivolò fuori dalla stanza (/dentro l'appartamento).
The thief slipped out of the room (/into the apartment).

■ Rodolfo fece scivolare dieci dollari (/le chiavi) nella mia mano e se ne andò.
Rudolph slipped ten dollars (/the keys) into my hand and left.

scommettere   to bet

■ Scommettiamo una cena (/centomila lire)?
Shall we bet a dinner (/a hundred thousand lire)?

■ Quel mio amico scommette somme molto forti sui cavalli (/sull'esito delle elezioni).
That friend of mine bets large amounts of money on horses (/on the results of the elections).

■ Scommetto che non c'era (/non ce la faranno/oggi nevica).
I bet it wasn't there (/they won't make it/it's going to snow today).

scoprire   to find out; to discover; to spot; to show; to sight; to take off; to unveil

■ Non riuscirono mai a scoprire chi fosse quell'individuo.
They could never find out who that guy was.

■ Hanno scoperto la verità (/la causa del disastro ferroviario/il colpevole/una legge matematica).
They found out the truth (/the cause of the railway disaster/the culprit/a law of mathematics).

■ Chi scoprì la penicillina (/l'elettricità/quel virus)?
Who discovered penicillin (/electricity/that virus)?

■ Quel regista ha scoperto molte star.
That movie director has discovered lots of stars.

■ Hanno scoperto il fuggitivo (/molti errori nella contabilità).
They spotted the fugitive (/many mistakes in the accounting).

■ Il suo ragazzo non vuole scoprire i suoi sentimenti.
Her boyfriend doesn't want to show his feelings.

■ Hanno scoperto terra!
They sighted land!

■ Scopri la pentola.
Take the lid off (the pot).

■ Oggi scopriranno una statua.
Today they will unveil a statue.

■ Scopri le tue carte.
Lay your cards on the table.

■ Hai scoperto l'America! (*idiomatic*)
Aren't you clever!

scoprirsi   to throw off; to uncover oneself; to take off one's hat; to prove oneself

- Di notte mi scopro sempre.
  At night I always throw my covers off.

- Tutti gli uomini si scoprirono in segno di rispetto.
  All the men took off their hats as a gesture of respect.

- Col passare degli anni non si scoprì una vera amica.
  As the years went by, she did not prove herself a true friend.

- Attento a non scoprirti. (*boxing*)
  Careful not to drop your guard.

scrivere   to write; to spell; to record; to say

- Da giovane mio padre scriveva musica.
  My father used to write music when he was young.

- Come si scrive il suo nome?
  How is your name spelled?

- Scrivimi due righe presto.
  Drop me a line soon.

- Quello studente scrive male.
  That student has bad handwriting (or writes badly).

- Lei deve scrivere qui il dare e l'avere.
  You must record the debit and the credit here.

- Come scrive Freud . . .
  As Freud says . . .

scrivere (a/di/in/per/su qc/qco)   to write (by/about/in/to/for/on sb/sth)

- Devo scrivere la lettera (/la domanda) a mano o a macchina?
  Should I write the letter (/application) by hand, or should I type it?

- Scrivimi qualcosa di Beatrice.
  Write me something about Beatrice.

- Potresti scrivere il tuo nome in maiuscolo (/minuscolo/corsivo/stampatello/tedesco).
  You could write your name in capital letters (/lowercase/in italics/in block letters/in German).

- Ho scritto negli Stati Uniti (/a Princeton) per avere informazioni.
  I have written to the United States (/Princeton) to get information.

- Ferdinando scrive per il teatro (/per quella rivista/in versi/in prosa).
  Ferdinand writes for the theater (/for that magazine/poetry/prose).

- Quel professore ha scritto molto su questo argomento (/di astronomia).
  That professor wrote a lot on this subject (/about astronomy).

- Scrivilo sulla lavagna (/sul foglio/sul muro/sulla sabbia).
  Write it on the blackboard (/sheet/wall/sand).

scrivere a qc che + *subj*/**di** + *inf*   to write to sb to + inf

- Hai scritto a loro che vengano subito?
  Did you write to them to come right away?

- Gli ho scritto di non venire.
  I wrote to him not to come.

scriversi   to write each other/one another

- Non si scrivono più.
  They don't write each other anymore.

scuotere   to shake (up); to stir; to shrug

- Il terremoto scosse la loro casa. Il nonno scosse la testa.
  The earthquake shook their house. Grandpa shook his head.

- Tutti furono scossi dalla sua morte (/da quell'esperienza).
  All were shaken by his death (/that experience).

- Una brezza leggera scuoteva le foglie.
  A gentle breeze was stirring the leaves.

- Il ragazzo scosse le spalle e se ne andò.
  The boy shrugged his shoulders and left.

scuotersi   to shake (off): to awake

- Dovete cercare di scuotervi di dosso la tristezza (/il sonno/questi pregiudizi/la paura).
  You must try to shake off your sadness (/your sleepiness/these prejudices/your fear).

- A primavera molti animali si scuotono dal letargo.
  In the spring many animals awake from hibernation.

scusare   to excuse

- Devi scusare il comportamento di Giovanni.
  You must excuse John's behavior.

- Mi scusi, signora Longhi.
  Excuse me, Mrs. Longhi.

scusarsi di qco/di + *inf*   to apologize for sth/for + ger

- Ci scusammo del nostro ritardo.
  We apologized for our delay.

- Il signor Amato si scusò di essere venuto un giorno prima (/non aver comprato i fiori/non aver telefonato).
  Mr. Amato apologized for having come a day early (/not having bought the flowers/not phoning).

sedere   to sit; to take a seat

- La bambina sedeva vicino alla madre.
  The little girl was sitting near her mother.

■ Mettiti a sedere.
   Take a seat.

■ Non c'erano più posti a sedere.
   There were no more seats available.

sedere a/in/su   to sit at/in/on

   ■ La ragazza sedeva a tavola (/al banco/allo sportello/alla turca).
      The girl was sitting at the table (/at the counter/at the window/cross-legged).

   ■ Il ragazzo sedeva in una poltrona (/in terra/in sella/su una sedia/su uno sga-
      bello/sul letto/sul divano/sui gradini della chiesa).
      *The boy was sitting in an armchair (/on the ground/in the saddle/on a
      chair/on a stool/on the bed/on the couch/on the steps of the church).*

   ■ Lo zio di Guido sedette in tribunale (/in Parlamento) per molti anni.
      Guy's uncle sat in court (/Parliament) for many years.

sedersi (a + *inf*)   to sit down (to + *inf*)

   ■ Si sieda, signor Nannini. Siediti, Giovanni. Sedetevi, bambini.
      Sit down, Mr. Nannini. Sit down, John. Sit down, children.

   ■ Dobbiamo sederci a discutere questa faccenda (/mangiare).
      We must sit down to discuss this matter (/eat).

sedurre   to seduce; to entice; to fascinate

■ È una bellezza che seduce.
   It is a beauty that seduces (one).

■ Non lasciarti sedurre dalle loro promesse!
   Don't be enticed by their promises!

■ Lo sedussero con la speranza di un forte guadagno.
   They enticed him with the hope of easy money.

■ Questa idea mi seduce.
   This idea fascinates me.

segnare   to mark; to note down; to keep score; to score; to say; to indicate; to read;
   to scratch

■ Segnerò i brani da imparare a memoria (/i verbi in blu/i colli da spedire/il prezzo
   dei vari articoli).
   *I'll mark the passages to memorize (/the verbs in blue/the packages to ship/the
   prices of the various articles).*

■ La sua faccia era segnata da una profonda cicatrice.
   His face was marked by a deep scar.

■ Signorina Ragni, segni per favore il nome del cliente (/il giorno e l'ora/il loro
   numero di telefono/l'indirizzo a cui mandare il pacco/le cose importanti).
   *Miss Ragni, please note the name of the client (/the day and time/their telephone
   number/the address to send the parcel/the important things).*

■ Chi segna i punti? (*card game*)
   Who's keeping score?

■ Quel giocatore (di hockey) ha segnato al decimo minuto del primo tempo.
That (hockey) player scored at the tenth minute of the first half.

■ L'orologio segna le sei.
The clock says six o'clock.

■ Il barometro segna pioggia.
The barometer indicates rain.

■ Quanto segna il contatore?
What's the reading on the meter?

■ Chi ha segnato il tavolo?
Who scratched the table?

segnarsi   to cross oneself

■ Le vecchiette si segnarono entrando in chiesa.
The little old ladies crossed themselves as they entered the church.

seguire   to follow; to shadow; to do the same; to keep up with; to go (with); to supervise; to help; to take; to watch; to continue

■ Andate avanti, io vi seguo più tardi.
Go ahead. I'll follow you later on.

■ Quel cane la segue dovunque.
That dog follows her everywhere.

■ Segua questa strada fino alla chiesa, poi giri a destra, signora Amato.
Follow this road as far as the church and then turn right, Mrs. Amato.

■ La polizia segue tutti i movimenti dei due indiziati (/una nuova pista).
The police are following all the movements of (or shadowing) the two suspects (/a new lead).

■ Devi seguire le prescrizioni del medico (/i tuoi impulsi/i consigli di tuo padre/ le istruzioni/la moda).
You must follow the doctor's orders (/your impulses/your father's advice/ the directions/the latest fashion).

■ Il poliziotto aveva avuto l'ordine di seguirli.
The policeman had been ordered to shadow them.

■ Se un tuo amico si buttasse dalla finestra, tu lo seguiresti?
If a friend of yours jumped out of a window, would you do the same?

■ Quel giornalista segue gli sviluppi della situazione (/le novità editoriali/la politica estera).
That journalist is keeping up with developments in the situation (/the latest books /foreign politics).

■ L'architetto sta seguendo i lavori di restauro.
The architect is supervising the restoration work.

■ Mia nipote segue i bambini di Maria coi compiti.
My niece helps Mary's children with their homework.

- Che corsi segui quest'anno?
  Which courses are you taking this year?

- Il fratello di Sabrina ha seguito tutte le partite di calcio dei mondiali.
  Sabrina's brother watched all the soccer games of the World Cup.

- L'articolo segue a pagina 5.
  The article continues on page 5.

- Segue.
  To be continued.

1. sentire   to hear, listen; to find out; to know

- Non hai sentito il campanello (/una voce/uno sparo)?
  Didn't you hear the bell (/a voice/a shot)?

- Non riesco a sentire: c'è troppo rumore.
  I can't hear. There's too much noise.

- L'ho sentita cantare (/entrare/sussurrargli qualcosa/piangere).
  I heard her sing (/come in/whisper something to him/cry).

- Il nonno di Andrea non ci sente bene.
  Andrew's grandfather can't hear well.

- Hai sentito l'ultima?
  Did you hear the latest?

- Devi sentire tutte e due le campane. (*idiomatic*)
  You must hear both sides.

- Non vollero sentire ragioni.
  They didn't listen to reason.

- Hai sentito la radio (/il concerto/la canzone)?
  Did you listen to the radio (/concert/song)?

- Sentimi bene.
  Listen to me.

- Senti che cosa vogliono.
  Find out what they want.

- Vorrei sentire il tuo parere.
  I'd like to know your opinion.

  farsi sentire   to make oneself heard; to speak up

  - Si fecero sentire.
    They made themselves heard (or They spoke up).

  sentire parlare di qc/qco   to hear about sb/sth

  - Non ho mai sentito parlare di lei (/lui/loro/ciò) (*or* Non ne ho mai sentito parlare).
    I've never heard about her (/him/them/that).

  - Non ne voglio sentir più parlare.
    I don't want to hear about it anymore.

2. sentire   to feel

- Sento fame (/sete/sonno).
  I feel hungry (/thirsty/sleepy).
- Senti come è morbido.
  Feel how soft it is.

sentirsi   to feel

- Come ti senti? —(Non) mi sento bene.
  How are you feeling? —I'm (not) feeling well.
- Il signor Funari si sente stanco (/depresso/eccitato/triste/felice/offeso/
  grato/obbligato/amareggiato/commosso/turbato/debole/forte/sfinito).
  *Mr. Funari feels tired (/depressed/excited/sad/happy/hurt/grateful/obliged/
  embittered/moved/upset/weak/strong/exhausted).*

sentirsi + *inf*   to feel + (that, like)

- Mi sento svenire.
  I feel like I'm going to faint.

(non) sentirsi di + *inf*   (not) to feel like + ger

- (Non) mi sento di uscire (/partire/finire i compiti).
  I (don't) feel like going out (/leaving/finishing my homework).

(non) sentirsela (di + *inf*)   (not) to feel up to (+ *ger*)

- Non me la sentivo di dirle cosa era successo.
  I didn't feel up to telling her what had happened.

separare   to separate

- Volevano che chiesa e stato fossero separati.
  They wanted church and state to be separated.
- Il poliziotto separò i due ragazzi che si picchiavano.
  The policeman separated the two boys who were fighting.

separare qc/qco da   to separate sb/sth from

- I due campi erano separati da un profondo fossato.
  The two fields were separated by a deep ditch.
- Dobbiamo separare il bianco dal tuorlo (/la crusca dalla farina/il bene dal
  male/il vero dal falso).
  *We must separate the egg white from the yolk (/bran from the flour/good
  from evil/truth from falsehood).*

separarsi   to separate, leave; to split up, get a legal separation

- All'incrocio ci dovremo separare.
  At the intersection we'll have to separate.

■ L'idea di andare in Australia li attira, ma non vogliono separarsi dal loro vecchio padre.
The idea of going to Australia appeals to them, but they don't want to leave their old father.

■ I due scalatori si erano già separati dal gruppo.
The two climbers had already left the group.

■ I genitori di Antonio si sono separati dieci anni fa, ma non si sono mai separati legalmente.
Anthony's parents split up ten years ago but never got a legal separation.

seppellire   to bury; to hide; to file away; to outlive; to forget

■ L'hanno seppellita nella tomba di famiglia.
They buried her in the family vault.

■ Il giardiniere aveva seppellito i soldi in giardino, vicino al rosaio.
The gardener had buried the money in the garden, near the rosebush.

■ Si dice che l'abbiano seppellito vivo.
They say he was buried alive.

■ La donna seppellì il documento in un cassetto.
The woman hid the document in a drawer.

■ Hanno seppellito questa pratica (/l'inchiesta).
They have filed away these papers (/the inquiry).

■ La loro nonna li seppellirà tutti.
Their grandmother will outlive them all.

■ Dovete seppellire quei tristi ricordi (/il passato). (*fig*)
You must forget those sad memories (/the past).

seppellirsi   to bury oneself

■ Mia sorella si è seppellita fra i libri (/in un paesino di campagna). (*fig*)
My sister buried herself in her books (/in a small country village). (fig)

servire   to serve; to be of use/service; to help; to use; to need

■ Servivano la stessa causa (/la patria/due padroni).
They served the same cause (/their country/two masters).

■ Il cameriere serviva il cappuccino con le brioches.
The waiter was serving cappuccino with croissants.

■ La stanno servendo, signore?
Are you being served, sir?

■ La metropolitana (/Questo ospedalc) servirà anche quelle zone.
The subway (/This hospital) will serve those areas as well.

■ La memoria l'ha mal servito.
His memory served him badly.

■ Chi serve? (*tennis*)
Who's serving?

■ In che cosa posso servirla?
How may I help you?

■ Questo non mi serve più.
I don't need this anymore.

■ A cosa serve questo?
What is this (used) for?

■ Che cosa ti serve? —Mi serve un martello (/il tuo aiuto/molto denaro).
What do you need? —I need a hammer (/your help/a lot of money).

servire a + *inf*   to serve, help to + *inf*

■ Le note servono a spiegare il testo.
The notes serve to explain the text.

■ Questo può servire a giustificare il suo comportamento.
This may serve to justify his behavior.

■ La lettura serve a migliorare la conoscenza di una lingua.
Reading helps to improve one's knowledge of a language.

servire di/come qco   to serve as sth

■ Quello che è successo gli servì di scusa (/pretesto).
What happened served him as an excuse (/a pretext).

■ L'hanno servito di barba e capelli. (*idiomatic*)
They taught him a lesson.

servire in qco   to serve in sth

■ Giovanni ha servito per molti anni in marina (/nell'esercito/nel comitato).
John served in the navy (/army/committee) for many years.

■ Serve in casa loro da molti anni come cuoco (/autista).
He has been serving in their house for many years as a cook (/driver).

servire da/come qc/qco   to serve as sb; to use, be used as sth

■ L'amico di Marco servì da interprete (/guida).
Mark's friend served as interpreter (/guide).

■ Questa stanza gli servirà da ufficio.
This room will serve as an office for him.

■ Questa scatola può servire da tavolino.
This box can be used as a table.

servirsi   to help oneself; to serve oneself; to be a customer; to use/make use of

■ Perché non ti servi?
Why don't you help (or serve) yourself?

■ Mi servo in quel negozio e mi trovo bene.
I am a customer of that store, and I'm happy with it.

■   Ti puoi servire della mia automobile (/di un esempio classico/di un inter-
prete/delle tue gambe/del registratore).
*You can use my car (/a classical example/an interpreter/your legs/a tape
recorder).*

sfidare   to challenge, defy; to brave

■   Luigi li sfidò a poker (/al biliardo/alle bocce).
Louis challenged them to poker (/pool/bocce).

■   La sfido a presentarmi le prove di ciò che dice (/fare quello che faccio io), signor
Mannino.
*I defy you to produce evidence of what you are saying (/to do what I do), Mr.
Mannino.*

■   Tu vuoi sfidare il tempo.
You want to defy (the passing of) time.

■   Sfidarono il pericolo (/la morte/la furia del vento).
They braved the danger (/death/the fury of the wind).

■   Sfido! (*or* Sfido io!)
Of course!

sfidarsi   to challenge each other/one another

■   I due campioni si sono sfidati.
The two champions challenged each other.

sforzare   to strain; to force

■   Non dovresti sforzare la vista (/la voce) in questo modo.
You shouldn't strain your eyes (/voice) this way.

■   I ladri hanno sforzato la finestra (/la porta).
The thieves have forced the window (/door).

sforzare qc a + *inf*   to force sb to + *inf*

■   Devi sforzarli a leggere di più (/fare qualcosa).
You must force them to read more (/to do something).

sforzarsi di + *inf*   to strive, try hard to + *inf*

■   Sforzati di capirlo (/farti capire).
Try hard to understand him (/make yourself understood).

sfuggire   (auxiliary *essere*) to escape; to slip; to avoid

■   Mi è sfuggito di mente il nome di quello studente.
The name of that student escaped my mind.

■   Sono sfuggiti alla morte per un pelo. (*fig*)
They escaped death by the skin of their teeth. (fig)

■   Si è lasciato sfuggire di bocca i nomi dei complici.
He let the names of his accomplices slip out.

■ Si è lasciata sfuggire il segreto.
She let the secret slip out.

■ Ti sei lasciato sfuggire un'occasione d'oro.
You let a marvelous opportunity slip by.

■ Quei ragazzi sono riusciti a sfuggire il pericolo.
Those kids managed to avoid danger.

significare   to mean; to signify; to stand for

■ Cosa significa questo termine?
What does this word mean?

■ *Amour* in francese significa "amore".
Amour *in French means "love."*

■ Quel ragazzo non significa niente per lei.
That boy doesn't mean anything to her.

■ Quell'atteggiamento significa disapprovazione.
That attitude signifies disapproval.

■ Il verde significa speranza.
Green stands for hope.

simpatizzare (con/per qc/qco)   to hit it off (with sb); to take a liking (to sb); to sympathize (with sb/sth)

■ Il nuovo studente ha simpatizzato con i suoi compagni.
The new student has hit it off with (or taken a liking to) his schoolmates.

■ Simpatizzavano per il movimento dei poveri.
They sympathized with the movement of the poor.

sistemare   to arrange; to fix; to settle; to find a job; to leave (somewhere)

■ I nomi (/libri) vanno sistemati in ordine alfabetico (/in biblioteca).
The names (/books) must be arranged in alphabetical order (/in the library).

■ Adesso ti sistemo io!
I'll fix you!

■ Dobbiamo sistemare i conti (/questa faccenda).
We must settle the accounts (/this matter).

■ Spero che riescano a sistemare la vertenza.
I hope they will be able to settle the lawsuit.

■ Sono riusciti a sistemarlo in una fabbrica.
They managed to find him a job in a factory.

■ Non puoi sistemare la tua stanza?
Can't you tidy up your room?

sistemarsi   to settle (down); to get married

- Si è sistemato a Torino.
  He settled in Turin.

- I figli del signor Tosi si sono sistemati nel nuovo appartamento.
  Mr. Tosi's children have settled down in the new apartment.

- Tutti i suoi nipoti si sono sistemati.
  All of her grandchildren got married.

smettere (di + *inf*)   to stop, quit (+ *ger*)

- Smettila.
  Stop it.

- Ha smesso di piovere (/nevicare/grandinare).
  It has stopped raining (/snowing/hailing).

- È ora di smetterla.
  It is time to stop.

- Devi smettere di lamentarti (/bere/dire sciocchezze/telefonargli).
  You must stop complaining (/drinking/talking nonsense/phoning him).

smontare   to dismantle; to disassemble, take to pieces; to drop (a person); to stop (work); to get off duty; to refute; to dampen; to discourage

- Abbiamo già smontato tutti gli scaffali.
  We have already dismantled all the shelves.

- Il tecnico ha smontato il televisore e ha sostituito il pezzo.
  The technician disassembled the TV set and replaced the part.

- L'autobus la smontò davanti al teatro.
  The bus dropped her in front of the theater.

- I nostri muratori smontano alle cinque.
  Our masons stop work at five.

- Le sentinelle smontano alle sei.
  The sentries get off duty at six.

- L'avvocato difensore ha smontato l'accusa.
  The attorney for the defense refuted the accusation.

- Non voglio smontare le loro speranze (/il loro entusiasmo).
  I don't want to dampen their hopes (/enthusiasm).

- Questo insuccesso l'ha smontata.
  This failure discouraged her.

smontare da qco   to get off (means of transportation); to dismount

- Solo una persona è smontata dal treno (/dall'autobus).
  Only one person got off the train (/bus).

- Sofia smontò da cavallo.
  Sophia dismounted (from the horse).

smontarsi   to be, become disheartened, discouraged

- Paolo si smonta troppo spesso. (*fig*)
  Paul gets disheartened too often.

- Non devi smontarti alle prime difficoltà. (*fig*)
  You shouldn't lose heart (or get discouraged) at the first difficulties.

soddisfare   to please; to gratify; to satisfy

- È facile soddisfare quest'ospite.
  It is easy to please this guest.

- Non dovrebbero soddisfare tutti i desideri della loro figlia.
  They shouldn't gratify all the wishes of their daughter.

- Quel pasto non aveva soddisfatto la nostra fame.
  That meal had not satisfied our hunger.

soffiare (su/via/in)   to blow (on/away/in); to puff; to huff; to hiss; to whisper; to steal; to squeal

- A Trieste in questi giorni soffia un vento gelido.
  An icy wind is blowing these days in Trieste.

- Dovete soffiare dell'aria in quei palloni.
  You must blow some air into those balloons.

- Hai mai visto come soffiano il vetro a Murano?
  Have you ever seen how they blow glass in Murano?

- Soffia il naso alla bambina.
  Make the little girl blow her nose.

- Se soffi sulla candela, la spegni.
  If you blow on the candle, you'll blow it out.

- Non soffiare nel fuoco. (*also fig*)
  Don't blow on the fire (or Don't stir up trouble).

- Attento, il vento ti soffierà via il cappello!
  Careful—the wind will blow your hat off!

- Le scale lo fanno soffiare come un mantice.
  Stairs make him huff and puff.

- Il gatto soffiò quando la vide.
  The cat hissed when he saw her.

- Tuo fratello le soffiava qualcosa nell'orecchio.
  Your brother was whispering something in her ear.

- Gli ha soffiato la ragazza (/la palla).
  He has stolen his girlfriend (/the ball) from him.

- I due arrestati hanno soffiato.
  The two (who were) arrested squealed.

soffiarsi   to blow

- Soffiati il naso.
  Blow your nose.

- Il ragazzo si soffiava sulle dita per riscaldarle.
  The boy was blowing on his fingers to warm them up.

soffrire   to suffer; to stand, bear

- Margherita soffre da anni di mal di testa.
  Margaret has been suffering from headaches for years.

- Quel paziente soffriva di cuore (/colite/artrite/asma/sclerosi multipla).
  That patient was suffering from heart disease (/colitis/arthritis/asthma/multiple sclerosis).

- Le mie piante hanno sofferto per il gelo.
  My plants have suffered from the frost.

- Hanno sofferto la fame (/la sete/il freddo/il caldo/una forte perdita).
  They suffered hunger (/thirst/cold/heat/a serious loss).

- Non lo posso soffrire.
  I can't stand him.

- Non posso soffrire questo rumore.
  I can't bear this noise.

  non poter soffrire di + *inf*   not to be able to stand to + inf

  - Non posso soffrire di vederti trattare così.
    I can't stand to see you treated that way.

sognare   to dream (of), have a dream

- Hai mai sognato in lingua straniera?
  Have you ever dreamed in a foreign language?

- Sognavano un avvenire migliore. (*fig*)
  They were dreaming of a better future.

- Non me lo sono mica sognato!
  I didn't just dream it!

- Gabriella sognava a occhi aperti.
  Gabrielle was daydreaming.

  sognare di + *inf*   to dream; to imagine + *ger*; to dream of

  - Ho sognato di morire (/volare/essere in Egitto).
    I dreamed I was dying (/flying/in Egypt).

  - Chi avrebbe mai sognato di rivederti qui (/vincere alla lotteria)! *or* Chi si sarebbe mai sognato di rivederti qui (/vincere alla lotteria)!
    Who would have ever imagined seeing you here again (/winning the lottery)!

■   Quando era giovane Alfredo sognava di andare in Nuova Zelanda (/fare l'attore).
When he was young, Alfred dreamed of going to New Zealand (/being an actor).

sognare che   to dream (that)

■   Ho sognato che eri partito (/che avevi comprato una Ferrari).
I dreamed you had left (/bought a Ferrari).

sognarsi di qc/qco   to dream of sb/sth

■   Mi sono sognato di te (/della mia giovinezza).
I dreamed of you (/my youth).

sognarsi di + *inf*   to dream (that)

■   Mi sono sognato di essere nella giungla (/lavorare con te).
I dreamed I was in the jungle (/I was working with you).

■   Non sognarti di poter venire con noi. (*fig*)
Don't think you can come with us.

sognarsi che   to dream (that)

■   Si è sognata che eri morto.
She dreamed you were dead.

solere   to be used to

■   Si suol dire così.
They say thus.

■   Solevano dare grandi feste (/andare a casa d'estate).
They used to (would) give big parties (/go home in the summer).

sollevare   to raise; to lift; to rouse; to cheer; to boost; to relieve

■   Lo studente sollevò la mano (/un'obiezione/gli occhi dal libro).
The student raised his hand (/an objection/his eyes from the book).

■   Quel ragazzo solleva pesi.
That boy lifts weights.

■   Il bambino cercò di sollevare la grossa pietra, ma era troppo pesante.
The child tried to lift the big stone, but it was too heavy.

■   Sollevarono il popolo contro la dittatura.
They roused the people against the dictatorship.

■   Le tue parole mi hanno molto sollevato.
Your words have cheered me greatly.

■   Dobbiamo sollevare il morale delle truppe.
We must boost the troops' morale.

■   Mi avete sollevato da una grande fatica (/un grave compito).
You have relieved me of some hard work (/a heavy task).

■ Il comandante è stato sollevato dal suo incarico.
The commander was relieved of his post.

sollevarsi to rise, get up

■ L'aquilone non riusciva a sollevarsi.
The kite could not rise.

■ La gente si sollevò in massa contro la polizia.
The people rose together (or en masse) against the police.

■ Sollevati subito da terra!
Get up from the ground right away!

somigliare to take after sb; to resemble; to look like

■ Filippo somiglia alla madre.
Philip takes after (or resembles) his mother.

■ Il vostro cane somiglia al mio.
Your dog is like (or resembles) mine.

■ La signora Franchi somiglia alla donna nel ritratto.
Mrs. Franchi resembles the woman in the painting.

■ I capelli della bambina somigliavano alla stoppa.
The little girl's hair looked like straw.

somigliarsi to be alike

■ I due fratelli si somigliano molto.
The two brothers are very much alike.

■ I gemelli di mia cugina si somigliano come due gocce d'acqua. (*idiomatic*)
My cousin's twins are as alike as two peas in a pod. (idiomatic)

sommergere to flood; to sink; to cover

■ L'acqua ha sommerso i campi.
The water has flooded the fields.

■ Le ondate sommersero la nostra barca.
The waves sank our boat.

■ Lo hanno sommerso di insulti. (*fig*)
They covered him with insults. (fig)

sommergersi to submerge; to sink, go under

■ Il sottomarino si sommerse.
The submarine went under.

■ La nave si sommerse.
The ship sank.

sopportare   to stand, endure; to bear

■ Quel ragazzo non sopporta il caldo (/il freddo/le persone noiose).
That boy can't stand the heat (/the cold/boring people).

■ Non lo sopporto più.
I can't stand him anymore.

■ Mi dispiace che tu debba sopportare quel peso (/quella responsabilità).
I'm sorry that you have to bear that burden (/responsibility).

  non sopportare di + *inf*   not to stand to + *inf*

  ■ Il padre non poteva sopportare di sentirla parlare così.
  Her father could not stand to hear her talk like this.

sopprimere   to suppress; to abolish; to kill; to delete; to cut out

■ La rivolta fu soppressa con grande spargimento di sangue.
The revolt was suppressed with great bloodshed.

■ Quella carica (/Quella normativa) sarà soppressa.
That post (/regulation) will be abolished.

■ L'hanno soppresso perché era un testimone pericoloso.
They killed him because he was a dangerous witness.

■ Si devono sopprimere le seguenti clausole.
The following clauses must be deleted.

■ Le censura ha soppresso alcune scene di quel film.
The censors have cut out some scenes from that movie.

sorgere   (auxiliary *essere*) to rise; to raise; to crop up

■ Il sole sorge alle sei.
The sun rises at six.

■ Mi hai fatto sorgere dei dubbi.
You raised some doubts in my mind.

■ Sorsero molte impreviste difficoltà.
Many unforeseen difficulties cropped up.

sorpassare   to surpass; to pass; to exceed, go too far

■ Lo stipendio sorpassa le sue aspettative.
His salary surpasses his expectations.

■ È vietato sorpassare in curva.
It is forbidden to pass a car on a curve.

■ Devi stare attento a non sorpassare il limite di velocità.
You have to be careful not to exceed the speed limit.

■ Temono che quel fiume abbia già sorpassato il livello di guardia.
They are afraid that the river has already exceeded the danger level.

■ Il signor Guadagni questa volta ha superato ogni limite.
Mr. Guadagni went too far this time.

sorprendere   to surprise, be taken by surprise; to catch; to take advantage of

■ Fui sorpreso di vederli là.
I was surprised to see them there.

■ Mi sorprese la sua reazione (/la sua risposta/il prezzo di quell'articolo).
His reaction (/answer/The price of that item) surprised me.

■ Le loro dimissioni ci hanno sorpreso.
Their resignations took us by surprise.

■ La grandine li sorprese nel mezzo del bosco.
The hail caught them in the middle of the woods.

■ L'hanno sorpreso mentre rubava (/mentre comprava la droga/con le mani nel sacco).
They caught him stealing (/buying drugs/red-handed).

■ Hanno sorpreso la tua buona fede.
They took advantage of your trust.

    sorprendersi   to be surprised

    ■ Non mi sorprendo più di niente.
    Nothing surprises me anymore.

    ■ Non dovresti sorprendertene.
    You shouldn't be surprised (by it).

sorridere (a qc/di qco)   to smile (at/on sb/sth); to appeal

■ Non t'ho visto sorridere alla festa.
I didn't see you smile at the party.

■ La ragazza mi sorrise quando mi vide.
The girl smiled at me when she saw me.

■ La vita (/La fortuna/Il futuro) gli sorride. (*fig*)
Life (/Fortune/The future) smiles on him.

■ La possibilità di andare con lei non mi sorride.
The possibility of going with her does not appeal to me.

sospendere (a/in/per)   to suspend; to hang (up); to interrupt; to stop; to put off; to adjourn

■ Le ostilità (/Quegli studenti) sono state sospese (/sono stati sospesi).
The hostilities (/Those students) were suspended.

- Hanno sospeso la pubblicazione di quel giornale (/la sentenza).
  The publication of that paper (/judgment) has been suspended.

- Paolo era lì sospeso a mezz'aria.
  Paul was suspended there in midair.

- Un lampadario di Murano era sospeso in mezzo alla sala.
  A Venetian Murano chandelier was hanging in the middle of the room.

- Il programma (/Il trattamento) sarà sospeso per alcuni giorni.
  The program (/treatment) will be interrupted for a few days.

- I lavori (/pagamenti) devono essere sospesi.
  The work (/payments) must be stopped.

- La partenza (/L'indagine/La ricerca) deve essere sospesa.
  The departure (/inquiry/research) must be put off.

- La seduta (/Il processo) è stata sospesa (/sospeso).
  The meeting (/The trial) was adjourned.

sospettare   to suspect; to have a suspicion; to think

- Sospettavano da tempo un attentato terroristico (/un inganno).
  They had suspected a terrorist attack (/a trick) for some time.

- Loro non sospettano minimamente quello che sta succedendo.
  They don't have the slightest suspicion of what is happening.

- Nessuno sospetterebbe tanto coraggio in lei.
  No one would think she has so much courage.

sospettare qc di qco   to suspect sb of sth

- Lo sospettavano di furto con scasso (/bigamia/omicidio).
  They suspected him of burglary (/bigamy/murder).

sospettare che + *subj*   to suspect, think (that)

- Sospettano che sia un agente della CIA (/un ladro).
  They suspect him of being a CIA agent (/a thief).

- Non avrei mai sospettato che lei potesse comportarsi così.
  I never would have thought that she could behave that way.

sospettare di qc   to distrust sb

- Il signor Ferri sospetta di tutti.
  Mr. Ferri distrusts everybody.

sospettarsi   to distrust each other/one another

- Si sospettano.
  They distrust each other.

sospirare   to sigh; to long for

- Mammina, non sospirare.
  Mommy, don't sigh.

- Quella ragazza ha pianto e sospirato tutto il giorno.
  That girl cried and sighed all day long.

- Sospirarono di sollievo vedendola.
  They sighed with relief seeing her.

- Sospira il ritorno del figlio (/le vacanze/la promozione).
  She longs for her son's return (/for vacation/for a promotion)

- Per favore, non farti sospirare. (*idiomatic*)
  Please don't make us wait for you.

sostenere   to support; to bear; to maintain; to stand; to back up; to hold; to take; to resist; to nourish; to carry on; to strengthen

- Pilastri sostengono il tetto (/il balcone).
  Pillars support the roof (/the balcony).

- Lo sostenevo con il braccio.
  I supported him with my arm.

- Gli ho promesso di sostenere la sua candidatura.
  I promised him that I would support his candidacy.

- Il padre della ragazza ha sostenuto tutte le spese del matrimonio.
  The girl's father bore all the expenses for the wedding.

- Sostiene che non l'ha fatto.
  He maintains that he didn't do it.

- Sostengo l'innocenza dell'accusato.
  I maintain the innocence of the accused.

- Il nostro amico non poté sostenere il dolore (/la prova/la luce del sole).
  Our friend could not stand the pain (/the test/sunlight).

- L'accusa di omicidio è sostenuta da prove convincenti.
  The accusation of murder is backed up by convincing evidence.

- Quell'uomo non sostiene bene il vino.
  That man does not hold his wine well.

- Non credo che quell'attrice sosterrà quella parte.
  I don't think that actress will take that role.

- Dovrò sostenere gli esami in luglio.
  I'll have to take my exams in July.

- Le nostre truppe hanno sostenuto coraggiosamente l'urto del nemico.
  Our troops have bravely resisted the enemy attack.

- La carne sostiene.
  Meat nourishes (or is nourishing).

- Non sanno neanche sostenere una conversazione in spagnolo!
  They can't even carry on a conversation in Spanish!

- Gli hanno fatto un'iniezione per sostenere il cuore.
  They have given him a shot to strengthen his heartbeat.

sostenere di + *inf* to assert (that)

- L'accusato sostiene di essere innocente (/non aver visto niente).
  The accused asserts he is innocent (/did not see anything).

sostenersi to support oneself on; to lean on/against sth; to stand up

- La vecchia signora si sosteneva con le stampelle.
  The old lady supported herself on crutches.

- Il mendicante si sosteneva alla ringhiera.
  The beggar was leaning against the railing.

- La tua teoria non si sostiene.
  Your theory doesn't stand up.

sostituire qc/qco to replace; to substitute for sb/sth; to act for sb; to take sb's place

- Hanno sostituito la vecchia caldaia (/macchina) con una nuova.
  They replaced the old furnace (/car) with a new one.

- Marco (/Il signor Panini) sostituirà il giocatore (/il signor Andreani come presidente).
  Mark (/Mr. Panini) will replace the player (/Mr. Andreani as president).

- Devo sostituire il professore che è andato in Italia.
  I have to substitute for the professor who went to Italy.

- In certe ricette si può sostituire la margarina al burro.
  In some recipes one can substitute margarine for butter.

- Il vicepresidente sostituirà il presidente nella prossima seduta.
  The vice-president will be acting for the president at the next meeting.

- Il figlio ha sostituito il padre nella direzione dell'azienda.
  The son took his father's place in the management of the business.

sottomettere (qc a qco) to subdue, subject (sb to sth); to submit, to subordinate

- Hanno sottomesso quelle tribù.
  They subdued those tribes.

- Hanno sottomesso i prigionieri (/quei ragazzi) a sevizie (/una prova).
  They subjected the prisoners (/those boys) to torture (/to a test).

- Quel ragazzo vorrebbe sottomettere tutti alla sua volontà.
  That boy would like to submit everybody to his will.

- Il caso (/Il problema) fu sottomesso al giudice (/alla nostra attenzione).
  The case (/problem) was submitted to the judge (/our attention).

■   Devi sottomettere il piacere al lavoro (/il tuo interesse a quello della collettività).
       You must subordinate work to pleasure (/your interest to the interest of the community).

    sottomettersi   to submit oneself

    ■   Si è sottomesso alle autorità.
       He submitted himself to the authorities.

    ■   Si farebbero uccidere piuttosto che sottomettersi.
       They would rather be killed than submit.

sottoscrivere   to subscribe; to sign; to donate; to adhere

■   Ho sottoscritto un abbonamento a quella rivista.
       I subscribed to that magazine.

■   Non possiamo sottoscrivere il vostro operato.
       We cannot subscribe to (or sanction) your behavior.

■   Tutti hanno sottoscritto quella lettera (/quella dichiarazione/quella petizione/quel contratto).
       Everybody signed that letter (/declaration /petition/contract).

■   Abbiamo sottoscritto per una forte somma a favore degli alluvionati.
       We donated a large sum to the flood victims.

■   Hanno sottoscritto a quel programma (/a quella proposta).
       They have adhered to that program (/proposal).

sottrarre   to subtract; to deduct; to purloin; to steal; to rescue

■   Sottrarre dieci da diciassette. (*math*)
       Subtract ten from seventeen.

■   Devi ancora sottrarre le spese.
       You still have to deduct expenses.

■   Il cassiere ha sottratto una grossa somma di denaro.
       The cashier stole a large amount of money.

■   Un impiegato ha sottratto dei documenti (/delle lettere).
       An employee stole some documents (/letters).

■   Mi ha sottratto alla morte (/al pericolo).
       He rescued me from death (/danger).

    sottrarsi   to escape; to shirk, evade; to back out

    ■   Non puoi sottrarti al tuo dovere (/alla giustizia).
       You cannot shirk your duty (/evade justice).

    ■   Carlo non può sottrarsi a quell'obbligo.
       Charles cannot back out of that obligation.

spaccare   to break; to split; to chop

- Il bambino ha spaccato il vetro della finestra con un sasso.
  The little boy broke the windowpane with a stone.

- Il loro nonno spaccava le pietre con lo scalpello.
  Their grandfather used to split stones with a chisel.

- Questo è spaccare un capello in quattro! (*idiomatic*)
  This is splitting hairs! (idiomatic)

- O la va o la spacca. (*proverb*)
  It's do or die. (proverb)

- Potresti spaccare un po' di legna con l'accetta?
  Could you chop some wood with the hatchet?

  spaccarsi   to break; to split

  - Ti spaccherai la testa!
    You'll break your head!

  - Il ghiaccio (/La terra) si spaccò sotto di loro.
    The ice (/ground) broke under them.

  - Questo è un tipo di legno che non si spacca facilmente.
    This is a kind of wood that doesn't split easily.

sparare (a qc/qco)   to shoot (at sb/sth); to fire; to lash out

- Spararono tre proiettili senza colpirlo.
  They shot three bullets without hitting him.

- Gli ordinarono di sparare al bersaglio (/al cervo/ai soldati nemici).
  They ordered him to shoot at the target (/deer/enemy soldiers).

- Tu non sai sparare, devi imparare a sparare.
  You can't shoot. You must learn to shoot.

- Il calciatore sparò il pallone in rete.
  The soccer player shot a goal.

- Spararono molti colpi di cannone (/a salve).
  They fired many gunshots (/in salvos).

- Il cavallo sparava calci.
  The horse lashed out.

  spararsi   to shoot oneself

  - Si è sparato nella gamba.
    He shot himself in the leg.

spargere   to strew; to scatter; to spread; to shed

- La bambina sparse fiori sulla tomba del nonno.
  The little girl strewed flowers on her grandfather's grave.

■   Hanno sparso il sentiero di ghiaia.
They scattered gravel on the path.

■   Le tue lettere erano sparse dappertutto.
Your letters were scattered everywhere.

■   Hanno sparso brutte voci su di lui.
They spread bad rumors about him.

■   Penso che a loro piaccia spargere la zizzania. (*fig*)
I think they like to spread discord.

■   La mia amica ha sparso molte lacrime amare per lui.
My friend shed many bitter tears for him.

spargersi   to disperse; to scatter; to spread

■   Tutti si sparsero per il parco.
Everybody dispersed (or scattered) in the park.

■   La voce si è già sparsa dappertutto.
The rumor has already spread everywhere.

sparire   (auxiliary *essere*) to disappear; to fade away

■   Mi è sparito l'orologio.
My watch has disappeared.

■   È vero che le sono sparite le rughe?
Is it true that her wrinkles have disappeared?

■   Non ti sembra che la mia cicatrice sia quasi sparita?
Don't you think that my scar has almost faded away?

spaventare   to frighten

■   Quell'improvviso tuono ha spaventato i bambini.
That sudden thunder has frightened the children.

■   Non credere che le tue parole mi spaventino.
Don't think your words frighten me.

spaventarsi   to be frightened, scare

■   Non spaventarti, non è niente.
Don't be frightened. It's nothing.

■   Quel bambino si spaventa di tutto.
That little boy is frightened by everything.

■   Quel cavallo si spaventa facilmente.
That horse scares easily.

spegnere   to turn/switch off; to extinguish; to blow out

■   Per favore, spegni la luce (/la televisione/la radio).
Please turn (or switch) off the light (/television/radio).

- Sono due ore che i pompieri cercano di spegnere il fuoco.
  The firefighters have been trying for two hours to extinguish the fire.

- Devi spegnere la candela.
  You have to blow out the candle.

spegnersi   to go out/off; to die out; to pass away; to fade away

- Il fiammifero (/fuoco) si sta spegnendo.
  The match (/fire) is going out.

- Improvvisamente la luce si spense.
  Suddenly the light went off.

- Il condizionatore si è spento un'altra volta.
  The air conditioner died again.

- Il loro zio si spense durante la notte.
  Their uncle passed away during the night.

- La speranza si spense col passar del tempo.
  Hope faded as time passed.

spendere   to spend

- Ho speso un occhio della testa (/un patrimonio/molto/poco/tutto quello che avevo guadagnato).
  I spent a mint (of money) (/a fortune/a lot/a little/all I had earned).

- Quanto hai speso per quella collana (/tuo figlio)?
  How much did you spend for that necklace (/on your son)?

- Quel ragazzo spende e spande. (*idiomatic*)
  That boy throws his money around. (idiomatic)

- Ho speso tutte le mie forze in quel progetto. (*fig*)
  I spent all my energies on that project.

sperare   to hope (for)

- Lo spero da molto tempo.
  I have been hoping for it for a long time.

- Spero che lo faranno.
  I hope they'll do it.

- Spero di sì (/no).
  I hope so (/not).

- Che cosa possiamo sperare? Non abbiamo più nulla da sperare.
  What can we hope for? We don't have any hope left.

- Tutto lo fa sperare.
  It looks very promising.

sperare in qc/qco   to hope for sth; to trust in sb

■   Speravamo nella sua guarigione (/in un aumento di stipendio/nel loro ritorno/nell'aiuto degli amici/in un avvenire migliore/in bene).
We hoped for his recovery (/a salary raise/their return/help from our friends/a better future/the best).

■   Speriamo in Dio.
Let's trust in God.

sperare (*past tense only*) + che + *conditional*   to expect (that)

■   Non speravo che saresti venuto.
I didn't expect (that) you would come.

sperare di + *inf*   to hope (that)/to + *inf*

■   Spero di poter venire con voi (/ricevere presto buone notizie/essere promosso/non avervi annoiato).
I hope I can come with you (/I'll get good news soon/I'll be promoted/ I didn't bore you).

sperare + *subj*   to hope (that)

■   Spero che loro non vengano (/oggi non nevichi/le sue condizioni migliorino/vi divertiate).
I hope they aren't coming (/it won't snow today/his condition improves/ you'll have fun).

spiegare   to spread (out); to explain; to expound; to tell; to unfurl; to deploy; to account for

■   La madre aveva spiegato la bella tovaglia ricamata.
The mother had spread out the beautiful embroidered tablecloth.

■   Il grosso uccello spiegò le ali.
The large bird spread its wings.

■   Spiegami il significato di questa parola.
Explain the meaning of this word to me.

■   Era difficile spiegare il problema (/il concetto filosofico).
It was difficult to explain the problem (/philosophical concept).

■   Il professore spiegò il teorema.
The professor expounded on the theorem.

■   Devo spiegarti quello che devi fare?
Do I have to tell you what to do?

■   Puoi spiegarmi quello che è successo?
Can you tell me what happened?

■   I miei nipoti spiegarono le vele (/la bandiera).
My nephews unfurled the sails (/the flag).

- Spiegarono le truppe.
  They deployed the troops.

- Come si spiega questa differenza di cinquecento dollari?
  How can this difference of five hundred dollars be accounted for?

spiegarsi   to explain to oneself; to mean; to make oneself clear

- Non riesco a spiegarmi il loro comportamento.
  I can't explain (to myself) their behavior.

- Mi spiego?
  Do you see what I mean?

- Vedo che non mi sono spiegato.
  I can see I haven't made myself clear.

spingere qc/qco a/in/in avanti/contro/dietro/dentro/fuori   to push, drive sb/sth
to/forward/against/behind/inside/out; to carry

- Non spingere il pulsante (/la porta).
  Don't push the button (/the door).

- Questo l'ha spinto al suicidio (/alla rovina).
  This pushed him to suicide (/ruin).

- Spingiamo il tavolo in avanti (/contro il muro/dietro alla porta).
  Let's push the table forward (/against the wall/behind the door).

- Spingilo dentro (/fuori).
  Push it in (/out).

- Il vento spinse la zattera sulla spiaggia (/fuori rotta).
  The wind drove the raft to the beach (/off course).

- Non dovresti spingere la tua ambizione (/i tuoi scherzi) fino a quel punto.
  You shouldn't carry your ambition (/jokes) that far.

spingere qc a + *inf*   to drive sb to + *inf;* to urge; to incite

- Solo la miseria (/la fame) poteva spingerli a mendicare (/rubare).
  Only poverty (/hunger) could drive them to beg (/to steal).

- Il padre li spingeva a studiare di più, ma loro non l'ascoltavano.
  Their father urged them to study more, but they wouldn't listen.

- Temono che qualcuno possa spingere gli operai a scioperare.
  They are afraid somebody may incite the workers to go on strike.

spingersi   to push; to venture; to throw oneself

- Spingiti avanti (/indietro/dentro/fuori).
  Push forward (/backward/in/out).

- Il ragazzo si spingeva tra la folla.
  The boy was pushing (his way) through the crowd.

- Decidemmo di non spingerci fino alla Foresta Nera.
  We decided not to venture as far as the Black Forest.

- Mio cognato si è spinto in un affare rischioso.
  My brother-in-law threw himself into a risky business.

spogliare   to undress; to strip

- La mamma spoglia i bambini perché devono fare il bagno.
  Mother is undressing the children because they have to take a bath.

- I nemici hanno spogliato la città dei suoi tesori artistici.
  The enemy stripped the city of its art treasures.

- Il vento ha spogliato gli alberi delle ultime foglie.
  The wind has stripped the trees of their last leaves.

  spogliarsi   to get undressed; to strip; to slough off

  - Spogliati!
    Get undressed!

  - San Francesco si spogliò di tutto quello che aveva.
    Saint Francis stripped himself of all that he had.

  - La serpe si spoglia della pelle a primavera.
    The snake sloughs off its skin in the spring.

sporcare   to make dirty; to soil; to stain

- Beppino ha sporcato la tovaglia di vino (/il tappeto di fango).
  Joe dirtied (or soiled) the tablecloth with wine (/the carpet with mud).

- Hai sporcato il nostro nome (/la nostra fama). (*fig*)
  You sullied our name (/stained our reputation). (fig)

  sporcarsi   to get dirty

  - Quel bambino si sporca sempre quando mangia.
    That kid always gets dirty when he eats.

  - Non voglio sporcarmi le mani. Non hai un paio di guanti di gomma da prestarmi?
    I don't want to dirty my hands. Don't you have a pair of rubber gloves to lend me?

  - Non ti sporcare le mani in questa storia! (*fig*)
    Don't dirty your hands with this story! (fig)

  - Giovanni si è sporcato la camicia (/i pantaloni) di sugo (/di caffè).
    John dirtied his shirt (/pants) with sauce (/coffee).

  - Questa camicetta si sporca facilmente.
    This blouse gets dirty easily.

  sporcarsi a + *inf*   to lower oneself + *ger*

  - Non mi sporco a trattare con voi.
    I won't lower myself (by) dealing with you.

sposare   to marry; to wed; to embrace

- Teresa dice che vuole sposare un uomo alto e bello.
  Theresa says she wants to marry a tall, handsome man.

- Dopo solo una settimana le chiese di sposarlo.
  He proposed to her after only a week.

- Li sposò il capitano della nave (/il sindaco/il cugino vescovo).
  The ship's captain (/The mayor/Their cousin the bishop) married them.

- Mio cugino ha sposato la figlia a un uomo anziano (/un suo amico/un ricco vedovo).
  My cousin married off his daughter to an elderly man (/a friend of his/a rich widower).

- L'ha sposata contro il volere del padre.
  He married her against his father's will.

- Hanno sposato la causa dei poveri (/il nuovo partito).
  They embraced the cause of the poor (/the new party).

  sposarsi (con qc)   to marry (sb); to get married (to sb)

  - Si è sposata con un irlandese (/un avvocato/un compagno d'infanzia).
    She married an Irishman (/a lawyer/a childhood friend).

  - Si sono sposati due anni fa (/in Italia/in primavera/a Napoli/in una chiesetta in montagna/alle sei di mattina).
    They got married two years ago (/in Italy/in the spring/in Naples/in a small church in the mountains/at six in the morning).

sprofondare (in)   (auxiliary *essere;* if the verb is followed by a direct object, auxiliary *avere*) to sink (to/into); to give way; to collapse

- Il *Titanic* sprofondò nel fondo del mare.
  The Titanic *sank to the bottom of the sea.*

- Dopo l'incidente (/la festa) Edoardo è sprofondato in uno stato depressivo (/in un profondo sonno).
  After the accident (/party) Edward sank into a state of depression (/a deep sleep).

- I nostri piedi sprofondavano nella neve (/nel fango/nella melma).
  Our feet were sinking in the snow (/in the mud/in the slime).

- Durante il terremoto improvvisamente il terreno sprofondò sotto di loro.
  During the earthquake the ground suddenly gave way under them.

- Ho paura che la neve farà sprofondare il tetto del garage.
  I am afraid the snow will cause the garage roof to collapse.

  sprofondarsi   to bury oneself; to sink

  - Mia nipote si è sprofondata nello studio (/nel lavoro/nella lettura).
    My niece has buried herself in her studies (/work/reading).

  - Le piaceva sprofondarsi in quella poltrona a leggere.
    She liked to sink into that armchair to read.

spronare   to spur on

- Sofia spronò il cavallo e partì al galoppo.
  Sophia spurred the horse on and galloped away.

  spronare qc a + *inf*   to goad sb into + *ger*/to + *inf*

  - Lo devo sempre spronare a fare le cose (/lavorare/studiare).
    I always have to goad him into doing things (/working/studying).

stabilire   to establish; to fix; to ascertain; to decide; to make

- La causa dell'incendio non è mai stata stabilita.
  The cause of the fire has never been established.

- Stabiliamo i fatti.
  Let's establish the facts.

- Sperano di stabilire relazioni diplomatiche con quel paese.
  They hope to establish diplomatic relations with that country.

- Resta da stabilire la data della riunione.
  The date of the meeting remains to be fixed.

- Dovete stabilire se quello che vi hanno detto è vero.
  You must ascertain if what they told you is true.

- Stabilirono di partire la settimana dopo.
  They decided to leave the following week.

- Non abbiamo ancora stabilito la data della partenza.
  We have not yet decided on the departure date.

- Non riusciamo a stabilire un collegamento.
  We cannot make a connection.

  stabilirsi   to settle

  - Mia figlia vorrebbe stabilirsi a Torino.
    My daughter would like to settle in Turin.

  - Dove pensa di stabilire la sua residenza, professor Galli?
    Where do you plan to establish your residence, Professor Galli?

stampare   to print; to leave; to imprint

- Hanno in programma di stampare una nuova edizione di quel dizionario.
  They plan to print a new edition of that dictionary.

- Lo stamperanno su una carta speciale (/su seta)
  They'll print it on special paper (/silk).

- Ai bambini piace stampare le proprie orme sulla sabbia.
  Children like to leave their footprints in the sand.

- Le tue parole sono stampate nella mia mente.
  Your words are imprinted (or engraved) in my memory.

- Quando Carla l'ha visto, gli ha stampato un bacio sulla guancia.
  When Carla saw him, she planted a kiss on his cheek.

stamparsi   to imprint

■   Quell'immagine mi si è stampata nella memoria.
That picture is imprinted (or engraved) in my memory.

stancare   to tire (out); to weary

■   Andare in bicicletta la stanca.
It tires her to ride a bike.

■   La passeggiata li ha stancati.
The walk tired them.

■   Il suo chiacchierare senza sosta mi stanca.
Her nonstop chatting tires (or wearies) me.

stancarsi   to get tired; to strain

■   Ho paura che i bambini si stanchino troppo.
I am afraid the children may get too tired.

■   Ci siamo tutti stancati di questa musica.
We all got tired of this music.

■   Non stancarti gli occhi!
Don't strain your eyes!

stancarsi di + *inf*   to tire of + *ger*

■   Si sono stancati di ripeterlo (/lavorare).
They became tired of repeating it (/working).

stare   (auxiliary *essere*) to stay; to be; to be about; to stand; to side; to be located; to fit; to suit; to live; to depend

■   I bambini vogliono stare alzati stasera.
The children want to stay up tonight.

■   Devi stare in casa (/a letto), non puoi ancora uscire (/alzarti).
You must stay indoors (/in bed). You can't go out (/get up) yet.

■   La bambina era così spaventata che stette sveglia quasi tutta la notte.
The little girl was so frightened that she stayed awake most of the night.

■   Starò da mia nonna (/Gabriella) per due o tre giorni.
I'll stay at my grandmother's (/Gabrielle's) for two or three days.

■   Buongiorno, signor Sacco. Come sta? —Sto bene, grazie, e Lei?
Good morning, Mr. Sacco. How are you? —I'm fine, thank you. And you?

■   Bambini, state zitti (/buoni/attenti a non farvi male).
Kids, be quiet (/good/careful not to hurt yourselves).

■   Tu stai sempre a dieta.
You're always on a diet.

- Sua madre stava alla finestra a osservarla.
  Her mother was at the window watching her.

- Non c'è proprio da stare allegri.
  There's nothing to be happy about.

- Cinque sta a dieci come due sta a quattro.
  Five is to ten as two is to four.

- Non stare indietro (/in disparte).
  Don't stand back (/aside).

- Quel bambino non può stare fermo (/diritto).
  That child can't stand still (/up straight).

- Quel ragazzo è così debole che non può stare in piedi.
  That boy is so weak that he can't stand up.

- Loro con chi stanno? —Stanno coi Repubblicani.
  Who do they side with? —They side with the Republicans.

- La loro casa sta a dieci chilometri da Genova.
  Their house is located ten kilometers from Genoa.

- Come le stanno le scarpe nuove? —Le stanno strette.
  How do the new shoes fit her? —They're tight on her.

- Questo colore le sta bene, signora Bechi.
  This color suits you, Mrs. Bechi.

- Dove stanno di casa i tuoi amici? —Stanno in via Roma, al primo piano di quella casa color terra di Siena.
  Where do your friends live? —They live on Via Rome, on the first floor (i.e., the second floor in the U.S.) *of that sienna-colored house.*

- Franco sta con i genitori.
  Frank lives with his parents.

- Se stesse in me, non lo farei.
  If it depended on me, I wouldn't do it.

- Tutto sta se loro manderanno i soldi.
  It all depends on whether they'll send the money.

stare/starci to contain, hold

- In questa bottiglia ci sta quasi un litro.
  This bottle contains (or holds) almost a liter.

- Nel nuovo stadio ci staranno tremila persone.
  The new stadium will hold three thousand people.

stare + *ger* to be + *ger*

- Stavo studiando (/mangiando/dormendo/scrivendo) quando mi hai chiamato.
  I was studying (/eating/sleeping/writing) when you called me.

stare a qc + *inf*   to be for (up to) sb to + *inf*

■   Stava a te giudicare la situazione (/dircelo/pensarci/decidere).
It was for you to judge the situation (/tell us/think about it/decide).

stare per + *inf*   to be about to + *inf*

■   Stavo per telefonarle (/venire da Lei), signora Graziani.
I was about to call you (/come to your house), Mrs. Graziani.

■   Stavo per dirglielo quando sei arrivato.
I was about to tell her/him, when you arrived.

■   Sta per piovere.
It is about to rain.

stare a + *inf*   to go to + *inf*

■   Sono stato a fare quattro chiacchiere con Giovanni (/mangiare la pizza/ guardare le vetrine di Natale).
I went to have a chat with John (/eat pizza/look at the Christmas windows).

stimare   to consider; to think highly of; to appraise

■   Tutti lo stimano un bravissimo ragazzo (/un grande artista).
Everybody considers him a very good kid (/a great artist).

■   È stimato da tutti.
Everyone thinks highly of him.

■   Non è stimato molto.
They don't think much of him.

■   Devono far stimare la loro casa (/la collana).
They have to have their house (/the necklace) appraised.

stimarsi   to consider oneself

■   Puoi stimarti sano come un pesce! (fig)
You can consider yourself as sound as a bell!

studiare   to study; to learn; to practice; to examine

■   Studiano medicina (/il comportamento degli scimpanzé/i loro avversari/la loro parte/il carattere dei criminali/la situazione/questo problema).
They are studying medicine (/chimpanzees' behavior/their opponents/their part/the character of criminals/the situation/this problem).

■   Ho studiato per tre anni con (*or* sotto la guida di) un buon maestro (/all'Università di Napoli).
I studied for three years under a good teacher (/at the University of Naples).

■   Studiano sodo (/molto poco/di malavoglia).
They study hard (/very little/unwillingly).

■   Devo studiare questa poesia a memoria.
I have to learn this poem by heart.

- Hai già studiato il pianoforte oggi?
  Have you already practiced the piano today?

- I suoi genitori non hanno potuto farla studiare.
  Her parents couldn't afford to pay for her studies.

- Dobbiamo studiare il loro piano di lavoro (/la loro proposta).
  We have to examine their work plan (/proposal).

  studiarsi   to observe oneself; to watch

  - I due contendenti si studiavano.
    The two rivals were watching each other.

  studiarsi di + *inf*   to try to + *inf*

  - Angela si studia sempre di ubbidire (/fare del suo meglio).
    Angela always tries to obey (/to do her best).

subire   to undergo; to suffer; to be damaged/tortured/sentenced/defeated

- Quella ragazza ha dovuto subire un grave intervento (/un interrogatorio).
  That girl had to undergo a serious operation (/an interrogation).

- Quella banca inglese ha subito serie perdite finanziarie.
  That English bank suffered serious financial losses.

- La loro casa ha subito forti danni durante il terremoto.
  Their house was seriously damaged during the earthquake.

- Dicono che i prigionieri abbiano subito ore di tortura.
  They say that the prisoners were tortured for hours.

- L'omicida subì una condanna a quindici anni di carcere.
  The murderer was sentenced to fifteen years in prison.

- Le truppe nemiche hanno subito una sconfitta.
  The enemy troops were defeated.

succedere (a/su/in)   (auxiliary *essere*) to happen; to succeed; to follow

- Che cosa succede? —Niente di grave.
  What's happening? —Nothing serious.

- Che cosa le è successo?
  What happened to her?

- Tiberio succedette ad Augusto.
  Tiberius succeeded Augustus.

- I figli gli succedettero nell'azienda.
  His sons succeeded him in the business.

- Chi le succederà sul trono?
  Who will succeed her to the throne?

- L'effetto succede alla causa.
  The effect follows the cause.

succedersi   to follow one another, one upon/after another

- I giorni si succedono.
  The days follow one another.

- Si succedettero molte ribellioni.
  Many rebellions followed, one after another.

sudare   to sweat, perspire; to work hard; to toil

- Il paziente sudava molto.
  The patient was sweating profusely.

- Sudai freddo vedendolo.
  I was in a cold sweat at seeing him.

- Sudavamo tutti per il caldo.
  We all were perspiring from the heat.

- Gli sudano le mani quando è agitato.
  His hands perspire when he is upset.

- Sudano per guadagnarsi la vita.
  They work hard to earn a living.

- Hanno sudato sette camicie. (*fig*)
  They have toiled hard.

suggerire   to suggest; to prompt

- Il dottore suggerì una nuova medicina.
  The doctor suggested a new medicine.

- Non devi suggerire agli altri studenti.
  You must not prompt the other students.

  suggerire a qc di + *inf*   to advise sb to + *inf*

  - Le suggerii di non uscire con lui (/di comprargli una cravatta).
    I advised her not to go out with him (/to buy him a tie).

suonare   (auxiliary *avere* when the verb is followed by a direct object; otherwise *essere*) to play; to ring; to blow; to go off; to sound; to strike

- Ernesto suona la viola nell'orchestra di Genova.
  Ernest plays the viola in the Genoa orchestra.

- Io suono a orecchio (/a prima vista).
  I play by ear (/sight).

- Mi suoneresti qualcosa al piano?
  Would you play something on the piano for me?

- Hai suonato il campanello?
  Did you ring the bell?

■ Il campanello è suonato.
  The bell rang.

■ Perché hai suonato il clacson?
  Why did you blow your horn?

■ La sveglia è suonata ma nessuno si è alzato.
  The alarm went off but no one got up.

■ Hanno suonato l'allarme (/il campanello/la ritirata/un do minore).
  They sounded the alarm (/the bell/the retreat/a C minor).

■ Quella parola (/Questo verso) non suona bene.
  That word (/verse) does not sound good.

■ Le tue parole suonarono come una condanna (/false).
  Your words sounded like a condemnation (/false).

■ L'orologio suonava le sei.
  The clock was striking six.

■ Gliele suonarono. (*idiomatic*)
  They gave him a good thrashing.

superare   to surpass; to pass; to exceed; to go too far; to cross; to cover; to recover; to overcome; to be over (number of years); to get over

■ Questa volta il figlio ha superato il padre.
  This time the son surpassed the father.

■ Il successo della commedia ha superato le mie aspettative.
  The success of the play surpassed my expectations.

■ La macchina della polizia ci superò.
  The police car passed (or overtook) us.

■ Tuo padre temeva che tu non avessi superato tutti gli esami (/la prova).
  Your father was afraid you had not passed all your exams (/the test).

■ La produzione di macchine supera la richiesta.
  The car production exceeds the demand.

■ Penso che abbiate superato il limite.
  I think you went too far.

■ Non abbiamo ancora superato il fiume (/il burrone).
  We haven't crossed the river (/ravine) yet.

■ Avevano già superato un'enorme distanza quando si spezzò la cinghia, e non poterono proseguire.
  They'd already covered an enormous distance when the belt broke, and they couldn't go on.

■ Superarono tutte le difficoltà (/un grave pericolo).
  They overcame all the difficulties (/a serious danger).

■ Credo che la signora Alessio abbia superato i cinquant'anni.
I think Mrs. Alessio is over fifty.

■ Devi superare quel muro.
You have to get over that wall.

superare qc/qco in qco   to surpass sb/sth in sth; to be more + *adj* than

■ Eugenio lo supera in intelligenza.
Eugene surpasses him in intelligence (or *Eugene is more intelligent than he*).

■ Il Monte Bianco supera le altre montagne in altezza.
Mont Blanc is taller than the other mountains.

■ Tu lo superi in altezza di almeno cinque centimetri (/due pollici).
You are at least five centimeters (two inches) taller than he is.

■ La loro macchina supera la mia in velocità.
Their car is faster than mine.

■ Sono certo che li superiamo in numero.
I am certain that we outnumber them.

supporre che + *subj*   to suppose (that); to assume (that)

■ Supponi che loro non vengano.
Suppose they aren't coming.

■ Supponiamo che le cose stiano così.
Let's assume that such is the case.

■ Luigi viene alla festa? —Suppongo di sì (/di no).
Is Louis coming to the party? —I (/don't) suppose so.

supporre di + *inf*   to imagine

■ Supponete di essere in Italia (/vederla con un altro uomo/vincere la lotteria).
Imagine yourselves in Italy (/seeing her with another man/winning the lottery).

sussurrare   to whisper; to murmur; to rustle; to gossip

■ Lidia le ha sussurrato qualcosa all'orecchio.
Lydia whispered something in her ear.

■ Il ruscello sussurrava tra gli alberi.
The brook murmured among the trees.

■ Sentivo le foglie sussurrare nel vento.
I heard the leaves rustle in the breeze.

■ Parecchi sussurrano contro di lui.
Many people are gossiping about him.

svegliare   to wake (sb) up; to awaken; to arouse

- A che ora devo svegliarti? —Svegliami alle sette, per favore.
  At what time should I wake you up? —Wake me up at seven, please.

- La luce (/Ogni minimo rumore) la sveglia.
  Light (/The slightest noise) wakes her up.

- Devi svegliare la curiosità (/l'interesse) di quel ragazzo.
  You must awaken the curiosity (/interest) of that boy.

- Cerca di svegliare l'appetito (/l'intelligenza) del bambino.
  Try to arouse the child's appetite (/intelligence).

  svegliarsi   to wake (oneself) up; to rouse oneself; to become aware

  - Mi sono svegliato presto stamattina.
    I woke up early this morning.

  - Con l'età si è svegliato.
    He became more aware as he got older.

T

tacere   to keep quiet; to stop talking; to fall/be silent; to say nothing about, not mention; to omit

- Taci!
  Be quiet (or Stop talking)!

- Fa tacere tuo figlio, per favore.
  Please make your son keep quiet.

- La mitragliatrice improvvisamente tacque.
  The machine gun suddenly fell silent.

- La storia tace questi fatti.
  History is silent on these facts.

- Su questi avvenimenti le fonti tacciono.
  The sources say nothing about these events.

- L'accusato tacque il nome del complice.
  The accused did not name his accomplice.

- Tu hai taciuto un particolare importante.
  You omitted an important detail.

tagliare   to cut (across/down/off/out); to carve; to mow; to snip; to intersect

- La mamma tagliò una fetta di pane e me la diede.
  Mom cut a slice of bread and gave it to me.

- L'ho tagliato col coltello (/con le forbici/con la sega/con la lametta).
  I cut it with a knife (/the scissors/a saw/a blade).

- Devo tagliarlo in due o tre?
  Should I cut (or carve) it in two or three (pieces)?

- Stamattina abbiamo tagliato per il parco.
  This morning we cut across the park.

- Quando tagli quell'albero?
  When will you cut down that tree?

- Giovanni ha tagliato un pezzo di formaggio (/i rami di quell'albero).
  John cut off a piece of cheese (/the branches of that tree).

- Dobbiamo tagliare la ritirata (/i viveri) al nemico.
  We must cut off the enemy's retreat (/supplies).

- Se tu mi tagli il vestito, io lo cucio.
  If you cut out a dress for me, I'll sew it.

- Taglia. (*card game*)
  Cut.

■ Tagliamo corto.
Let's cut it short.

■ Si è fatta tagliare i capelli da un parrucchiere italiano.
She had her hair cut by an Italian hairdresser.

■ Il giardiniere ha tagliato l'erba.
The gardener mowed the grass.

■ Quel ragazzo le ha tagliato una ciocca di capelli.
That boy snipped off a lock of her hair.

■ Prendi il sentiero che taglia quella strada.
Take the path that intersects that road.

■ Il corridore italiano ha tagliato per primo il traguardo.
The Italian runner crossed the finish line first.

■ Quella tua amica taglia i panni addosso a tutti. (*idiomatic*)
That friend of yours tears everybody to shreds. (idiomatic)

tagliarsi   to cut oneself; to shave

■ La bambina si è tagliata col coltello.
The little girl cut herself with the knife.

■ Dovresti tagliarti le unghie: sono troppo lunghe.
You should cut your nails. They're too long.

■ Perché non ti tagli la barba (/i baffi)?
Why don't you shave your beard (/mustache)?

tardare   to be delayed, be late; to arrive late

■ Il treno tardò mezz'ora a causa dell'incidente.
The train was delayed half an hour because of the accident.

■ Cerca di non tardare all'appuntamento.
Try not to be late for the appointment.

■ Gli aiuti tardarono e loro furono perduti.
The help arrived late, and they were lost.

tardare a + *inf*   to be late (in) + *ger*

■ Hanno tardato a dare il permesso (/consegnare la merce/rispondere).
They were late (in) giving permission (/delivering the goods/answering).

telefonare (qco) a qc   to telephone (sth to) sb

■ Quando hai telefonato al signor Tedeschi? —Gli ho telefonato ieri sera.
When did you phone Mr. Tedeschi? —I phoned him last night.

■ Quando telefoni a tua moglie? —Le ho telefonato un'ora fa.
When are you going to phone your wife? —I phoned her an hour ago.

■ Ho telefonato la notizia ai miei nonni.
I phoned the news to my grandparents.

telefonarsi   to phone each other/one another

- Si telefonano tutte le sere.
  They phone each other every night.

telegrafare   to telegraph, wire, cable

- Stamattina ho telegrafato le quotazioni al signor Savini (/a Milano).
  This morning I cabled the quotations to Mr. Savini (/Milan).

- I suoi genitori le telegrafarono gli auguri per il suo compleanno.
  Her parents wired her greetings for her birthday.

  telegrafare di + *inf*   to telegraph + *inf*

  - Gli hanno telegrafato di partire subito.
    They wired him to leave at once.

temere   to fear, dread; to worry; not be able to stand

- Non avete nulla da temere.
  You have nothing to fear.

- Temo di sì (/di no).
  I fear so (/not).

- Non temevano la morte (/il castigo/il duro lavoro/le difficoltà).
  They did not fear death (/punishment/hard work/difficulties).

- Temo la legge (/il peggio).
  I fear the law (/the worst).

- Quel ragazzo teme le sgridate del padre.
  That boy dreads his father's scoldings.

- Non temere, non succederà niente (/ti aiuteremo).
  Don't worry. Nothing will happen (/We'll help you).

- Questi fiori temono il freddo (/il caldo).
  These flowers can't stand the cold (/the heat).

- Teme l'umidità (la luce/il calore).
  Store in a dry (/dark/cool) place.

  temere per qc/qco   to be worried about sb/sth

  - Temono per lei (/la salute del figlio).
    They are worried about her (/their son's health).

  temere che + *subj*   to fear, be afraid (that)

  - Temo che non sia vero.
    I fear it isn't true.

  - Temevo che (non) venissi.
    I was afraid you would (not) come.

temere di + *inf*   to be afraid of + *ger*

- La vecchia signora temeva di scivolare (/essere in ritardo).
  The old lady was afraid of slipping (/being late).

- Non temi di sbagliare (/dimenticartene)?
  Aren't you afraid of making a mistake (/forgetting it)?

tendere   to stretch; to tighten; to hold (out); to strain; to draw; to tend; to lean to

- Per favore, tendi quell'elastico.
  Please stretch that rubber band.

- Tutti tendevano il collo per vederla.
  All were stretching their necks to see her.

- Devi tendere le corde del violino (/le redini).
  You must tighten the violin strings (/reins).

- La mendicante tese la mano.
  The beggar held her hand out.

- Non tendere così tanto quella corda o si romperà.
  Don't strain that rope so much or it will break.

- L'arciere tese l'arco.
  The archer drew the bow.

- Questo piatto tende al dolce.
  This dish is on the sweet side.

- Questo ragazzo (/Quel paziente) tende alla malinconia (depressione).
  This boy (/That patient) tends toward melancholy (/depression).

- Tu tendi verso la sinistra, vero?
  You lean to the left, right?

tendere a + *inf*   to tend to, be inclined to + *inf;* to aim at + *ger*

- Il professor Tassi tende a crederle (/parlare troppo).
  Professor Tassi is inclined to believe her (/talk too much).

- La signora Ruggero tende a esagerare tutto (/essere triste).
  Mrs. Ruggero tends to exaggerate everything (/be sad).

- Le parole di Roberto tendevano a chiarire questo punto.
  Robert's words aimed at explaining this point.

tendersi   to contract

- I muscoli dell'atleta si tesero.
  The athlete's muscles contracted.

1. tenere   to hold

- Non sono sicuro che questa fune terrà (/queste viti terranno).
  I am not sure that this rope (/these screws) will hold.

- La ragazza teneva in mano una moneta (/un bastone).
  The girl was holding a coin (/a stick) in her hand.

- Non tenne quella carica a lungo.
  He didn't hold that office for long.

- Ogni settimana si terrà una riunione.
  A meeting will be held every week.

- Quel tenore può tenere una nota per molto tempo.
  That tenor can hold a note for a long time.

- Tutti lo tenevano in grande considerazione.
  Everyone held him in high esteem.

- Questo bicchiere terrà un litro.
  This glass may hold a liter.

tenere qc per   to hold sb by

- Il padre lo teneva per il braccio (/la mano).
  His father was holding him by the arm (/hand).

tenere indietro   to hold back

- La polizia teneva indietro la gente.
  The police were holding the people back.

- Si tenga indietro.
  Stand back.

tenere (su)   to hold on/up

- Tieni su la testa.
  Hold your head up.

- Tieni duro, non cedere.
  Hold on; don't give up.

- Questi pilastri tengono su il soffitto.
  These pillars are holding up the ceiling.

tenere a + *inf*   to like, want + *inf*

- Tengo a spiegarti quello che è successo.
  I want to explain to you what happened.

- Terrei molto a incontrarlo.
  I would very much like to meet him.

tenersi   to keep (out/away from)

- Tenetevi pronti. (*idiomatic*)
  Be ready.

- Michele preferì tenersi lontano dai luoghi dove era stato con lei.
  Michael preferred to keep away from the places where he'd been with her.

- Sarebbe meglio che ti tenessi fuori dalle loro beghe.
  It would be better for you to keep out of their quarrels.

2. tenere   to keep

■   Ho tenuto il vino in fresco.
    I kept the wine in a cool place.

■   Quando era piccola, mia figlia teneva un diario.
    When she was small, my daughter kept a diary.

■   In Inghilterra ricordati di tenere la sinistra, non la destra!
    In England remember to keep to the left, not to the right!

■   Posso tenere il cappotto? Mi tiene caldo.
    May I keep my coat on? It keeps me warm.

■   Se arrivi prima al cinema, puoi tenermi un posto?
    If you get to the (movie) theater first, can you keep a seat for me?

■   Dovresti tenere il cappello in testa (/le spalle rilassate/la bocca chiusa).
    You should keep your hat on (/shoulders relaxed/mouth shut).

■   Fa piuttosto freddo. Perché non teniamo chiusa la finestra?
    It's rather cold. Why don't we keep the window closed?

■   Perché non venite a tenermi compagnia?
    Why don't you come keep me company?

■   Tenetelo d'occhio prima che combini un altro pasticcio.
    Keep an eye on him before he creates another mess.

tenere qc in piedi   to keep sb standing

■   Mi ha hanno tenuto in piedi nella pioggia.
    They kept me standing in the rain.

tenersi a qco   to stick to sth; to follow; to hold on to

■   Vorrei che Lei si tenesse al testo (/ai fatti).
    I would like for you to stick to the text (/facts).

■   Ci si deve tenere alle istruzioni del manuale (/agli ordini del dottore).
    One needs to follow the instructions in the manual (/the doctor's orders).

■   Dobbiamo tenerci alla ringhiera.
    We must hold on to the banister.

3. tenere (a)   to take up room, occupy; to follow; to have; to be proud of, care about

■   Questo tavolo tiene troppo posto. Devo spostarlo.
    This table takes up too much room. I must move it.

■   Il quadro teneva tutta la parete.
    The picture occupied the whole wall.

■   Ugo non sa che strada tenere.
    Hugh does not know which course to follow.

■   La mia insegnante di italiano tiene le sue lezioni il martedì.
    My Italian teacher has her classes on Tuesdays.

- Quello scrittore tiene molto ai premi che ha ricevuto.
  That writer is very proud of the awards he received.

- Quella ragazza tiene molto ai vestiti (/alla sua collezione di bambole).
  That girl cares a lot about clothes (/her doll collection).

tentare   to try; to tempt; to test; to touch

- Dobbiamo tentare ogni via.
  We must try every way.

- Tentar non nuoce. (*proverb*)
  There's no harm in trying.

- È un'idea che mi tenta.
  It is a tempting idea.

- Non tentarmi, sono a dieta (/devo lavorare).
  Don't tempt me. I'm on a diet (/I must work).

- Volevano tentare la tua onestà.
  They wanted to test your honesty.

- Il cieco tentava il terreno con un bastone.
  The blind man was testing (or touching) the ground with a stick.

  tentare di + *inf*   to try to + *inf*

  - Abbiamo tentato di persuaderlo (/telefonargli/convincerli), ma senza
    riuscirci.
    We tried to persuade him (/phone him/convince them), but without success.

testimoniare   to testify; to give testimony; to attest

- Il tuo amico ha testimoniato a favore o a sfavore dell'imputato?
  Did your friend testify for or against the defendant?

- Credo che abbiano testimoniato il falso (/il vero).
  I believe they gave false (/truthful) testimony.

- Maria è stata chiamata a testimoniare.
  Mary was called as a witness.

- Questi fatti testimoniano l'onestà di quell'impiegato (/la verità dell'asserzione).
  These facts attest to the integrity of that employee (/the truth of the statement).

tingere (di, in)   to dye

- Ho tinto la camicia di rosso.
  I dyed the shirt red.

  tingersi (di)   to become stained; to tinge, dye

  - Il cielo si tinse dei colori dell'alba.
    The sky was tinged with the color of dawn.

■   Non credo che il signor Romani si tinga i capelli.
I don't think Mr. Romani dyes his hair.

tirare   to pull; to draw; to move; to throw; to blow; to drag; to be tight; to print

■   Non tirare quella corda (/le redini/la porta/la maniglia/l'allarme)!
Don't pull that rope (/the reins/the door/the handle/the alarm)!

■   Devi tirargli le orecchie, perché non ha ubbidito.
You have to pull his ears, because he didn't obey.

■   Puoi tirare la tenda, per favore?
Can you draw the curtain, please?

■   L'aratro era tirato da un vecchio cavallo.
The plow was drawn by an old horse.

■   Quando è finalmente arrivata, abbiamo tirato un respiro.
When she finally arrived, we drew a breath (of relief).

■   Tirate una linea.
Draw a line.

■   Oggi il camino (/la pipa) tira bene.
Today the chimney (/my pipe) is drawing well.

■   Tira la sedia vicino al tavolo.
Move the chair near the table.

■   Il bambino le tirò un sasso.
The child threw a stone at her.

■   Oggi tira un vento gelido.
Today an icy wind is blowing.

■   Non tirare la storia in lungo.
Don't drag out the story.

■   Questa sottana le tira sui fianchi, signora Pierini.
This skirt is tight around your hips, Mrs. Pierini.

■   Quante copie hanno tirato del tuo libro?
How many copies of your book did they print?

tirare fuori   to draw out; to throw out (of); to stick out

■   Il turista tirò fuori una mappa della città.
The tourist drew out a map of the city.

■   Il tuo bambino ha tirato qualcosa fuori dalla finestra.
Your child threw something out of the window.

■   Tira fuori la lingua.
Stick your tongue out.

tirare giù   to throw down; to lower

■   Potresti tirarmi giù le chiavi della macchina?
Could you throw down my car keys?

- Tirate giù il sipario.
  Lower the curtain.

tirare qc per qco   to pull sb by sth

- Il ragazzo tirava il bambino per la mano (/il gatto per la coda).
  The boy was pulling the child by his hand (/the cat by the tail)

tirare su   to roll up; to raise; to bring sb up; to cheer up

- Tira su il finestrino, per piacere.
  Roll up the (car) window, please.

- Tira su la testa.
  Raise your head.

- L'ha tirata su la nonna.
  Her grandmother brought her up.

- Le tue parole mi hanno tirato su.
  Your words cheered me up.

tirare via   to take away; to pull (out)

- Hanno tirato via il manifesto.
  They took the poster away.

- Il dentista gli ha tirato via un dente oggi.
  The dentist pulled one of his teeth today.

tirare a + *inf*   to try to + *inf*

- Tirano a indovinare.
  They are taking a wild guess.

- Tirano a campare.
  They (try to) get by.

tirarsi   to draw (back/aside/away)

- Non tirarti indietro (/in disparte/lontano).
  Don't draw back (/aside/away).

tirarsi dietro   to pull behind; to drag after

- Il ragazzo si tirò dietro il cancello.
  The boy pulled the gate (shut) after him.

- Perché devi sempre tirarti dietro il tuo amico?
  Why do you always have to drag your friend after you?

tirarsi su   to get up, stand up; to roll up, pull up; to take off

- Tirati su.
  Get (Stand) up.

- Tirati su le maniche.
  Roll your sleeves up.

- Tirati su i calzoni (/le calze).
  Pull up your trousers (/socks).

- Tirati via il cappotto.
  Take off your coat.

- Si è tirato addosso l'odio di tutti.
  He made himself the object of everybody's hatred.

toccare   to touch (on); to feel; to handle; to call at; to fall; to sweep; to happen

- Non toccare!
  Don't touch!

- Hanno toccato il fondo. (*also fig*)
  They have touched the bottom.

- Le parole di tua madre mi hanno toccato il cuore.
  Your mother's words touched my heart.

- Tocca ferro! (*idiomatic*)
  Knock on wood! (literally: *Touch iron!*) (idiomatic)

- L'insegnante ha soltanto toccato questo argomento.
  Our teacher only touched on this subject.

- La mamma gli toccò la fronte perché pensava che avesse la febbre.
  Mom felt his forehead because she thought he was running a temperature.

- Si prega di non toccare la frutta.
  Please don't handle the fruit.

- La nave non tocca Napoli.
  The ship does not call at Naples.

- La maggior parte del lavoro (/Tutta la responsabilità) toccò a lui.
  Most of the work (/All the responsibility) fell on him.

- Il tuo vestito è troppo lungo, tocca terra.
  Your dress is too long. It sweeps on the ground.

- Mi dispiace molto per quello che ti è toccato.
  I am very sorry about what happened to you.

- Il prigioniero (/Mio figlio) non tocca cibo da tre giorni.
  The prisoner (/My son) has not eaten for three days.

- Ti farò toccar con mano quanto sbagli.
  I'll make you realize how wrong you are.

- Quella donna toccherà la cinquantina.
  That woman must be about fifty.

- A chi tocca? —Tocca a te. (*games*)
  Whose turn is it? —It's your turn (or *It's your move*).

- Gli è sembrato di toccare il cielo con un dito. (*idiomatic*)
  He thought he was in heaven. (idiomatic)

toccarsi   to touch oneself, each other/one another

■   Paolo si toccò la fronte.
Paul touched his forehead.

■   Erano così vicini da toccarsi.
They were so close they were almost touching each other.

■   I due palazzi si toccano.
The two buildings touch each other.

togliere   to take (away/from/off/out of); to do away with; to remove; to relieve; to get out of

■   Togli quell'ombrello, per favore.
Please take away that umbrella.

■   Dobbiamo togliere di mezzo queste difficoltà.
We must do away with these difficulties.

■   Togliete due da dieci. (*math*)
Take two from ten.

■   Quell'uomo non le tolse gli occhi di dosso.
That man did not take his eyes off her.

■   Togli il cappello (/i guanti/le scarpe/la giacca) a Simone.
Take off Simone's hat (/gloves/shoes/jacket).

■   Togli il dieci per cento dal totale.
Take off ten percent from the total.

■   Togli le mani di tasca (/le dita di bocca/il dito dal naso).
Take your hands out of your pockets (/your fingers out of your mouth/your finger out of your nose).

■   Non puoi togliere quella macchia?
Can't you remove that stain?

■   Questo mi toglie ogni responsabilità (/un gran peso).
This relieves me of every responsibility (/a great burden).

■   L'hanno tolto di mezzo.
They got him out of the way (or They killed him).

togliersi   to get off/out (of); to take (off); to satisfy

■   Togliti da quella sedia.
Get out of that chair.

■   Cerca di toglierti dagli impicci.
Try to get out of trouble.

■   Togliti la giacca (/il cappello/il grembiule).
Take off your jacket (/hat/apron).

■   Si è tolta un capriccio (/una curiosità/la voglia di fare un viaggio).
She satisfied a whim (/her curiosity/a longing to take a trip).

■   Togliti di mezzo.
Get out of the way.

tollerare   to tolerate; to put up with; to stand

■   Giovanni non tollera il caldo (/l'aspirina).
John does not tolerate the heat (/aspirin).

■   Non posso tollerare il tuo comportamento (/questo ronzio).
I can't tolerate your behavior (/this buzzing).

■   Tuo padre ha tollerato la tua villania per troppo tempo.
Your father has put up with your rudeness for too long.

■   Non posso tollerare la sua presenza.
I can't stand his presence.

> **non tollerare che** + *subj*   not to tolerate sb's + *ger*
>
> ■   Non posso tollerare che Giorgio parli così con sua madre (/risponda in quel modo/sia così villano).
> *I cannot tolerate George's speaking to his mother like that (/answering that way/being so rude).*

tradire   to betray, deceive, be unfaithful

■   La sua eccitazione tradiva la sua paura.
His excitement betrayed his fear.

■   Tradiresti la patria (/i tuoi ideali/una causa/un segreto)?
Would you betray your country (/your ideals/a cause/a secret)?

■   Se la memoria non mi tradisce, questo è successo ad Assisi.
If my memory does not deceive me, this happened in Assisi.

■   Li hai traditi!
You have deceived them!

■   Beppe tradisce la moglie e Maria tradisce il marito.
Joe is unfaithful to his wife, and Mary is unfaithful to her husband.

> **tradirsi**   to betray oneself; to give oneself away
>
> ■   Con quell'affermazione il criminale si tradì.
> *With that statement the criminal betrayed himself.*
>
> ■   Ti sei tradito!
> *You gave yourself away!*

tradurre   to translate; to carry out; to express; to take

■   Questo articolo va tradotto dal tedesco in italiano.
This article must be translated from German into Italian.

■   Quello scrittore ha tradotto in italiano molte opere di Faulkner.
That writer translated many works of Faulkner's into Italian.

■ Saprai tradurre in pratica quel progetto?
Will you be able to carry out that project?

■ Quel pittore ha saputo tradurre sulla tela un senso di solitudine.
That painter managed to express a sense of solitude in his painting.

■ L'hanno già tradotto in carcere.
They have already taken him to prison.

tradursi   to result; to manifest, show

■ Speriamo che tutti i nostri sforzi si traducano in un miglioramento delle condizioni di lavoro.
Let's hope that all our efforts result in an improvement of working conditions.

■ La gioia dei bambini si tradusse in risate.
The children's joy showed in their laughter.

trafficare   to traffic, deal, trade; to bustle about, run around

■ Credo che traffichino in droga (/armi).
I believe they traffic (deal) in drugs (/arms).

■ Mio zio trafficava con gli Stati Uniti in legname.
My uncle used to deal in lumber with the United States.

■ Tua suocera è sempre lì a trafficare.
Your mother-in-law is always running around (busy).

trascinare   to drag; to sway

■ Il bambino trascinava la coperta.
The child was dragging the blanket.

■ Non camminare trascinando i piedi.
Don't drag your feet when you walk.

■ Il poliziotto trascinò il ladro al commissariato.
The policeman dragged the thief to the police station.

■ La corrente trascinò i due bambini.
The current dragged the two children away.

■ Quel dittatore sapeva trascinare la folla.
That dictator could sway the crowd.

trascinarsi   to drag (oneself) along; to drag on

■ Il nonno a malapena si trascina.
Granpa can hardly drag himself along.

■ Temono che quel processo si trascinerà per molti mesi.
They are afraid that trial will drag on for many months.

trasferire   to transfer

- Il signor Marchi è stato trasferito da Milano a Torino (/in un altro stabilimento) due anni fa.
  Mr. Marchi was transferred from Milan to Turin (/to another factory) two years ago.

- Hanno trasferito la loro proprietà ai figli.
  They transferred (or conveyed) their property to their children.

  trasferirsi   to move

  - I Rossi si sono trasferiti in campagna (/in città) qualche anno fa.
    The Rossis moved to the country (/city) a few years ago.

trasformare (in qc/qco)   to transform; to turn (into sb/sth); to change

- Il principe fu trasformato in un ranocchio.
  The prince was transformed into a frog.

- Questa relazione va trasformata in qualcosa di più positivo.
  This relationship must be transformed into something more positive.

- Il re Mida trasformava in oro qualunque cosa toccasse.
  King Midas turned whatever he touched into gold.

- I soldi l'hanno trasformata.
  Money has changed her.

  trasformarsi in qc/qco   to change into sb/sth

  - Il bruco (/La rana) si trasformò in farfalla (/principe).
    The caterpillar (/The frog) changed into a butterfly (/a prince).

trasmettere   to transmit; to broadcast; to send

- La malaria è trasmessa dalle zanzare del genere anofele.
  Malaria is transmitted by mosquitoes of the genus Anopheles.

- Il motore (/Quel cavo) trasmette il movimento alle ruote.
  The motor (/That cable) transmits movement to the wheels.

- Stasera trasmetteranno un concerto di musica sinfonica (/il discorso del presidente/la partita Roma–Napoli) in diretta.
  Tonight they will broadcast a concert of classical music (/the president's speech/the Rome–Naples game) live.

- Mi devono ancora trasmettere le istruzioni.
  They still have to send me the instructions.

  trasmettersi   to be transmitted

  - Certe caratteristiche fisiche si trasmettono di madre in figlio.
    Some physical characteristics are transmitted from mother to son.

■   Come si trasmette l'elettricità?
How is electricity transmitted?

trattare   to treat; to deal in/with; to be about, be the matter; to handle; to take care; to negotiate; to have anything to do (with)

■   Al pronto soccorso gli hanno trattato la ferita con un antisettico.
At the emergency room they treated his wound with an antiseptic.

■   L'hanno trattata con gentilezza (/bene/coi guanti/da idiota).
They treated her kindly (/badly/with kid gloves/like an idiot).

■   Non mi piace il vostro modo di trattare la gente.
I don't like the way you treat people.

■   Trattano in cotone.
They deal in cotton.

■   Non abbiamo mai trattato con quella società.
We have never dealt with that company.

■   Di che cosa tratta quel libro (/film)?
What is that book (/movie) about?

■   Il signor Gentili sa come trattare i suoi impiegati (/le cose fragili).
Mr. Gentili knows how to handle his employees (/fragile things).

■   In quel negozio trattano male i forestieri.
They treat foreigners badly in that store.

■   Stanno trattando la pace (/il cessate il fuoco/un prestito).
They are negotiating peace (/the cease-fire/a loan).

■   Io non voglio trattare con certa gente.
I don't want to have anything to do with certain people.

trattarsi   to treat oneself

■   Tu ti tratti molto bene!
You treat yourself very well!

trattarsi di qco + *inf*   to be the matter/question

■   (Non) si tratta di vita o di morte.
It is (not) a matter of life and death.

■   Si tratta solo di schiacciare un bottone.
It is only a matter of pressing a button.

■   Si tratta di decidere se dovete farlo o no.
The question is whether you must do it or not.

tremare   to tremble; to shake; to shudder

■   Davanti a lui tremava tutta Roma.
All Rome trembled before him.

■   Il bambino tremava come una foglia.
The child was trembling like a leaf.

■   Mi tremano le ginocchia (/le gambe) quando vado dal medico.
    My knees (/legs) shake when I go to the doctor.

■   Il terremoto ha fatto tremare tutta la casa.
    The earthquake shook the whole house.

■   I fiori tremavano nella brezza.
    The flowers were quivering in the breeze.

■   Tremarono quando videro quella scena raccapricciante.
    They shuddered when they saw that horrifying scene.

tremare di qco/per qc/qco   to tremble with sth/for sb

   ■   Il bambino tremava di freddo (/paura).
       The child was trembling with cold (/fear).

   ■   La voce gli tremava per l'emozione.
       His voice was trembling with emotion.

   ■   Tremiamo per lei (/i nostri figli). (*fig*)
       We fear for her (/our children).

tremare a + *inf*   to tremble to + *inf*

   ■   Tremavano persino a parlarne.
       They trembled even speaking of it.

trovare   to find; to meet; to achieve; to think

■   Ho trovato le chiavi nel cassetto (/nel baule).
    I found the keys in the drawer (/in the trunk).

■   Rosanna non ha ancora trovato casa (/marito/lavoro).
    Roseanne has not found a house (/a husband/a job) yet.

■   L'ho trovato invecchiato (/depresso/pronto a partire/a letto/a casa).
    I found him aged (/depressed/ready to leave/in bed/at home).

■   L'ho trovato scritto sul giornale di ieri che sono morti nell'incidente.
    I found it written in yesterday's paper that they died in the accident.

■   Non trovare scuse per non venire!
    Don't find excuses not to come!

■   Lo hanno trovato colpevole.
    They found him guilty.

■   Puoi essere sicuro di trovarlo al bar.
    You can be sure to meet (or bet on meeting) him at the bar.

■   Trovarono fama e gloria.
    They achieved fame and glory.

■   Non trovo che dovresti dirlo.
    I don't think you should say it.

■   Questa macchina è molto bella, non trovi?
    This car is very nice, don't you think?

trovare qc che + *verb*   to find sb + *ger*

- L'ho trovata che leggeva (/mangiava/dormiva/giocava).
  I found her reading (/eating/sleeping/playing).

trovarsi   to be; to happen; to meet; to get on; to feel; to be found

- A quell'epoca mi trovavo a Milano.
  At that time I was in Milan.

- La mia casa si trova vicino alla banca.
  My house is near the bank.

- Si trovano nei guai.
  They are in trouble.

- Mi trovavo a passare di lì.
  I happened to be passing there.

- Troviamoci là alle sette.
  Let's meet there at seven.

- Come ti trovi coi nuovi colleghi?
  How are you getting on with your new colleagues?

- Qui mi trovo come a casa mia.
  I feel at home here.

- Questo libro si trova in tutte le librerie.
  This book can be found in all the bookstores.

truccare   to make up, rig; to mark; to doctor/soup up

- L'hanno truccata da clown.
  They made her up as a clown.

- Si teme che abbiano truccato le elezioni (/la partita).
  It is feared they rigged the election (/the game).

- Loro truccano le carte.
  They mark the cards.

- Credo che il motore della sua macchina sia truccato.
  I think his car's engine is souped up. (informal)

truccarsi   to wear makeup; to put makeup on; to disguise oneself

- Quella ragazza si trucca troppo.
  That girl wears too much makeup.

- L'attrice si era truccata da Ofelia.
  The actress made herself up as Ophelia.

- Si era truccato per non farsi riconoscere.
  He had disguised himself in order not to be recognized.

truffare   to cheat; to swindle

■   È stata truffata.
She was cheated.

■   Quell'uomo ha truffato parecchi uomini d'affari.
That man swindled many businessmen.

tuffare   to dip

■   Il ragazzo tuffò i remi (/la testa) nell'acqua.
The boy dipped the oars (/his head) into the water.

tuffarsi   to plunge; to dive

■   L'uomo si tuffò nell'acqua (/dal trampolino).
The man plunged into the water (/from the diving board).

■   Si sono tuffati negli affari.
They dove into business.

■   L'aeroplano si tuffò.
The plane nosedived.

■   Si tuffò nello studio.
He buried himself in his books.

tuonare   (auxiliary *essere* or *avere* when referring to weather; otherwise *avere*)
to thunder

■   Ha (È) tuonato tutto il giorno.
It has thundered all day long.

■   I cannoni tuonarono per tutta la notte.
Cannons thundered the entire night.

■   Il prete tuonò contro i peccatori.
The priest thundered (or railed) against the sinners.

U

ubbidire (a qc/qco)   to obey (sb/sth); to comply (with sb/sth); to respond

- Devi ubbidire ai tuoi genitori (/ai superiori/alla tua coscienza).
  You must obey your parents (/superiors/conscience).

- Si deve ubbidire agli ordini.
  Orders should be obeyed.

- Dobbiamo ubbidire alle leggi (/alle leggi della natura).
  We must comply with the laws (/laws of nature).

- Il mio cane non ubbidisce al fischio.
  My dog doesn't respond to the whistle.

- L'aereo non ubbidisce più ai comandi.
  The plane no longer responds to the controls.

ubriacare   to make, get (sb) drunk; to intoxicate; to daze

- Poco vino basta a ubriacarla.
  A little wine is enough to make her drunk.

- Era ubriacata dal suo trionfo (/dal caldo).
  She was intoxicated by her triumph (/the heat).

- Tutto questo rumore mi ha ubriacato.
  I'm dazed from all this noise (or All this noise has dazed me).

- Tutti quei complimenti (/Tutte quelle promesse) l'avevano ubriacata.
  All those compliments (/promises) had gone to her head.

  ubriacarsi   to get drunk

  - Quell'uomo si ubriaca molto spesso.
    That man gets drunk very often.

uccidere   to kill; to murder; to assassinate

- L'amante l'ha uccisa con un coltello (/con un fucile).
  Her lover killed her with a knife (/rifle).

- Questo disinfettante uccide tutti i germi.
  This disinfectant kills all the germs.

- Questo caldo (/quest'afa/quest'angoscia/questa noia) mi uccide.
  This heat (/humidity/anxiety/boredom) is killing me.

- La fatica e le continue sofferenze (/I dispiaceri) lo uccideranno.
  Fatigue and endless suffering (/Sorrows) will kill him.

- Il gelo ha ucciso le mie piante di rosmarino.
  The frost killed my rosemary plants.

■ L'imperatore fu ucciso da un anarchico.
The emperor was assassinated by an anarchist.

uccidersi   to kill oneself

■ Si è ucciso dalla disperazione (/con un colpo di pistola).
He killed himself in despair (/with a pistol shot).

uguagliare (qc in qco)   to equal, make equal; to tie; to match (sb in sth)

■ Quel pianista (/Quell'artista) ha uguagliato il suo maestro.
That pianist (/artist) equaled his master.

■ Hanno uguagliato il record dei russi.
They tied (or equaled) the Russians' record.

■ Ricordati: le entrate devono uguagliare le uscite.
Remember: Income must equal expenditures.

■ Nessuno può uguagliarlo in forza (/eloquenza/astuzia/abilità/cultura).
Nobody can match him in strength (/eloquence/shrewdness/ability/learning) (or
Nobody can equal his strength).

ungere   to oil, grease; to butter; to anoint; to bribe

■ Devo ricordarmi di ungere questa serratura (/questo ingranaggio).
I must remember to oil this lock (/gear).

■ Hai già unto la tortiera?
Did you already grease the cakepan?

■ Il vescovo unge la fronte dei bambini che devono essere cresimati.
The bishop anoints the forehead of the children to be confirmed.

■ Ungimi, ungimi, non riuscirai a comprarmi. (*fig*)
Butter me, butter me, you won't be able to buy me. (fig)

ungersi   to apply oil/lotion; to get grease on oneself

■ Mia nipote si unge sempre con la crema antisolare prima di prendere il sole.
My niece always applies sunblock before sunbathing.

■ Suo marito, per controllare l'olio nella macchina, si è unto tutto.
Her husband got grease all over himself when checking the oil in his car.

unire   to unite; to combine; to put together, join; to link; to connect

■ Li uniscono gli interessi comuni.
Common interests unite them.

■ Sono idee (/principi/esigenze) che uniscono.
They are ideas (/principles/needs) that unite (people).

■ Unite tutti gli ingredienti e cuocete a fuoco moderato.
Combine all the ingredients and cook at moderate heat.

■ Abbiamo deciso di unire le nostre risorse.
We decided to combine our resources.

■ Se arriveranno altre persone, dovremo unire due tavoli.
If more people come, we'll have to put two tables together.

■ Se uniamo due assi con la colla ne otteniamo una più lunga.
If we join two boards with glue, we'll get a longer one.

■ Devi unire questi due punti con una retta.
You have to join these two points with a straight line.

■ Un nuovo traforo unirà i nostri due paesi.
A new tunnel will link our two countries.

■ Le due città saranno unite da una ferrovia.
The two cities will be connected by a railroad.

unirsi   to join (together); to blend; to unite

■ Le due società si unirono per battere la concorrenza (/per conquistare nuovi mercati).
The two companies joined together to beat the competition (/to secure new markets).

■ Perché non ci uniamo a loro per andare al cinema?
Why don't we join them to go to the movies?

■ Questi due colori si uniscono molto bene.
These two colors blend very well.

■ "Proletari di tutto il mondo, unitevi!"
"Workers of the world, unite!"

■ Si sono uniti in matrimonio.
They were united in matrimony.

urgere   to be urgent; to be needed urgently

■ Urge una riforma radicale dell'assistenza medica.
A radical reform of health insurance is urgently needed.

usare   to use; to exercise; to wear; to be in fashion; to be the custom

■ Posso usare il tuo scooter?
May I use your scooter?

■ Usa la testa, non le mani.
Use your head, not your hands.

■ Bisogna usare prudenza (/attenzione).
One must exercise prudence (/attention).

■ D'inverno la signora Damiani usa molto la pelliccia.
In winter Mrs. Damiani wears her fur coat a lot.

■ Non mi piacciono gli articoli "usa e getta".
I don't like disposable (literally: use and throw away) articles.

■ Quelle scarpe non si usano più.
Those shoes are no longer in fashion.

- Da noi (/loro) si usa così.
  This is our (/their) custom.

- In campagna (/in città/all'estero/in Italia) si usa così.
  This is the custom in the country (/in the city/overseas/in Italy).

usare + *inf*   to be used to, accustomed to + *inf*

- Usavano passare l'estate in montagna (/alzarsi presto).
  They used to spend the summer in the mountains (/to get up early).

usare qco per + *inf*   to use sth to + *inf*

- La donna usò un mattone per difendersi.
  The woman used a brick to defend herself.

- Perché non usi un altro coltello per tagliare la carne?
  Why don't you use another knife to cut the meat?

uscire   (auxiliary *essere*) to leave (sth/*place*); to go, come out; to come (from/off/up);
to be drawn; to emerge; to get (out); to be discharged

- Sono usciti dieci minuti fa.
  They left ten minutes ago.

- L'hanno assalito mentre usciva dall'ufficio (/dal bar/dal teatro).
  They attacked him as he was leaving his office (/the bar/the theater).

- Il treno esce dalla stazione.
  The train is leaving (or going out from) the station.

- Il corridore è uscito dal gruppo.
  The runner left the pack.

- La mamma è uscita a piedi o in macchina?
  Did Mom go out on foot or by car?

- Dopo la morte del marito non esce più molto.
  Since her husband's death, she doesn't go out much.

- Da questa catena di montaggio escono cinquecento macchine alla settimana.
  Five hundred cars come off this assembly line every week.

- Il secondo volume sta per uscire.
  The second volume is about to come out.

- Quello scrittore esce da una delle migliori università italiane.
  That writer comes from one of the best Italian universities.

- Suo figlio è uscito vincitore (/secondo).
  Her son came out a winner (/second).

- Esce fumo da quella finestra.
  Smoke is coming out of that window.

- Il numero 12 non esce da mesi.
  Number 12 has not come up for months. (lottery)

- Il suo nome è uscito per primo.
  His/her name was drawn first.

- Quell'uomo uscirà domani dall'ospedale.
  That man will be discharged tomorrow from the hospital.

- Il sole uscì dalle nuvole.
  The sun emerged from the clouds.

- Ne siamo usciti con onore.
  We emerged with honor.

- Credo che stia uscendo del gas.
  I think gas is escaping.

- Il chiodo esce di qualche centimetro dalla porta.
  The nail is sticking a few centimeters out of the door.

- Il fiume è uscito dal letto.
  The river has overflowed its banks.

far uscire da qco   to get from

- Da tre litri puoi far uscire quattro bottiglie.
  You get four bottles from three liters.

- Da questo scampolo non puoi far uscire un vestito.
  You cannot get a dress from this remnant.

uscire da qco   to get out of/through sth

- Il ladro uscì dalla finestra.
  The thief got out through the window.

- Esci dalla macchina.
  Get out of the car.

uscire di qco   to slip (out from) sth

- Il vaso le uscì di mano e cadde.
  The vase slipped out of her hands and fell.

- Il loro indirizzo le è uscito di mente.
  Their address slipped her mind.

- Gli è uscito di bocca il tuo nome.
  He let your name slip out.

uscire di casa/carica/prigione/strada/tutela/scena   to leave the house
(/home)/office/prison/to go off the road/to come of age/to leave the stage,
to exit

- Quando una figlia esce di casa, le cose cambiano.
  When a daughter leaves home, things change.

- Usciranno di carica fra due anni.
  They will leave office in two years.

- Non credo sia ancora uscito di prigione.
  I don't think he is out of prison yet.

- La macchina uscì di strada.
  The car went off the road.

- Quando uscirà di tutela entrerà in possesso di una grande proprietà.
  When he comes of age, he will come into possession of a large estate.

- Dopo lo scandalo quel senatore uscì di scena.
  After the scandal, that senator left the stage.

- Amleto esce di scena.
  Hamlet exits.

uscire in qco   to end in sth; to lead to/into sth

- Quella via esce in Piazza Manzoni.
  That street leads into Manzoni Square.

uscire a + *inf*   to go out to + *inf*

- Dove vai? —Esco a prendere una boccata d'aria.
  Where are you going? —I'm going out to get some fresh air.

uscire + *ger*   to go out + *ger*

- È uscito fischiando (/cantando/ridendo).
  He went out whistling (/singing/laughing).

V

vacillare   to sway; to wobble; to flicker; to be shaky; to be unsteady; to waver; to stagger in/out; to vacillate, be undecided

- Il vecchio vacillò.
  The old man swayed.

- La luce vacillò e si spense.
  The light flickered and went out.

- La memoria della nonna a volte vacilla.
  Grandmother's memory is shaky at times.

- Dopo aver bevuto così tanto, quell'uomo vacilla sulle gambe.
  After drinking so much, that man is unsteady on his legs.

- La loro fede vacilla.
  Their faith is wavering.

- Uscirono dal bar vacillando.
  They staggered out of the bar.

- Vacillavo fra due opinioni contrarie.
  I vacillated between two opposite opinions.

vagliare   to sift; to sieve; to weigh (up), examine

- Vagliare mezzo chilo di farina.
  Sift half a kilo of flour.

- Dobbiamo vagliare i pro e i contro.
  We must examine the pros and cons.

- Il comitato ha vagliato tutte le proposte.
  The committee weighed (or examined) all the proposals.

valere   (auxiliary *essere*) to be worth; to have authority; to be valid; to be equivalent to

- L'ho pagato centomila lire, ma vale molto di più.
  I paid a hundred thousand lire for it, but it is worth much more.

- Questa macchina vale venti milioni.
  This car is worth twenty million.

- Il capitano vale più del tenente.
  A captain has more authority than a lieutenant.

- Questo regolamento (/Questa dichiarazione/Il mio passaporto) non vale più.
  This law (/This declaration/My passport) is no longer valid.

■ La partita non vale.
   The game is not valid (does not count).

■ Quello è un tecnico che vale molto.
   That is a very good technician.

■ Questa è roba che vale. Quella è roba che non vale niente.
   These are valuable things. That is useless junk.

■ Che vale parlare così tanto?
   What is the use of talking so much?

■ Un pollice vale due centimetri e mezzo.
   An inch is equivalent to two and a half centimeters.

vale a dire (che)   it means; that is to say, i.e.

■ Questo vale a dire che dobbiamo partire subito.
   That means that we must leave right away.

■ Ti chiamerò presto, vale a dire prima della fine di questa settimana.
   I'll call you soon—that is to say, before the end of this week.

valere la pena   to be worthwhile, worth it

■ Non ne vale la pena.
   It is not worthwhile.

■ Questi sono due articoli che vale la pena di leggere.
   These are two articles worth reading.

far valere   to assert

(■) Dovresti far valere i tuoi diritti (/la tua autorità).
   You should assert your rights (/your authority).

farsi valere   to make oneself appreciated

■ Loro sanno come farsi valere.
   They know how to make themselves appreciated.

■ Dovresti imparare a farti valere.
   You should learn how to make yourself appreciated.

valersi di   to take advantage of; to make use of

■ Si sono valsi dei miei suggerimenti.
   They took advantage of my suggestions.

■ Si è valsa del mio nome.
   She made use of my name.

vantare   to boast; to claim rights

■ Firenze vanta tanti musei.
   Florence boasts many museums.

■ Gli eredi vantano diritti anche su questa proprietà.
The heirs claim rights to this property too.

vantarsi   to boast; to brag

■ Benedetto si vanta sempre delle sue capacità.
Benedict is always boasting about his abilities.

■ Di che cosa ti vanti?
What are you boasting about?

■ Il signor Vanni si vanta delle sue ricchezze (/dei suoi successi).
Mr. Vanni brags about his wealth (/successes).

■ Non faccio per vantarmi, ma . . .
I don't mean to brag, but . . .

vantarsi di + *inf*   to boast of + *ger*

■ Si vanta di essere il migliore della classe.
He boasts of being the best in the class.

variare   to vary, change; to differ; to fluctuate

■ La richiesta di certi prodotti varia con la stagione.
The demand for certain products varies with the season.

■ Vorrei che tu variassi la dieta (/le letture).
I would like you to vary your diet (/readings).

■ L'età a cui i bambini cominciano a parlare varia.
The age at which children start speaking varies.

■ Pensano di variare il percorso della gara automobilistica.
They are planning to change the course of the car race.

■ Da qualche settimana il suo umore varia.
His mood has been changing for some weeks.

■ I gusti variano dall'uno all'altro.
Tastes differ (or People have different tastes).

■ I cambi variano a seconda del mercato.
Exchange rates fluctuate according to the market.

vedere   to see; to show; to decide; to read

■ Hai visto un fantasma (/un bel film/Giovanni)?
Did you see a ghost (/a good movie/John)?

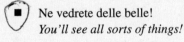 Ne vedrete delle belle!
You'll see all sorts of things!

■ Vorrei vederlo morto (/povero/felice).
I would like to see him dead (/poor/happy).

- Non vedo perché dovrei farlo (/parlargli/lavorare).
  I don't see why I should do it (/speak to him/work).

- Vedemmo che non c'era più niente da fare.
  We saw there was nothing more to be done.

- Bisogna vedere se le cose stanno veramente così.
  It must be seen if things are really that way.

- Vedere per credere. *(proverb)*
  Seeing is believing. (proverb)

- Si veda (Vedere) pagina 15.
  See page 15.

- Vedi sopra (/sotto).
  See above (/below).

- A mio modo di vedere, questa è la decisione giusta.
  In my opinion, this is the right decision.

- Si vede ancora la macchia (/la cicatrice)?
  Does the stain (/scar) still show?

- Io non so cosa dargli, veda Lei.
  I don't know what to give him. You decide.

- Ha visto quell'articolo sul giornale di oggi?
  Did you read that article in today's paper?

vedere qc/qco + *inf*   to see sb/sth + *inf/ger/ptp*

- Quando l'avete vista pattinare (/recitare/cadere/rubare)?
  When did you see her skate (/act/fall/steal)?

- Abbiamo visto cadere il ciclista.
  We saw the cyclist fall.

- Ho visto cadere una stella.
  I saw a star falling.

vedere qco   to go to (a show, etc.)

- Avete visto l'ultima commedia di Dario Fo (/quella mostra/la partita)?
  Did you go to Dario Fo's last play (/that exhibit/the game)?

vedere che   to see to it that

- Signorina, veda che questa lettera sia pronta stasera.
  Miss, see to it that this letter is ready tonight.

vedere di + *inf*   to try to + *inf*

- Vedrò di trovare quel libro (/telefonarle).
  I'll try to find that book (/phone her).

far vedere qco a qc   to show sth to sb, to let sb see sth

- Mi faccia vedere la patente.
  Show me your driver's license.

- Fammi vedere cosa hai comprato.
  Let me see what you bought.

farsi vedere   to show up, show one's face; to see, be examined by a doctor, dentist, etc.

- Non si è fatto vedere stamattina.
  He has not shown up this morning.

- Perché non ti fai mai vedere?
  Why don't you ever show your face?

- Fatti vedere presto.
  Come see us soon.

- Dovresti farti vedere dal medico.
  You should see a doctor.

vederci   to be able to see

- Con questi occhiali non ci vedo bene.
  I can't see well with these glasses.

- Mia nonna ci vede ancora bene anche senza occhiali.
  My grandmother can still see well even without glasses.

vedersi   to see oneself, each other/one another; to meet

- Si vide allo specchio: un vecchio.
  He saw himself in the mirror: (he was) an old man.

- Ci vediamo alle sette, va bene?
  Let's meet at seven, okay?

- Non si vedono da molto tempo.
  They haven't seen each other for a long time.

- Allora ci vediamo stasera dai Rossi (/da mia zia)?
  So are we going to meet at the Rossis' (/at my aunt's) tonight?

- Ci vediamo sempre in autobus (/in treno/a scuola/per strada).
  We always meet on the bus (/on the train/at school/in the street).

- Si vide perduto (/sconfitto/salvo).
  He saw himself lost (/defeated/safe).

vegliare   to stay awake; to keep vigil; to watch (over)

- Abbiamo vegliato fino a tardi ieri sera (/all'alba).
  We stayed awake till late last night (/until dawn).

- Vegliavano al capezzale del padre.
  They were keeping vigil at their father's bedside.

- Hanno vegliato in preghiera.
  They spent the night in prayer.

- Dio veglia su di noi.
  God is watching over us.

vendere   to sell

- Vendono libri.
  They sell books.

- L'hanno venduto all'asta (/a buon mercato/al miglior offerente/per un milione/ per pochissimo).
  They sold it at auction (/cheaply/to the highest bidder/for one million/for very little).

- Loro vendono all'ingrosso (/al dettaglio/a credito/a peso).
  They sell wholesale (retail/on credit/by weight).

- Sai vendere la tua merce.
  You know how to sell your merchandise.

- Venderebbe l'anima al diavolo. (*fig*)
  He would sell his soul to the devil. (fig)

1. venire   (auxiliary *essere*) to come (along/away/off/in/out); to arrive

- Penso che stia venendo qualcuno.
  I think someone is coming.

- Gli è venuta una bellissima idea (/venuto un dubbio).
  A very nice idea (/A doubt) came to him.

- Le sono venute le lacrime agli occhi.
  Tears came to her eyes.

- Perché non vieni insieme a noi?
  Why don't you come along with us?

- Sono venuti via dal paese molto tempo fa.
  They left their village a long time ago.

- Dopo molte lunghe discussioni sono venuti a patti.
  After many long arguments they came to an agreement.

- Non so se sia già venuta la posta.
  I don't know whether the mail has already arrived.

- Finalmente è venuta la primavera (/l'ora di partire).
  At long last, spring (/the time to leave) has arrived.

- "Bambini, è venuta la mia ora", disse il vecchio.
  "Children, my time has come," the old man said.

■ Siamo venuti alla conclusione che dovete restare qui.
We've reached the conclusion that you must stay here.

venire a + *specific place*   to come to + *specific place*

■ A che ora sono venuti a casa (/scuola/lezione/letto/teatro) ieri?
What time did they come home (/to school/to class/to bed/to the theater)
yesterday?

venire a + *city/town*   to come to + *city/town*

■ I miei genitori sono contenti che io venga a Roma con te.
My parents are glad I am coming to Rome with you.

venire a + *article* + *destination*   to come to + *article* + *destination*

■ Non credevo che lui sarebbe venuto al cinema (/allo zoo/all'aeroporto/alla
partita/all'agenzia di viaggi) con te.
I didn't think he would come to the movies (/zoo/airport/game/travel
agency) with you.

venire da + *house/office*   to come to + *house/office*

■ Verrò con te da loro (/da Maria/dal dottore), te lo prometto.
I'll go with you to their house (/to Mary's/to the doctor's), I promise.

venire da qc/qco   to come, derive from sb/sth

■ Quel ragazzo viene da buona famiglia.
That boy comes from a good family.

■ Credi che "agronomo" venga dal greco?
Do you think "agronomist" comes from Greek?

■ Da che ti viene tanta sicurezza?
Where does all your self-confidence come from?

venire da + *city/town*   to come from + *city/town*

■ Vengono da Milano (/New York).
They are coming from Milan (/New York).

venire da + *article* + *country/place*   to come from + *country/place*

■ Da dove viene quello studente? —Viene dall'Italia (/dalla Spagna/
dall'Egitto/dal Perù)/dagli Stati Uniti/dai Paesi Bassi).
Where does that student come from? —He comes from Italy (/Spain/
Egypt/Peru/the United States/the Netherlands).

■ Il vento viene dal mare (/dal lago/dai monti/dall'ovest).
The wind comes from the sea (/the lake/the mountains/the west).

■ Quest'olio viene dalle mie terre.
This oil comes from my estate.

- Vengono dal cinema (/dall'aeroporto/dallo zoo/dalla biblioteca).
  They are coming from the movie theater (/airport/zoo/library).

venire giù /su/dentro/fuori   to come + *adverb*

- Perché non vieni giú (/su/dentro/fuori)?
  Why don't you come down or *downstairs (/up/upstairs/inside/outside)?*

- La neve veniva giù fitta (/lenta).
  The snow was coming down thickly (/slowly).

- A questo punto Giorgio venne fuori con la sua famosa frase.
  At this point George came out with his famous sentence.

- Mi viene su il sapore dell'aglio.
  The taste of garlic keeps coming back.

- Venite avanti.
  Come forward (/up).

- Antonio mi veniva dietro.
  Anthony was coming after me.

- Lei veniva dopo di me (/prima di me) nella fila!
  You were in line behind me (/before me)!

- Dalle indagini è venuto fuori un particolare interessante.
  An interesting fact emerged from the investigations.

- La macchina stava per venirmi addosso, quando qualcuno gridò: "Attento!"
  The car was about to hit me, when somebody shouted, "Watch out!"

venire in + *country (singular)*   to come to + *country (singular)*

- Quando sono venuti in Italia (Francia/Spagna) i tuoi cugini?
  When did your cousins come to Italy (/France/Spain)?

venire in + *article* + *country (plural)*   to come to + *article* + *country* (plural)

- Quando è venuta negli Stati Uniti sua sorella?
  When did your sister come to the United States?

venire in + *destination*   to come, come to + *destination*

- Perché non vieni con me in banca (/palestra/ biblioteca)?
  Why don't you come with me to the bank (/gym/library)?

venire per + *inf*   to come (in order) to + *inf*

- Siete venuti per chiacchierare o per lavorare?
  Did you come to chat or to work?

venire via   to come off

- La maniglia della porta è venuta via.
  The door handle came off.

- Se non attaccherai quel bottone, verrà via.
  If you don't sew that button, it will come off.

2. venire   to cost; to be drawn; to fall; to owe; to turn out

- Quanto vengono queste scarpe?
  How much do these shoes cost?

- La cena verrà trentamila lire a testa.
  The dinner will cost thirty thousand lire a head.

- È venuto il 23.
  The number 23 was drawn. (lottery)

- Natale viene di domenica quest'anno.
  Christmas falls on a Sunday this year.

- Mi vengono diecimila lire da te.
  You owe me ten thousand lire.

- Com'è venuto il vestito? —È venuto troppo stretto.
  How did the dress turn out? —It turned out too tight.

- Il dolce è venuto bene.
  The cake came out (or turned out) well.

- Ho fatto la somma e mi è venuto dieci.
  I've done the addition, and the result is ten.

venire + *article* + *illness*   to catch + *illness*

- Le è venuto (/sono venuti) il morbillo (/gli orecchioni).
  She has caught the measles (/the mumps).

venire da + *inf*   to feel like + *ger*

- Mi viene da piangere (/ridere/tossire).
  I feel like crying (/laughing/coughing).

venire + *ptp*   to be + *ptp*

- Le sue opere vennero ammirate (/scelte/criticate/vendute).
  His works were admired (/chosen/criticized/sold).

- Quel matematico viene considerato un genio.
  That mathematician is considered a genius.

venire su   ~~to grow~~

- Vengono su sani quei bambini.
  Those children are growing up healthy.

- L'insalata viene su bene quest'anno.
  Lettuce is growing well this year.

far venire + **qc/qco**   to send for, call sb/sth

- Bisogna far venire subito il dottore.
  We must send for the doctor right away.

- Bisogna far venire un tassì (/un'ambulanza).
  We need to call a taxi (/an ambulance).

farsi venire qco   to have sth sent

- Si è fatta venire il vino (/il vestito/il libro) dalla Spagna.
  She had the wine (/dress/book) sent from Spain.

vergognarsi (di qc/qco)   to be ashamed (of sb/sth); to be shy

- Non ti vergogni? Vergognati!
  Aren't you ashamed? Shame on you!

- Si vergognano della loro umile origine (/del loro figlio/di quello che hanno fatto).
  They are ashamed of their humble origin (/their son/what they did).

- Mi vergogno di me stesso.
  I am ashamed of myself.

- Quella ragazza si vergogna di tutto e di tutti.
  That girl is very shy.

vergognarsi di + *inf*   to be ashamed of + *ger;* to be embarrassed to + *inf*

- Quella studentessa si vergogna di parlare (/cantare) in pubblico.
  That student is ashamed of speaking (/singing) in public (or That student is embarrassed to speak [/sing] in public).

- Mi vergogno di chiederglielo.
  I'm embarrassed to ask him for it.

versare   to pour (out); to spill; to pay; to deposit; to shed

- Dovresti versare il vino nei bicchieri.
  You should pour the wine into the glasses.

- Gli assediati versavano olio bollente dalle mura della città.
  The besieged were pouring oil from the city walls.

- Il panettiere versò la farina dal sacco.
  The baker poured the flour from the bag.

- Non sono stata io a versare il profumo sul copriletto.
  It wasn't I who spilled the perfume on the bedspread.

- Dobbiamo versare la prima rata.
  We must pay the first installment.

- Hanno versato una larga somma in banca (/nel conto).
  They deposited a large amount of money in the bank (/in the account).

Il ragazzo versa in pericolo di vita. (*idiomatic*)
The boy is in danger (of death). (idiomatic)

■ La madre versava il brodo.
The mother was ladling out the broth.

■ Maddalena lo disse senza versare una lacrima.
Madeleine said it without shedding a tear.

versarsi　to spill; to pour (oneself); to flow

■ Si è versata del vino sul vestito.
She spilled wine on her dress.

■ Una folla immensa si versava sulla piazza.
A large crowd was pouring (or flowing) into the square.

■ Tutte le sere il nonno si versava un bicchierino di sambuca.
Every night Grandfather would pour himself a little glass of sambuca.

vestire　to dress; to suit; to become

■ La mamma sta vestendo il bambino.
Mother is dressing the baby.

■ Mia nipote vestiva l'orsacchiotto.
My niece was dressing her teddy bear.

■ Non gli va il modo in cui vesto.
He doesn't like the way I dress.

vestirsi　to dress (oneself); to wear

■ Quel bambino non è ancora capace di vestirsi da solo.
That child cannot dress himself yet.

■ Si è vestita da pagliaccio.
She dressed up as a clown.

■ Va a vestirti.
Go and get dressed.

■ La signora Ravera si sa vestire. Si veste sempre con gusto (/con eleganza/alla moda).
Mrs. Ravera knows how to dress. She always dresses with taste (/elegantly/fashionably).

■ In questo albergo ci si deve vestire per la cena.
In this hotel one has to dress for dinner.

■ Vestiti bene!
Dress up!

■ La loro madre si veste sempre di blu.
Their mother always wears blue.

■ Dobbiamo vestirci con abiti pesanti perché farà molto freddo là.
We must wear heavy clothes because it will be very cold there.

viaggiare (a/in/per)   to travel (/for/in/on)

■ Il loro padre viaggiava spesso per affari (/in incognito).
Their father often traveled on business (/incognito).

■ Gli piace viaggiare per mare (/per terra/in macchina/in treno/in aereo/in prima classe).
He likes to travel by sea (/by land/by car/by train/by plane/first class).

■ Il signor Pasquini ha viaggiato tutto il mondo.
Mr. Pasquini has traveled all over the world.

■ Il nostro treno viaggia con quaranta minuti di ritardo.
Our train is forty minutes late.

vietare (qco a qc)   to prohibit, forbid (sth to sb)

■ La caccia è vietata in questi mesi.
Hunting is prohibited during these months.

■ La legge vieta la vendita di film pornografici.
The law prohibits the sale of pornographic movies.

■ Il dottore gli ha vietato il vino.
The doctor forbade him wine.

■ Vietato fumare (/farsi trainare).
No smoking (/towing).

■ L'entrata è vietata ai minori di sedici anni.
No admittance to those under sixteen.

■ La legge lo vieta.
The law doesn't allow it.

vietare a qc di + *inf*   to prohibit, prevent sb from + *ger;* to forbid sb to + *inf*

■ Il dottore gli vietò di alzarsi.
The doctor prohibited him from getting up.

■ Niente vi vieta di farlo (/partire subito).
Nothing prevents you from doing it (/leaving at once).

■ Il dottore gli ha vietato di fumare.
The doctor forbade him to smoke.

vigilare   to watch (over); to be on the alert

■ Erano vigilati da due poliziotti.
They were watched over by two policemen.

■ Devi vigilare, se vuoi che tutto vada bene.
You must be on the alert if you want everything to be all right.

vincere   to win; to defeat; to overcome; to master

■ Chi ha vinto? —Ha vinto la maggioranza (/la loro squadra).
Who won? —The majority (/Their team) won.

- Vinsero la battaglia (/la guerra).
  They won the battle (/the war).

- Arturo ha vinto il primo premio (/duecentomila lire alla lotteria/la causa/la partita/la corsa).
  Arthur won first prize (/two hundred thousand lire in the lottery/the case/the game/the race).

- Vinsero l'esercito nemico.
  They defeated the enemy army.

- Devi cercare di vincere la timidezza (/la paura/tutte le difficoltà).
  You have to try to overcome your shyness (/fear/any difficulties).

- È un uomo che non sa vincere le sue passioni.
  He is a man who cannot master his passions.

- Nessuno lo vince in bontà (/astuzia).
  No one outdoes him in goodness (/outwits him).

vincersi   to control oneself

- La ragazza non riuscì a vincersi e scoppiò in lacrime.
  The girl could not control herself, and (she) burst into tears.

violare   to violate, desecrate; to break; to invade

- Il segreto epistolare (/Il segreto) non va violato.
  The privacy of letters (/pledge of secrecy) must not be violated.

- Vandali hanno violato quella chiesa (/l'altare/molte tombe in quel cimitero).
  Vandals desecrated that church (/the altar/many tombs in that cemetery).

- I diritti dell'uomo non vanno violati.
  Human rights must not be violated.

- Non dovete violare la legge (/i sigilli).
  You must not break the law (/the seals).

visitare   to visit (applies only to places and doctors; for people, *andare a trovare*)

- Quando siamo andati in Italia abbiamo visitato quattro città, dieci musei, otto gallerie d'arte e non so quante chiese.
  When we went to Italy, we visited four cities, ten museums, eight art galleries, and I don't know how many churches.

- Il nuovo direttore ha visitato tutti gli uffici.
  The new manager visited all the offices.

- Il dottore la visitò.
  The doctor gave her an examination.

- Devo andare a farmi visitare dall'oculista.
  I have to go to the eye doctor.

- I miei amici mi hanno fatto visitare la città.
  My friends gave me a tour of the city.

vivere   (auxiliary *essere;* if the verb is followed by a direct object, auxiliary *avere*) to live; to make a living; to go through

■ Mia nonna è vissuta solo fino a novantasei anni.
My grandomother lived to ninety-six years of age.

■ Il nonno di Alberto ha vissuto una lunga vita (/una vita felice/una vita tranquilla/una doppia vita).
Albert's grandfather lived a long (/happy/peaceful/double) life.

■ Il suo nome (/La sua fama) vivrà per sempre.
His name (/His fame) will live on forever.

■ Hanno vissuto un brutto momento (/attimi di angoscia/avventure terribili).
They lived through some bad moments (/moments of anguish/terrible adventures).

■ Antonio vive da gran signore.
Anthony lives like a lord.

■ Non riescono a guadagnarsi da vivere.
They cannot make a living.

vivere a + *city/town/***in** (+ *art*) **qco**   to live in *city/town/*sth; to be alive

■ Quei miei amici non vivono più a Roma.
Those friends of mine do not live in Rome anymore.

■ Credo che vivano ancora in un paesino del Piemonte, nella casa in cui sono nati.
I believe they're still living in a small village in Piedmont, in the house where they were born.

■ Vivono in pace (/nel timore di essere riconosciuti).
They live in peace (/fear of being recognized).

■ Questa pianta vive nell'acqua (/in questo clima/nel deserto del Sahara).
This plant lives in the water (/in this climate/in the Sahara Desert).

■ Queste tradizioni vivono ancora in certe regioni d'Italia.
These traditions are still alive in some regions of Italy.

vivere di qco   to live by/on sth

■ Il signor Manzini vive di espedienti (/di carità/di speranza/del suo stipendio).
Mr. Manzini lives by his wits (/on charity/on hope/on his salary).

■ Gli abitanti di quella regione vivono di caccia e di pesca.
The inhabitants of that region live by hunting and fishing.

■ Tu potresti vivere di carote (/riso).
You could live on carrots (/rice).

vivere per qc/qco   to live for sb/sth

■ Angelo vive per il suo lavoro (/i suoi figli/la pallacanestro).
Angelo lives for his work (/his children/basketball).

viziare   to spoil; to foul

- I nonni viziano troppo tuo figlio.
  The grandparents spoil your son too much.

- Spesso un figlio unico è viziato.
  An only child is often spoiled.

- Tutto questo fumo vizia l'aria.
  All this smoke fouls the air.

    viziarsi   to get spoiled

-    Crescendo in quell'ambiente si è viziato.
     He got spoiled growing up in that environment.

volare   (auxiliary *avere* when the action in itself is considered; *essere* in other cases)

    to fly (away); to blow away; to pass quickly; to speed

- Quel ragazzo non ha mai volato.
  That boy has never flown.

- Gli uccelli (/Gli aeroplani) volano.
  Birds (/Planes) fly.

- Il nostro aereo volava a un'altitudine di 10.000 piedi.
  Our plane was flying at an altitude of 10,000 feet.

- Il vento fece volare il giornale (/il pallone del bambino/le foglie).
  The wind made the newspaper (/the child's balloon/the leaves) fly away.

- La farfalla è volata via.
  The butterfly flew away.

- La notizia volò per tutta la città. (*fig*)
  The news flew (spread quickly) all over town. (fig)

- Come vola il tempo!
  How time flies!

- Nel bar volavano schiaffi. (*fig*)
  Fists flew in the bar. (fig)

- I bambini facevano volare gli aquiloni.
  The children were flying kites.

- Gli è volata via la sciarpa.
  His scarf has blown away.

- Questi due anni sono volati.
  These two years passed quickly.

- L'automobile volava sull'autostrada (/attraverso la vallata).
  The car was speeding along the expressway (/through the valley).

volere   to want, like; to ask; to expect; to look for; to will; to need; to take

- Volevo una rivista da leggere.
  I wanted a magazine to read.

- Vorrei qualcosa di freddo da bere.
  I would like something cold to drink.

- Fate come volete.
  Do as you like.

- Quanto vuoi per la macchina?
  How much are you asking for the car?

- Tu vuoi troppo da lui.
  You expect too much from him.

- Tua moglie ti vuole.
  Your wife is looking for you.

- Dio lo vuole.
  God wills it.

- Questo bambino vuole molta attenzione.
  This child needs a lot of attention.

- Questa preposizione vuole l'accusativo.
  This preposition takes the accusative.

- Se segui le mie indicazioni non ti puoi perdere, neanche se vuoi.
  If you follow my directions, you can't get lost—not even if you try.

- Chi troppo vuole, nulla stringe. (*proverb*)
  Grasp all, lose all. (proverb)

  volere + *inf*   (*Note*: In compound tenses, if *volere* is followed by a verb requiring *essere*, the auxiliary *avere* or *essere* can be used. See the first example.)   to want to + *inf;* to wish + *subject* + *vb:* to refuse to + *inf;* to mean to + *inf;* to look like

  - I ragazzi hanno voluto andare a casa (*or* I ragazzi sono voluti andare a casa).
    The kids wanted to go home.

  - Voglio essere ubbidito.
    I want to be obeyed.

  - Vorrebbero venire ma non possono.
    They would like to come, but they can't.

  - Vorrei essere ricco.
    I wish I were rich.

  - Oggi la mia macchina non vuole funzionare.
    Today my car refuses to run.

■   Volevo telefonarti ma non ho avuto tempo.
    I meant to call you, but I didn't have the time.

■   Vuol nevicare.
    It looks like snow.

volere che + *subj*   to want sb + *inf;* shall + *inf;* to wish; to think

■   Non voglio che tu venga domani.
    I don't want you to come tomorrow.

■   Vuole che apra (/chiuda) la finestra (/la porta), signora Marchi?
    Shall I open (/close) the window (/door), Mrs. Marchi?

■   Vorrei che tu gli parlassi (/dessi il libro/dicessi la verità).
    I wish you would talk to him (/give him the book/tell him the truth).

■   Vuoi che non ci sia nessuno che la possa aiutare?
    Do you think there is anyone who can help her?

voler bene a qc   to love sb; to be fond of sb

■   Antonio le ha detto che le vuol bene e che la vuole sposare.
    Anthony told her he loves her and wants to marry her.

■   Le vogliono bene come a una figlia.
    They love her like a daughter.

■   Tutti gli vogliono bene.
    Everyone is fond of him.

volersi bene   to love each other/one another

■   Si sono sempre voluti molto bene.
    They have always loved each other very much.

voler dire   (auxiliary *essere*) to mean; to be important

■   Cosa vuoi dire?
    What do you mean?

■   Vuol dire molto avere una buona istruzione (/dei buoni amici).
    It is important to have a good education (/good friends).

volerci   (*auxiliary essere*) to take; to be necessary, required; to need

■   Quanto tempo ci vuole per andare in centro?
    How long does it take to go downtown?

■   Ci sono volute due ore.
    It took two hours.

■   Per una camicetta ci vogliono due metri di stoffa.
    For a blouse, two meters of fabric are necessary.

■   Ci vogliono troppi soldi per comprare quella macchina.
    It takes too much money to buy that car.

- Per quell'incarico ci voleva dell'esperienza.
  Some experience was required for that task.

votare   to devote: to dedicate; to pass; to vote

- La signora Antonini ha votato la vita alla famiglia (/ai poveri/alle opere di carità).
  Mrs. Antonini has devoted (or dedicated) her life to her family (/the poor/charity).

- Il progetto di legge è stato votato.
  The bill passed.

- Votate per (/contro di) lui.
  Vote for (/against) him.

- Si voterà per acclamazione (/per alzata di mano/appello nominale).
  We are going to vote by acclamation (/a show of hands/roll call).

- Credo che voteranno contro la proposta.
  I believe they are going to vote against the proposal.

- Oggi andiamo a votare.
  We are going to the polls today.

  votarsi   to devote oneself

  - Si è votata a Dio.
    She devoted herself to God.

vuotare   to empty; to drain; to clean (out)

- Ho vuotato un baule (/una valigia/le tasche).
  I emptied a trunk (/a suitcase/my pockets).

- In agosto la città si vuota.
  In August the city empties (out).

- Devono vuotare lo stagno (/la piscina).
  They have to drain the pond (/swimming pool).

- Il ragazzo vuotò il bicchiere (/il piatto).
  The boy drained his glass (/cleaned his plate).

- Le hanno vuotato l'appartamento.
  They cleaned out her apartment.

- In quel ristorante mi hanno vuotato le tasche. (*fig*)
  They cleaned me out in that restaurant. (fig)

- Dovettero vuotare l'acqua dalla barca.
  They had to bail out the boat.

- L'uomo ha vuotato il sacco. (*idiomatic*)
  The man spilled the beans. (idiomatic)

Z

zoppicare   to walk with a limp; to be wobbly, be shaky

- Zoppicava quando l'ho vista ieri.
  She was limping when I saw her yesterday.

- Questo tavolino zoppica.
  This little table is wobbly.

- Questo è un ragionamento che zoppica.
  This is a lame argument.

- Quel mio studente zoppica un po' in matematica.
  That student of mine is a little shaky in math.

Glossary

abandon   abbandonare, lasciare

abase oneself   abbassarsi

abate   calmarsi

abdicate   abdicare

(be) able   potere, sapere, riuscire

(be) able to do it   farcela

(be) able to see   vederci

abolish   abolire, levare, eliminare, sopprimere

abort   abortire

(be) about   trattarsi di

(be) about to   prepararsi a, stare per

abridge   ridurre

abrogate   abolire

absolve   assolvere

absorb   assorbire

(be) absorbed   raccogliersi, concentrarsi

abstain   astenersi, guardarsi

abuse   abusare

accelerate   accelerare

accentuate   marcare

accept   accettare, ammettere, assumersi, dire di sì, ricevere

acclaim   acclamare

accompany   accompagnare

accomplish   assolvere

account for   spiegare

accuse   accusare

accustom   abituare

achieve   trovare

acknowledge   riconoscere

acquire   acquistare, conquistare

acquit   assolvere

act   agire, operare, fare (1), rappresentare, sostituire, fungere

adapt   adattare, ridurre

add   aggiungere

address   parlare, dirigere, indirizzare, destinare

adhere   aderire, sottoscrivere

adjourn   aggiornare, sospendere

adjust   adattare, correggere

admire   ammirare

admit   ammettere, convenire, ricevere, riconoscere, concedere, accettare

adopt   adottare

adore   adorare

advance   avanzare, muovere

advertise   far conoscere

advise   consigliare, avvisare, suggerire

affect   affettare, colpire, incidere, influire, interessare

afford   permettere, permettersi

(be) afraid of   temere

(be) against   essere contro

(be) an agent for   rappresentare

agitate   agitare

agree   combinare, convenire, incontrarsi, intendersi, fissare, accettare, consentire

aid   aiutare

aim   tendere, dirigere, aspirare

alienate   allontanare

(be) alike   somigliarsi

(be) alive   vivere

alleviate   alleviare, ingannare, addolcire

allow   permettere, lasciare, concedere, consentire, ammettere

allude   alludere

(be) almost   (length of time) mancare poco a

amaze   sbalordire

(be) amazed   meravigliarsi

amuse   divertire

anesthetize   addormentare

animate   animare

annotate   commentare

announce   partecipare

annul *or* **cancel**   annullare

anoint   ungere

answer   rispondere

anticipate   prevenire

apologize   scusarsi

appeal   attirare, *(find favor)* incontrare

appear   apparire, mostrarsi, parere, figurare, presentarsi, *(as)* costituirsi, *(suddenly)* pararsi

appease   levarsi

applaud   applaudire

apply   applicare, *(oil/lotion)* ungersi

appoint   costituire

appraise   stimare

appreciate   quotare

approach   avvicinare

approve   applaudire

argue   discutere

arouse   svegliare, eccitare

arrange   combinare, disporre, distribuire, sistemare

arrest   arrestare, catturare

arrive   arrivare (1), venire (1), giungere

ascend   salire

ascertain   stabilire, determinare, accertare, accertarsi

(be) ashamed   vergognarsi

ask   chiedere, chiedersi, domandare, pretendere, interrogare, pregare, consigliarsi, volere

aspirate   aspirare

aspire   aspirare

assassinate   uccidere

assemble   montare, raccogliere

assert   far valere, accampare, sostenere, imporsi

assess   accertare

assign   affidare, assegnare, distribuire, destinare

assimilate   assorbire

associate   associare, praticare

assume   assumere, ammettere, mettere il caso, supporre, fingere

assure   assicurare, garantire

attach   dare (2), attaccare

attain   raggiungere

attempt *or* **risk**   osare

attend   assistere, partecipare, intervenire, ascoltare, incaricarsi

attest   testimoniare

attract   attirare, *(attention)* imporsi

attribute   imputare

avail oneself   approfittarsi

avoid   evitare, girare, sfuggire

awaken   svegliare

award   dare (2), assegnare, distribuire

(be) aware   sapere

babble   balbettare

back out   sottrarsi

back up   confortare, sostenere

bake   cuocere, fare (5)

balance   bilanciare, quadrare

ban   condannare

bandage   bendare

bang   sbattere

banish   allontanare, confinare

baptize   battezzare

base   basare, derivare, fondare

battle   lottare

be   essere (1, 3), risultare, tenere (3), correre, riuscire, stare, restare, esistere, trovarsi, figurare, dovere, costituire, *(profession, weather, math, age)* fare (2)

be + *adj (idiomatic)*   avere + *noun*

be + *ptp*   venire + *ptp*

be on   fare (2), funzionare

be on the alert   vigilare

be taken by surprise   sorprendersi

be (there)   esserci

be very hot   bruciare

bear   produrre, soffrire, permettere, sopportare, sostenere

beat   battere, sbattere

beckon   accennare

become   diventare, farsi, essere (1), *(aware)* svegliarsi, *(confused)* confondersi, *(lively)* animarsi, *(member)* entrare, *(more marked)* accentuarsi, *(overcast)* coprirsi, *(part of)* inserirsi, (*popular/a success*) imporsi

become *or* **suit**   vestire

beg   chiedere

begin   cominciare, mettersi, aprirsi

begrudge   rimproverare

behave   agire, comportarsi

  behave like   fare da

believe   credere, fidarsi, prestarsi

belong   appartenere, essere di qc

bend   piegare, inclinare, *(down)* abbassarsi

bestow   dispensare, concedere

bet   scommettere, giocare

betray   tradire

better   migliorare

  (be) better   convenire

beware   guardarsi

bewilder   imbarazzare

(be) beyond   eccedere

bid good morning/good evening/good night/good-bye   dire buongiorno, *etc.*

bind   legare, impegnare

bite   mordere, abboccare

blame   rimproverare, accusare, biasimare

blast   brillare

bleed   sanguinare

blend   unirsi, fondersi

bless   benedire

blind   accecare

blindfold   bendare gli occhi

blink   battere gli occhi

block   impedire, bloccare, interrompere

bloom   aprirsi

blow   tirare, suonare, soffiare, fondersi, saltare (in aria), volare, *(off)* portare via, spegnere, far saltare

(be) a blow   ferire

blur   confondere

(get on) board   imbarcare

boast   vantare, vantarsi

boil   bollire, cuocere, fare (5)

bomb   bombardare

bombard   bombardare

book   impegnare, fissare

boost   sollevare, incoraggiare

border   confinare

bore   annoiare

  (be) boring   addormentare

(be) born   nascere

borrow   farsi prestare

bother   disturbare

bound   limitare

bow   piegarsi

brag   vantarsi

brand   marcare

brave   sfidare

break   far saltare, rompere, spaccare, lacerare, violare, risolvere, penetrare, lasciare, interrompere, abbattersi, ridursi, sciogliere, dissolvere, *(oneself of sth)* correggersi, *(open)* forzare, *(up/off)* lasciarsi/piantarsi

brew   bollire

bribe   ungere, comprare

brighten   rallegrare

bring   portare, introdurre, causare, attuare, determinare, *(about/forth)* far nascere, *(down)* far saltare, ridurre, accampare, *(to end)* concludere, *(together again)* riunire, *(up)* tirare su, *(up-to-date)* aggiornare

broadcast   trasmettere, comunicare, mandare

broaden   allargare

brush (*teeth*) lavarsi i denti
bud gettare
build fabbricare, costruire, fare (4), alzare
build up accavallarsi
bump (*against*) battere contro, (*into*) incontrare (per caso)
(be a) burden pesare
burn (down) bruciare, (*out*) bruciarsi/fulminarsi
burst rompere, invadere
bury seppellire
bustle (about) trafficare
butter ungere
button (up) abbottonare, abbottonarsi
buy comprare, farsi, fornirsi di
cable telegrafare
call chiamare, chiamarsi, dirsi, riunire, battezzare, toccare
calm (down) calmare
camp campeggiare, accamparsi
can fare (7), potere, sapere
cancel sciogliere
capsize capovolgere, capovolgersi, rovesciarsi
capture catturare, arrestare, conquistare
care badare
   (not) care (non) guardare (2)
(be) careful (make sure) badare
caress accarezzare
carry portare, imbarcare, spingere, sostenere, proseguire, esercitare, continuare, realizzare, operare, tradurre in pratica, compiere, eseguire, attuare
carve tagliare, fare (4), incidere
cast fondere, gettare, lanciare, calare
catch contrarre, catturare, attaccare, prendere, sorprendere, cogliere, venire, afferrare, raggiungere, (*fire*) incendiarsi
   (be) catching attaccare
cause creare, causare, procurare, provocare, produrre

(be) caused dipendere
cauterize bruciare
cave in cedere
cease cessare, passare
cede cedere
celebrate celebrare, bagnare
center concentrare
certify dichiarare
challenge sfidare
change mutare, transformare, girare, cambiare, variare, diventare, convertirsi, (*radically*) capovolgere
characterize distinguere
charge far pagare, praticare, caricare, chiedere, accusare, imputare
charge *or* **entrust** incaricare
cheat truffare, ingannare
check accertare, guardare
cheer sollevare, (*up*) tirare su, rallegrare
cherish accarezzare
chew masticare
chirp cantare
chitchat chiacchierare
choose scegliere, adottare
chop spaccare
christen battezzare
circulate correre
cite citare
claim reclamare, pretendere, (*rights*) vantare
clap battere (le mani), applaudire
clean pulire, (*out*) vuotare
cleanse lavare
clear chiarire, discolpare, (*up*) risolvere
climb salire, montare, fare (6)
cling attaccarsi
close chiudere, (*down*) chiudere/concludere, (*gently*) accompagnare
(be) close avvicinarsi
cloud chiudersi

clutch   afferrarsi

coach   allenare, preparare

collaborate   collaborare

collapse   sprofondare

collect   esigere, raccogliere

collide   investire

combine   unire, combinare

   (be) combined   riunirsi

come   venire (1), uscire, avanzarsi, *(about)* determinare, *(earlier)* anticipare, *(in)* entrare/accomodarsi, *(off)* venire via, *(on)* accendersi, saltare, andare via, *(out)* uscire, balzare, *(to boil)* bollire, *(to conclusion)* concludere, *(to halt)* arrestarsi, *(to head)* maturare, *(to agreement)* accomodarsi, *(to agreement/understanding)* aggiustarsi, *(to life)* animarsi, *(true)* compiersi, realizzarsi, *(undone)* disfarsi, *(up)* arrivare/offrirsi

comfort   confortare

command   comandare, imporre, raccomandarsi

commemorate   ricordarsi

commence   cominciare

commend   raccomandare

comment (on)   commentare

commit   commettere, affidare

compare   paragonare

compel   forzare

compensate   compensare

compete   gareggiare, misurarsi

complain   reclamare, lagnarsi, lamentarsi

complete   compiere

comply   ubbidire, aderire

compose   comporre

compromise   compromettere, esporsi

conceal   nascondere, dissimulare

conceive   immaginare

concentrate   concentrare

concern   riferirsi

   (be) concerned   interessare, interessarsi

conclude   concludere

condemn   condannare

conduct   condurre, dirigere

confer   abboccarsi

confess   confessare

confide   affidare

confine   obbligare, consegnare, confinare

   (be) confined   confinarsi

(be in) conformity   corrispondere

confront   affrontare

confuse   confondere

congratulate   congratularsi, felicitarsi, rallegrarsi

connect   unire, collegare, legare

conquer   conquistare

consent   accogliere

consider   pensare, guardare (2), stimare, considerare, dare, guidicare, contarsi, stimare

   (be) considered   passare per

consist   costituire, comporre, consistere

console oneself   confortarsi

constitute   costituire

construct   costruire

consult   consultare, interrogare

(be) consumed by   distruggersi

(be) contagious   attaccare

contain   contenere, stare, starci

   (be) contained   entrarci

contemplate   considerare

contend   combattere

(be) content   accontentarsi

continue   continuare, procedere, seguire, proseguire

contract   contrarre, tendersi

contravene   contravvenire

contribute   contribuire, collaborare

control   dominare, comandare, vincersi

converge   convergere

(be) conversant with   conoscere

convert   convertire

convince   convincere

convince *or* **persuade oneself**   convincersi, persuadersi

cook   cucinare, cuocere, fare (5)

correct   correggere

correspond   corrispondere, incontrarsi

corrode   mordere

cost   costare, venire (2), essere (3)

count   contare

cover   coprire, sommergere, compiere, superare

crash   cadere (2), *(down)* cascare

crave   desiderare (molto)

create   creare, fare (4)

(be) creditor for   avanzare

criticize   commentare

crop up   sorgere

cross   attraversare, superare, passare, accavallare, incrociare, segnarsi, *(out)* cancellare

crow   cantare

crowd together   addossarsi

cry   piangere

cry *or* **call for**   gridare

cultivate   coltivare

cure   guarire

curse   maledire

curtail   ridurre, abbreviare

(be the) custom   usare

(be a) customer   servirsi

cut   tagliare, *(down)* ridurre, *(off)* interrompere/incidere, *(out)* sopprimere

cut (sth) out   piantare

(be) cut out for   nascere

cycle through   attraversare in bicicletta

damage *or* **hurt**   nuocere

dampen   smontare

dance   ballare

dare   osare, permettersi

(be) daring   osare

date   datare

daze   ubriacare

deal   trafficare, trattare, *(out)* distribuire/dispensare, *(with)* maneggiare

debate   discutere, dibattere

debilitate   provare

deceive   illudere, giocare, tradire, ingannare

decide   decidere, fare (3), stabilire, destinare, giudicare, vedere, disporre, risolvere

declare   dire, protestare, dichiarare, pronunciarsi

decline *or* **refuse**   rifiutare

decrease   calare

dedicate   votare, dedicare

deduct   sottrarre, scaricare

deem   giudicare

defeat   disfare, battere, vincere

defend   difendere

define   definire, determinare

deflect   deviare

defy   sfidare

(be) delayed   tardare

delete   sopprimere, cancellare, distribuire, emettere, consegnare

delude   illudere

demand   reclamare, esigere

demolish   abbattere, demolire, condannare

demonstrate   dimostrare, manifestare, provare

denote *or* **mean**   indicare

deny   negare, rifiutare

depart   partire

depend   dipendere, stare, disporre

depend on it   non dubitare

depict   rappresentare, dipingere

deploy   spiegare

deposit   depositare, versare

depress   deprimere

deprive   privare

derive derivare

descend discendere, scendere

describe rappresentare, presentare, descrivere, qualificarsi

desecrate violare

desert lasciare, disertare, abbandonare

deserve meritare

design progettare

designate dichiarare

destine destinare

destroy distruggere

detail comandare

determine determinare

  (be) determined fissarsi

detest odiare

develop formarsi

deviate deviare

devise elaborare

devote dedicare, destinare, votare, impegnarsi

dial *(number)* comporre, formare un numero

dictate dettare

die morire, mancare, cadere (2), *(out)* spegnersi

differ variare

dilute allungare

dim abbassare

dip tuffare, bagnare

direct dirigere, indirizzare

(be) disagreeable dispiacere

disappear sparire

disapprove biasimare

disassemble smontare

discharge licenziare, scaricare

  (be) discharged uscire

disclose anticipare

discourage smontare

discover scoprire

discuss discutere, agitare

disguise mascherare, truccare

disgust disgustare

dishearten abbattere, buttare giù

dismantle smontare

dismiss licenziare, allontanare

dismount smontare

dispel dissolvere

dispense dispensare, sciogliere, spargere

display esporre

displease dispiacere

dispose disporre

dissolve sciogliere, dissolvere

dissuade *or* **deter** dissuadere

distinguish distinguere, distinguersi, farsi notare

distort forzare

distress addolorare

  (be) distressed addolorarsi

distribute distribuire, consegnare

distrust sospettare

disturb disturbare

dive tuffarsi

divert deviare, divertire

divest privare

divide dividere, distinguere

do fare (1), compiere, *(away with)* togliere, *(business)* lavorare, *(same)* seguire, *(sth to excess)* eccedere, *(without)* privarsi

  (be) done with finire

doctor/soup up truccare

dodge (around) evitare

dominate dominare

donate sottoscrivere

doubt dubitare

drag tirare, trascinare

drain vuotare

draw estrarre, tendere, tirare, chiudere, *(attention)* farsi notare, *(away)* allontanarsi/aspirare, *(near)* avvicinare, *(out)* tirare fuori/cavare, *(up)* elaborare, *(upon oneself)* attirarsi

(be) drawn   venire (2), uscire

dread   temere

dream   sognare

dress   vestire, *(wound)* bendare, condire, *(up as)* mascherarsi, *(well)* figurare

drink   bere, *(to excess)* eccedere

drive   piantare, portare, fare (6), andare in macchina, guidare, condurre, *(away)* cacciare, *(back)* respingere, spingere, indurre, affondare, *(through)* attraversare in macchina

drop   calare, cadere (2), *(person)* smontare, abbassarsi, abbandonare

drown   affogare, coprire

dry   asciugare

(be) due *or* **result**   derivare

(be) due/bound   dovere

duel   battersi

dwell   *(in)* abitare, *(on)* intrattenersi

dwindle   ridursi

dye   tingere

earn   guadagnare, meritare, *(one's living)* mantenersi

ease   calmare

eat   mangiare, *(to excess)* eccedere

eclipse   eclissare

economize   risparmiare

educate   istruire

elect   eleggere

electrocute   fulminare

elevate   elevare

eliminate   eliminare

elope   fuggire

embark   imbarcare

embarrass   imbarazzare

(be) embarrassed   vergognarsi

embrace   abbracciare, sposare

emerge   uscire

emit   emettere

emphasize   accentuare

employ   praticare, occupare

empty   vuotare, rovesciare

encircle   accerchiare

enclose   circondare, includere

encourage   incoraggiare, animare, proteggere

end   finire, morire, andare a finire, uscire, *(up)* finire/concludersi

(come to an) end   compiersi

endanger   compromettere

endorse   girare

endure   sopportare, resistere

enforce   eseguire, applicare

engage   praticare, *(in conversation)* intrattenere

(be) engraved   incidersi

engross   assorbire

enjoy   divertirsi, godere, gustare

enlarge   allargare

enliven   animare

(be) enough/sufficient   bastare

entail   comportare, imporre, implicare

enter   entrare

entertain   divertire, intrattenere

entice   attirare, sedurre

entrust   affidare, raccomandare

envelop   avvolgere

equip   fornire

(be) equivalent to   valere

eradicate   eliminare

erase   cancellare

erect   elevare

escape   scappare, salvarsi, evitare, fuggire, sfuggire, sottrarsi, riparare

escort   accompagnare

espouse   abbracciare

establish   stabilire, creare, fondare, costituire, fissare

estimate   misurare

etch   incidere

evade   sottrarsi, ingannare

even   uguagliare

(be) evident   mostrare

exact   esigere

exaggerate   esagerare, calcare

examine   esaminare, interrogare, studiare, vagliare

   (be) examined   (by *doctor, dentist,
etc.*) farsi vedere

exceed   superare, sorpassare

excel   eccellere

exchange   darsi, incrociarsi, scambiare,
barattare

excite   provocare, eccitare

exclude   escludere

excuse   scusare, perdonare, esonerare

execute   eseguire

exempt   dispensare, esonerare

exercise   esercitare, usare

exert   esercitare

exhibit   esporre

exhort   esortare

exist   esistere, essere (1)

   (be in) existence   esistere

expand   allargarsi

expect   aspettarsi, immaginarsi,
prevedere, volere, sperare, pretendere

experience   conoscere

explain   spiegare, esporre, interpretare

explode   saltare (in aria), far saltare

exploit   giocare

expose   esporre

expound   spiegare, interpretare

express   esprimere, dire, manifestare,
tradurre

extend   distendersi, continuare

extinguish   spegnere

extol   celebrare

extract   estrarre, cavare

fabricate   fabbricare

face   affrontare, guardare (1)

fade   languire, *(away)* spegnersi/sparire

fail   fallire, abbandonare, abortire,
cadere (2), respingere, bocciare, *(to express)* tradire

   (not) fail to   non mancare

fall   cadere, scendere, discendere, venire
(2), calare, *(asleep)* addormentarsi,
(down) cascare/cadere (1)/abbattersi,
(down again) ricadere, *(ill)* ammalarsi, *(in
love)* innamorarsi, *(silent)* tacere

falter   esitare

(be) familiar with   conoscere

familiarize   familiarizzare

fascinate   sedurre

(be in) fashion   usare

(be) fashionable   andare molto

fasten   fissare, legare, *(oneself)* assicurarsi

favor   guardare (2), proteggere

fear   temere

feed   mangiare, nutrire

feel   avere, toccare, sentire (2), accusare, avvertire, trovarsi, provare,
(again) risentire, *(fulfilled)* realizzarsi,
(hot) bollire, *(like)* parere/venire da/an-
dare/girare, *(pity)* compatire

   feel up to   fidarsi, sentirsela

feign   fingere, figurare

fence   circondare

fidget   ballare

fight   battersi, litigare, combattere,
lottare

file away   seppellire

fill   riempire, caricare, impregnare,
(with indignation) indignare

   fill up   *(with gas)* fare il pieno (di
benzina)

filter passare

find trovare, dichiarare, *(guilty)* condannare, *(guilty/not guilty)* giudicare, *(job)* sistemare, *(out)* informarsi/sentire (1)/scoprire

finish finire

fire sparare, scaricare, cuocere

(be on) fire bruciare

fit entrare, aderire, stare, andare, *(for)* misurare, *(in)* quadrare, *(in with)* combinarsi, *(well, of shoes)* calzare

(be) fit prestarsi

fix assegnare, fissare, determinare, incidere, aggiustare, stabilire, sistemare, accomodare

flap sbattere

flash lampeggiare

flavor condire

flee fuggire

flicker vacillare

fling lanciare

flood sommergere, invadere

flop cadere (2)

flounder dibattersi

flow versarsi, scaricarsi, gettare, *(through)* bagnare, *(toward)* discendere

fluctuate variare

flutter battere, dibattere

fly andare, dirigersi, volare, *(flag)* battere

fold chiudere, *(up)* piegare

follow seguire, accettare, tenere (3), succedere, accompagnare, *(treatment)* curarsi

(be) fond voler bene

fondle accarezzare

fool oneself illudersi

(be) for essere per

forbid proibire, vietare

force forzare, sforzare, imporre, obbligare

forecast prevedere

foresee prevedere

forestall prevenire

foretell indovinare

forewarn prevenire

forget dimenticare, seppellire

forgive perdonare

forgo rinunciare

form costituire, contrarre, creare, formare

form a line/circle disporsi in fila, in cerchio

forsake abbandonare

forward proseguire

foul viziare

found fondare, basare

(be) found trovarsi

free scaricare, sciogliere, liberare

freeze gelare

frequent praticare

frighten spaventare

(be) frightened spaventarsi

fulfill sciogliere, onorare

(be) fulfilled compiersi

fumble about (for) cercare

function funzionare

(be) funny far ridere

furnish fornire

gain guadagnare, ottenere, cavare

gather raccogliere, riunirsi, convenire

gauge misurare

gaze fissare

get diventare, prendere, ottenere, ricevere, procurare, portare, montare, *(accustomed)* abituarsi, *(advanced degree)* laurearsi, *(ahead)* riuscire, *(angry)* scaldarsi, *(around)* girare, *(back together)* riunirsi, *(bored)* annoiarsi, *(confused)* confondersi, *(covered)* coprirsi, *(deeply involved)* buttarsi, *(depressed)* abbattersi, *(dirty)* sporcarsi, *(disconcerted)* confondersi, *(discouraged)* deprimersi, *(disgusted)* disgustarsi, *(disheartened)* abbattersi/smontarsi, *(done/through)* concludere/sbrigare, *(drunk)* ubriacarsi, *(engaged/involved)* impegnarsi, *(excited)* accendersi/eccitarsi/accalorarsi, *(flat tire)* bucarsi, *(grease on oneself)* ungersi, *(hold of)* afferrare/impadronirsi, *(in)* passare, *(indignant)* indignarsi, *(information)* informarsi, *(inspiration)* ispirarsi, *(into)* mettersi/inserirsi/cacciarsi/entrare/introdursi, *(into one's head)* mettersi in mente/fissarsi, *(involved)* occuparsi, *(irritated)* irritarsi, *(killed)* ammazzarsi, *(legal separation)* separarsi, *(less rigid)* allentarsi, *(longer)* allungarsi, *(lost)* perdersi, *(married)* sposarsi/sistemarsi, *(mixed up)* confondersi, *(more serious)* aggravarsi, *(nervous)* irritarsi, *(off)* scendere/smontare/discendere, *(off/out)* togliersi, *(off duty)* smontare, *(on)* salire/trovarsi, *(oneself up-to-date)* aggiornarsi, *(out)* uscire/scendere/togliere/andarsene, *(out from)* uscire, *(out of it)* cavarsela, *(out of prison)* uscire di prigione, *(over)* superare, *(ready)* preparare/disporsi, *(rid of)* guarire/scaricare/disfarsi/correggersi/cavarsi/eliminare, *(sb interested)* interessare, *(sick)* disgustarsi, *(spoiled)* viziarsi, *(sth done)* combinare, *(sth out)* cavare, *(sth out of sth)* guadagnarci, *(swell-headed)* montarsi, *(tall)* alzarsi, *(through)* collegarsi/sbrigarsi, *(tired)* stancarsi, *(to like)* affezionarsi, *(undressed)* spogliarsi, *(up)* alzarsi/levarsi/tirarsi su/sollevarsi, *(upset)* agitarsi, *(weather/time)* farsi, *(wet)* bagnarsi, *(worse)* aggravarsi

give corrispondere, dare (1), praticare, allungare, *(assistance)* assistere, *(back)* rendere/restituire, *(birth)* dare alla luce, *(in/way)* cedere, *(name/nickname)* imporre (nome/soprannome), *(nod)* salutare, *(off)* dare (1), *(one's opinion)* pronunciarsi, *(one's regards)* salutare, *(oneself away)* tradirsi, *(oneself to despair)* disperarsi, *(oneself up)* costituirsi/abbandonarsi, *(rise to)* causare, *(sth as a gift)* regalare, *(testimony)* testimoniare, *(the*

idea) far nascere (l'idea), *(up)* rinunciare/disperare/abbandonare/cessare/abolire/lasciare, *(up hope)* condannare/disperare, *(up one's job)* licenziarsi, *(way)* sprofondare/abbandonarsi

(be) glad rallegrarsi

glide away scivolare

glitter brillare

go andare, portarsi, stare a, funzionare, dirigersi, marciare, allontanarsi, fare (6), passare, *(and see)* guardare, *(as far as)* arrivare/giungere, *(away)* andare via, *(back)* ritornare/risalire, *(bankrupt)* fallire, *(by)* basarsi, *(down)* scendere/discendere/calare *(measure)*/abbassarsi, *(fast)* correre, *(faster)* accelerare, *(flat)* smontarsi, *(into)* entrare, *(into/to + room of the house)* andare in + *room of the house,* *(off)* suonare/scattare, *(off the road)* uscire di strada, *(on)* continuare/proseguire procedere, *(on board)* imbarcarsi, *(out)* uscire, *(out/off)* spegnersi, *(over)* ripetere, *(to show, etc.)* vedere, *(to sleep)* addormentarsi, *(through)* attraversare, *(together)* combinarsi, *(too far)* superare/sorpassare/esagerare, *(under)* fallire, *(up)* aumentare, *(up/upstairs)* salire, *(up again/upstream)* risalire, *(with)* seguire

goad spronare

gossip bisbigliare, chiacchierare, sussurrare, parlare

graduate licenziare

grant accontentare, accogliere, convenire, concedere, ascoltare

grant custody affidare

grasp afferrare, capire, abbracciare

gratify soddisfare

grease ungere

greet salutare

grieve addolorare, piangere

grill cuocere, fare (5)

grow coltivare, venire su, farsi, diventare, essere (1), crescere

grow fond of attaccarsi, affezionarsi

grow tall   allungarsi

grumble   mormorare

guarantee   assicurare, garantire

guard   guardare (1), proteggere

guess   indovinare, immaginare, pensare

guide   guidare

gush   gettare

(be) had or **taken in**   cascarci

hail   acclamare

halt   bloccare, arrestare

hamper   imbarazzare, impedire

hand   dare (2), *(in)* consegnare, rassegnare, *(out)* distribuire, *(over)* cedere

handle   sbrigare, prendere, toccare, trattare, maneggiare

hang   attaccare, pesare, mettere, pendere, *(down)* ricadere, *(loosely)* ballare, *(out)* esporre/distendere, *(up)* sospendere

happen   accadere, avvenire, capitare, succedere, trovarsi, toccare, essere (1), arrivare (2), *(again)* ripetersi

harm   nuocere

harness   attaccare

harvest   raccogliere

hasten   affrettare, accelerare

(be) hatched   nascere (1)

hate   odiare

have   avere (1), portare, tenere (3), fare (3), prendere, godere, dovere, bisognare, avere da, *(anything to do with)* trattare/entrarci, *(at one's disposal)* disporre, *(authority)* valere, *(breakfast)* fare colazione, *(consultation)* consigliarsi, *(dream)* sognare, *(flat tire)* bucare, *(fun)* divertirsi, *(in store)* preparare, *(influence on)* influire, *(meeting)* abboccarsi, *(miscarriage/abortion)* abortire, *(not)* mancare, *(one's beard/mustache/hair shaved)* farsi radere la barba/i baffi/i capelli, *(sth sent)* farsi venire qco, *(source)* nascere (1), *(suspicion)* sospettare

head   dirigersi

heal   guarire, chiudersi

heap   coprire

hear   sentire (1), sapere, *(again)* risentire, *(talk about)* sentire parlare di

heat   scaldare, accalorare

help   aiutare, facilitare, servire, seguire prestarsi, contenersi

   (need) help   *(in stores)* desiderare

hesitate   esitare

hide   nascondere, mascherare, seppellire, coprire

hire   assumere

hiss   soffiare

hit   colpire, scaricare, *(it off)* simpatizzare, *(nail on the head)* indovinare

hold   accogliere, mordere, tenere (1), coprire, disporre, occupare, celebrare, sostenere, stare, starci, contenere, tendere, occupare, *(back)* tenere indietro, *(by)* tenere per, *(one's own)* difendere, *(out)* tendere, *(out against)* resistere, *(tight)* afferrarsi

honor   onorare

hop   saltare

hope   sperare

(be) hot   cuocere

huff   soffiare

hug   abbracciare

hull   brillare

hunt   cacciare

hurl   buttare, sbattere, lanciare

hurry   affrettarsi, correre, sbrigarsi

hurt   ferire

identify   riconoscere, identificare

idle   girare a vuoto (in folle)

ignore   ignorare

illuminate   illuminare

imagine   immaginare, pensare, figurarsi, sognare, fingere, supporre, rappresentarsi

(be) imbued   ispirarsi

implicate   implicare

imply implicare

import importare

(be) important importare, contare, voler dire

impose imporre

impregnate impregnare

imprint stampare

improve migliorare, correggere, acquistare, elevarsi, *(one's mind)* istruirsi

impute imputare

incite spingere

(be) inclined inclinare, pendere

include includere, abbracciare

increase montare, migliorare, allargare, aumentare, aggravare, *(speed)* accelerare

incur incorrere

indicate segnare, indicare

induce indurre, provocare

(be) indulgent compatire

infer concludere

inflame incendiare

inflict on oneself prodursi

influence influire

inform informare, avvisare, partecipare, comunicare, istruire

inhabit abitare

inhale aspirare

inherit ereditare

inject iniettare, *(illegal drugs)* bucarsi

injure nuocere

inquire informarsi, domandare

insert introdurre, inserire

insist insistere, battere

inspire ispirare

  (be) inspired ispirarsi

instill comunicare

institute istruire

instruct istruire

insult offendere

insure assicurare

intend destinare, intendere, contare

(be of) interest interessare

  (be) interested interessarsi, guardare (2)

interfere intervenire, interessarsi, disturbare

intern confinare

interpret interpretare

interrogate interrogare

interrupt interrompere, sospendere, fermare

intersect incrociarsi, tagliare

intervene intervenire

interview intervistare

intoxicate ubriacare

introduce presentare, introdurre, far conoscere

invade invadere, violare

invalidate viziare

invest investire

invite invitare

involve comportare

irritate irritare

issue emettere

jam bloccarsi, disturbare

jilt piantare

join unire, associarsi, aggiungersi, raggiungere, entrare, *(forces)* collegarsi

joke scherzare

jot down buttare giù

judge giudicare, basarsi

jump saltare, balzare

just think figurarsi

keep tenere (2), mantenere, impedire, durare, osservare, parare, insistere, continuare, badare, seguire, *(quiet)* tacere, *(score)* segnare, *(sb busy/under pressure)* impegnare, *(sb standing)* tenere in piedi, *(vigil)* vegliare

kick battere, cacciare, sparare, *(oneself)* mordersi

kid scherzare

kill uccidere, ammazzare, sopprimere, finire, morire, gelare, eliminare

kiss baciare

knead lavorare

knit lavorare a maglia

knock bussare, battere, sbattere, abbattere, distendere, eliminare, rovesciare, *(down)* buttare giù

know conoscere, sapere, sentire (1)

  (not) know ignorare

lacerate lacerare

lack mancare

lament lamentare

lance incidere

languish languire

lap leccare

lash out sparare

last durare, mantenersi, bastare

(be) late tardare, farsi desiderare

laugh ridere, burlarsi

launch lanciare

lay appoggiare, distendere, addossare

lead guidare, condurre, andare, aprire, portare, menare, andare a finire, indurre, finire, uscire

leak tenere (3), imbarcare, colare, perdere, fare acqua

lean inclinare, pendere, addossare, appoggiare, sostenersi

leap balzare, saltare

learn imparare, studiare

lease affittare

leave lasciare, uscire, partire, abbandonare, stampare, depositare, andare via, andarsene, allontanarsi, separarsi

  (be) left avanzare, restare

lend prestare, dare (2)

lengthen allungare

let lasciare, permettere, affittare, *(choose)* fare *or* lasciar scegliere, *(down)*

calare/sciogliere, *(oneself fall)* abbandonarsi, *(know)* avvisare/avvertire, *(out)* allargare/gettare, *(see)* far vedere

lick leccare

lie *(down)* distendersi, *(heavily)* pesare, *(in)* consistere, *(prevaricate)* mentire

lift levare, sollevare

light accendersi, animarsi, *(up)* illuminare/accendere

  (be) lit up illuminarsi

lighten alleggerire, illuminarsi

(be) lightning lampeggiare

like piacere, gustare, volere, parere, andare, tenere, quadrare, *(better/best)* preferire

(be) like essere (1), fare (da), avvicinarsi

(be) likely dovere

limber up sciogliere

limit limitare

line up disporsi in fila

link unire, *(up)* legare/collegare

listen sentire (1), ascoltare, badare

live vivere, abitare, stare, esistere, *(on)* nutrirsi, *(one's part)* investirsi, *(temporarily, as in camp)* accamparsi

liven up animare

load imbarcare, *(down/up)* caricare

loan prestare

loathe odiare

locate determinare

  (be) located stare, trovarsi

lock chiudere (a chiave)

long desiderare (molto), sospirare

  (be) longing/dying morire dalla voglia

look presentarsi, dimostrare, apparire, guardare (1), *(and see)* guardare (1), *(after)* assistere/occuparsi/ badare, *(around)* cercare/guardarsi, *(at)* osservare, *(better)* guadagnarci, *(for)* cercare/volere, *(good/smart)* figurare, *(like)* parere/somigliare, *(onto)* dare su, *(out for)* badare

loom   apparire

loosen   allentare

lose   perdere, scappare, giocarsi, *(hair or teeth)* cadere (2), lasciarci, *(hope)* disperare, *(measure)* calare

(be) **lost**   benedire

love   amare, volere bene, adorare

lower   abbassare, tirare giù, *(away)* calare, *(oneself)* sporcarsi/ridursi

(be) **lucky/unlucky**   capitare bene/male

lull   addormentare

(be) **made of**   essere di

maintain   sostenere, mantenere

make   fare (1), realizzare, stabilire, creare, diventare, commettere, mettere, praticare, fabbricare, presentare, rendere, qualificare, *(clear)* chiarire, *(cry)* far piangere, *(detour)* deviare, *(dirty)* sporcare, *(drunk)* ubriacare, *(easier)* facilitare, *(equal)* uguagliare, *(for)* dirigersi, *(fun)* ridere/scherzare/giocarsi/burlarsi, *(happy)* rallegrare, *(hole)* bucare, *(indignant)* indignare, *(it)* farcela, *(living)* vivere, *(math)* dare (2), *(member of)* associare, *(mistake)* sbagliare, *(money)* guadagnare, *(name for oneself)* farsi conoscere, *(note)* notare, *(oneself)* rendersi, *(oneself appreciated)* farsi valere, *(oneself clear)* spiegarsi, *(oneself comfortable)* accomodarsi, *(oneself heard)* farsi sentire, *(oneself known)* farsi riconoscere, *(oneself respected)* imporsi, *(out)* distinguersi, *(profit)* guadagnare, *(progress)* migliorare, *(sacrifices)* sacrificarsi, *(sb a subscriber)* abbonare qc, *(sb get off)* far scendere qc, *(sb laugh)* far ridere qc, *(sb talk)* far parlare qc, *(sb work)* far lavorare qc, *(short)* abbreviare, *(sleepy)* addormentare, *(sth lighter)* alleviare qco, *(sth square)* quadrare qco, *(sth turn/spin)* far girare qco, *(sth work)* far funzionare qco, *(speech)* parlare, *(sure)* accertarsi/procurare/assicurarsi/preoccuparsi, *(up)* truccare, *(up for)*

riparare/compensare, *(up one's mind)* decidersi, *(use of)* valersi, *(weak)* buttare giù, *(worse/more serious)* aggravare

manage   riuscire, guidare, cavarsela, dirigere, difendersi, poter farcela, arrivare

manifest   manifestare, tradursi

march   marciare, entrare

mark   marcare, segnare, notare, distinguere, truccare

marry   sposare

mask   mascherare

master   vincere, dominare, impadronirsi

match   uguagliare, combinare, accompagnarsi, *(clothing)* andare

matter   importare

(be the) **matter/question**   trattarsi

mature   maturare

may/might   potere

may be   può darsi

mean   voler dire, significare, spiegarsi, destinare, volere, andare a finire

it means, that is to say (i.e.)   vale a dire

measure   misurare

meet   incontrare, conoscere, trovarsi, vedersi, rispondere, incrociarsi, riunirsi

mellow   addolcire, maturare

melt   colare, disfare, fondere, sciogliersi

(be a) **member**   appartenere

mend   aggiustare, accomodare, *(one's way)* correggersi

mention   citare, menzionare, accennare, parlarne, *(not)* tacere

"don't mention it"   s'immagini

merge   fondere

mind   dispiacere, guardare (2), interessarsi, pensare, badare, notare, occuparsi

mine   estrarre

mingle   mescolare, confondersi

miscalculate   sbagliare

misfire scattare

mispronounce sbagliare

miss mancare, perdere, fallire, sbagliare, scappare

(be) **missing** mancare

misspell sbagliare

mistake scambiare per, confondere

(be) **mistaken** ingannarsi, sbagliarsi

mix mescolare, *(up)* confondere

moan lagnarsi

mold plasmare

molt mutare

mount montare, salire, balzare

mourn piangere, lamentare

move muovere, allontanare, portarsi, trasferirsi, tirare, commuovere, passare, *(up)* anticipare

(be) **moved** commuoversi

mow tagliare

murder ammazzare, uccidere

murmur mormorare, sussurrare

must dovere, bisognare

mutter masticare, mormorare

name dedicare

(be) **nearly/almost** mancare poco che

(be) **necessary** occorrere, importare, bisognare, volerci

need meritare, mancare, volere, servire, dovere, *(only)* bastare, *(urgently)* urgere

(be) **needed** andare

need (help) *(in store)* desiderare

neglect abbandonare

negotiate trattare

nickname battezzare

nod accennare di sì (col capo)

"not at all" s'immagini

note notare, *(down)* segnare

notice accorgersi, osservare, notare, avvertire

notify avvertire

nourish nutrire, sostenere

obey ubbidire, ascoltare

object opporsi, osservare

oblige impegnare

observe osservare, celebrare, *(oneself)* studiarsi

obstruct impedire

obtain ottenere

occupy occupare, abitare, tenere (3), *(oneself)* occuparsi

occur avvenire, presentarsi, operarsi, prodursi

offend offendere

(be) **offended** offendersi, dispiacersi

offer offrire, presentarsi

officiate celebrare

oil ungere

omit tacere

ooze colare

open (up) aprire, allargare, *(illegally)* manomettere, *(onto)* rispondere

operate agire, lavorare, operare, comandare, intervenire

oppose opporre

(be) **opposed** opporsi

ordain ordinare

order ordinare, disporre, comandare, imporre

organize organizzare

ought dovere

outlive seppellire

(be) **over** *(number of years)* superare, *(with)* finire di

overburden oneself caricarsi

overcome superare, vincere

overdo esagerare

overindulge abusare

overlap accavallare

overload aggravare

overlook   elevarsi, ignorare, dare su

overshadow   eclissare

overturn   capovolgere, rovesciare

owe   dovere, venire (2)

own   avere

paint   dipingere, fare (4)

parry   parare

part   lasciarsi, *(separate)* dividere

participate   partecipare

pass   sorpassare, emettere, superare, votare, promuovere, allungare, *(away)* spegnersi, *(by)* passare, *(for)* passare per, *(quickly)* volare

  (be) passed   passare

pause   arrestarsi

pawn   impegnare

pay   pagare, dare (2), versare, corrispondere, rispondere, *(attention)* ascoltare/badare/curarsi, *(in advance)* anticipare

peep   guardare (1)

penetrate   penetrare

perceive   accorgersi

perform   eseguire, dare (2), fare (1), operare

permit   permettere, consentire

persist   persistere, durare, insistere

perspire   sudare

persuade   persuadere, convincere

  (be) persuaded   persuadersi, convincersi

phone   telefonare

pick   cogliere, *(out)* scegliere, *(up)* raccogliere

picture   figurarsi, immaginarsi

pierce   penetrare, lacerare

pile up   accavallarsi

pitch   piantare

pity   compatire

place   disporre, mettersi, addossare

plan   progettare, proporsi, pensare

plant   coltivare, *(with)* piantare

play   suonare, giocare, interpretare, incontrare, prodursi, *(market)* giocare in borsa, *(the part of)* fare (1), *(with)* scherzare

plead   difendere, pregare, *(guilty)* confessarsi

please   piacere, soddisfare

please + *command*   prego + *command*

(be) pleasing   piacere

pledge   impegnare

plunge   tuffarsi

ply   investire

point (at)   indicare, *(out)* mostrare/far osservare/far notare/accentuare/accennare

pollute   inquinare

pool   associare

(be) popular   incontrare

portray   dipingere, rappresentare, rendere

(be) possible (that)   non escludere che

pounce   buttarsi

pour   piovere, colare, *(oneself)* versarsi, *(out)* versare

practice   esercitarsi, praticare, studiare, *(profession)* esercitare

  (be in) practice   praticare

pray   pregare

preach   predicare

prefer   preferire

(be) prejudiced against   prevenire

prepare   preparare, cucinare, disporre

present   presentare

presume to be   dare per

pretend   darsi, fingere, pretendere, figurare, mostrare

prevail   prevalere

prevent   prevenire, impedire, vietare

prick oneself   bucarsi

print   stampare, tirare

proceed   procedere

process elaborare

procure procurare

produce produrre, rendere, fabbricare

profess pretendere

prohibit proibire, vietare

prolong allungare

(be) prominent campeggiare

promise promettere

promote promuovere, proteggere

  (be) promoted passare

prompt suggerire

pronounce pronunciare

propose proporre, dichiararsi, presentare

protect proteggere, salvare, riparare, parare, difendere, *(oneself)* guardarsi

protest protestare

prove provare, dimostrare, *(one's innocence)* discolparsi, *(oneself)* scoprirsi/mostrarsi

provide provvedere, prevedere, fornire, disporre

provoke provocare, eccitare

puff soffiare

pull tirare, *(behind)* tirarsi dietro, *(down)* abbattere/abbassare/calcarsi, *(out)* tirare via, *(up)* tirare su

punch (a hole) bucare

purchase acquistare

purloin sottrarre

push spingere, *(back)* cacciare

put mettere, *(forward)* avanzare, *(in order)* ordinare, *(off)* sospendere, *(on)* assumere/mettersi, *(on lighter clothes)* alleggerirsi, *(on makeup)* truccarsi, *(on shoes)* calzare, *(sth into sth)* inserire, *(to sleep)* addormentare, *(together)* unire, riunire, *(up)* esporre/attaccare, *(up with)* tollerare

puzzle imbarazzare

qualify qualificarsi

quarrel bisticciare, litigare

quarry estrarre

quench cavarsi

question discutere, interrogare, sospettare

quicken accelerare, forzare

quit lasciare

quiver tremare

quote citare, quotare

rain piovere

raise alzare, alzarsi, tirare su, aumentare, sollevare, elevare, sorgere, assumere, *(a number exponentially)* elevare

raze radere

reach giungere, arrivare, portarsi, raggiungere, guadagnare, *(out)* allungare

read leggere, correre, segnare, vedere, interpretare

realize rendersi conto, accorgersi, realizzare, capire, avvertire

reap raccogliere

rebel (against) ribellarsi

rebuke rimproverare

recall ricordare

receive ricevere, accogliere, raccogliere, arrivare (2)

recognize riconoscere

recommend raccomandare, consigliare

record scrivere, accogliere, incidere

recount raccontare

recover guarire, superare

rectify riparare

reduce ridurre

reel barcollare

refer riferirsi, parlare

reflect riflettere

  (be) reflected riflettersi

refrain astenersi

refuse rifiutare, negare, dire di no, opporre, volere, *(to admit)* escludere

refute smontare

register depositare

regret pentirsi

  (cause) regret dispiacere

rehearse provare

reject respingere, rifiutare, bocciare

relapse ricadere

relate riferire, descrivere

relax distendere, allentare

release scattare, liberare, sciogliere

relieve togliere, sollevare, esonerare, alleggerire, *(stress)* scaricarsi

rely fidare, affidarsi, fondarsi

remain restare, *(in office)* durare

remember ricordare

remind ricordare

remove togliere, eliminare, levare

rend lacerare

renounce rinunciare

rent affittare

repair riparare, accomodare, aggiustare

repeat ripetere, *(oneself)* ripetersi

repel respingere

repent pentirsi, battersi

replace sostituire

reply rispondere

report riferire, informare

represent rappresentare, figurare

repress contenere

reproach rimproverare

request pregare, invitare

require esigere, obbligare

rescue liberare, sottrarre

resemble somigliare

reserve fissare, *(for)* destinare

(be) reserved abbottonare

resign licenziarsi, rassegnare, adattarsi

resist resistere, sostenere

resolve risolvere, decidere

respond rispondere, ubbidire

(be) responsible for rispondere

rest riposare, appoggiare

restore restituire

restrict limitare

result risultare, derivare, dipendere, tradursi

retire confinarsi

return ritornare, restituire, corrispondere, respingere, rendere

reveal manifestare

reverse rovesciare

reward compensare

rid oneself liberarsi

ride montare, *(animals)* cavalcare

(be) ridiculous far ridere

rig truccare

ring suonare

ripen maturare

rise alzarsi, montare, aumentare, nascere (2), elevarsi, salire, sorgere, crescere, sollevarsi, levarsi

risk rischiare, giocarsi

roast fare (5), cuocere

roll ballare, *(up)* tirare su/avvolgere

rouse sollevare, svegliare, accalorare

rule comandare, *(over)* dominare

run correre, andare, funzionare, dirigere, presentarsi, *(across)* attraversare, *(away)* battersela/fuggire/scappare, *(down)* scaricarsi, *(in)* entrare, *(into)* incontrare, *(over)* investire, *(risk)* rischiare

rush buttarsi

rustle sussurrare

sacrifice sacrificare

sail navigare

salute salutare

satisfy soddisfare, cavarsi

sauté far saltare

save risparmiare, salvare, avanzare, parare, evitare

say dire, fare (2), segnare, scrivere, *(hello/good-bye)* salutare, *(more)* far parlare, *(nothing)* tacere, *(prayers)* pregare

scald oneself   bruciarsi

(be, get) scared   spaventarsi

scatter   spargere

scent   odorare

scold   rimproverare

scorch   bruciare

score   realizzare, marcare

scour   battere

scratch   segnare

scream   gridare

sculpt   fare (4)

(be at) sea   navigare

search   cercare

season   condire

second   appoggiare

secrete   elaborare

secure   fermare, assicurare

seduce   sedurre

see   vedere, riconoscere, abbracciare, interessarsi, provvedere, curare, occuparsi

seek   cercare, *(advice)* consigliarsi

seem   parere, mostrarsi, presentarsi

seize   cogliere, catturare, prendere, afferrare, impadronirsi

sell   vendere, *(cheap)* regalare

send   mandare, trasmettere, *(away)* allontanare, *(for)* chiamare/far venire/mandare a prendere

sentence   condannare

separate   separare, dividere

serve   servire

   (have) serve oneself right, deserve   meritarselo

set   dare (1), legare, *(aside for)* destinare, *(fire)* incendiare, *(to do)* mettersi, *(up)* costituire

settle   stabilirsi, sbrigare, definire, comporre, determinare, sistemare, depositarsi, aggiustare, decidere, fissarsi

sew securely   fermare

shadow   seguire

shake   tremare, ballare, agitare, scuotere

   (be) shaky   barcollare, vacillare, zoppicare

share   associarsi, partecipare, dividere

shatter   fulminare, dissolvere

shave   radere, tagliarsi

shed   versare, spargere

shell   bombardare

shelter   proteggere

shield   parare

shift   scaricare

shine   brillare

shock   colpire, disgustare

shoot   gettare, buttare, cacciare, sparare, *(down)* abbattere, *(movie/scene)* girare (un film/una scena)

shorten   abbreviare

should   dovere

shout   gridare

show   mostrare, dimostrare, provare, manifestare, dare (2), fare (2), scoprire, vedere, presentare, rappresentare, tradursi, introdurre, insegnare, far vedere, *(on one's face, up)* farsi vedere, *(signs)* accennare, *(traces)* risentire

   (be) shown   fare (2)

shroud   avvolgere

shrug   scuotere

shudder   tremare

shuffle   mescolare

shut   chiudere, confinare

(be) shy   vergognarsi

(be) sick of   disgustarsi

side   stare

sieve   vagliare

sift   vagliare

sigh   sospirare

sight   scoprire

sign   firmare, sottoscrivere, *(on)* imbarcarsi

signify   significare

simmer   cuocere

simulate   affettare

sing   cantare

sink   affondare, sommergere, sprofondare, abbandonarsi, colare

sit   sedere, *(down)* sedersi/accomodarsi

skip   saltare

slacken   allentare

slam   bloccare, sbattere

slaughter   abbattere, ammazzare

sleep   dormire

slice   affettare

slide   scivolare

slip   scappare, sfuggire, uscire, scivolare, introdurre

slope down   discendere

slough off   spogliarsi

smart   bruciare

smash   rompere

smell   sapere, odorare

smile   sorridere

smoke   fumare

smuggle   introdurre

snap   scattare

snip   tagliare

soak   bagnare, impregnare, assorbire, bere

soften   addolcire

soil   sporcare

solve   sciogliere, risolvere

soothe   calmare

(make) sorry   dispiacere

sort out   scegliere

sound   suonare, *(like)* parere

span   cavalcare

spare   risparmiare, perdonare, evitare

sparkle   lampeggiare, ridere, brillare

speak   parlare, dire, mormorare, *(briefly)* accennare, *(up)* farsi sentire

speculate   giocare (in borsa)

speed   volare, *(up)* lanciare/accelerare

spell   scrivere

spend   *(money)* spendere/finire, *(night)* dormire, *(time)* passare/occupare

spice   condire

spill   versare, rovesciare

spin   girare

split   spaccare, *(up)* dividersi/separarsi

spoil   viziare

sponsor   offrire

spot   scoprire

spout   gettare

spread   allargare, distendere, spargere, *(out)* spiegare/allargarsi/distribuire

spread *or* **trespass on**   invadere

spring   scattare, balzare, derivare

sprinkle   bagnare

sprout   gettare, nascere (2)

spur on   spronare

squander   mangiarsi

square   quadrare

squeal   soffiare, cantare

stage   rappresentare

stagger   barcollare, vacillare

stain   sporcare, tingersi

stall   bloccarsi

stammer   balbettare

stamp on   calcare

stand   sostenere, sopportare, soffrire, stare, tollerare, *(not)* non sopportare/temere/significare/figurare/distinguersi, *(out)* campeggiare, *(up)* tirarsi su/intervenire/sostenersi/levarsi/difendere

stare   guardare (1), fissare

start   cominciare, procedere, attaccare, aprire, fondare, muovere, partire, ritornare, *(to grow)* nascere (2)

state   dichiarare, dire, indicare, esporre, disporre, protestare

station   distribuire

stay   stare, restare, fermarsi

stay awake   vegliare

steal   rubare, soffiare, sottrarre,

steer clear of   evitare

step in   intervenire

stew   cuocere, fare (5)

stick   attaccarsi, bloccarsi, aderire, cacciare, mettere, applicare, tenersi, tirare fuori

stimulate   aiutare

sting   bruciare

stir   muovere, agitare

stop   fermare, smettere, finire, cessare, arrestare, sospendere, bloccare, impedire, intrattenersi, interrompersi, *(by)* passare, *(talking)* tacere, *(work)* smontare

strain   colare, passare, stancarsi, tendere, sforzare

strengthen   sostenere

stress   accentuare, calcare

stretch   allungare, tendere, muovere, distendere, allargare

strew   spargere

stride along   camminare

strike   calare, colpire, battere, accendere, balzare, suonare, *(by lightning)* fulminare

strip   disfare, spogliare

strive   sforzarsi, lottare

stroke   accarezzare

struggle   dibattersi, lottare

study   studiare, prepararsi

stuff   cacciare, riempire

stun   sbalordire

stunt   fermare

subdue   sottomettere

subject   sottomettere

submerge   sommergersi

submit   sottomettere, presentare

subordinate   sottomettere

subscribe   abbonarsi, sottoscrivere, quotarsi

subside   cessare

substitute   sostituire

subtend   insistere

subtract   sottrarre

succeed   riuscire, succedere, giungere

(be a) success   incontrare

(be) successful   arrivare (2), riuscire

sue   querelare, citare, fare causa

suffer   soffrire, patire, subire, risentire

suffice   bastare

suggest   suggerire, dettare, proporre, indicare

suit   stare, convenire, adattarsi, accomodare, vestire, fare (2), convenire

summon   citare, chiamare, riunire, convocare

(be) superior   eccellere

supervise   seguire

supply   provvedere, fornire

support   sostenere, aderire, confortare, appoggiare, mantenere

suppose   supporre, immaginare, mettere (il caso)

(be) supposed (to)   dovere

suppress   sopprimere, abolire, eliminare

(be) sure   non dubitare, guardare

surpass   sorpassare, superare

surprise   sorprendere, meravigliare

(be) surprised   meravigliarsi, sorprendersi

surrender   arrendersi

surround   circondare, limitare, abbracciare

survive   salvarsi

suspect   sospettare

suspend   sospendere

swallow   buttare giù, bere, inghiottire

swap   scambiarsi

swarm   invadere

sway   trascinare, vacillare

swear   giurare

sweat   sudare

sweep   toccare

sweeten   addolcire

swim   nuotare, *(across)* attraversare

swindle   truffare

symbolize   figurare

sympathize   simpatizzare

tackle   affrontare

take   prendere, portare, condurre, tradurre, togliere, *(action against)* querelare, *(advantage)* valersi/sorprendere/abusare/approfittare, *(after)* somigliare, *(again)* ripetere, *(away)* tirare via, *(away/off/out)* levare, *(care)* provvedere/trattare/guardare/curare/interessarsi/incaricarsi/risparmiarsi/pensare, *(exam)* dare (un esame), *(good care not to)* guardarsi bene, *(Holy Communion)* comunicarsi, *(ill)* ammalarsi, *(interest)* interessarsi, *(into account)* contare, *(into consideration)* esaminare, *(into custody)* fermare, *(legal steps)* agire, *(liberty)* permettersi, *(liking)* simpatizzare, *(notice)* curarsi, *(off)* partire/scoprire/cavarsi/tirarsi su, *(offense)* offendersi/risentirsi, *(on/upon)* assumere, *(on board)* imbarcare, *(out stitches)* disfare, *(part)* partecipare, *(pleasure in)* godere, *(possession of)* impadronirsi, *(prisoner)* catturare, *(refuge)* riparare, *(root)* attaccare, *(seat)* sedersi/accomodarsi, *(shelter)* ripararsi, *(ship)* imbarcarsi, *(sb by mistake)* scambiare, *(sb's place)* sostituire, *(time)* metterci/volerci/seguire/sostenere/menare/conquistare/chiedere/adottare/volere, *(to)* portare/dare, *(to pieces)* smontare, *(trouble)* disturbarsi/ preoccuparsi, *(turn for)* mettersi, *(up)* occupare/assorbire/abbracciare, *(up/in)* raccogliere, *(up room)* tenere (3)

  (be) taken in   abboccare

talk   parlare, chiacchierare, cantare, *(to each other again)* risentirsi

  "there is talk of"   si parla di

tally   corrispondere, quadrare

tamper with   manomettere

tap   battere, incidere

tape (record)   incidere

taste   sapere, gustare, essere (3), *(like)* parere

teach   insegnare, istruire

  (be a) teacher   insegnare

tear   lacerare, *(to pieces)* demolire

tease   scherzare

telegraph   telegrafare

telephone   telefonare

tell   dire, raccontare, riferire, comunicare, spiegare, dettare, distinguere

  (fore)tell   indovinare

tempt   tentare

tend *or* **be inclined**   tendere

tender *or* **bid**   offrire

test   provare, tentare

testify   testimoniare

thank   ringraziare

thaw   sciogliere

thicken   legare

think   pensare, credere, immaginare, stimare, parere, sospettare, trovare, volere, considerare, dire, riflettere, pretendere, fare, giudicare

threaten   minacciare

throb   battere

throw   buttare, gettare, lanciare, sbattere, cacciare, tirare, spingersi, scoprirsi

thrust   piantare, affondare, *(oneself)* cacciarsi

thunder   tuonare

tie   legare

  (be) tied   attaccarsi

(be) tight   tirare

tighten   tendere

till   lavorare

tilt   inclinare

tinge *or* **dye**   tingere, tingersi

tip   pendere

tire (out)   stancare

toast   brindare

toil   sudare, affannarsi

tolerate   tollerare

toss   gettare, lanciare, agitarsi, girarsi

touch   toccare, tentare

tour   girare

tower (over)   elevarsi

trade   trafficare

traffic   trafficare

train   istruire, allenare, coltivare
  (be) trained   formarsi
tramp   camminare
transfer   trasferire, cedere
transform   trasformare
translate   tradurre, rendere
transmit   comunicare, trasmettere
travel   viaggiare, correre
tread   calcare, *(on)* camminare
treat   trattare, curare
tremble   tremare
trouble   disturbare, affannare
trust   fidare, affidarsi, sperare, prestarsi
try   cercare, tentare, provare, studiarsi, vedere, tirare, misurare, procurare, *(case)* giudicare, *(hard)* sforzarsi
try on *or* **have a fitting**   provare
tumble (down)   cascare
turn   girare, abbassare, adattare, ridurre, dirigere, farsi, piegare, *(age)* compiere, *(into/to)* diventare/trasformare/finire/convertire, *(off)* chiudere/spegnere, *(on)* accendere/aprire, *(out)* risolversi/venire (2), *(out to be)* dimostrarsi/risultare, *(over)* capovolgere/rovesciare, *(upside down)* rovesciare, *(weather)* mettersi
twinkle   brillare
twist   contrarre, forzare
type   battere (a macchina)
uncover oneself   scoprirsi
(be) undecided   vacillare
undergo   subire, *(surgery)* operarsi
understand   capire, intendersi, risultare
undertake   impegnarsi
undo   disfare, annullare
undress   spogliare
(be) unfaithful   tradire
unfurl   spiegare
unite   unire, fondere
unload   scaricare
unmake   disfare
unpack   disfare

unravel   disfare
(be) unsteady   vacillare
untie   sciogliere
unveil   scoprire
unwrap   disfare
uphold   accogliere
upset   dispiacere, rovesciare, buttare
urge   esortare, insistere, spingere
(be) urgent   urgere
use   usare, servire
  (be of) use/service   servire
  (be) used *or* **would**   usare
  (be) used as   servire da
  (be) used to   solere
  make use   servirsi
usher   introdurre
utter   dire, pronunciare, emettere, lanciare
vacate   liberare
vacillate   vacillare
(be) valid   valere
vanish   dissolversi, eclissarsi
vary   variare
venture   spingersi
vest   parare
vex   irritare
vie   gareggiare
violate   contravvenire, violare
visit   visitare, andare a trovare
voice   esprimere
vote   votare
vouch   rispondere, garantire
vow   giurare
wait   aspettare
wake   svegliare
walk   camminare, fare (6), *(with a limp)* zoppicare
wander   allontanarsi, girare
want   volere, desiderare
  want to see   cercare
warm (up)   scaldare
warn   prevenire, avvisare

warrant   garantire

wash   lavare, pulire, bagnare

waste   buttare, sacrificare, perdere

watch   guardare (1), osservare, seguire, *(over)* vigilare/vegliare

water   piangere, bagnare

wave   salutare, agitare

waver   vacillare, esitare

wax   crescere

wear   avere (2), portare, durare, vestire, usare, *(shoes)* calzare

weary   stancare

wed   sposare

weep   piangere

weigh   pesare, bilanciare, considerare, *(heavily)* incidere, *(up)* vagliare

welcome   accogliere, ricevere

   "You're welcome"   prego

wet   bagnare

whet   eccitare

whip   montare, sbattere

whisper   sussurrare, bisbigliare, soffiare

widen   allargare

wield   maneggiare

will   volere, destinare

win   vincere, *(over)* conquistare/prendere/acquistare/guadagnare/attirarsi

wind up   caricare

wipe   pulirsi

wire   telegrafare

wish   desiderare, augurare, volere

withstand   resistere

wobble   vacillare

   (be) wobbly   zoppicare

wonder   domandarsi, chiedersi

word   esprimere

work   lavorare, funzionare, operare, coltivare, agire, *(hard)* sudare, *(out)* accomodarsi

   (make) work   far lavorare

worry   preoccupare, preoccuparsi, affannare, temere, pensare, *(oneself)* affannarsi

   "don't worry"   dubitare

   (be) worried about   temere, preoccuparsi

worship   adorare

(be) worth   valere, meritare

(be) worthwhile   meritare

(be) worthy of   essere da

wound   ferire, ferirsi

wrap   bendare, *(up)* avvolgere

write   scrivere, fare (4), *(commentary)* commentare, *(down)* notare

(be) wrong   sbagliare, sbagliarsi

yell   gridare

yield   cedere, produrre, rendere, gettare, arrendersi, dare (2)